MW00476443

SPACES BETWEEN US

SPACES BETWEEN US

Queer Settler Colonialism and Indigenous Decolonization

Scott Lauria Morgensen

FIRST PEOPLES
New Directions in Indigenous Studies

University of Minnesota Press
Minneapolis
London

Publication of this book was made possible, in part, with a grant from the Andrew W. Mellon Foundation.

Portions of chapter 1 were previously published as "Settler Homonationalism: Theorizing Settler Colonialism within Queer Modernities," *GLQ: A Journal of Lesbian and Gay Studies* 16, no. 1–2 (2010): 105–31; reprinted by permission of the publisher. Portions of chapter 4 were previously published as "Arrival at Home: Radical Faerie Configurations of Sexuality and Place," *GLQ: A Journal of Lesbian and Gay Studies* 15, no. 1 (2009): 67–96; reprinted by permission of the publisher. Portions of chapter 5 were previously published as "Rooting for Queers: A Politics of Primitivity," *Women and Performance: A Journal of Feminist Theory* 15, no. 1 (2005): 251–89; and as "Back and Forth to the Land: Negotiating Rural and Urban Sexuality among the Radical Faeries," in *Out in Public: Reinventing Lesbian/Gay Anthropology in a Globalizing World*, ed. Ellen Lewin and William Leap (Malden, Mass.: Blackwell Publishers, 2009), 143–63. Portions of chapter 6 were previously published as "Activist Media in Native AIDS Organizing: Theorizing the Colonial Conditions of AIDS," *American Indian Culture and Research Journal* 32, no. 1 (2008): 35–56; reprinted by permission of the American Indian Studies Center, UCLA; copyright 2008 Regents of the University of California.

Copyright 2011 by the Regents of the University of Minnesota

All rights reserved. No part of this publication may be reproduced, stored in a retrieval system, or transmitted, in any form or by any means, electronic, mechanical, photocopying, recording, or otherwise, without the prior written permission of the publisher.

Published by the University of Minnesota Press
111 Third Avenue South, Suite 290
Minneapolis, MN 55401-2520
http://www.upress.umn.edu

Library of Congress Cataloging-in-Publication Data

Morgensen, Scott Lauria.
  Spaces between us : queer settler colonialism and indigenous decolonization / Scott Lauria Morgensen.
      p.   cm. — (First peoples : New directions in indigenous studies)
   Includes bibliographical references and index.
   ISBN 978-0-8166-5632-5 (hc : alk. paper) — ISBN 978-0-8166-5633-2 (pb : alk. paper)
   1. Indian gays—History.   2. Indian gays—Colonization.   3. Frontier and pioneer life—United States—History.   4. Colonists—United States—Sexual behavior.   5. Two-spirit people—United States—History.   6. Radical Faeries (New Age movement).   7. Decolonization—United States—History.   I. Title.
   E98.S48M67   2011
   325'.30973—dc23   2011017145

Printed in the United States of America on acid-free paper

The University of Minnesota is an equal-opportunity educator and employer.

18 17 16 15 14   10 9 8 7 6 5 4

To all those who left us too soon

Contents

Preface

> In writing close to the other of the other, I can only choose
> to maintain a self-reflexively critical relationship towards the
> material, a relationship that defines both the subject written and
> the writing subject, undoing the I while asking, "what do I want
> wanting to *know* you or me?"
>
> —TRINH T. MINH-HA, *Woman, Native, Other*

THIS BOOK MAKES THREE CENTRAL CLAIMS at the intersections of queer, Native, and settler colonial studies and related fields. First, in the United States, modern queer cultures and politics have taken form as normatively white, multiracial, and non-Native projects compatible with a white settler society. Although queer hegemonies may be disrupted by challenging whiteness or nationalism, that alone may not fully disturb their conditioning by settler colonialism, which aims to amalgamate subjects in a settler society as "non-Native" inheritors, and *not* challengers of the colonization of Native peoples on occupied Native lands. Second, within broad transnational alliances (focused here in the United States), Native queer and Two-Spirit activists directly denaturalize settler colonialism and disrupt its conditioning of queer projects by asserting Native queer modernities. By repudiating heteropatriarchy as a colonial project, recalling subjugated Native knowledges, and forming alliances that trouble settler sovereignty and pursue decolonization, Native queer and Two-Spirit activists have created critical theories and movements to which all people can respond. Third, settler colonialism and its conditioning of modern sexuality produce an intimate relationship between non-Native and Native queer modernities that I interpret as conversations. Non-Native and Native queer politics formed by telling different kinds of stories about the meaning of indigeneity to queer people, which entered them into power-laden conversations that nevertheless remained open to creative transformation.

Native and non-Native queer politics formed their relationship in the spaces between them produced by settler colonialism. Settler societies create spaces that are at once material and symbolic, as Sherene Razack argues, an insight I extend by interpreting them as intimately relational.[1] Such spaces appear in specific places: Indigenous lands, whether sustained by collective claims of Indigenous sovereignty, stolen and possessed by settlers, or traversed and contested by Natives and non-Natives within settler society. In these places, interchanges of Native and non-Native people locate them in power-laden spaces of relationship, which this book interprets for queer Natives and non-Natives as conversations. My account takes particular inspiration from Katie King's account of debates in feminist theory as "conversations in U.S. women's movements."[2] King explained feminist debates over difference not as interruptions of feminist politics, as some Western feminists have claimed, but as formations worthy of study as contentious, border-crossing deliberations. Asking how "feminist objects of knowledge . . . are made and materialized over time in political production," King investigated in regard to any object the

> histories of its production over time, the contests for meanings within which
> it is embedded, the political contours that are the circumstances out of which
> it is fabricated, and the resources and costs of its making, contesting, and
> stabilizations. (xvi)

King contextualized this work as the study of "conversations," or "units of political agency in action in theoretical discourse," which she distinguished from "'debates' as political contour from theoretical contents." Examining not only "formal writing or circulating manuscripts" but also "oratory, group production, private oralities, [and] publications," King asked how historical deliberations as conversations produced the objects and subjects of U.S. women's movements (56). This response to the racial and national contestation of feminism recognized conflict as productive to feminist thought and as deserving of study. King's account suggests at once a theory of feminist knowledge production and a method for engaging it. The analytic category "conversations" invokes intersubjective social activity, as would be made apparent by ethnography, oral history, or archival or literary study of texts written and circulated for deliberation. But King's work engages such evidence from within a genealogy of discursive registers that link or split varied claims and contexts. Several implications for theory and method follow. Thinking in these terms invites one to read narratives as relating across differences that become meaningful in the contested spaces of conversation. In turn, interpreting claims in conversation will reveal failures of recognition—as people speak past one another, or in mutual ignorance—as well as moments of confrontation, as evidence of interrelationship. Finally, as discursive fields that are multiple, contradictory, and actively contested, conversations center the incitement by power relations of creative possibilities.

King's model informs my account of the formation of queer knowledges even as I extend it to address Native and settler colonial studies. King theorized how feminist claims across differences of social location and geography become interreferential in a U.S. context. My work examines and then displaces the settler state by interpreting U.S. queer politics across the national differences of Native peoples and sovereignties. Here, "conversations" indexes interactions among non-Native and Native queers not within or as "U.S." queer movements but as distinct queer projects within the transnational relationships formed by Native and non-Native people in a settler society. Indigenous feminist thought is helpful in modeling the interpretation of knowledge production under such conditions. For instance, Andrea Smith's "intellectual ethnography" of Native feminists portrays activists as theorists who challenge settler colonialism from within "unlikely alliances," where transnational ties among Native people and with non-Natives work to defend Native nations and pursue decolonization on Indigenous feminist terms.[3] My engagements with activist dialogues across the national differences of queer Natives and non-Natives is a feminist and trans-allied effort to disturb the centrality of white cisgender gay men—a location that could describe me—as hegemonic subjects in the definition of queer modernities on settler colonial terms.[4] To some degree, my work responded in this way to models of feminist reflection on questions of "home," such as white antiracist feminist accounts of whiteness, or the responses by feminist ethnographers to anthropology's coloniality that led Kamala Visweswaran to call for "homework" as a condition of fieldwork.[5] Yet my research confronts a problem that self-reflection cannot contain: contested spaces of knowledge production where interlocutors' competing claims tell more in their differences with one another than any single narrative can tell alone. In response, I learned from feminist scholars who examine politicized knowledge production as its situated participant, and thence as potential subjects of critique as well as interlocutors in modeling change.[6] My intent is to explain the historical formation of

Native and non-Native queer politics, in alliance with Indigenous, feminist, queer, trans, and Two-Spirit critiques that already displace the settler colonial processes I examine.[7]

The Introduction explains my theoretical analysis of settler colonialism conditioning the formation of Native and non-Native queer modernities in conversation. It draws from and advances Native, critical race, feminist, and queer studies by centering Indigenous feminist and queer thought and Native queer and Two-Spirit activism.

Part I, "Genealogies," examines the historical precedents and diachronic registers of conversation that condition the movements examined in this book. Chapter 1, "The Biopolitics of Settler Sexuality and Queer Modernities," explores how "settler sexuality" queers Native peoples to attempt their elimination compatibly with asserting racialized heteropatriarchal control over subject people of color placed on Native lands. The queering of white settlers then depends on the existence of a settler colonialism that conditions both heteronormative and queer gender and sexual politics on stolen land, which Native queer and Two-Spirit activists resist. Chapter 2, "Conversations on Berdache: Anthropology, Counterculturism, Two-Spirit Organizing," then examines how twentieth-century examinations of berdache formed key contexts where non-Native and Native queer subjects and politics formed in relationship.

Part II, "Movements," traces how these genealogies are manifested in historical and ethnographic cases of late-twentieth-century non-Native and Native queer politics. The chapters trace three qualities of modern non-Native queer projects—the pursuit of cultural authenticity, ancient roots, and global purview—inspired by Native American indigeneity or challenged by Native queer and Two-Spirit people. Chapter 3, "Authentic Culture and Sexual Rights: Contesting Citizenship in the Settler State," traces how desires for cultural authenticity linked queer politics in the United States to what Elizabeth Povinelli has called "liberal settler multiculturalism" while being challenged by multiracial and transnational queer alliances led by Two-Spirit activists. Chapter 4, "Ancient Roots through Settled Land: Imagining Indigeneity and Place Among Radical Faeries," examines how non-Native gay counterculturists pursued multiple desires for queer indigeneity that, while contested by antiracist critique, confronted their settler formation only in relationship to Native gay and Two-Spirit men. Chapter 5, "Global Desires and Transnational Solidarity: Negotiating Indigeneity among the Worlds of Queer Politics," explains the globalism of U.S. queer modernities as effects of settler colonialism by tracing how homonationalism and white settler queer primitivism may link within white queer politics and diasporic queer of color critiques until resituated by the transnationalism of Two-Spirit organizing.

Chapter 6, "'Together We Are Stronger': Decolonizing Gender and Sexuality in Transnational Native AIDS Organizing," explains how Native activist critiques of heteropatriarchy in Native communities, settler states, and global arenas mark the settler colonial biopolitics of health governance and incite global Indigenous alliances for decolonization. The Epilogue returns to the implications Native queer and Two-Spirit activisms carry for queer non-Natives and all people to critically transform settler colonialism.

Abbreviations

AAA	American Anthropological Association
AICH	American Indian Community House
AIDS	Acquired Immune Deficiency Syndrome
AIGL	American Indian Gays and Lesbians
AIM	American Indian Movement
APA	American Psychiatric Association
AQA	Association for Queer Anthropology
ARGOH	Anthropological Research Group on Homosexuality
BDSM	bondage and discipline, sadism and masochism
BLW	Black Leather Wings
CAAN	Canadian Aboriginal AIDS Network
FACT	Faeries of All Colors Together
GAA	Gay Activists Alliance
GAI	Gay American Indians
GLBTQ	gay/lesbian/bisexual/transgender/queer
GLF	Gay Liberation Front
HIV	human immunodeficiency virus
HRC	Human Rights Campaign
IAC	International AIDS Conference
IDUs	intravenous drug users
IHS	Indian Health Service
MACT	Men of All Colors Together
MSM	men who have sex with men
NAISA	Native American and Indigenous Studies Association
NASTAD	National Alliance of State and Territorial AIDS Directors
NCPC	Naraya Cultural Preservation Council
NE2SS	North-East Two-Spirit Society
NGLTF	National Gay and Lesbian Task Force

NGO	nongovernmental organization
NGTF	National Gay Task Force
NIH	National Institutes of Health
NNAAPC	National Native American AIDS Prevention Center
OCAP	Ownership, Control, Access, and Possession
PRI	Partido Revolucionario Institucional
PSDN	Pacific Sexual Diversity Network
S/M	sadomasochism
SOLGA	Society of Lesbian and Gay Anthropologists
UN	United Nations
YMCA	Young Men's Christian Association

WE ARE CAUGHT UP IN ONE ANOTHER, we who live in settler societies, and our interrelationships inform all that these societies touch. Native people live in relation to all non-Natives in the context of the power relations of settler colonialism, though they never lose inherent claims to sovereignty as Indigenous peoples. Non-Natives live in relation to Native people—whether or not they know this, whether or not they recognize that Indigenous peoples exist—as though Native lands, societies, or cultures were theirs to inherit, control, or enjoy. Settler societies engender a normative relationality between the designations "Native" and "settler" that imbues histories of intermingling, interdependence, or the attempted erasure of indigeneity as a marker of national difference. The distinction between "Native" and "settler" informs all power in settler societies and their relations with societies worldwide.[1]

This book examines how settler colonial power relations among Native and non-Native people define the status "queer." It argues that modern queer subjects, cultures, and politics have developed among Natives and non-Natives in linked, yet distinct, way opatriarchy relegates Native people an  queered statuses as racialized populatio Native nationality and settle Native lands. Modern sexuality comes into existence when the heteropatriarchal advancement of white settlers appears to vanquish sexual primitivity, which white settlers nevertheless adopt as their own history. When modern sexuality queers white settlers, their effort to reclaim a place within settler society produces white and non-Native queer politics for recognition by the state. Yet memories and practices of discrepant sexual cultures among Indigenous peoples and peoples of color persistently trouble the white settler logics of sexual modernity. For instance, Native modes of kinship, embodiment, and desire such as those today called

politics of recognition

1

"Two-Spirit" produce Native queer modernities that denaturalize settler colonialism. The comparative studies in this book show settler colonialism as the context in which non-Native and Native people produce modern queer subjects, cultures, and politics.

A methodological shift in Native studies heralded by such scholars as Linda Tuhiwai Smith and Robert Warrior theorizes settler colonialism by tracing the "intellectual histories" (Warrior) and methods of Native peoples practicing survival, resistance, and decolonization.[2] Scholarship in settler colonial studies must support this turn, as when Patrick Wolfe theorizes settler colonialism as "a structure, not an event" that calls for a sustained denaturalizing critique.[3] Andrea Smith calls on Native studies to refuse its "ethnographic entrapment" in the description of Native cultures and instead become an interdisciplinary site for explaining and transforming a world defined by settler colonialism.[4] She promotes this shift by invoking queer theory, which displaced the description of sexual minorities in gay/lesbian studies by theorizing heteronormativity as a power relation that conditions all subjects and social life.[5] Scholars at the intersections of Native and queer studies have responded to these calls by demonstrating that each field is intrinsic to the other.[6] Smith explains that "the heteronormativity of settler colonialism" has subjected Native and non-Native people to settler colonial rule and regimes of modern sexuality. In this context, "queer" statuses accrue to nonheteronormative identities—such as gay, lesbian, bisexual, transgender, or queer—after colonial heteropatriarchy first redefines embodiment, desire, and kinship to eliminate Native culture, control racialized populations, and secure, in Sherene Razack's term, a "white settler society." In this book, *queer* will refer to statuses produced by the heteropatriarchal power of white supremacist settler colonialism. My analysis joins critics of homonormativity in arguing that all "queer" statuses are not equivalent.[7] Jasbir Puar critiques "homonationalism" as the process whereby whiteness and imperialism create U.S. queer subjects as "regulatory" over peoples queered by U.S. rule.[8] I resituate Puar's account to argue that in a white settler society, queer politics produces a *settler* homonationalism that will persist unless settler colonialism is challenged directly as a condition of queer modernities.[9] Native and queer studies must regard settler colonialism as a key condition of modern sexuality on stolen land, and use this analysis to explain the power of settler colonialism among Native and non-Native people.

This book investigates how settler colonialism produces what I call "non-Native queer modernities," in which modern queers appear definitively not Native—separated from, yet in perpetual (negative) relationship to, the original peoples of the lands where they live. The phrase suggests a settler colonial logic that disappears indigeneity so it can be recalled by modern *non*-Natives as a relationship to Native culture and land that might reconcile them to inheriting conquest.[10] Thus, "non-Native" signifies not a racial or ethnic identity but a location within settler colonialism. Non-Native queer modernities naturalize settler colonialism when they confront queer differences as racial or diasporic in a manner that sustains Native disappearance. If queer subjects align with whiteness or homonationalism, their settler colonial roots may seem clear. But even multiracial and transnational queer critiques of racism and imperialism can erase Native people and naturalize settler colonialism in ways that indirectly or directly define queer modernity as not Native. This book examines "Native queer modernities" as projects that formed historically precisely to displace the settler colonial logics that sustain "non-Native queer modernities."

Native queer cultures and politics critique colonial heteropatriarchy by asserting Indigenous methods of national survival, traditional renewal, and decolonization, including within Two-Spirit identity. My analysis of the distinctions among non-Native and Native queer modernities invokes the critical models of queer of color, queer diasporic, and queer/migration critiques and women of color and transnational feminisms as they interact with Native queer and Two-Spirit critiques. My analysis is that of a white queer critic within multiracial, normatively white, and non-Native queer spaces, whose settler colonial conditions I denaturalize in response to Native queer critics who are pursuing Indigenous decolonization.

While confronting the seeming intractability of settler colonial power relations, this book shows how subjects acted creatively to transform them. It affirms the Foucauldian insight, highlighted by Judith Butler, that power is the very condition of agentive action—a transformative context for its repetition and potential destabilization.[11] The reproduction of norms and their critique require close reading to ascertain which forms of creativity might produce decolonizing ends. I am not suggesting that non-Native and Native queer modernities share the same origin, for only Native queer modernities recall a life unconditioned by settler colonialism and their relationship formed precisely by negotiating discrepancies. Feminist ethnographer Anna Tsing theorizes the creative effects of discrepancies encountering power-laden relationship in the form of "friction," as when global hegemonies engage local situations to elicit heated exchanges along unexpected routes of interpretation and negotiation.[12] I examine the settler colonial power relations conditioning non-Native and Native queer modernities as a frictional space producing contrasting yet interdependent accounts in the form of "conversations." Here I invoke Katie King's mapping of debates in U.S. women's movements over differences of gender, race, and nation as discursive spaces existing within a power-laden interrelationship, which she called "conversations."[13] I interpret non-Native and Native queer modernities as forming within the intimate relationships of conversation, in which their friction produced a multiplicity of narratives for textual and ethnographic interpretation, while mapping genealogies wherein their differences became interreferential amid the persistent and transforming power of settler colonialism. Queer subjects in a settler colonial situation become caught up in one another from within the creative and constrained spaces of conversations and the power relations they produce and negotiate. This book critically engages those conversations to clarify histories and incite change.

Conversations on Queerness, Indigeneity, and Settlement

Citational Tactics: *Another Mother Tongue* and *Living the Spirit*

Closely reading articulations among white and Native narratives of queer modernity maps their relational, yet ultimately divergent, locations on Native lands and in settler society. During the 1980s, Native and white lesbian and gay writers in the United States produced deeply interreferential texts, as demonstrated by the San Francisco organization Gay American Indians (GAI)—the first group of its kind in the United States, formed in 1975— and white lesbian writer Judy Grahn. Although GAI's membership came from across North America, its focus was to serve Native people in the San Francisco Bay Area, where Grahn also resided. Their work situated their distinct liberations within a Native or white settler relationship to queer locations on Native land and in a settler society.

Judy Grahn's award-winning book *Another Mother Tongue: Gay Words, Gay Worlds* (1984) narrated U.S. lesbian and gay history as a colonial desire of non-Natives for a sense of place on Native land.[14] Grahn cited recent research, notably accounts of Native American history reprinted in Jonathan Katz's *Gay American History* (1976), and she also took inspiration from accounts of a primal gay spirituality, as described in Arthur Evans's *Witchcraft and the Gay Counterculture* (1978). Grahn argued that by respecting gender and sexual diversity, Native American societies and other ancient or Indigenous peoples traditionally recognized a primal truth shared by all gay men and lesbians, a claim backed for her by anthropological and colonial accounts of berdache. She implicitly, and at times directly, addresses her readers as non-Natives identified with Euro-American culture—for lack of a clearer description, white people—who look to ancient or Indigenous cultures for inspiration. Such claims were not original with Grahn, though she focused on lesbians rather than gay men, as Arthur Evans had done in *Witchcraft and the Gay Counterculture*, and explained their oppression through a lesbian-feminist analysis of heteropatriarchy. She sought to shift lesbians and gay men from narratives of perversion to identification as a subjugated people seeking liberation. She describes white U.S. gay men and lesbians as needing Native cultural authenticity to learn to speak in their own "mother tongue." Yet, as her title indicates, that tongue remains "another" when modern non-Natives adopt Indigenous identifications in their pursuit of liberation.

Grahn's concept of an Indigenous nature for lesbians and gay men appears as a subtext when she juxtaposes her narrative to italicized passages addressing her first lover, Von (Yvonne). Here Grahn appears to fulfill an old love whose survival in an earlier era would have been eased by the knowledge she now has. We learn that in 1959, Von brought the eighteen-year-old Grahn out into a lesbian relationship when they were living in rural towns in eastern New Mexico. Grahn explains to Von what she sees as a universal gay pattern strongly linked to berdache. She recalls a sense of an absent history defining her life and Von's in a region now, ironically, marked by proximity to the histories that will save them:

> We had no idea of the gay customs barely suppressed or still functioning in the Indian cultures around us, Von, as we grew up each in her isolated small Anglo town. By the time we were eighteen, we were cut off from our own Euro-American people by their hostility toward the very essence of our lives, our Gayness . . . We felt and acted rejected, alienated, and thoroughly "queer." I know that if we could have known anything about the Navajo nadle, of the Bo-the of the Crow, of the Hwame women of the Pima, so much of our alienation and terror would have left us. We could have understood our own behavior, or specialness, as a gift as well as a burden and as an asset to our society as well as its apparent nemesis. We could have played the American game of cowboys and Indians with a brand-new twist.[15]

Grahn argues that Native histories of acceptance oppose efforts by white people to "queer" their own. But she also identifies whites as settlers, having inherited from a history of wars a proximity and contrast to "the Indian cultures around us." Positing an Indigenous embrace for queer exiles from a white settler society lets her imagine switching allegiances to play "Indians" against her own people. Philip Deloria, in *Playing Indian*, explains that white Americans associate marginality and resistance with the Indian as an internal antagonist to settler society, which then lets them impersonate indigeneity when they launch social critiques that reconcile them to settler society. Grahn admits that the Native histories she seeks remain "barely suppressed or still functioning" in the very Native communities near her hometown. Yet her story displaces that intimacy with occupation by investing in emptied Native land as a past and present home. She wishes that she and Von had known of Native "gay roles":

> we might have recognized more personal reasons for the deep attraction we both felt for the ancient Indian cultures everywhere present in the Southwest. You and I often went out into the deserts and mesas to walk arroyos near abandoned stone villages, peering into vine-filled underground kivas amber with October light, turning over the fine-ground sand potsherds left from hundreds of years ago. We did not particularly collect anything. We just went there to feel the oldness of the places, to think about what might have been. We felt at home there, as "at home" as we felt anywhere. We took comfort in this feeling.[16]

The desires for Native roots Grahn voices here later sparked the intellectual journeys of her book—where, Renée Bergland's work suggests, the Indian recurs as a ghost defining and motivating the narration of a settler subject.[17] Yet Grahn also names her youthful desires as queer—or, more precisely, queered in the sense of estranged from her "own Euro-American people." She defends a universal "Gayness," but her first sense of belonging to indigeneity arose not from that knowledge but from the "thoroughly 'queer'" experience of being exiled from white settler society and then taking comfort in imagining her own indigenized emplacement. White settler heteropatriarchy creates queers who resolve their exile through land-based relationships to disappeared Native people. Grahn's liberatory vision of a global and transhistorical Indigenous "Gayness" offers a more deeply *queer* relationship to inheriting white settler colonialism on Native lands. Her book narrates Native peoples as part of a disappeared past that white settlers inherit, and that grants queer exiles solace and a means for them to come "home."

Grahn's deferral of Native people from her narrative of a modern queer present is interrupted at a crucial moment more than halfway through the book. In a widely cited passage, she responds to the existence of Native gay and lesbian activists:

The day I saw a poster declaring the existence of an organization of Gay American Indians, I put my face into my hands and sobbed with relief. A huge burden, the burden of isolation and of being defined only by one's enemies, left me on that enlightening day. I understood then that being Gay is a universal quality, like cooking, like decorating the body, like singing, like predicting the weather. Moreover, after learning about the social positions and special offices fulfilled by Indians whose tribes once picked them for the task of naming, healing, prediction, leadership, and teaching precisely because they displayed characteristics we call gay, I knew that Gayness goes far beyond simple sexual/emotional activity. What Americans call Gayness not only has distinct cultural characteristics, its participants have long held positions of social power in history and ritual among people all over the globe.[18]

Like her story of growing up next to, yet apart from, Native peoples, Grahn's affirmation of Native activists is mediated by their distance. Without her having had any prior interaction with Gay American Indians, reading the poster simultaneously triggers and authorizes the desires she describes in her book. If the mere "existence of an organization of Gay American Indians" can launch her chain of associations, then Grahn seems to be primed to make Native peoples facilitate cathartic healing for her life as a white lesbian settler on Native land. While the chronology in this passage must be read against the one in her letters to Von, the passage suggests that she views Native gay and lesbian organizing as something apart from her own. Thus, rather than projecting indigeneity as something far off in space or time, only to be drawn upon to liberate white settlers, Grahn *only* meets Native people in the *same* temporal and spatial horizons of her queered life within relational locations defined by settler colonialism.

Members of Gay American Indians told quite different stories about, and *for,* Native people, yet they also ultimately adapted Grahn's narrative to their own ends. After the formation of GAI, cofounders Barbara Cameron (Lakota) and Randy Burns (Paiute) received invitations to explain their work to non-Native gays and lesbians. In a 1976 interview in the *Advocate* (reprinted in *Gay American History*), Cameron and Burns call GAI a support group for Native lesbians and gay men, which Cameron describes as "first and foremost a group for *each other.*" Cameron also says, "I really align myself with Indians first and gay people second."[19] The group's leaders describe their desire to educate Native people and to ensure that, as Cameron puts it, "Indians know that there *are* gay Indians, both sexes" (Katz, 334). As Burns explains:

In the Indian community, we are trying to realign ourselves with the trampled traditions of our people. Gay people were respected parts of the tribes.
Some were artists and medicine people. So we supply speakers from the group
to appear at Indian gatherings. Sometimes we are booed or jeered, but it doesn't
last long. (Ibid., 333)

Cameron and Burns present GAI's aim as only secondarily to educate non-
Natives. In this interview, they do not divulge information about historical
gender roles in Native societies, and non-Natives are not invited to identify
with Native histories. But they do urge readers of the *Advocate* to recognize the value of Native lesbians and gays organizing with one another and
within Native communities as signs that they are resisting the power of settler colonialism and racism, which condition the sexism and homophobia
they face.

The GAI History Project was begun in 1984 to record Native histories of
gender and sexual diversity and members' own lives and produced the landmark collection *Living the Spirit: A Gay American Indian Anthology* (1988).[20]
Contributors described these histories in various national contexts, and
encouraged pantribal identities that could cross and link these contexts.
No contributor argued that Native gays and lesbians represent the original
nature of all sexual minorities, or that Native histories also belong to non-
Natives. Rather, Midnight Sun (Anishnaabe) and Maurice Kenney (Mohawk)
affirm themes in the memoirs of Clyde M. Hall (Shoshone-Bannock), Erna
Pahe (Navajo), and others: histories of gender and sexual diversity in particular nations can be reaffirmed by their members, while pantribal activism
can link them for mutual inspiration.[21] Hall argues that "if traditions have
been lost," they "need to be researched and revived" to support "groups
and societies for gay Indians" that, like "the contemporary pow-wow," can
form a "modern Indian tradition" meeting needs among Native people
today.[22] Burns presents these insights as GAI's having created an urban
network reminiscent of Renya Ramirez's account of "Native hubs." In her
reading, San Francisco Bay Area American Indian communities defined
home as a site of movement for Native people traversing settler colonial
diasporas, where they reasserted national identities while also forming
broader solidarities.[23] Burns explains that many GAI members "had never
lived in cities" and that "our dream was to return someday to our reservations and help our people—and many of us have returned." In the city,
GAI "re-created the kinship ties of the traditional Indian family" as an
"extended family for gay Indians," meant for "not only those of us who

live in the San Francisco Bay area, but for our many family and friends who regularly visit from other areas."[24] He argues that the diverse knowledge that GAI assembled about Native traditions let members identify as "Indian, yet contemporary and pantribal" (5).

Living the Spirit presents its contributors as mobile subjects who remain linked to tradition and peoplehood. Images by Hulleah Tsinhnahjinnie (Seminole-Muscogee-Dine) portray Native people—marked as women, yet open to more gendered readings—wearing traditional regalia in or near urbanized landscapes. In "Hin-mut-toe-ta-li-ka-tsut (Thunder Clouds Going over Mountains)," a Native woman in traditional dress sits astride a horse grazing against a backdrop of rolling hills that stretch to the horizon, while intercut by a crowded freeway. Among many possible readings, I mark the narrowed background motion of cars articulating the subject's glance behind and the horse's potential movement into a broad landscape to suggest prior and sustained mobility against the time-space of colonial modernity. Tsinhnahjinnie disrupts the tradition/modernity split by portraying Native women asserting subjectivity by linking modern mobility to a sustained relationship to national culture. Whether traditions are landed behind or before them, or right where they now stand, the woman and horse mark a capacity to remain linked to them while traversing incompletely settled lands near, but not within, the routes of colonial discipline. A relationship of travel to ancestral emplacement also opens the book's second section, "Gay American Indians Today." Here, Hall begins a commentary on Native gay men by invoking the Shoshone-Bannock reservation where he lives. He says that while this land "is a harsh place . . . of temperature extremes and a difficult life," after many travels he chose to return to where he had been raised by his grandmother as one of "the 'old peoples' children' . . . having been taught the knowledge, traditions, songs, and lifeways of the tribe." Here where his people long have lived,

> there is something that exists for an Indian person nowhere else: the sense of belonging, of family and of the land. You are not only a person, alone, but an extension of a family and a group of people, a 'tribe,' that has existed before the written word.[25]

Hall is "not saying that we should all go 'back to the blanket' or return to the reservation. But somehow, there should be a blending of the old with the new," so "gay Indians today" can realize "respect" for themselves and one another in "a resurgence of that old pride and knowledge of place"

(104). If for Hall, place is an ancestral and tribal location, he and other contributors also name it as the place of Native gay community, as a border-crossing activity that recalls the many landed traditions of Native nations wherever Native gay people may go.

Given the era when *Living the Spirit* appeared—in the wake of Grahn's work and other studies of the berdache—the contributions are notable for not affirming white queer desires to claim Indigenous sexual or spiritual nature. One potential link to them appears in the introductory poem by Paula Gunn Allen (Laguna), "Some Like Indians Endure." This poem reso-nates with *Another Mother Tongue* and the San Francisco lesbian-feminist communities in which Allen and Grahn participated, even as it invokes lesbian collectivity to enable a theory of Native lesbian resistance.[26] The poem invites the reader to understand "dykes" as having lived and suffered like "Indians," in that they "used to live as tribes" and were "massacred," but "always came back."[27] As in *The Sacred Hoop*, Allen adapts qualities of a white lesbian-feminist story of matriarchal roots to link ancient Europe to the Americas as Indigenous sites opposed to heteropatriarchy, so as to affirm the traditional respect and power accorded to women and lesbians among Native people. I agree with Jace Weaver and Lisa Tatonetti in read-ing Allen as affirming a decolonizing positionality for Native women and lesbians that refuses colonial appropriation.[28] Nevertheless, given that indi-genizing lesbians opens the book in a way that white lesbians or other non-Natives could connect to their own lives, it bears noting that the book's subsequent contributions do not repeat the poem's theme and, at times, markedly displace it, as when Chrystos (Menominee) offers a scathing dis-missal of cultural appropriation in her poem "Today Was a Bad Day like TB."[29] Allen's poem might be better read as addressing a Native audience, as the book suggests, in that it asserts that Native lesbians and gays have belonged to their nations throughout the past and that they endure today because their nationality (Indian) and gender and sexuality (dyke) are inseparable.

Nevertheless, *Living the Spirit* forms a strong association with white queer desires by adapting them to its self-determining project. The first hardcover edition reprints as its frontispiece and on the back cover Grahn's entire state-ment beginning "The day I saw a poster declaring the existence of an orga-nization of Gay American Indians . . ." Bookending *Living the Spirit* in this way may seem to invite reading the text and GAI as consonant with Grahn's desires, or as meant to satisfy them. However, given that the contributors do not discuss the quotation, it appears instead as one possible point of entry into a distinctive text. St. Martin's Press originally advertised the book for sale to the very gay and lesbian readers prepped to consume Native culture as representing their roots. GAI hired as the book's coordinating editor Will Roscoe, whose analyses of Native histories reflected his responsible relationship to GAI in this book and to the Zuni nation in his *The Zuni Man-Woman* (1991). Yet Roscoe later wrote texts on queer spirituality that invited non-Native queer people to adopt Native culture as part of their own spiritual nature.[30] Decisions by St. Martin's Press or by Roscoe to market *Living the Spirit* to gay and lesbian non-Natives might explain why Grahn's words were featured. But I am more interested in their potential resonance with the book's contributors, who appear to engage with them, even if not explicitly. When GAI was new, the non-Natives who paid it most heed—Roscoe, Katz, Grahn—were white people acting within long histories of adapting Native culture to gay and lesbian liberation. Insofar as GAI members engaged them, it showed their ability to adapt non-Native desires to their own ends. To repeat, both GAI and *Living the Spirit* addressed Native queer people by highlighting historical ties to Native traditions so that they might transform their own and their peoples' subjugation to colonial heteropatriarchy from within a transnational Native movement that remained distinct from non-Native queer politics. *Living the Spirit* was the first book to quote Grahn to a Native queer audience. Thus, the words of a prominent lesbian writer could be seen to affirm the impact of Gay American Indians on gay and lesbian politics, reinforcing the value of the group's telling its story in its *own* words.

Grahn's words also could be adapted to GAI's own goals. Cameron and Burns defended Native gays and lesbians to *Native* communities by arguing that their societies (to quote Grahn) "once picked them for the task of naming, healing, prediction, leadership, and teaching because they displayed characteristics" that Native people in Western terms now "call gay." Although Grahn was addressing non-Natives, her words, in this context, have the different effect of inviting solidarity among Native peoples in opposing colonial heteropatriarchy. Most importantly, no contributors address her claim that Native traditions bequeath to non-Native gay men and lesbians "positions of social power in history and ritual among people all over the globe" because "Gay is a universal quality." If Allen potentially intimates such a story, even she does not invite its extrapolations, but locates non-Native lesbians in solidarity with Native peoples. For Grahn, non-Natives already embody a queer indigeneity that can liberate queer settlers on Native lands. Native activists may adapt this language to claim forms of historical and contemporary leadership in their nations while forging transnational alliances for decolonization. As meanings that shift across distinct yet relational locations in a settler society, these readings indicate that non-Native and Native queer modernities arise diversely within the power-laden intimacies of conversation.

Relational Locations: Ethnography and History of Queer Politics

This book explains narrative relationships among queer subjects by situating them within ethnographic and historical accounts of U.S. queer politics. My involvement in northern California queer movements in the 1980s and 1990s produced an initial ethnographic study of them. That work grew into a broader historical account of U.S. queer politics as non-Native by comparison to the histories of Native queer politics documented by Native activists. This research path responded to anticolonial, transnational, and Indigenous feminist criticism, which, as a scholar in women's and gender studies, I apply to queer anthropology to transform its colonial legacies.

A persistent form of storytelling about indigeneity in late-twentieth-century U.S. gender/sexual politics sparked my inquiry into its conditions and effects. As that politics shifted among lesbian/gay and LGBT coalitions, radical queer politics that challenged homonormativity, and the adoption of *queer* as an "umbrella" term for minority rights, I recurrently heard participants tell that Native American societies historically honored people like themselves with social esteem and spiritual gifts. This story promised them a sexual nature, an authentic culture, or both simultaneously, while enabling them to claim forms of cultural belonging through ancient roots. While the terms in the story shifted once berdache was displaced by Two-Spirit, cisgender gay men remained central within them, as if they were also descriptive of women and trans people; and stories centering trans people reframed similar sources to different ends. Historians might reference these stories to Walter Williams's *The Spirit and the Flesh* (1986) or Leslie Feinberg's *Transgender Warriors* (1996), but I encountered them in classrooms, bookstores, political activism, theater productions, and friendship networks that preceded publication of these books. Whether people agreed or disagreed with these stories, their recurrence kept the question of Native history central to the determination of queer truths.

My research began in the mid-1990s as an ethnography of how such storytelling in U.S. queer politics articulated multiracial communities and antiracist activism. I engaged social networks already linked to my life in northern California and nationally by asking how stories about indigeneity formed utopian narratives that attempted to unify queer communities across their differences. I noted the tension between a promise in such stories to heal racism and the evidence that racism persisted among their narrators. Although I sought at the time to pursue an antiracist queer account of colonial discourse in solidarity with queer of color activists, it soon became clear that the stories I examined exceeded this scope and also required a targeting of queer antiracism. In the 1990s, queers of color and their white antiracist queer allies critiqued queer movements that represented their "community" as a multiracial and global yet unitary group— notably when those movements sought to "include" a "diversity" within otherwise white middle-class spaces. Antiracist activists challenged queer racism, economic inequality, and imperialism by critiquing how white middle-class queers linked their liberation to acceptance within their own racialized class and state. But such efforts were stymied when queer movement leaders agreed with critics to oppose inequalities by arguing that their work had already bridged them: with a queer *culture* linking queers to one another more than to any other group; with a queer *history* linking all queers across time; or within a queer *world* on a global scale. These claims readily invoked as key evidence Native American history and extrapolated it onto Indigenous peoples worldwide. Yet if activists ever criticized such claims as being "racist," they failed to comprehend fully what they confronted: for, invoking Native roots for queer culture and history already presented a means to mediate racism; and if critics sought to address racism by working for "inclusion" of queers of color, that could help to diversify the very politics where those stories still circulated.

This book aims to answer this conundrum, by shifting my ethnography of queer spaces where I lived to studying their formation in relation to the spaces they elided: those formed by Native queer and Two-Spirit activists. My shift was driven by a recognition that I, the narrators of the aforementioned stories, and the antiracist movement that sought to disrupt them all were positioned in relation to Native queer people as non-Native. In retrospect, it became clear to me that both the queer "racism" and "antiracism" I had known arose from a *non-Native* relationship to imagining indigeneity. Yet I first encountered them within the milieu of a settler society, which presumes and naturalizes Native people's absence or disappearance. Non-Native writers such as Williams and Feinberg popularized Two-Spirit people's voices even as Two-Spirit activists were mobilizing in cities like San Francisco, Toronto, and New York and in rural Native communities, all of which made Native queer people seem ubiquitous in late-twentieth-century queer politics. Yet this was happening within settler societies, where queer movements functioned without the participation of Native people even though many members felt they were entitled to narrate Native history as their own. During the 1990s, I met different stories only by moving *outside* normatively white queer politics to attend to Native queer activist space, including women of color feminist spaces where Native queer women provided leadership. Here I heard very different stories from Native narrators. Many claimed a relationship to traditions of gender and sexual diversity in their nations, which some extended to include all Native queer people. Others argued that however inspiring tradition might be, their Native queer identities today were most important. These claims were not exclusive but interlinked. Amid their differences, I heard Native narrators express a desire to join with and lead their peoples in a collective struggle for decolonization.[31] Throughout the 1990s, Native queer people were defining their lives autonomously, practicing—to borrow Audra Simpson's phrase—an "ethnographic refusal" of non-Native anthropological or queer inquiry. My research responded to this politicization of anthropological knowledge by what might by called an "ethnographic repudiation" of white queer ethnography of Native people. In its place, I pursued ethnographic and historical study of the *non*-Native queer spaces where I lived and I increasingly responded directly to Native queer activist critiques.

The project thus became comparative of non-Native and Native queer politics once it was repositioned, politically and methodologically, in relationship to Native queer and Two-Spirit activists. I traced historical ties between non-Native and Native queer politics in literature by Native activists now housed in libraries and archives. I requested and received critical engagement from Native queer activists across the United States and Canada, and they interviewed me about my work. Much of the literature I cited had received little or no attention in earlier writing by non-Natives, despite its importance in the historical growth of Native queer and Two-Spirit activism. I thus became a non-Native critic who was engaging Native activists against colonial methodologies that would frame the Native activist texts I discuss as "discoveries" by a non-Native scholar. Instead, I cite Native queer activist texts as a distinctive body of critical theory to which queer non-Natives already were intellectually and politically accountable, and to which my now-comparative and historical study of non-Native queer politics offered a response. The material in this book in fact *triangulates* two readings—my own and those shared by Native queer and Two-Spirit activists—to critically examine non-Native queer politics, even as my reading remains responsible to Native activists.

My approach decidedly departs from the gay and lesbian anthropology of berdache—not to separate from its history, but to traverse it with a critical difference. During the late twentieth century, gay and lesbian anthropologists revisited prior work on berdache or conducted new research with the intention of affirming Native gender and sexual diversity. Yet that work also served to advance their own non-Native gender and sexual politics, and reinforced their anthropological authority to determine Native truth while leaving their desire for it unexamined. By investigating the non-Native and, most centrally, white queer subjects that produced and consumed berdache, I displace the distancing effects of classic anthropology with critical insider research of constituencies in which I am already located. I then cite Native queer and Two-Spirit people as critical theorists of their own lives who require no anthropological translation and whose claims still retain the power to interrupt it. My project thus engages anthropology by interpreting the effects of anthropological knowledge in queer cultures and politics. Certain qualities of ethnography are important to it, such as its recurrent return to the social geography of the San Francisco Bay Area that produced intertwined histories of Native and gender/sexual politics.[32] I evaluate the anthropology of berdache as a legacy of the Society of Lesbian and Gay Anthropologists (SOLGA), which provided crucial support to my work, and is now known as the Association for Queer Anthropology (AQA), committed to studying sexuality and gender in context of studies of race, class, nationality, colonization, and globalization. AQA is accommodating an interdisciplinary approach in anthropology that regards queerness less as an object of representation and more as an action to be taken on the field. Queer*ing* anthropology may denaturalize and destabilize disciplinary norms, which this book contributes to by *unsettling* anthropology's settler colonial formation and holding it accountable to the interdisciplinary and political work of decolonizing queer knowledge production.

I agree with anthropologists who question colonial desires for Native history, as, for instance, in Towle and Morgan's critique of the "third gender" concept in U.S. transgender politics or Sue-Ellen Jacobs's response to Two-Spirit criticism of gay and lesbian anthropology.[33] But my work differs by not suggesting that such desires will be resolved by producing a better anthropology of Native culture. I focus not on Native or non-Native people but on the genealogies of settler colonialism that produce non-Native and Native queer modernities in relationship. I examine non-Native tales of Native truth—anthropological or popular, romantic or objectivist, colonial or anticolonial—as claims conditioned by the persistent power of settler colonialism. I compare them to Native narratives that address non-Natives without beginning or ending in non-Native logics. The interrelated quality of these narratives becomes apparent even as the capacity of non-Native narratives to contain Native truth is displaced. Narrating non-Native and Native queer projects in conversation thus inspires a new theory of settler colonialism and resistance to its power.

Theorizing Settler Colonialism and Queer Modernities

Theories of settler colonialism in Native studies and Indigenous feminist and queer critique inspire my argument that modern sexuality produces non-Natives in relation to Native people in the multiracial space of a white settler society. I hold queer theories particularly accountable to the study of settler colonialism, in response to the critical implications of Native queer modernities modeled by Native queer and Two-Spirit activisms.

Settlers naturalize their presence on Native land as rightful, final occupants so that the question of conquest can appear to be "settled." Naturalization addresses settlers' "illegitimacy"—at times, their "central dilemma," in Amy den Ouden's words—by asserting their presence on settled land as incontestable.[34] Settler colonialism is naturalized whenever conquest or displacement of Native peoples is ignored or appears necessary or complete, and whenever subjects are defined by settler desires to possess Native land, history, or culture. Settler colonialism thus must be denaturalized not only in social and political spaces but also in definitions and experiences of subjectivity. By more fully understanding its naturalization, critiques may destabilize it within settler societies and all spaces that those societies inform.

I explain settler colonialism's naturalization by evaluating proposals of Native disappearance and settler replacement. Patrick Wolfe defines settler colonialism along "the logic of elimination," which seeks the erasure of Native peoples to facilitate their replacement by settlers.[35] Recognizing that genocide studies after Raphael Lemkin correlates genocide to extermination, Wolfe argues that genocidal practices are among the techniques that may serve the logic of elimination. He notes that settlers may pursue the elimination of Native peoples by trying not to destroy but to produce life, through the amalgamation of Native peoples into settler society and the narrowing or erasure of claims on Native nationality. For instance, blood quantum and other racial and colonial methods for determining Native identity enact narratives of "dilution," anticipating Native people's disappearance, and define self-identified Native people and people of mixed Indigenous heritage as "non-Native."[36] Many Native studies scholars use "genocide" precisely to name this array of destructive and productive practices. I affirm such usage even as I appreciate Wolfe's use of the term, which in its breadth also references a method by settlers to replace Native people by naturalizing their own proliferation. Jean O'Brien explains how settlers founded colonial New England in narratives of the inevitable disappearance of Native people, in an extenuated, conflictual, and incomplete process that persists even as New England Native peoples continue to resist erasure today.[37] Dale Turner evaluates the erasure of Native peoples within Canadian "White Paper liberalism," in which regressive Native identity is contrasted to the progressive individuality and modern freedoms conferred by attempts to re-create Native peoples as citizens of the settler state.[38] Native studies scholars expose these ruses of settler colonialism's logic of elimination by arguing the integrity and renewal of Indigenous governance and Indigenous relationships to land, language, and peoplehood, as these trace "intellectual histories" (in Robert Warrior's term) that displace settler authority while affirming Native modernities as creative assertions of survival and resistance.[39]

Philip Deloria and Renée Bergland point out that when white settlers in the United States proclaim civilization's advance, they also confirm their (il)legitimacy by resituating the Native peoples they (seem to) supplant as part of their own histories and inner lives. Bergland examines the appearance of Native people as ghosts of inspiration within narratives of white settler lives and society. Deloria traces how white settlers adapt indigeneity's putative opposition to civilization through "Indian impersonation," which performs opposition to settler rule as well as the authority to claim it for themselves as settler subjects. In both accounts, settlers supplant *and* incorporate indigeneity to attain settler subjectivity. Racialized by white supremacy, these acts appear civilizational—vanquishing Native adversaries mirrors calls to civilized people to control primitive drives. Yet they are also nostalgic for an indigeneity that modern people must transcend, even while incorporating it as part of their history. In a settler society, then, the very demand upon settlers to replace Natives simultaneously incites white settler desires to be intimate with the Native authenticity that their modernity presumably replaces. Indigeneity's civilizational replacement thus is complementary to the settler pursuit of primitivism. Impersonating indigeneity and believing in colonial modernity are noncontradictory acts, given that settlers preserve Native authenticity as a history they must possess in order to transcend. If Indian impersonation seems to be an appropriation of Native culture, Deloria and Bergland argue that white settlers in fact perform an indigeneity they imagine from their desires to belong to stolen land. Nostalgic quests for roots that modern nationals transcend also defined the growth of modern European nationalism more generally; but in settler societies, this path articulated the difference of Native peoples whom settlers must supplant, incorporate, and transcend in order to become modern subjects of a settler nation.[40] Thus, settler colonialism is naturalized not only in Native people's seeming "disappearance" from a modern, settled landscape, but also in indigeneity's recurrent appearance within and *as* settler subjectivity. Whether erasing or performing indigeneity, omitting or celebrating it, settlers practice settlement by turning Native land and culture into an inheritance granting them knowledge and ownership of *themselves.* If settlement thereby presumes Native authenticity's disappearance, it does *not* follow that Native people are absent from representation. James Cox observes that narratives encoded by Native disappearance mark the presence of indigeneity, in that the persistence of Native peoples surviving and resisting colonization remains outside the frame, inspiring settler narratives to deny their existence and reinforce their erasure.[41] Deloria, Bergland, and Cox thus show that within the racial and national frame of white settler colonialism, settlers and Natives are produced in relation to each other when the former arise *as settlers*, naturalizing an emplacement produced through their own and others' displacement by narrating Native elimination.

These analyses explain white-supremacist settler colonialism once we recognize that a normative relation of "Natives" to "settlers" articulates a multiracial and transnational settler society and the locations within it of non-Native peoples of color. Histories of white settler colonialism and its logic of elimination in the Americas and the Pacific must theorize its coproduction with the transatlantic slave trade and the African diaspora, franchise colonialism in Asia and Africa, and global migrations of indentured labor, all of which inform the globalization of European capital and empire.[42] This context suggests that the relationality of "settler" to "Native" in a white settler society has the effect of excluding non-Native people of color from the civilizational modernity that white settlers seek when they appear to eliminate Native peoples only to elide the subjugation of non-Native people of color on stolen land. In the United States, African diasporic peoples, migrant Asian, Latin American, African, and Middle Eastern laborers, and conquered Chicano/a and Latino/a peoples are located distinctly from the settler status inherited by representatives of Anglo whiteness—even if they might accede to that status if the interpretation of their racialization changes. For instance, the relationality of "Native" and "settler" invokes intimacies among Native and African diasporic peoples in opposition to and in complicity with settlement: as Native peoples rejected, or practiced, African enslavement; as free blacks participated in settler conquest or joined Natives in resisting; and as Native and black peoples had to debate their ancestral relationships in relation to the hegemony of a white-supremacist color line. Yet, while conditioned by these complex histories, solidarity and kinship ties among Native and black peoples have not been erased as a potential site for challenging white-supremacist settler colonialism.[43]

Scholars debate the degree of accountability of white people or people of color for the status and power of "settlers" in relation to Native peoples in white settler societies. Bonita Lawrence and Haunani-Kay Trask have called on non-Native people of color in white settler societies to ask themselves how their histories of racial subjugation and antiracist resistance might be compatible with settler colonial elimination of Native peoples and their sovereignty.[44] Nandita Sharma and Cynthia Wright respond to Lawrence by citing colonial and postcolonial studies on the colonization of diasporic peoples of color and the perpetuation of racism and genocide by postcolonial nationalism, and propose that colonial legacies can be disrupted by cosmopolitan subjects forming multiracial, transnational "commons" in the local and global spaces they now inhabit.[45] Sharma and Wright transpose critiques of the imperial nation-state and postcolonial cultural nationalism onto Indigenous peoples and settler societies without sufficiently considering literature on Indigenous decolonization, which disturbs the colonial modern state-form and presents alternative forms of nationality that displace colonial, racialist, and heteropatriarchal domination.[46] They also do not address how diasporic scholars of color and white antiracist allies are accountable to the struggles of Native nations, including how a white settler academy empowers them to argue that non-Natives are not settlers or that Native people should not defend their nations. Nevertheless, I agree with them that to say that all non-Natives are settlers may fail to explain how settler colonialism conditions non-Natives by "race" or migrant/immigrant status, while stymieing efforts to link Native, diaspora, and critical race studies in defending Native decolonization.[47] I find most compelling the self-reflective assertions by non-Native people of color of their status, role, or power as settlers—as when Asian American allies of the Hawaiian sovereignty movement critique participation by Asians in U.S. settler colonization of Hawai'i, or when diasporic Palestinians voice solidarity with Indigenous Americans who also ally with Palestinians in struggle against Israeli settlement of Palestinian lands.[48] More such analysis is needed within diaspora and critical race studies to displace accounts of colonization and resistance that normalize whiteness. White radicals often fail to note the racial specificity of their settler colonial inheritance. If they project their experience into theorizing the responsibility of non-Natives to demonstrate Indigenous solidarity, they may *reproduce* white supremacy by not considering how people of color negotiate settler colonialism—perhaps within Indigenous solidarity that white people will not share.

My project shifts questions of status—such as "Who is the settler?"—to ask instead how subjects are produced by social processes: "Who, under what conditions, inherits the power to represent or enact settler colonialism?" It thus responds to political demands that subjects who inherit the power of settler colonialism challenge their inheritance, which I do by investigating and clarifying the genealogies through which such subjects might arise. For instance, white-supremacist settler colonialism distinguishes "Native" from "settler" so as to naturalize whiteness in teleologies of modernity, civilization, and citizenship that predict Indigenous elimination and settler replacement. White subjects may appear—if their locations by nation, class, gender, sexuality, and disability can be made to match—as the settlers differentiated from the Natives whose lands and histories they inherit. Yet this definition is troubled immediately by the logic of elimination's having operated precisely via amalgamation. Lawrence and Malinda Maynor Lowery explain that the Native identities of mixed-blood Native people are invalidated by their racialization as white or black through the policing of Native status and the redrawing of the color line.[49] Maria Saldaña-Portillo further explains how mixed Indigenous ancestry is produced by national projects of *mestizaje* to replace specific Indigenous identifications or land claims, and that whether conforming to white supremacy or indigenizing mestizos/as such projects can remain in tension with Native communities that retain a traditional collective identity.[50] In light of these complexities, we cannot assume that all who are forcibly aligned with whiteness, blackness, or *mestizaje* are "non-Native," even though their lives may be meaningfully defined by a lived difference from Native nationality and collectivity.

The logic of elimination defines "Native" as an ever-disappearing location that includes or excludes Native people as this benefits conquest. To presume an absolute distinction of "Native" from "non-Native" invariably misses this historically porous definition. At the same time, even subjects structurally opposed by racism may recognizably share status as non-Native in relation to the difference of indigeneity in a settler society. Racialization under white supremacy will grant non-Natives distinct, often mutually exclusive, abilities to represent or enact settler colonial power. But all non-Natives still will differ in their experiences of settler colonialism from the experiences of Native peoples.[51]

The logic of elimination defines a normative relationality of "Native" to "settler" precisely by positioning non-Native people of color *outside* a power relation that all defined as Native are made to *inhabit*. Native people become *marked* within the power relation that purportedly *eliminates* them, in direct relation to how non-Native people of color are *absented* from the very power relation *producing* them as racialized populations in a white settler society on "emptied" land. My reading of white settler colonization triangulates normative statuses assigned to whiteness, indigeneity, and non-Native peoples of color, while noting how histories of amalgamation, mixed heritage, and *mestizaje* cross their putative borders. I then explain distinctions among Natives and non-Natives by referring to the work of sovereign Native nations and their members within alliance politics. Native nations are defining and defending sovereign distinctions from non-Native peoples and societies by producing innovative theories of alliance: to bridge differences of status defining membership; to embrace differences in the community such as "race," gender, and sexuality; to link varied nations transnationally; and to connect their national or transnational work with allied non-Natives. The alliances emerging in Native activism are pursuing, as Andrea Smith notes, "unlikely" routes to ensure survival and defend sovereignty, as modeled for Smith by Indigenous women activists.[52] I focus on such alliance work as theorized and practiced by Native queer, Two-Spirit, and HIV/AIDS activists, which Qwo-Li Driskill and Chris Finley argue is needed both to bridge the diversity of Native queer/Two-Spirit communities and to realign their communities and nations in struggle against heteropatriarchy.[53] Formation of such alliances in Native politics does not presume that those it joins across differences are wholly distinct. For instance, activist responses to the Arizona anti-immigrant law SB1070 deepened alliances of Tohono O'odham and Chicano/a activists in ways that respected the national integrity of O'odham people and lands, facilitated Indigenous identification among Chicano/a activists, and recognized that racial profiling of "illegal immigrants" targeted all people with Indigenous features. As a result, Tohono O'odham and Chicano/a solidarity with migrants emerged through negotiating distinct, yet linked, Indigenous heritage.[54] When my

analysis addresses the difference of Native nationality as it troubles settler society and refracts the lives of non-Natives, I intend not to police the
boundaries of Native identity, but rather to focus on accounts by Native
people that demonstrate how their lives are interdependent and bridge the
differences imposed by colonial exclusion and domination. The national
and transnational models of alliance by Native queer and Two-Spirit people
emerge as projects to which all non-Native queers can be accountable, in
contrast to settler colonial desires for a relationship to indigeneity outside
of a situated politics of alliance.

In sum, in a multiracial, transnational white settler society, the relation
of "Native" to "settler" articulates distinctions of Native from non-Native,
but *these two comparisons are neither identical nor parallel.* The teleological
binary Native/settler is perpetually complicated by the *non*binary relations
of diverse non-Natives and Native peoples across commonalities and differences. Nevertheless, no degree of complication in either comparison removes
the meaningful difference indigeneity continues to make in a settler society, as in Native sovereignty struggles and national and transnational Native
alliances. If settlers ever do learn who they are, they will recognize themselves at the least as those who are meant to *replace.* Native disappearance
haunts settler subjectivity and illuminates all cultures and politics in a
settler society. Regardless of whether non-Natives think they inherit the
power of settler colonialism, all can ask how it produces them in roles that
may sustain it and its naturalization.

Queering Colonial Relationalities

Interdisciplinary theory of settler colonialism rarely entertains the degree
of complexity I invite while defying the naturalization of settlement by centering Native people. Among theories that address European settler colonialism by emphasizing relations with Native peoples, one long in circulation is Mary Louise Pratt's "contact zone" indicating a power-laden space
of cultural creativity in colonial situations.[55] Pratt's innovation was to shift
colonial studies from narrating imperial power and Native subjection to
focus on their relational formation, while highlighting the critical agency
of Native peoples and contacts in which Natives influenced colonists while
colonists relied on Natives for self-definition. While Pratt acknowledged the
diverse racialization of colonial situations, her term often is used to reference "Native/settler" relations without explaining the multiracial scope of
settler societies. Nevertheless, any reflection of white settler logics in the

term—the *appearance* that a relation of disappearing "Natives" to civilizational white "settlers" defines social life—is precisely what makes "contact zone" useful to my reading of the settler histories of modern sexuality. Inspired by Indigenous feminist and queer critiques of sexual colonization, and with the United States as my context, I argue that modern sexuality arises in white settler society as a "contact zone," defined by attempting to replace Native kinship, embodiment, and desire with the hegemony of "settler sexuality," or the heteropatriarchal sexual modernity exemplary of white settler civilization. I adapt Foucault's history of sexuality by reading "modern sexuality" as the array of discourses, procedures, and institutions that arose in metropolitan and colonial societies to distinguish and link primitive and civilized gender and sexuality, while defining racial, national, gendered, and sexual subjects and populations in biopolitical relationship. I analyze the subjection of Native societies to colonial heteropatriarchy as a proving ground for the biopolitics of settler colonialism, which defines modern sexuality as "contact" between queered indigeneity and its transcendence by settler sexuality. My approach affirms the work of Saidya Hartman, Allan Punzalan Isaac, Eithne Luibhéid, and other scholars in examining the formation of modern sexuality as settler sexuality in the United States amid the terrorizing racial and heteropatriarchal regulation of diasporic and colonized African, Asian, Latin American, and Arab and Middle Eastern peoples, including mestizo/a Latin Americans racialized in an Anglo context beyond normative whiteness or authentic indigeneity.[56] Mindful of this array of intersections, I focus on the sexual colonization of Native peoples as a key site through which settler colonialism conditions the diversely racialized subjects produced within queer modernities.

Indigenous feminist theorists explain settler colonialism *as* sexual colonization. Andrea Smith theorizes it as sexual violence, through which the conquest of land and bodies advances heteropatriarchal rule over Native peoples and establishes it throughout settler society.[57] Kim Anderson, Bonita Lawrence, and Chris Finley, among others, explain heteropatriarchy as a genocidal method for isolating, dispersing, and eliminating Native peoples, including through internalization as a norm of discipline and violence in Native communities.[58] Indigenous feminist theorists and women's movements invite decolonization by challenging heteropatriarchy as a colonial legacy; some also note that colonial violence targets persons marked by gender or sexual diversity so as to queer Indigenous *peoples* to colonial heteropatriarchal rule. Their work informs Indigenous queer critiques and allied work in queer studies.[59] Deborah Miranda explains Spanish conquest in California as defined by the "extermination of the *joyas*," a process Finley links to the genocidal effects of colonial biopower, which Mark Rifkin investigates in U.S. state efforts to produce Native peoples as heteronormative private-property owning citizens of a settler nation.[60] Qwo-Li Driskill focuses Indigenous queer critiques through an "erotics of sovereignty" to answer the violences of heteropatriarchal colonization with the body-based and collective work of decolonization.[61] Forty years of Native queer and Two-Spirit organizing in the United States and Canada anticipated and pursued these insights by recalling memories of Indigenous embodiment, desire, and kinship that challenge the heteropatriarchal logics of settler modernity. Anguksuar Richard LaFortune, cofounder of American Indian Gays and Lesbians (Minneapolis) and the International Two-Spirit Gathering, recognizes Two-Spirit organizing as a "movement," while saying that "what is happening, actually, is that we are remembering who we are and that our identities can no longer be used as a weapon against us."[62] Native queer and Two-Spirit activists negotiating colonial discourses join Indigenous queer and feminist scholars in critiquing heteropatriarchy as crucial to struggle for decolonization.

Andrea Smith and Qwo-Li Driskill argue that queer theory reproduces the violences of settler colonialism unless these are examined as conditions of the social worlds in which its practitioners live.[63] Smith and Driskill join queer of color, queer diasporic, and queer/migration critiques in regarding all queer formations as conditioned by colonization, racialization, diaspora, and globalization. But they also demonstrate how theories of queer temporality, racialization, and diaspora must shift to address settler colonialism. If settler colonialism is produced by processes of elimination and replacement and by teleologies of modernity and civilization, it immediately invites theory of temporality. Smith goes beyond Lee Edelman's theory of queer temporality displacing heteronormative futurity in the image of the queer child—one José Esteban Muñoz evaluates as "always already white"—to assert that

> an indigenous critique must question the logic of "no future" in the context of genocide, where Native people have already been determined by settler colonialism to have no future. If the goal of queerness is to challenge the reproduction of the social order, then the Native child may already be queered.[64]

Indigenous feminist and queer critics explain that by queering Native *peoples* as threats whose conquest will establish colonial heteropatriarchy, canceling the future of the Native child produces the future of white settler society as genocide. Yet Smith notes that to recall what was queered within Native society itself constitute a queer critique of heteropatriarchy.

Smith and Driskill also question antiracist and diasporic queer theories that erase Native peoples. If queer and diaspora theories valorize dislocation, Smith argues, then Native peoples will appear excessively local or national and, hence, insufficiently queer. Smith answers Gayatri Gopinath's assertion that "queerness is to heterosexuality as diaspora is to the nation" by asking if "perhaps we can understand Indigenous nationhood as already queered."[65] Driskill argues that "Two-Spirit critiques" locate Native queer and Two-Spirit people "as productive, if not central, to nationalist, decolonial agendas . . . not [as] an assimilationist move but a move against the colonial powers that have attempted to dissolve or restrain Native sovereignties."[66] According to Driskill, Native queer and Two-Spirit people do not accommodate and reinforce heteronormative nations, as occurs along the "autological" mode of settler citizenship critiqued by Elizabeth Povinelli, or the postcolonial nationalisms disrupted by diasporic queer critics.[67] Rather, from Driskill's "erotics of sovereignty" to the Two-Spirit and Native HIV/ AIDS activism recounted in this book, Native queers lead their peoples in reimagining modes of embodiment, desire, and collectivity that defy their queered encounters with settler colonialism. Their redefinitions of nationality are informed by Smith's account of Native feminists whose "models of nationhood . . . do not have the heteronormative, patriarchal, nuclear family as their building block," but produce national belonging that, "rather than a commitment to national chauvinism and insularity," performs creative solidarities and "unlikely alliances" in pursuit of Indigenous decolonization.[68]

Following Indigenous feminist and queer critics, I understand *queer* to be a location constituted by white-supremacist settler colonialism that will be unascertainable until this condition is explained. My argument is less "intersectional" than genealogical, in that nothing in the history of white-supremacist settler colonialism or the globalization of European capital and empire that it facilitates is separable from what is perceived as "queer." But a stronger implication is epistemological: eliding such analyses will leave queer studies empty of meaning. The problem is not that white, class-privileged, national inheritors of settler colonialism have been central to queer accounts. The problem is that all conclusions drawn from such accounts fail to explain not only all who are excluded from them but also all who are *included:* because the only possible explanation of queerness under white-supremacist settler colonialism is one that also interrogates that condition. Queer studies must examine settler colonialism as a condition of its own work. A queer critique of location, temporality, or belonging that naturalizes its relationship to settler colonialism no longer will be considered transgressive. Native queer appeals to national traditions or liberation, in turn, no longer will be considered normative if their effect is to denaturalize settler heteropatriarchy and homonationalism while investing Native decolonization in feminist and queer social change. All this follows once settler colonialism and Indigenous decolonization become a focus of queer studies.

My account recognizes in Native queer and Two-Spirit projects a *discrepancy* in relation to settler colonial biopolitics and the "contact zone" of settler sexuality. Native queer and Two-Spirit people recall languages, memories, and relations that exceed colonial epistemic authority, and their relationship to these formations answers the queered conditions of Native people under settler rule. Their projects thus disrupt the temporality of settler colonialism, which predicts indigeneity's erasure by positing authenticity as a past split from a progressive present. Native queer and Two-Spirit people perform instead the queer temporality of Native modernity, wherein tradition is precisely not primordial but an articulation of memory and survival with life in a settler colonial situation. I recognize Native queer modernities arising discrepantly from non-Native queer modernities precisely when they engage in power-laden conversation. In so doing, Native queer people may act as Chela Sandoval theorized for U.S./Third World feminists, who traversed and displaced the boundaries of modernist social movements in a *differential* oppositional consciousness.[69] Or, they may practice what Muñoz named for queers of color as *disidentification* from the totalizing binary of opposition or assimilation by working "on and in" power to expose and disrupt its effects.[70] Women of color feminism and queer of color critique resonate with Indigenous queer critiques when their objects and claims are recognized as conditioned by the settler colonial power that Native queer and Two-Spirit activists displace.

By way of response, this book examines how non-Natives formed modern queer identities, cultures, and politics in the United States while participating in a white settler society. I explain variation among non-Native queer projects by their degree of consonance with white-supremacist settler colonial power, which establishes the heteronormative binary sex/gender systems on Native land. My account both affirms and extends that of scholars of homonormativity and homonationalism. Locating homonationalism within a critique of settler colonialism suggests that this phenomenon is unlikely to describe the alignments of only *some* queers with neoliberal or imperial power. All queer modernities under white-supremacist settler colonialism respond to its power, the very power Native queer and Two-Spirit critiques continue to contest. Several implications follow.

Queer critics must not be satisfied once they identify homonationalist defenders of civilization as if this means that their work is done—indeed, as if antiracism, anti-imperialism, or anticolonialism are not routes to the practice of homonationalism. In a white settler society, seeking homonationalist alignment with the settler state creates non-Native queer modernities as normatively white appeals to settler citizenship. Read strictly within the normatively white and non-Native frame of white settler colonialism, modern queers *are* homonationalists. Here, homonationalist aspirations will traverse the normative routes of settler citizenship, by aspiring to civilizational modernity, but also by incorporating and transcending the primitivity that settlers definitively supplant *and* recall. American and Native studies show that settler citizens in the United States are at once civilizationalists and primitivists. In this context, homonationalism will define modern queers within quests to achieve settler citizenship; and civilizationalist and primitivist practices will derive from and express homonationalism. Thus, while queer scholars today must continue to target white-supremacist and imperialist forms of homonationalism, the problem this book addresses is somewhat different. For some time, I have been preoccupied with the settler colonial and homonationalist implications of queer projects produced within the horizons of liberal multicultural logics of inclusion, equity, and democracy, and their interdependence with radicalisms pursuing anti-oppression, structural change, and revolution. I am especially concerned by any suggestion that queer radicalism initiates queer modernities that queer liberalisms only secondarily normalize for a heteropatriarchal society. Queer radicalisms and liberalisms arise interdependently within white-supremacist settler colonialism and perform settler homonationalism when they traverse primitivist *and* civilizationalist trajectories of queer liberation.

Although my arguments are specific to the racial and national contexts of the United States, they are applicable to other white settler societies. Yet the U.S. context remains key because of the global hegemony asserted by U.S. queer projects. Settler colonialism is part of all power projected by the United States as "domestic" or global acts. Therefore, the distinctly "non-Native" and settler form of U.S. queer modernities can sustain wherever U.S. queer subjects, cultures, or politics go. I join ethnographers of transnational sexualities in being skeptical that U.S. queer formations overwrite local or national creativity among queer people worldwide.[71] Nevertheless, scholars of queer globalization should ask how the settler colonial formation of U.S. queer modernities articulates across borders. If modern queers become settlers in the United States, then this path to queer modernity may create queers as settlers even if they travel, or appear elsewhere. I propose all of these implications without attempting to write "outside" the colonial conditions I critique. White queer critics are called to undertake a critique of settler colonialism—by Indigenous feminist and queer critiques, and the critique of settler colonialism in Native studies—and that is what this book endeavors to do.

Nevertheless, this book examines non-Native and Native queer modernities not so much to critique non-Native queers as colonial but to ask why and how diverse non-Native *and* Native queer people arise within intimately relational and power-laden conversations, with effects that as often as not blur easy distinctions of "colonial" from "anticolonial." The book explains non-Native queer modernities as forming within the friction of conversations with discrepant Native queer modernities denaturalizing settler colonialism. Neither chosen nor denied, these conversations are not utopian; but they nevertheless form creative zones of contact and transformation whose outcomes are not preordained. Interreferential moments in conversation show that the meaning of non-Native or Native queer subjectivity appeared by engaging relational claims. Apparently close ties nevertheless led to communicating in divergent registers, even as distant projects cited similar registers, with often distinct effects. I examine these effects by oscillating between synchronic and diachronic contexts and local and mobile spatializations. My genealogical readings hinge on narrative spaces—testimonies, newsletters, books, research reports, visual media; community centers, performances, rural camps, and public activism—near which I was located in my historical and ethnographic research. I examine "communities" as inexplicable except within the relations of culture and power marked by genealogy. My effort to mediate multiple voices in interlinked accounts is also a contribution to their dialogue. Thus, in the end, more than a study *of* conversation, this book *is* a kind of conversation, as well as an effort to transform those in which it arose and that it examines.

Part I Genealogies

Chapter 1   The Biopolitics of Settler Sexuality and Queer Modernities

MODERN SEXUALITY ARISES IN SETTLER SOCIETIES as a function of the biopolitics of settler colonialism. In the United States, the sexual colonization of Native peoples produced modern sexuality as "settler sexuality": a white and national heteronormativity formed by regulating Native sexuality and gender while appearing to supplant them with the sexual modernity of settlers. Queer modernities in a settler society are produced in contextual relationship to the settler colonial conditions of modern sexuality.

White settlers promulgating colonial heteropatriarchy queered Native peoples and all racialized subject populations for elimination and regulation by the biopolitics of settler colonialism. Achille Mbembe has adapted Giorgio Agamben's account of biopower to colonial situations by explaining colonial rule as "necropolitics," or a positioning of the space-time of the colony in a state of exception to Western imperial rule.[1] Mbembe invites revisiting the racialization and sexualization of colonial situations, including in white settler societies in the Americas that formed multiracial societies from the transatlantic slave trade, colonized indentured labor, and genocidal control of Indigenous peoples under European settlement. However, to pursue such an account, scholars must explain how the colony comes to be located in a state of exception in context of white-supremacist settler colonialism and the logic of Indigenous elimination. Mbembe's account limited its analysis to modern regimes of colonial biopolitics that arose in the nineteenth-century European franchise colonization of Africa and Asia. As a practice that is not past but continues today, the biopolitics of *settler* colonialism requires specific study.[2] This chapter names necessary elements to such an account, narrowed to explain the settler colonial necropolitics that queered Native peoples in the Americas by targeting modes of embodiment, desire, and kinship that Native queer and Two-Spirit people reclaim as their and their peoples' histories.

31

I argue that the biopolitics of settler colonialism produces settler sexuality as the context traversed by non-Native and Native people formulating queer modernities. The queering of Native peoples defined not only settler sexuality, broadly, but also the definition of queer subjects *among* white settlers: as a primitive, racialized sexual margin akin to what white settlers attempted to conquer among Natives. When queer white settlers reversed such discourses—notably by laying claim to the colonial object berdache[3]—they argued their inclusion in settler society by traversing normative paths to settler citizenship, which incorporate and transcend ties to Native roots to achieve national belonging. Non-Native queer modernities form by gathering a multiracial, transnational constituency as a diversity that exists in a non-Native relationship to disappearing indigeneity. Yet, narrating Native disappearance distinguishes non-Native queer modernities from the survival of Native queer people, who negotiate settler sexuality by recalling knowledges and practices queered by colonial heteropatriarchy. Native people defined unique identities, including Two-Spirit, as modern, decolonizing Native critiques of settler colonialism and its structuring of non-Native queer projects. This chapter grounds my interpretation of non-Native and Native queer modernities within a genealogy of white-supremacist settler colonialism as the condition of sexual modernity and its contestation in a settler society.

Modern Sexuality and Settler Colonial Biopolitics

Interdisciplinary theory of biopower has yet to investigate the specificity of settler colonialism, but its analysis can inform diversely racialized and transnational settler colonial formations and, in turn, be transformed by them. European settler colonization of Indigenous peoples produced modes of biopower that condition all modern sexuality. Multiple forms of colonization defined racialized and Indigenous peoples in settler societies in the Americas in the context of white-supremacist settler colonization's logic of elimination. Patrick Wolfe explains European settler colonialism by distinguishing the material conditions and discursive effects of settler from franchise colonies, where the latter are defined by European control at a distance or as a minority, while the former pursue the wholesale replacement of Native peoples to establish a white settler majority. Wolfe notes that in American settler societies, this distinction parallels the contrast between the genocidal elimination and amalgamation of Native peoples, which clears land for white settlers, and their brutal creation and reproduction of subject racialized populations through the transatlantic slave trade and indentured colonized labor to make settled lands productive.[4] Nevertheless, as for Mbembe, theory of colonial biopolitics generally is defined only by reference to franchise colonies—for example, European colonization of Africa and Asia in the nineteenth and twentieth centuries, where long-standing modes of biopower in Western sovereignty shifted into modern regimes of biopolitics. If such times or places focus our definitions of "colonialism" and "biopolitics," we will not comprehend how settler colonization in the Americas from the sixteenth century functioned alongside colonization in Africa and Asia within modes of biopower to produce the biopolitics of settler colonialism. Foucault argued that biopower and its biopolitical regimes appear at a historical shift, as the premodern right of the sovereign to mete out death in punishment—to "let live and make die"—changes as modern states utilize disciplinary power to "make live" racialized national populations and to "let die" all excluded from this life-making project.[5] Giorgio Agamben counters that, rather than an effect of the historical shift Foucault names, biopower is a core condition of Western sovereignty inherited from Roman law. For Agamben, both sovereign power over death and the modern state's power over life exhibit biopower, whereas Foucault's genealogy of modern biopolitics describes just one, historically recent, elaboration of biopower into a form that now appears ubiquitous.[6] Agamben does not reject Foucault's periodization of a premodern power over death being modified by modern biopolitics, but he does redefine biopower as constituting Western sovereignty in the enactment of the state of exception.

If the European contexts examined by Foucault and Agamben are viewed in relationship to settler colonization in the Americas, one can see with Agamben that the sovereign rule imposed by colonial powers from the sixteenth to the eighteenth centuries already functioned as biopower, by positioning Native peoples perpetually in the state of exception. Here, Mbembe's theory of the colony as exception demands being correlated to Wolfe's account of settler colonialism as a logic of elimination, to recognize Native peoples being positioned within the state of exception by projects of white settler replacement. The logic of Indigenous elimination provided a necessary premise for any subsequent subjection of African, Asian, or Pacific peoples within the colonial state of exception on putatively emptied land. Moreover, as Mark Rifkin argues, that logic grounds settler colonial biopolitics in "the *geopolitical* project of defining the territoriality of the nation" when attempting to control Indigenous people and supplant Indigenous sovereignty.[7] No account of biopolitics will explain a multiracial and transnational settler society or its projections into a colonized and globalized world unless its foundational conditioning by the biopolitics of settler colonialism and the logic of Indigenous elimination structures our theory of the exception and the colonial exercise of sovereignty.

In the Americas and, specifically, the United States, the biopolitics of settler colonialism was constituted by the imposition of colonial heteropatriarchy and the hegemony of settler sexuality, which sought both the elimination of Indigenous sexuality and its incorporation into settler sexual modernity. Theorists of sexuality who address biopower and colonization are indebted to Ann Stoler's efforts to locate Foucauldian accounts of modern sexuality within colonial studies.[8] Although Foucault omitted colonialism from his work on sexuality, Stoler demonstrated how the histories he traced in Europe explain those of imperial metropoles and colonial societies producing modern sexuality and "race" as biopower.[9] Stoler displaced more common readings of Foucault's history of sexuality in queer theory, which tended to frame European societies and their normative whiteness as roots of modern sexuality, and to pay secondary or no attention to race or colonialism. In particular, early queer accounts of Foucault's history of modern sexuality did not emphasize his reading of it as a mode of biopolitics, by which he described modern regimes that produce subjects of life by deploying state racism to define populations for regulation. Stoler argued that linking theories of biopolitics and colonialism shifts trajectories of queer theory that would interpret Foucault's history of sexuality as "a history of western desire."[10] In light of colonial histories, Europe is Western only to the extent that it is metropolitan—a center of colonial empires—which means that neither Europe nor Western cultural legacies will be understood without first studying their formation in relationship to both settler and franchise colonial societies. Stoler and other scholars in colonial studies examined how racial and national formations of sexuality produced the biopolitics of colonial regimes.[11] As Stoler notes, a focus on modes of reproduction has accounted poorly for nonheteronormative sexualities and genders, and still requires critically queer readings. Yet work in colonial strudies shows—in concert with Foucault's work, but against limits he put on it—that modern sexuality may have arisen first *in* colonial societies, including settler colonial societies, if not in their relationship to European imperial states. On this basis, Stoler explains the sexual and racial regimes of metropolitan and colonial societies as based on a colonial "education of desire." Stoler here marks how colonial power deployed a sovereign power over death that nevertheless became complementary with a modern and disciplinary education of desire that produced normative subjects of life in relation to subject populations. She presents colonial biopolitics as what Foucault called a "society of normalization"—"a society where the norm of discipline and the norm of regularization intersect"—and shows that it formed subjects of life and populations marked for deadly regulation by educating them in their interdependent locations within colonial regimes.[12]

Stoler's account of colonial biopolitics can illuminate how the sexual colonization of Native peoples in the United States conditioned the settler sexuality that formed to control and supplant them. Yet, her focus on franchise colonies in the modern era of biopolitics distinguishes her work from accounts of white settler colonization in the Americas, including its periodicity across the shifting modes of biopower within Western law from the fifteenth to the nineteenth centuries. The specificities of these histories of biopower already appear in scholarship on sexuality and settler colonialism, which shows that in settler societies in the Americas, sexuality served as a primary locus in projecting settler colonial power. With Andrea Smith we see that the sexual violence of colonial heteropatriarchy enabled the European conquest of Native peoples as queer to colonial rule, including by targeting Native systems of gender and sexuality that conflicted with European colonial logics. Rifkin shows that colonial regulation of Native peoples for assimilation targeted kinship relations that appeared nonheteronormative as a way of maintaining settler colonial control. Smith's and Rifkin's work suggests that the violent disciplinary regulation of Native peoples taught settlers doing this work, or any non-Natives witnessing or inheriting its effects, the meaning of being subjected to modern sexuality as settler sexuality. It thus cannot be separated from the education of desire presented to subject racialized peoples and peoples assimilated into whiteness by the sexualized violence that defined a white-supremacist society. My focus on the sexual colonization of Native peoples does not suggest its separability or exclusivity, but instead asks how it illuminates the conditioning of a white settler society by this mode of colonization. Future studies can pursue this even more by, for example, investigating the triangulated histories of Native peoples, African diasporic peoples, and white settlers in the United States by linking Saidya Hartman's account on the terrorizing sexualization of enslavement or Jim Crow society with the colonial education of desire under white settler colonization of Native peoples.[13] A key contribution by Native and settler colonial studies to such comparisons would be to explain the conditioning of *each* case, *and* their relationship to each other, by the logic of elimination within white-supremacist settler colonialism. My review of these processes affirms that a shift in the genocidal logic of white settler sovereignty, from exacting death to regulating life, explains the queering of Native peoples by colonial heteropatriarchy as a state of exception within the biopolitics of settler colonialism. Modern sexuality appears as settler sexuality in this context. The queering of white settlers as outside the promise of modern sexuality then incites U.S. queer modernities to form as appeals to white settler hegemony, which queers of color and Native queer people also negotiate in distinct ways.

Sexual Colonization and Disciplinary Power

Early colonists recurrently exacted a terrorizing sovereign right of death in order to educate Native people in the new colonial moral order. While interpreting Peter Martyr's account of Vasco Núñez de Balboa's 1513 expedition in Panama, Jonathan Goldberg notes that Balboa's victorious arrival after battle at the house of the Indigenous king was framed by his condemnation and elimination of what he perceived to be gender and sexual transgression. On reportedly finding the king's brother and about forty other men dressed in women's apparel or living in sexual relationships, Balboa threw them out to be eaten alive by his dogs. Goldberg says that this act "retrospectively justifies" the conqueror's earlier slaughters in battle—in which Spanish soldiers killed Indians "as animals"—or, to quote Martyr, "hewed . . . in pieces as the butchers doo fleshe." For Goldberg, "post-facto, the body of the sodomite takes on an originary status, as the cause for what was done to the Indians in the first place."[14] Linking ascriptions of savagery to transgressions of a sexual nature thus defined European rule as sexual colonization.

The account of Balboa evokes qualities that inflected other early Spanish, French, and British encounters with Native peoples narrated by the category of berdache. This Orientalist term arose first to condemn Middle Eastern and Muslim men as racial enemies of Christian civilization, by linking them to the creation of berdache (in translation) as "kept boys" or "boy slaves" whose sex was said to have been altered by immoral male desire. Like the category berdache, the transgressions Balboa described did not mark just gender or sexual transgressions but the acts of powerful men that turned them or others against nature, resulting in an immoral and effeminized male leadership that invited and justified conquest. Such an account reflects how early-modern European systems of sex fostered misogynist hierarchies, in which transgressive desires could be feared for threatening a reversal of sex.[15] In this context, the privileges of manhood were defined restrictively by achievement, so that males whose age, class, nationality, or race made them capable of manhood still were exhorted to attain it. Manhood was achieved by *practicing* natural law, but it remained limited and malleable, particularly if unnatural desires created conditions to become unmanned and unsexed.[16] Because berdache in fact defined the primitivity not just of a distinctive subject but of the society of men producing it, the object extended early-modern European policing of sex. Persons marked as berdache became targets of violent efforts to reconfigure Indigenous society in colonial and masculinist terms, by exacting a responsibility from Indigenous men to defend colonial sexual morality in their own and all Indigenous people's lives. Moreover, by imputing sexual primitivity to racialized targets of conquest, early-modern narratives of berdache affirmed the fulfillment of natural sex and desire by conquerors. Berdache thus marked a relationality not only among Indigenous males, but also between Indigenous societies and the civilizational sex and sexuality of Europeans. Stoler's feminist accounts of colonial power indicate that imposition of colonial rule was justified by discovering signs of a primitive lack of differentiation between the sexes. Knowing European manhood's boundaries to be porous and needing reinforcement, and meeting Indigenous possibilities that threw such boundaries into question, early conquerors invoked berdache as if assigning a failure to differentiate sex to Indigenous people, but they did so to define sexual normativity for them *all*. Thus, if colonial observers invoked berdache to mark Indigenous difference, the aim was to teach both colonial *and* Indigenous subjects the relational terms of colonial heteropatriarchy. Earlier generations of feminist scholars argued that a bias in colonial tales of berdache erased female embodiment from accounts of Native gender and sexual diversity. But feminist critiques in the wake of Stoler and Smith note that the condemnation of Native male embodiment in colonial accounts of berdache established the masculinist and heteropatriarchal terms of colonial power. Thus, I invoke berdache to indicate not persons but a logic of sexual primitivity and civilization that created Indigenous people and colonists in relation to each other. In the process, colonial discourses of race and sexuality came to mark transgressive individuals and entire communities when they meted out spectacular death to educate Native peoples in the moral order of colonization.

Histories of colonial control over Indigenous male sexuality support Foucault's claim that a sovereign right of death joined the rationalizing management of populations to produce modern disciplinary power. Zeb Tortorici examined a 1604 case of sodomy accusations in Valladolid, Michoacán,

Mexico, that illuminates this transition. After the capture of two Indigenous Purépecha men "committing the *pecado nefando*—the nefarious sin
of sodomy," a regional investigation resulted in sodomy charges against
thirteen Indigenous and mestizo men, some of whom were relatives or in
long-term relationships.[17] For two months, legal and religious authorities
exacted confessions and implications that tried to determine the degree
of interest or culpability in the alleged acts for each of the accused while
threatening torture or public execution as punishments. Yet the investigation deferred its threatened outcomes to serve as a fact-finding exercise,
which mapped social networks along which the church and government
began to chart new routes for their authority in Indigenous communities.
Given that only six of the thirteen accused men were tried for sodomy, with
four of them executed, and others who evaded capture never pursued,
Tortorici suggests that in this era the intimation of sodomy among Indigenous men remained deadly but no longer drew an absolute response (5).
Public execution now appeared as a threatened end to a broader process
of surveillance and population management that sought more minute
control over sexual transgressions and Indigenous communities. Tortorici
historicizes this shift in managing sexuality within "the secularization of
colonial Mexican society," so that, "while in 1604 four of the Purépecha
men accused of sodomy were executed for their crimes, in the eighteenth
century men found guilty of sodomy were never executed for their crimes"
(67n77, 57). Yet the study of "sodomitical subcultures" (as Tortorici calls
them) remained a method for colonial authorities to study and control sexuality among Native peoples.

Scholars of Anglophone and Francophone North America also have
observed how gender and sexuality shaped colonial expansion and its shifts
toward disciplinary regimes of modern sexuality. The settlement of French
and British Canada and of colonial and postrevolutionary New England
produced strongly gendered modes of control over Native peoples, as war,
containment on reserves, and colonial law, economy, and religion redefined
roles for Native women and men in work, marriage, and community leadership.[18] Accounts of sexual and gender diversity appear most clearly when
British, French, and U.S. explorers and traders participated in the fur trade
or colonial expansion and met Native people whom they called berdache,
"warrior women," or other terms of fascination or contempt. In the mid-
nineteenth century, when most such accounts appear, persons so marked
were less often singled out for violence than subjected with their communities to military attack, containment, or removal. They also came to notice

in new colonial institutions such as Indian agencies, missionary churches, and boarding schools. Without needing to exact brute violence, these institutions used disciplinary education to try to break Native communities, languages, and cultural knowledges—as reflected in Captain Richard Pratt's Carlisle Indian School and his motto, "Kill the Indian, and save the man." Native people made colonial institutions sites for defying the erasure of Native identity or community, including at times by adopting colonial languages and educational methods in new forms of resistance.[19] But both colonial control and Native resistance were shaped by struggle over gender and sexuality, through the establishment on the colonial frontier of modern methods for the colonial education of desire.

The grounding of U.S. colonization in sexual regulation and discipline is demonstrated, for instance, by the history of the Crow Agency and the life of Osh-Tisch (Finds-Them-and-Kills-Them). Osh-Tisch was born in 1854 and was raised and recognized in Crow society as *boté* (or *badé*), a Crow role in which she lived consistently on Crow land to the age of seventy-five.[20] I use the pronoun *she* in line with the English usage of Pretty Shield, a member of Osh-Tisch's village, who later recalled Osh-Tisch as "a Crow woman" who was also "neither a man nor a woman." Will Roscoe reports from oral histories of Osh-Tisch's life that her community included many *botés*, as well as at least one "woman who had no man of her own," The Other Magpie, whom Osh-Tisch accompanied in sharing exploits in battle (30–32). After the establishment of the Crow Agency and other colonial institutions, Roscoe says, Crow people were "subjected to ongoing interference by representatives of the U.S. government," including in contests over *botés*, among whom Osh-Tisch was prominent. Robert Lowie said of Osh-Tisch that "former agents have repeatedly tried to make him don male clothes, but the other Indians themselves protested against this, saying that it was against his nature" (29). Walter Williams interviewed Crow tribal historian Joe Medicine Crow about his memories of Osh-Tisch, who died in 1929 when Medicine Crow was seven years old. "When I asked about the controversy over Osh-Tisch's clothing," Williams says, "he did not answer but told me to meet him the following day on the grounds of the Bureau of Indian Affairs offices. I arrived the next day and observed that the BIA building was surrounded by huge oak trees." Medicine Crow then reflected that

> One agent in the late 1890s . . . tried to interfere with Osh-Tisch, who was the most respected *badé*. The agent incarcerated the *badés*, cut off their hair, made them wear men's clothing. He forced them to do manual labor, planting these trees that you see here on the BIA grounds. The people were so upset with this

that Chief Pretty Eagle came into Crow Agency, and told [the agent] to leave the reservation. It was a tragedy, trying to change them.[21]

Both Lowie and Medicine Crow say that the agency established its rule by targeting *botés* for gendered and sexual reeducation, which sparked resistance by Crow leaders and their community. Yet, even as pressure for gendered and sexual conformity increased in schools and churches, resistance to it did not end. According to Roscoe,

> children were required to attend government-run boarding schools in which any expression or use of native language and customs was severely punished, boys and girls were segregated, and girls were not allowed to leave the school until husbands had been found for them. In such an environment, children with *boté* tendencies were quickly identified. According to Holder, when a Crow boy was found secretly dressing in female clothes in the late 1880s, "He was punished, but finally escaped from school and became a *boté*, which vocation he has since followed."[22]

Historical records indicate that Osh-Tisch lived as a *boté* for the rest of her life. In 1891 she took in "a three-year-old child" who was listed on a census as her "adopted son," but who four years later was recorded as a girl—suggesting that Osh-Tisch was fulfilling a role in Crow community of passing the life of *boté* to a next generation.[23] Yet, by her late age, it appeared to colonial authorities that no other Crow persons were living a traditional *boté* identity. Williams quotes Crow medicine man Thomas Yellowtail: "When the Baptist missionary Peltotz arrived in 1903, he condemned our traditions, including the *badé*. He told congregation members to stay away from Osh-Tisch and the other *badés*. He continued to condemn Osh-Tisch until his death in the late 1920s. That may be the reason why no others took up the *badé* role after Osh-Tisch died."[24]

Death thus still shaped sexual colonization in the era of containment and assimilation, but in new ways. Under colonial rule, Native people faced constant condemnation of gender and sexual transgression, which at times took shape as a violent education in a new life. But when public punishment—which now did not end in murder—failed to quell resistance, the deadly logic of regulation kicked in. After the passing of old resisters like Osh-Tisch, colonial education prevented a new generation from being raised so that an entire way of life seemed to have died out. Yet death recurs in more ways in Native people's memories of these changes. Williams presents oral histories of Lakota traditionalists who recalled the effects of colonial education. As one explains:

By the 1940s, after more Indians had been educated in white schools, or had been taken away in the army, they lost the traditions of respect for *winktes*. The missionaries condemned *winktes*, telling families that if something bad happened, it was because of their associating with a *winkte*. They would not accept *winktes* into the cemetery, saying "their souls are lost." Missionaries had a lot of power on the reservation, so the *winktes* were ostracized by many of the Christianized Indians. (182–83)

Williams quotes another telling of the "pressures put on *winktes* in the 1920s and 1930s":

The missionaries and the government agents said *winktes* were no good, and tried to get them to change their ways. Some did, and put on men's clothing. But others, rather than change, went out and hanged themselves. I remember the sad stories that were told about this. (182)

Williams also tells of a Navajo woman who had narrated her own story of being taken with her relatives as a child to the Carlisle Indian School:

Her cousin, a *nadle*, was also taken there. Since he was dressed as a girl, school officials assumed he was female and placed him in the girl's dormitory. The Navajo students protected him, and he went undiscovered.

Later, however, there was a lice infestation. The white teachers personally scrubbed all the girls, and were shocked when they found out that the *nadle* was male. The Navajo woman said, "They were very upset. He was taken from the school, and he never returned again. They would not tell us what happened to him, and we never saw him again. We were very sad that our cousin was gone." The family still does not know if the boy was sent to another school, or to prison, or was killed. (180)

In these stories from the late nineteenth century to the first half of the twentieth, death frames Native people's collective experiences of the erasure of gendered and sexual possibility: as exiles from the community's spiritual continuity; in so restricting life as to force persons to "choose" to die; and in being "disappeared" by the traceless authority of the bureaucratic colonial state. These are some of the results of shifting colonial authority from a brutal right of public execution to the normalization of death in regulatory regimes based on discipline. But disciplinary methods were no less terrorizing. They required *internalizing* the idea that life as *nádleeh*, *winkte*, *boté*, or a "woman who had no man" was impossible. And they suggest that the resistance of relatives and communities ultimately faced a colonial power determined to make loved ones literally disappear, into a death beyond knowledge of life or death. These are the terrorizing logics of a society of normalization, as Foucault and Stoler theorized, and they were implemented on the frontier of the settler state by controlling Native peoples as populations for the colonial education of modern sexuality.

Settler Sexuality, Native "Disappearance," and Queer Modernities

The sexual regulation of Native peoples by the biopolitics of settler colonialism in the United States was a proving ground for producing settlers as subjects of modern sexuality. The late nineteenth and early twentieth centuries saw institutions and discourses of modern sexuality proliferate along with the "closure" of the frontier as a central feature of national consciousness in a white settler society. Efforts to institute a colonial education of desire, as in the events at the Crow Agency or during the 1879–1918 tenure of the Carlisle Indian School, informed the modern sexuality that white settlers promoted as settler sexuality. Thus, far from reflecting the finality of conquest, this period was one of tense negotiations of active and contested settlement. Any iteration of modern sexuality in this time that placed Native people in the past knew itself to be a contingent claim that remained open to challenge. Given these conditions, modern sexuality was not a *product* of settler colonialism, as if it came into being in the United States after settlement. Rather, modern sexuality became a method *to produce* settler colonialism, and settler subjects, by facilitating ongoing conquest and naturalizing its effects. If this transpired in close relationship to Native people's institutionalized education in colonial heteronormativity, it arose more broadly in any promotions of sexual modernity within a settler colonial society defined by the seeming finality of Native disappearance and replacement.

Settler colonialism is a primary condition of the history of sexuality in the United States. Settler colonialism is present precisely when it appears not to be, given that its normative function is to appear inevitable and final. Its naturalization follows both the seeming material finality of settler society and discourses that frame settlers as "those who come after" rather than as living in relationship to Native peoples in a colonial situation. The denaturalization of settler colonialism thus must address social relationships and tales of Native disappearance. Narrating Native peoples as absent does not erase them so much as produce knowledge about them as necessarily disappeared. Jean O'Brien and James Cox point out that the absence of Native people in a story tells a story of the settler colonial conditions of its subjects and claims. Reexamining the history of modern sexuality by centering settler colonialism and its naturalization will show how these processes condition normative subjects of sexual modernity and the regulation and exclusion of subjects from its achievement.

Queer histories of modern sexuality tend to study non-Natives without examining their formation within settler colonialism. Yet histories of sexuality in queer of color and queer diasporic critiques and queer migration studies already mark settler colonialism for critique. Roderick Ferguson and Eithne Luibhéid examine how the historical subjection of queer people of color followed their being marked within U.S. society as emblems of the collective racial degradation or need for racial subjugation of peoples of color, as queered targets of white-supremacist rule.[25] Heteronormative national whiteness established its rule by sexualizing the racial, economic, and political subjugation of peoples of color in the name of protecting white settler society from queer endangerment by perversely racialized sexuality and gender. This process mirrors Indigenous feminist and queer studies that show the subjection of Indigenous peoples to have followed their collective queering by colonial heteropatriarchy, including by targeting subjects who stood apart from a colonial sex/gender binary. Luibhéid shows that the locations of non-Native racialized communities have been positioned in structurally similar ways with Native peoples by white-supremacist heteropatriarchal rule, and suggests that their very distinctive encounters with U.S. hegemony may be explained as interrelated effects of white settler colonialism. Echoing Wolfe, the colonial subjection of Native peoples facilitated their elimination so as to consolidate white settler hegemony over stolen and putatively emptied land, while the control of non-Native peoples of color reproduced their collective subjection for economic and social roles within a normatively non-Native multiracial and transnational settler society. These trajectories may conflict, if the experience of subjection or the struggle for liberation among non-Native people of color naturalizes the erasure of Native people as inevitable, necessary, or complete or has Native people's subjection as its effect.

I locate this queer history of racial and national power in a settler society because queer histories, even when informed by racial or national diversity, often give the impression that modern queer subjects, cultures, or politics come into being within the boundaries of whiteness. Histories of the formation of modern sexual minority identities and politics in the United States— or, derivatively, in Europe—indicate that nineteenth- and twentieth-century sexual sciences produced subjects one might recognize today as queer by designating forms of embodiment or desire as perversions that required scientific documentation, theorization, and regulation. Siobhan Somerville notes that in the United States, new sexual sciences enhanced correlations of race mixture and homosexuality to frame queerness as racialized by an imputed primitivity, which then reinforced mixed-race people and people of color negotiating the color line as traversing sexually liminal space.[26] Such narratives coincided with increased scientific and legal attention to diverse modes of embodiment and desire in sexual subcultures defined by race, nation, class, or gender, which new scientific categories never entirely contained. For instance, Kevin Mumford shows how social practices in the early twentieth century linked homosexuality to miscegenation within popular narratives and policing practices of white "slumming" for sexual adventure in African American districts of New York City and Chicago.[27] New policing of a variety of racialized sexual cultures fostered narratives of sexual marginality that elided those that did not devolve on some relation to whiteness, whether through social ties or teleologies of primitivity and modernity. Of course, some racialized sexual cultures were merely ignored by an emergent focus of new sexual sciences on the white subjects they controlled. People of color already experienced sexualized and racialized control independently of their targeting by new sexual sciences, which never superseded their sexualized colonial regulation as racialized *peoples*. New sexual sciences thus bore a unique relationship to their white subjects. Jennifer Terry explains that as sexual sciences defined primitivity as a queer margin of civilized sexuality, perversions were classified by representing white subjects as degenerates who had regressed to earlier stages of racial evolution.[28] Thus, white subjects could indeed appear, as racially perverse subjects, to have escaped prior control by white racial knowledge and to be in need of redoubled effort to define them within racialized discourse on sexual perversion. Yet their very narration was an effect of being *produced* in this moment as new objects for the sexualized power relations of white-supremacist settler capitalism and empire.

The racialization of white subjects of sexology by discourse on sexual primitivity became crucial to their subsequent efforts as members of a multiracial settler society to gain its embrace, respect, and citizenship. Subjects so marked reversed the discourses on perversion that described them to proclaim a minoritized form of sexual normality in need of scientific defense to achieve social recognition and rights in the state.[29] Yet in light of their racialization, such narratives also portray modern sexuality as a property of white subjects who can belong to white civilization but for accusations of sexual primitivity. Their adaptations of discourse on primitivity creatively challenged its premises when applied to themselves, but did not necessarily challenge the logic of colonial discourse in broader circulation—notably, as it defined citizenship in a white settler state. Thus, while their critiques did mean to disturb discourses on primitivity, they did not undermine the white-supremacist and colonial power producing such discourses and that remained to adapt them to new use.

I am less interested, however, in defining racial or colonial complicities among early U.S. sexual minorities than in asking what followed their embrace of primitivity as a nature in need of civic inclusion in a white settler society; for, if white sexual minorities traversed their primitivity in order to claim national whiteness, they followed a normative path to citizenship for white settler subjects. Deloria's argument that settler citizenship is based on the conquest and incorporation of primitivity—crucially, as disappeared Native American indigeneity—makes primitivity a resource that settler subjects access when asserting their national belonging. This is reflected in the scientific promotion of civilizational white heteronormativity—as, for instance, when modern sexuality discourses taught white men to tap and control their inheritance of primitivity. G. Stanley Hall's recapitulation theory of play, youth health movements in the YMCA, and the Boy Scouts of America invited white middle-class boys and men to explore primitive developmental stages, including via Indian impersonation, as methods to achieve the virile sex and sexuality of civilized adults. They then performed these methods educatively with white working-class youths to lift them into white citizenship, or with black youths to conform them to stages of manhood preceding the civilizational status of which they were presumed incapable and which they were denied.[30] In the United States, white sexual minorities first collectively identified and organized in a political culture that validated journeys to personhood for white male citizens by translating primitive roots coded as Native American into white settler modernity and its hegemonic role in a multiracial capitalist settler society. Embracing a primitive sexual nature linked to roots within Native culture articulated the defense of modern sexual minorities with normative assertions of settler citizenship.

In the history of U.S. queer modernities as white articulations of settler sexuality, none highlight this process more clearly than popularizations of the colonial object berdache to define their nature and purpose as an indigenized minority ready for integration into settler freedom. In the United States, sexological and homosexual emancipation discourse on berdache in the early to mid-twentieth century traced back to European writing that correlated sexual minorities to primitivity, in particular to Native Americans. The emergence of such connections from the mid-nineteenth century onward affirms Foucault's account that Europe witnessed a scientific documentation of marginal sexualities for biopolitical regulation even as their targets reversed such discourses to make science legitimate their nature and rights. Karl Heinrich Ulrichs and Magnus Hirschfeld pursued this work from the mid-nineteenth into the early twentieth centuries in what would be known as homosexual emancipationism. Their defenses of sexual primitivity in otherwise white and often class-privileged subjects—those who could claim civilizational status if not for their gendered and sexual state—explained that state as a nature that their societies could accept as part of sexual science.[31] This approach cited the apparent existence and acceptance of marginal sexual subjects in "primitive" societies as evidence that their nature had been known since human origins and could be scientifically and legally affirmed. Berdache appeared in this context and grew in significance over time.[32] Invoking ethnology's authority, sexologists such as Richard von Krafft-Ebing and Havelock Ellis cited accounts of Native American gender and sexuality, which other scholars codified from ethnological evidence for their use, as when C. G. Seligmann and Ferdinand Karsch-Haack produced anthropological writing linking textual citations and field observations of berdache for use by sexologists.[33] In cross-referenced writing—Seligmann the ethnologist cites key claims to Ellis; Ellis the sexologist cites ethnology that Seligmann later collated—sexology and ethnology reinforced their modern scientific authority to determine sexual and primitive truth.[34] The radical thinker and sexual rights advocate Edward Carpenter related a dynamic emancipationist argument directly from berdache.[35] Carpenter promoted the "intermediate type" as a sexual nature based in male homosexuality along two trajectories: a "heroic" sexual desire among normal men tied to ancient Greece, and a gender-transitive male homosexuality defined by berdache. His focus on the latter agreed with Ulrichs and Hirschfeld that this form best explained sexual intermediacy, through its apparent association with creativity and spirituality, or, in Carpenter's words, with the role of "diviners" mediating the mundane and spiritual worlds.

In these commentaries, a familiar figure appeared of a Native American male formally assuming women's social roles while engaging in sexual contact with other males. Interpreters read this figure in different ways: Krafft-Ebing described it as an intermediate sex in a feminized male body, whereas Ellis framed gender variation as a sign of normative sex imbued by same-sex desire. Yet, while being cited in different societies, the figure evoked Native Americans as a social type representing the acceptance of gender-transitive male and same-sex desire in primitive societies. Thus, by the 1930s, European scholars using a reverse discourse had defined berdache as an object of sexual science and as proof that the sexual primitivity of modern sexual minorities bore a global and transhistorical nature. The figure was evidence that across vast temporal and cultural differences, an authentic Indigenous culture communicated the nature of modern sexual minorities. Crucially, the racial and gender formation of these discourses is evident in correlations of masculinism and whiteness in both the object and its promotions. The violent colonial masculinism projected into berdache, and expressed in its use during sexual colonization, was not questioned once white European men promoted it, putatively, to defend "all" sexual minorities, but notably to draw connections between their lives and male embodiment and desire. Thus, the promotion of berdache naturalized specifically *masculinist* colonial discourses and generic or specific references to male embodiment and desire as focal points of the sexual nature and rights defined in sexology and homosexual emancipationism by white men. These gendered, racial, and colonial contours remained in all later citations of the object: at times as naturalized contexts within which modern sexual minorities became imaginable, but often as recurrent arenas of struggle owing to their recirculation by the object's travels.

A capacity to incorporate indigeneity as a primitive past for thereby indigenized modern white Europeans to transcend is a characteristic of colonial discourse on primitivity.[36] The thread I wish to follow here differs not ontologically, but genealogically; for, if a mode of primitivism ever "arrives" from Europe to the United States, it will immediately articulate the primitivism already constituting white-supremacist *settler* subjectivity and its modernity, nationality, and citizenship. Sexological and emancipationist discourse on berdache "arrives" in the United States as the very settler colonial context that produced the accounts it cites. Berdache discourse locates white "European" and other racialized sexual subjects in relation to a scientifically generalized indigeneity that, here, announces the specifically Native American locations to which all subjects already bear *landed* relationships. These relationships will be apparent if discourse on berdache is recognized as multiple and transnational, yet distinctly U.S. American when it is adapted into this specific white settler colonial context.

Sexual minority activists in the United States engaged discourse on berdache by translating sexology and homosexual emancipation into their
desire to claim the modern sexual rights of citizens in a white settler state.
I do not mean to imply that all activists agreed with the hegemony of white
settler colonialism. Some vociferously opposed all structural oppressions, as
was the case for Harry Hay's Marxist-inspired critiques of white racism and
capitalism as sources of antihomosexual prejudice.[37] Nevertheless, adapting
berdache to justify sexual rights for U.S. citizens reflects the desire of white
sexual minorities to absorb Native American roots as their own in order
to claim—even critically—the rights of settler citizenship. The Mattachine
Society, the first ongoing advocacy group for sexual minority rights in the
United States, was formed under the leadership of Hay and his use of emancipationist discourse on berdache as a model for modern social acceptance
of sexual diversity.[38] In the mid-twentieth century, Hay and U.S. homophile
activists continued to reference sexology and emancipationist writing on
berdache when discussing whether sexual minorities—gay men in particular—could be said to possess a sexual nature, or, inspired by Carpenter, a
spiritual nature.[39] In this regard, white men argued on behalf of all sexual
minorities that their civil rights and national belonging were affirmed by
berdache. This affirmation appeared in late-twentieth-century gay liberation
and lesbian/gay civil rights organizing (discussed in chapters 2 and 3). Such
claims motivated mid-twentieth-century U.S. sexual minority politics toward
seeking political inclusion in a settler society that was still consolidating its
rule over Native peoples, while framing Native peoples' importance to them
as a disappeared history that non-Natives sought to incorporate as their
own. The hegemonic effect of these discourses was to ground modern sexual minority identities and politics in the appropriation of Native culture
by white men who then represented the sexual nature of a universal social
minority. Despite appearing to reference to Native people, the activists'
purpose was to define *themselves* in relation to a primitivity projected onto
Native Americans whose disappearance they could recover and redeem.
Berdache became a naturalized backdrop to scientific and activist claims on
sexual modernity, and even its absence from citation remained consistent
with its function: to offer a Native past that sexual minorities could incorporate in their quest for sexual modernity. Embracing berdache did not
mean "going Native"—although that form of primitivism could be one of
its effects. Rather, it allowed white subjects in a settler society, led by white
men, to answer their settler colonial inheritance by accepting Native roots
as theirs to possess and replace.

Berdache is just one of many figures of Native disappearance that produces queer modernities in the United States as normatively white claims on settler citizenship. The settler colonialism conditioning the object will remain naturalized and hegemonic among U.S. queer subjects, cultures, and politics until that condition is addressed. Claims on queer modernity by non-Native people of color at times disrupt settler colonial power by confronting white supremacy or colonization. Also, for many queers of color, a history of mixed heritage with Native peoples complicates stories of Native disappearance and an assumed non-Native relationship to modern sexuality. But my reading of queer claims within settler colonial power relations indicates that even antiracist and anticolonial work by queers of color may become compatible with settler projects, notably when portraying sexual modernity as multiracial and transnational to achieve non-Native queer belonging in a multicultural settler state. Displacing any such effects can start by locating U.S. queer modernities in the biopolitics of settler colonialism that still impose non-Native, normatively white, and settler relationships on Native peoples, and by efforts of Native queer and Two-Spirit people to denaturalize settler colonialism. In the face of non-Native queer projects that invite embrace by the settler state, Native queer and Two-Spirit people have critically confronted discourse on their disappearance—even as icons of queer salvation—to pursue their own and their peoples' resistance to the colonial conditions of life on Native lands.

Native Resistance and Queer Modernities

Native queer and Two-Spirit activisms challenge non-Native queer modernities and settler colonialism when they recall legacies of resistance and form modern Native identities, cultures, and politics that affirm the survival and resurgence of Native peoples.

Deborah Miranda and Qwo-Li Driskill invoke both the historical violence of attempted erasure and collective reassertions of embodied subjectivity as methods for Native queer and Two-Spirit people to resist the colonial education of desire.[40] They suggest that these resistances are not unique to the present but, across important differences in historical and cultural context, form "dissent lines" (Linda Tuhiwai Smith's term) that locate Native queer and Two-Spirit people in genealogies of anticolonialism.[41] The histories recounted by Tortorici, Williams, and Roscoe portray Native people resisting the colonial education of desire by eluding control and escaping punishment, harboring one another from detection and harm, organizing collective protests, and raising new generations in traditional knowledge despite colonial attempts to regulate Native life. If resistance appeared in the refusal of Osh-Tisch or others to relinquish their identities and roles, it also took the form of collective responses to the targeting of particular persons. As Jace Weaver has noted, Native resistance to colonization has performed a "communitism" that links collective survival to activism for justice. Histories of sexual colonization show Native peoples resisting by recognizing that targeting of individuals sought to educate entire communities in new regimes as a means to establish colonial control. For instance, forcing *botés* into masculine dress and parading them as labor proclaimed colonial power over the entire Crow community and its values. But Chief Pretty Eagle's defiance of the agent and his defense of the *botés* in the 1890s reaffirmed those values by marking gender and sexuality as embodying the very traditions that the Crow elders chose to defend as a condition of the community's collective sovereignty.[42] In turn, the girls at the Carlisle Indian School who protected the *nádleeh* youth defended the truth of their loved one's life, even as they recognized that a colonial intent to erase that life also sought to erase their interdependence. Neither their inability to protect their cousin nor their loss can overwrite the fact that their resistance dignified their identity as Native people and sustained their collective ties. All these stories show that the lives the term "berdache" attempted to name did not represent a singular sexual minority but the webs of relationship and solidarity within Native communities.

These histories are important to accounts of queer modernities not merely as a historical precedent but because of the way they persist within the settler colonial hegemony of modern sexuality. Foucault acknowledged that the discourses and institutions of modern sexuality formed by subjugating knowledges of bodies and pleasures that exceeded its logic.[43] Subjugation produced those knowledges as elided or forgotten elements within the discursive elaborations of modern sexuality, thereby altering how they may be known among the "many silences" defining its power. Nevertheless, Foucault suggests, the production of subjugated knowledges in modern sexual regimes presented the ever-present possibility of their resurgence. This resistance would transpire in the field of power established by sexual modernity. But subjugated knowledges recalled knowledges that were never entirely imaginable on modern sexuality's terms, despite its purported totalization. Thus, to pursue subjugated knowledges as a mode of resistance is precisely to negotiate the power relations of modern sexuality. But subjugating knowledges also fractures the ruse of totalization in modern sexuality, which then must police its own interruption by logics that exceed what it purports to assert and contain.

Organizing among Native queer and Two-Spirit people developed in the late twentieth century precisely by recalling such subjugated knowledges of embodiment, desire, kinship, and peoplehood in modes of language, memory, and relationality that were discrepant from colonial modern definitions of sexuality and gender. Two-Spirit identity is a modern Native recollection of subjugated traditional knowledges that contests the terms of colonial modernity—in anthropological discourse, queer colonial desires, and the heteropatriarchy of settler and Native societies—through a resurgence of Native peoplehood. Yet, describing Two-Spirit with its many ascribed meanings as a Native queer modernity does not frame it only in terms of the present. By recalling and reimagining subjugated knowledges that exceed the temporality of settler colonialism, Two-Spirit does not merely imagine or invoke their existence but connects genealogically to their continuation through time. The muliplicity of languages, memories, and ontologies of embodiment, desire, kinship, and collectivity invoked by Two-Spirit already carried a power to provincialize Western universalisms (of sex, race, nation, humanity) and displace their imperialist ruses. Perhaps this is why Two-Spirit people were among the first Indigenous people targeted for settler colonial erasure, and why heteropatriarchy has remained foundational to sustaining conquest and settlement.

The discrepancy of Two-Spirit identity when proposed by Native queer people arose partly in its critical response to anthropological writing on berdache and to non-Native queer desires for Indigenous history. Yet historicizing Native queer and Two-Spirit activism as if it arose only in response to colonial hegemony suggests that Native resistance is always already derivative of what it resists: the totalizing power of settler colonization. In fact, by definition, settler colonialism is *a relationship* between something that may attempt totalization and all that it attempts (forever incompletely) to suppress. Indeed, settler colonialism's inherent relationality continually invokes interdependence, *not* independence—whether that to which it relates seems present or absent, in the imagination or in interactions with those who survive attempted erasure. Settler colonialism cannot create totalizing forms of power to wholly produce Native peoples as constructs of a colonial gaze or as mere reinterpreters of colonial ideas about "themselves." A perception that this is all that is possible *is* the logic of elimination at work, but it remains naturalized in the settler academy.

As a contemporary category, Two-Spirit has implications for anticolonial critiques that denaturalize settler colonialism. Its effort to link Native queer people to genealogies of subjugated knowledge challenges the temporal trap of colonial modernity that would locate Native people in an untouchable authenticity or an inevitable amalgamation with settlers. Two-Spirit articulates epistemologies that, by being recollected, are no longer forgettable, placing Native people in a relationship to languages, memories, and ontologies that are reimagined in a colonial frame while showing that that frame was never complete. In the process, Two-Spirit identity shows the power of settler colonialism to be relational, as it displaces the purported universality, inevitability, and finality of settler colonialism. Thus, Two-Spirit identity, like other Native queer modernities, does not derive from non-Native queer projects, or any colonial modern project, even as its formation and practice are entirely relational to what it contests.

In this light, Native queer and Two-Spirit activisms can be seen to engage, and contest, the settler colonial terms of modern sexuality in ways that remain distinct from the normative affirmation of those terms in non-Native queer modernities. This occurs in their discrepant engagement with the biopolitics of settler colonialism that defines modern sexuality in the United States as a "contact zone." Following Mary Louise Pratt, this term invokes Europeans and Indigenous peoples in colonial situations producing conflictual yet creative exchanges, in which "conditions of coercion, radical inequality, and intractable conflict" generate "the interactive, improvisational dimensions of colonial encounters."[44] Theorizing modern sexuality as a contact zone has several implications. First, recognizing that settler colonialism has not ended, "contact" is recognizable not only in the past or in local spaces but as pervasive throughout settler society and all that transpires within it. Indeed, modern sexuality *is* the contact zone, with all its manifestations meaningfully contextualized by a relationality of "Natives" to "settlers" on colonized land. Just as all modern sexual subjects and practices in the United States arose amid settler colonization and narratives of Native disappearance, Native people articulated modern sexuality as a colonial project while countering it with distinctive Indigenous knowledges and modes of resistance.

Second, modern sexuality acts as a contact zone independently of encounters among non-Native and Native people. For non-Natives, sexual modernity produces them as subjects of contact because this modernity presumes Native disappearance, by citing Native sexual pasts to inspire in non-Natives a sexual future. For Native people, in turn, sexual modernity incites contact by presenting itself as the modernity of settlers. Even Native people who embrace it do not erase its historical ties to colonization, while those who critique it disturb its conflation of coloniality with modernity and create alternative spaces for defining Native modernities, including Native queer and Two-Spirit activisms.

Thus, and third, while the image of a contact zone suggests that colonization is its context, settler formations in fact are being displaced by decolonizing Native claims on modernity. While they are interdependent with non-Native queer cultures and politics, Native queer modernities do not derive from them. Rather, they creatively articulate modern sexuality as settler sexuality by reimagining Indigenous knowledges of personhood and community that never ceased to trouble the supposed universality of settler claims. This book traces the cultural and political effects of this discrepancy in Native queer claims on modernity as a counterpoint to the ubiquitous, but not all-powerful, effects of settler sexual culture.

Perpetually negotiating the contact zone of sexual modernity but without being derivative *of* contact, Native queer and Two-Spirit projects mark the contingency, contradiction, and potential transformation of settler colonialism. Their effects arise as Native queer people negotiate, in Tsing's term, their "friction" with settler knowledges and power relations, including in conversation with non-Native queer formations. The very inevitability of such conversations is what returns them to a state of friction: the more they produce and sharpen their discrepancies, the more consistent their interactions become. In the process, whether long-standing or of recent invention, Native queer modernities join all Native resistances to settler sexuality in denaturalizing settlement. Native queer and Two-Spirit people thus trace distinctive intellectual histories linking subjugated knowledges to current reimaginings. Their claims mark and displace the conditions of settler society in which all non-Native queer modernities arise, and thereby propose routes to decolonization that address both Native and non-Native people.

Chapter 2   **Conversations on Berdache**

Anthropology, Counterculturism,

Two-Spirit Organizing

AMID THE MANY TALES OF INDIGENEITY animating queer modernities in the United States, one became iconic: the colonial object berdache.
While appearing to describe Native Americans, berdache presented a primordial mirror to the civilizational modernity of colonial and settler subjects. It cohered an object of knowledge that described a gender-transitive
and homosexual subject, defined by male embodiment, who received social
recognition in Native American societies. Over time, the object projected
a uniformity of sex, gender, sexuality, and indigeneity that let it represent
principles of human nature and culture. Disagreement over its definition
regularly called its qualities into question, but that very deliberation pro-
mulgated berdache as a key object of colonial desire for Indigenous and
sexual truth.

This chapter examines conversations on berdache as spaces that produced
queer modernities for non-Native and Native people in close relationship
in the late twentieth century. Berdache became popularized by debates in
the United States over the cultural or historical scope of modern queer subjects that appeared in textbooks, anthologies, and scholarly and popular
texts in anthropology and in gay, lesbian, trans, and queer studies. A generation or more of university students, human service professionals, and
general readers interpreted queer histories and cultures by considering the
relationship they bore to berdache. Among the many effects of the object's
circulation, deliberating Native history became a key medium for concep-
tualizing queer modernity.

Three contexts proved crucial to the career of the object berdache. Two
are obvious: gay and lesbian anthropology, and critical engagement with
anthropology by Native queer activists, including after the adoption of Two-
Spirit identity in the 1990s. The other may be less obvious: back-to-the-
land counterculturism where non-Native gay men imagined radical cultures

and politics. Among the myriad spaces of conversation on berdache, these three highlight a prehistory into the 1970s that shaped debates on ber-dache among non-Native and Native queers until the end of the century. Each space of conversation engaged one or both of the others, whether it acknowledged this interdependence or not, and with resonances that appear throughout this book. Each also indicates that, rather than being contained, its debates incited broader conversations beyond the object ber-dache that weighed the modernity of non-Native and Native queers in relation to the histories of Native culture and settlement. Thus, while I rec-ognize berdache as an object of knowledge, I interpret it less as an object than as a *context* of conversation: a cipher for a multifaceted discursive regime whose colonial hegemony remained contested while conditioning non-Native and Native claims on queer modernity. A history of berdache demonstrates that Native queer activism decisively interrupted it. Yet the object's logic still permeates popular and scientific conversations on queer modernities, inviting critical vigilance and deeper investigation of its effects.

Progressive Sexual Science: Berdache and the Anthropology of Homosexuality

In the mid-twentieth century, U.S. cultural anthropology's heritage as a set-tler science of American Indians transformed into a popular project promoting relativist accounts of cultural difference. In the wake of Franz Boas's public critiques of race essentialism, his students Alfred Kroeber, Ruth Benedict, and Margaret Mead offered ethnography as a method to translate primitive culture for the edification of modern society. Their relativism maintained a civilizational difference between the societies they portrayed and the West-ern, if not settler societies, whose modernity was to be educated by primi-tive peoples' insights into the human condition. Mead notably invited her U.S. audiences to incorporate such knowledge into the progressive promo-tion of respect for human differences. Her writings on gender and sexuality presented berdache as part of anthropology's application of primitivity to the self-fashioning of modern subjects of a settler society.

The popularity of berdache was enhanced when gay and lesbian politics articulated progressive legacies of U.S. anthropology. Gay and lesbian and allied anthropologists in the 1970s began to critique sexual conservatism in anthropology and U.S. society by forming the Anthropological Research Group on Homosexuality (ARGOH), later renamed the Society of Lesbian and Gay Anthropologists (SOLGA). Under these names, twentieth-century scholars linked the anthropology of homosexuality to the pursuit of sexual minority politics within anthropology. One of their first achievements was a host of new scholarship on berdache, which by the late 1980s circulated as an ideal object to inspire accommodating variation in modern societies. ARGOH's predominantly white scholarly network was also reflected among anthropologists of berdache whose work was later reevaluated by Native and non-Native critics. Although by the turn of the century changes in anthropology and queer politics shifted SOLGA beyond the Meadian defense of gender and sexual variation, a first generation of anthropologists of homosexuality established disciplinary authority by linking sexual minority politics to progressive anthropology through scholarship on berdache.[1]

U.S. anthropology of homosexuality linked research on homosexuality to the activist defense of gay and lesbian anthropologists. In the 1970s, the American Anthropological Association (AAA) and other professional societies became sites of challenge to the medical pathologization of homosexuality and of the defense of gay and lesbian scientists.[2] At the 1970 AAA business meeting, Clark Taylor proposed three resolutions affirming that the organization "recognizes the legitimacy and immediate importance" of research on homosexuality, "urges the protection of homosexual anthropologists" from discrimination, and goes "on record as urging the immediate legalization of all consensual sexual acts." All three were approved, though only narrowly, in a subsequent membership vote.[3] Little further organizing followed until Steve Holtzman and Steve Weinstein organized a first AAA panel on the topic "Homosexuality in Cross-Cultural Perspective" at the 1974 meetings, with Margaret Mead serving as respondent.[4] Participants recognized Mead not only for legitimating their work but also for affirming a link between the study of sexual diversity and its place within scholars' lives. As Taylor later remarked of her quietly acknowledged sexual history, "that was Margaret Mead at her best . . . relatively open about her bisexuality, absolutely tremendously supportive."[5] Attempts to coordinate AAA researchers on homosexuality continued until the 1978 establishment of ARGOH as an AAA interest group (although not an official AAA section).[6]

While the ARGOH charter stated its core aim as "to encourage and to support anthropological research on homosexual behavior," its initial work organized members to shift the culture and politics of their discipline.[7] A newsletter published proposals for panels, conferences, and books, as well as reports of ongoing research, and raised the profile of researchers who served as writers or officers. This paid off: while in 1979 Joseph Carrier reflected that "anthropological research on homosexuality is meager . . . it is therefore difficult to organize the few papers that people proffer into a coherent symposium theme," Walter Williams in 1984 announced that ARGOH members had hosted four AAA panels on sexuality, gender, and AIDS, and that, "combined with sessions on women, questions of sexuality and gender were so prominent . . . that they were practically a theme of the meetings."[8] Beyond promoting scholarship, ARGOH had an activist profile. After Larry Gross invited Evelyn Blackwood to be female copresident ("to make sure that women's issues receive the attention necessary, and to express our desire for more female membership and participation"), Blackwood encouraged ARGOH to become "the politically active group it was originally formed to be" by helping "the various minority groups of the AAA join forces in a coalition to consider issues relevant to all our groups."[9] Her sentiment led to the formation of an ARGOH Political Action Committee, which supported Paul Kutsche in his (unsuccessful) 1983 bid to join the AAA Committee on Ethics on a platform of adding sexual orientation to the AAA nondiscrimination statement. When the Committee on Ethics responded with AAA board approval by proposing to rescind *all* antidiscrimination protections, it provoked widespread protest among the membership. Kutsche and AAA section leaders put forward a "Resolution on Minority Anthropologists" directing the organization to affirm prior protections and add sexual orientation, age, and disability, which was adopted by the membership in 1986. Afterward, Kutsche observed that "ARGOH is now part of American anthropology's consciousness," as a group with a "ten-year history of defending gay and lesbian causes . . . which the executive office in Washington . . . listens to with respect."[10]

By promoting research on homosexuality and defending gay and lesbian anthropologists, ARGOH made sexual minority politics a basis for anthropological knowledge production. ARGOH's first members attested that scholars of homosexuality were not just gay men and lesbians, while many gay and lesbian anthropologists who did not study homosexuality joined ARGOH out of solidarity with other lesbians and gay men. Yet tensions quickly arose around ARGOH's projects. On the one hand, gay and lesbian anthropologists worked in a relativist tradition that defended cultural differences against the imposition of scholarly bias. This directed them to qualify or restrict their use of culturally specific terms such as "homosexual," "gay," or "lesbian" as analytic categories. On the other hand, ARGOH scholars pursued projects that came to be defined ever more explicitly as "lesbian or gay topics."[11] This direction narrowed the potential array of culture that ARGOH would study to one matching the interests of U.S. lesbians and gay men. By exerting their scientific authority, lesbian and gay anthropologists could represent self-selected "topics" as if they constituted a natural bundling of culture. Many ARGOH affiliates were aware of this dilemma and pursued studies that challenged the expectations of modern sexual minorities.[12] But if even these could be promoted and defended by ARGOH under the phrase "lesbian or gay topics," a disturbing conflation of modern sexual minorities with their own interruption let even their displacement re-center them in anthropological knowledge about sexuality and gender.

I contend that, rather than presenting a conundrum, this conflict between cultural variety and sexual politics energized ARGOH, in two crucial ways. First, the ARGOH charter grounded its research agenda in an argument that "'homosexuality'—in the sense of an exclusive sexual preference for persons of one's own gender—is descriptive of a minority of the members of any society."[13] Here, by arguing that human truth and its scientific study both correspond to a minoritizing theory of sexuality, ARGOH's promotion of science and of gay and lesbian political interests logically meshed. Second, ARGOH's work reached its fullest expression by modeling U.S. cultural anthropology in the legacies of Benedict and Mead. Their work had portrayed sexual variation in primitive cultures as lessons to a modern settler society (excluding the Native peoples it occupies) to accept its (non-Native) gender and sexual diversity. ARGOH described sexuality and gender among its objects—primarily Indigenous societies and Native Americans most prominently—to promote an acceptance of lesbians and gay men within U.S. society, and, by extrapolation, in other societies. The primitive to modern, Native to non-Native directionality of ARGOH's educative work renewed a midcentury U.S. anthropological project as a modern settler science, reconfigured to serve a modern and settler sexual minority politics.

In this context, gay and lesbian anthropology found a focal point in berdache. A study of the anthropological record for evidence of gender and sexual diversity immediately encountered berdache. Although neither Mead nor Benedict wrote a book on berdache, both generalized it as an object of primitive sexuality and gender that could explain a variety of sexual cultures. Their uses of the object match Mead's reading: "among many American Indian tribes the berdache, the man who dressed and lived as a woman, was a recognized social institution." The object's gendered relationship to sexuality remained a matter of debate: Benedict framed berdache as "homosexual," only to note instances when that reading did not apply; Mead said that berdache reflected a malleability in gender beyond "sexual inversion," although she thought they often were linked.[14] Yet both invoked berdache as proof that gender and sexual diversity could be affirmed.[15] Anthropologists cited their work as a benchmark for distinguishing cultural systems as affirming or rejecting gender and sexual diversity. In 1951, Clellan Ford and Frank Beach rejected the pathologization of homosexuality by centering berdache in their anthropological account of human variation. Introduced as "the most common form of institutionalized homosexuality," they define berdache as "a male who dresses like a woman, performs women's tasks, and adopts some aspects of the feminine role in sexual behavior with male partners." They note that "less frequently a woman dresses like a man and seeks to adopt the male sex role"—indicating that, while possibly related, such practices fall outside the term berdache.[16] The few other commentators who clarified berdache for anthropologists at this time also described a male-centered role accommodating sexual variation as one that called for scientific understanding.[17] Thus, in a trajectory beginning in the 1930s, U.S. anthropologists used berdache to deploy a modern theory of sexuality and gender in which subjects "express" a natural sexuality and sex, which societies do not produce but simply recognize through affirmation or rejection. In the process, by making Native Americans a benchmark of affirmation in relation to which other cultures appear constricting, berdache implicitly educated its audiences to rethink gender and sexual norms in their own, implicitly non-Native, societies.

Lesbian and gay anthropologists both sustained and shifted the object's coherence when they applied berdache to new work. They shared an interest in challenging prevailing beliefs about homosexuality by reframing berdache and anthropology around new questions, especially gender. When Charles Callender and Lee Kochems sought to cull a comprehensive data set from earlier anthropological writing on berdache, they questioned the centrality of homosexuality by describing an object defined by "gender-mixing" among males who adopt "dress, occupations, and behavior" of females in "the absence of sexual relations with others occupying these statuses."[18] By codifying cultures as data within authoritative claims on human variation that took berdache as a descriptor of social life, Callender and Kochems renewed classic U.S. anthropology through a recursive process—seeking Indigenous culture in the object; seeking the object in Indigenous cultures—that narrowed their claims even as the object's invention remained largely unexamined. Two years prior to their writing, Harriet Whitehead's account of berdache deferred its interpretation as homosexuality or "'Meadian' cultural variation" by asking, after Gayle Rubin, how sex/gender systems create stratification in modes of labor and value. Yet

Whitehead's feminist discussion of gender left intact the object's masculinist presumptions when she described it as a status created from men's
social "advantage" in response to "the possibility that women, within their
own department, might be onto a good thing. It was into this unsettling
breach that the berdache institution was hurled." She suggests that if persons in a berdache role were praised for proficiency in women's work, this
left women "subtly insulted" in their "anatomic aspect," while "through
him, ordinary men might reckon that they still held advantage that was
anatomically given and inalterable."[19] Here Whitehead repeats the colonial origin story of berdache as a product of Indigenous men's prerogative,
only now not to practice perversion but to appropriate women's spheres.
Whether or not she intended it, her assertion echoes radical feminist sus-
picions that male-to-female transsexuals enact a conspiratorial agenda of
male appropriation of women's power.[20] Whitehead expresses a misreading of berdache as Indigenous culture rather than as an object invented
to project colonial and masculinist expectations onto Indigenous peoples.
Still, whereas Callender and Kochems echoed Ford and Beach by codifying
Indigenous people as data for progressive anthropology, Whitehead was
the first scholar to question the Meadian approach by turning from culture
"accommodating" sexual and gender diversity to asking how it was produced within power relations.

   While circulation of Whitehead's work in anthropology and lesbian/
gay studies focused discussion of berdache in academia, the object's broader
popularization followed the work of Evelyn Blackwood and Walter Williams,
who reframed its masculinism in light of Blackwood's feminist critiques
while presenting the best evidence yet of ARGOH's scholarly leadership.
Blackwood was one of the first ARGOH members to critically engage the
group's focus on gay men and "continued emphasis on male homosexual
behavior as a general model for theoretical analysis."[21] As editor of a special
issue on the anthropology of homosexuality in *The Journal of Homosexuality*
(1985), later published as *The Many Faces of Homosexuality* (1986), Blackwood and her contributors collated old data and set new research models
that included "[bringing] women's sexual behavior within the purview of
the current discussion on homosexuality by separating it from the historical construction of male homosexuality and by examining the particular
cultural contexts of lesbian behavior."[22] Blackwood had already pursued
this goal by questioning the object's masculinism in her focus on "female
cross-gender roles" in historical Native American societies.[23] Her rereading of anthropological texts through the lens of gender not only defined

berdache apart from homosexuality but also discarded the object before addressing the female embodiment it erased. In discussing historical accounts of Native women chiefs, women identified as or acting as warriors, and women taking roles apart from "woman" or "man," Blackwood focused on "gender" as a field of power relations that enables multiple social roles. Her application of feminist theory to distinguish between various western and Plains Native societies according to their degree of gender egalitarianism also broke with the uniformity projected by berdache. Blackwood created new contexts for debating the presumptions naturalized within berdache. Yet her work remained compatible with the aim of a new, feminist anthropological authority to define Indigenous, gendered, and sexual truth. While her term "female cross-gender roles" displaced the focus on male roles and was less totalizing than berdache, its purpose remained to codify Indigenous sexual and gender diversity into an anthropological object. However distinct this term was meant to be, it gained broadest discussion in texts defined by homosexuality and berdache, so that "female cross-gender roles" appeared as a variation on efforts to define Native Americans for the anthropology of homosexuality.

Walter Williams engaged Blackwood while writing his book *The Spirit and the Flesh: Sexual Diversity in American Indian Culture* (1986), although he endeavored to establish berdache as a key term in the anthropology of homosexuality. Following his peers in defining it not as homosexuality but as an "alternative gender role," Williams parted from feminist critics by not studying the term within gendered power relations, and instead repeating earlier accounts by examining a male role that permitted discussion of female embodiment and feminist critique only secondarily. Yet this dissonance arose from an even deeper problematic in Williams's project, as the first to move past rereading older texts and conduct new ethnography of Native people. Seeking to claim that the roles described by the object persisted in Native societies today, Williams assigned the term "berdache" to any male-bodied Native people he met who identified or were identified by others as gay, homosexual, or a variety of traditional terms—although, he found, never *as* "berdaches." His use of the term reflected its ease of translation and importance among anthropologists, but it also indicates that Williams met Native people from within the expectations set by the object. For instance, his concluding appeal to feminist analysis makes sense if the object's correlation to male embodiment made it seem both accurate and a service to women to discuss female embodiment separately. Yet any exclusion produced by the term followed Williams's anthropological invest-ment in finding the object in Native people's lives, rather than asking how a history of the term or of the anthropological project it incited would need to be studied and displaced for Native peoples' lives to be representable.

Ultimately, however, Williams presents his anthropological commitments as effects of a deeper commitment to create knowledge serving sexual minority politics, one presumably—and at times explicitly—non-Native. Referencing the work of Judy Grahn and Will Roscoe, he notes that tales of berdache historically inspired U.S. sexual minorities, by "[supplying] a sense of roots, a feeling of being part of a long tradition in America."[24] Yet, in doing so, berdache promised sexual or gender liberation only inas-much as it first liberated non-Native and presumably white gays and les-bians from identifying as settlers and rewrote their lives on stolen Native land as somehow being a return to kinship with their own kind. Most non-Native gays and lesbians in the 1980s knew Native gays and lesbians only from the pages of Williams's book. Their kinship existed as a commodity, its spine standing out on a bookshelf at home or in a lesbian and gay book-store, if not as a story widely circulating that let them imagine that minori-tized sexuality made them more like Native people than the settler society in which they lived. The naturalized settler colonial context of this desire let Williams exhort his U.S. audience to let berdache lead them to

> question whether a separated gay subculture, a minority lifestyle built around same-sex preferences, is more preferable to integration of gender variance and male-male eroticism into the general family structure and the main-stream society. We can use the American Indian concept of spirituality to break out of the deviancy model, to reunite families, and to offer special benefits to society as a whole. (275)

In this non-Native application of anthropology to U.S. sexual politics, Wil-liams turns Native America into a cipher for achieving homonationalist belonging by white settler descendants in a renewed white settler society. But rather than representing an innovation of his book, Williams's claim evokes an earlier ethnography that narrated Indigenous gender and sexu-ality under U.S. colonial rule as a lesson for U.S. society. Like *Coming of Age in Samoa*, *The Spirit and the Flesh* appears to exist "inside" Native culture—until its conclusion reveals that its goal all along was to address, evaluate, and progressively change the normatively white readership of a white set-tler society.

The success of Williams's work served ARGOH's effort to produce ground-breaking anthropology in clear defense of sexual minorities and their politics. In 1986, subsequent to its leadership in the AAA antidiscrimination battle, the group presented the first ARGOH Award for "Distinguished Scholarship on a Lesbian or Gay Topic"—later renamed the Ruth Benedict Book Prize—to *The Spirit and the Flesh*. ARGOH described the book as a work that "breaks new ground in gay research and exemplifies a quality of research which will open the way for the publication of other anthropological works on lesbian or gay topics."[25] Yet the meeting announcing this award also became a site for reevaluating the group that granted it. Records show that the award presentation was followed by a discussion initiated by women members on "the need for gender parity in ARGOH sponsored sessions, and the need for ARGOH to be more sensitive to lesbian concerns." As newsletter editor Blackwood explained, "this discussion led (inevitably) to questions about ARGOH's purpose: whether it is supposed to provide support for research on gay and lesbian topics or serve as an association for lesbian and gay anthropologists." Following a proposal that ARGOH's name be altered "to reflect our identity as gay people," discussion was tabled and letters addressing these themes were invited for the 1987 newsletter.[26] During subsequent months, member letters affirmed that the group had a history of marginalizing women, including in its use of the term "homosexuality," while its name obscured its commitments to sexual minority politics. Echoing a suggestion by Sue-Ellen Jacobs, many members proposed the creation of an interest group for the study of homosexuality to be subsidiary to an association redefined by political identity. Here, activist lesbian and gay scholars seeking minority recognition in their discipline gained support from colleagues who put their research goals second to new activism. Debate resolved in 1987 when the group voted to rename itself the Society of Lesbian and Gay Anthropologists. The proposed research group never materialized; but by being absorbed into the broader work of SOLGA, the new name fulfilled ARGOH's purpose: to support research on homosexuality from within a deeper purpose of promoting sexual minorities and their politics within anthropology and beyond. Defining a group by its leadership—lesbian and gay anthropologists—held anthropology accountable to the identities and politics of sexual minorities, while feminist critique now affirmed that lesbians no longer would be peripheral to gay men.

SOLGA's admixture of scholarly and political goals gained their widest public recognition in 1991 through a last popularization of berdache in this period, Will Roscoe's monograph *The Zuni Man-Woman*. Roscoe came to the anthropology of berdache as an independent scholar whose study of the Zuni *lhamana* role appeared in a slide show he presented at Zuni Pueblo and elsewhere titled "The Zuni Man-Woman: A Traditional Gay Role." In the early 1980s, he invited the San Francisco group Gay American Indians to collaborate in new research and GAI appointed him coordinator of its History Project, which led to the anthology *Living the Spirit* and publication of Roscoe's bibliography and historical accounts of berdache. Roscoe's later transition to doctoral study and SOLGA participation continued his effort to offer gay men and lesbians a history through cross-cultural evidence of "gay roles," whose economic, political, and religious qualities indexed for him a universal "gay pattern" matching gay and lesbian desires.[27] Roscoe promoted berdache much like Carpenter and Mead by arguing that a predictable appearance of minoritized sexuality in societies worldwide offered a tool for promoting self-knowledge for gay men and lesbians and social tolerance. Such sentiments define his writing at the time, although he focused more narrowly on Native and colonial histories in *The Zuni Man-Woman*. The book was published to wide acclaim, including recognition by the AAA, which gave it the 1991 Margaret Mead Award as the best book to "interpret anthropological data in ways meaningful to the public."[28] The Mead Award acknowledged the book's broad popularity in sexual minority communities as well as Roscoe's efforts to communicate its contents to the Zuni people.

Roscoe's success affirmed SOLGA's effort to renew U.S. anthropology's progressive profile by promoting berdache as a tool of social change. SOLGA reprinted the comments Roscoe did not have the chance to read aloud on receiving the award, and which then became part of SOLGA's legacy.[29] He opens by saying,

> there is a way that holding this award now completes a circle that begins with the work of Margaret Mead and her teacher, Ruth Benedict. They also wrote about Native American berdaches and drew on the insights they gained to argue for grater social tolerance. And they also were passionate lovers of their own sex. But unlike Benedict and Mead, I do not have to hide this part of my life. Even so, the task of ensuring that anthropology is an inclusive profession is far from complete.

Roscoe then links the sexually diverse history of progressive U.S. anthropology (in which berdache already played a part) to SOLGA's current challenge to disciplinary homophobia as a barrier that, we now see, also affected Benedict and Mead. Citing SOLGA's discussions on gaining status as an AAA section, Roscoe notes that "many institutions of higher education still do not prohibit discrimination based on sexual preference," such that "should the Society of Lesbian and Gay Anthropologists affiliate with the Association, it might be the only unit that anthropologists will actually have to risk their jobs to join." He quotes Catherine Bateson's comment on Mead's sexual history, to the point that Mead "clearly believed that the keeping of these secrets was . . . a precondition to her availability to do the work that she felt was important."[30] The era of AIDS begs for an anthropological "spokesperson" to lead critique and change, he says, and closes by asking, "How then can we make sure that . . . individuals with the talents and disposition of Mead can again achieve her stature and prestige, and make the kind of social contributions that she was able to make?" With the moral force of receiving one of the AAA's highest honors, Roscoe eloquently models the activism of ARGOH/SOLGA by making knowledge of sexual diversity, notably berdache, challenge sexual conservatism as an expression of the heart of the discipline. He does not just assert that sexual minority politics and good anthropology are compatible, but argues that, in view of the legacy of a figure like Mead, they appear as one.

SOLGA did not uniformly acclaim Roscoe's book. In a review in the SOLGA newsletter, Blackwood noted that "it is clear from [Roscoe's] analysis that he thinks of berdache as male" and questioned the modern gay logics she perceived in his descriptions of Zuni life.[31] But her disagreement regarding what Roscoe said about berdache ends by recalling the common ground shaping why they, as anthropologists, debated it:

> I am willing to set aside these problems, because Roscoe gives us a compelling view of another way of looking at humanity, a vision of an alternate construction of social life, which may help to liberate our own warped sense of who we are as "Western" women and men. (59)

This sentiment echoes the long-standing work of ARGOH/SOLGA members to narrate sexual and gender diversity as a means to fulfill their own lives. It repeats progressive anthropology's civilizational investment in separating "Western" and settler societies from the Indigenous cultures that edify them. In each case, the anthropology of berdache makes Native culture crucial to gender and sexual liberation because it transforms U.S. sexual minorities' relationship to the history, culture, and power of settler colonialism.

Anthropological conversations popularized berdache as an Indigenous and sexual truth that defined normatively non-Native sexual minority subjects and politics within a white settler society.

"Without Sources, without Footnotes, without Doubt": Counterculturist Imaginings of Queer Indigeneity

Prior to its promotion in late-twentieth-century anthropology, gay and lesbian counterculturists invoked berdache to liberate queer indigeneity. In the 1970s, gay and lesbian radicals challenged heteropatriarchal capitalism, racism, and imperialism by pursuing back-to-the-land rural collectivism and primitivism, which gay men also linked to recalling berdache. One record of their work appears in *RFD*, a U.S. reader-written journal by and for rural gay men. Beginning in 1974, rural gay men's collectives edited *RFD* to portray ideal rural and Indigenous routes to gay liberation. Contributors cited texts, oral narratives, and intuition as evidence tracing gay nature to an Indigenous spiritual root modeled by berdache that reconciled them to their non-Native and normatively white inheritance of settlement. While a key group that arose from this history, the Radical Faeries, will be discussed later in this book, this section reads *RFD* as a record of prior and broader counterculturist conversations that popularized berdache as Indigenous grounds for liberating non-Native gay men on settled land.[32]

Gay back-to-the-land counterculturism resembled other such projects by creating a rural–urban formation, in which urban expatriates joined rural-raised participants on rural land and invited visitors to participate through travel and information exchange. *RFD* was proposed as a "country journal by gay men" at the Midwest Gay Pride Conference in 1974, where "18 people (gay men) who are into a gay or mixed rural collective life style" living near Iowa City joined to produce the first issue.[33] Over time the editorship shifted among rural gay collectives in Oregon, western North Carolina, central Tennessee, and northern New England.[34] The journal quickly gathered a readership similar to other counterculturist projects. The winter 1976 issue editors at Wolf Creek described themselves as "all young (if those of us in our thirties can be considered young), white, men. Almost all of us grew up outside of the large cities. But all of us have been nurtured by the cultural/political gay male circles in the large cities. Though some of us come from the working class, most of us come from the middle class."[35] In 1975, the journal's first survey reported 276 readers, nearly three out of four being gay-identified urban residents of Christian religious background with a median age of twenty-five.[36] The absence of race as a factor in the survey reflected the normative whiteness of the collectives and the journal's readers. Imagery and testimony in *RFD* invoked rural white gay men inheriting a settler culture while seeking Indigenous ties to land. The journal first represented "country" within gay reimaginings of European roots and settler homesteading, as in articles on building cabins, gardening, and cooking.[37] Yet these nostalgic images appeared within a counterculturist spirituality that traced gay men's nature to European neo-pagan knowledge. Amid references to pagan holidays and celebrations, some contributors argued for a special role for ancient European gay men, as in the Wolf Creek collective's opening to the winter 1976 issue:

> The original meaning of faggot is "a bundle of twigs or sticks used as kindling." In the middle ages the church used us gay men as kindling, or faggots, to burn witches. Witches were usually wise herbal healers, all strong women, often lesbians. Witches and faggots were enemies of the church because we were often country dwellers, lovers of the natural world and the communal good, rather than private greed. We were an obstacle to the development of merchantalism, which became capitalism. We are proud of our past. We are proud of being identified so closely with strong women . . . Though all of us are not sissy-men, we will no longer be ashamed of woman-identified men or the woman-identified man in all of us.[38]

Proclaiming politicized effeminacy and feminism, this story portrays white gay men and feminist women as antagonists to a Euro-American, capitalist, and Christian settler society that they might otherwise appear to represent but that their politics disavows and opposes.

Correlations between a European past and Native American indigeneity appeared in *RFD* after its first concerted reflection on spirituality, in the summer of 1977 "Spirituality Issue." Having invited readers to describe "faggot spirituality" in "traditional spirituality, Native religions, personal magic, and all sorts of combinations," the editors arranged from submissions an eclectic mélange in which a uniquely gay nature claimed Native roots.[39] Contributor Gary Lee Phillips from Lansing, Michigan, asserted this when he told how breaking from a career as a Catholic priest led to his "present state of spirituality," which for him affirmed that

> there is a special magick in gayness. It has been recognized in most human cultures at one time or another. We as gay people, both women and men, have provided more than our share of saints and martyrs, priests and nuns, witches and warlocks, seers and prophets. This is not a coincidence.[40]

A gay adaptation of European religious histories to a global spirituality was evoked by Jada Joyous of San Francisco, who combined "feminism and sissy consciousness, socialism and anarchism, pagan-gypsy/trippy-hippie love-power, wholistic health and meditation, with Catholicism and Judaism, witchcraft and voodoo thrown in for spice." But Joyous grounded these ties in a new realization:

> Adding further spice to the brew is a new sense of gay history, connecting us to centuries of earth rituals (and persecutions) of faggot-witches. We have always been religious people, and have been in positions of religious honor in many Native cultures.[41]

In 1977, Joyous and Phillips assign newness to a story echoing the Iowa City collective in 1974, although here pagan Europe marks a more primordial human nature recognizable in "Native cultures." A grounding of gay spirituality in Native American roots also appeared in narratives invoking the "shaman," following the popularization of Carlos Castaneda's writing on psychotropics as Indigenous conduits to spiritual insight.[42] The term spoke to Caradoc from Berkeley, who found his practice as a priest in a European pagan coven situated more deeply: "I found in the craft a way of sharing my magic and vision, which are after all the basic function and obligation of a shaman."[43] The issue closed by affirming this notion in editor Jam's summation: "there's a great shaman/sorcerer/wisewoman inside you, more ***** than you can imagine, the key is your gayness."[44] Jam's inclusion of "wisewoman" after (Native) shaman and (European pagan) sorcerer suggests that gay spirituality will reflect gendered effeminacy and feminist stakes, although these represent a "key" to a *deeper* potential marked by Native spirituality.

Although submissions to the Spirituality Issue do not mention berdache by name, qualities associated with the object appear as references to a general Indigenous gay nature and a specific Native archetype for counterculturist white gay men. These cohere most forcefully in drawings by Jamal Redwing that are published in the issue without comment. Their absence of narrative contextualization suggests their legibility to *RFD*'s audience as aspects of a mythos that white gay counterculturism sought to create. Redwing's first image, "Faggot Shaman Poet Butterfly Dancer," most directly evokes berdache by representing a gay male figure embodying Native American religious life. A nude male in an effeminate and sexually suggestive pose dances in a butterfly headdress at a pueblo, along one wall of which three similarly attired dancers are silhouetted. The dancers' link of effeminacy to religious practice—"faggot shaman"—is stylized to project gay counter-culturist desire, as "dancer" and "poet" evoke the creative life Carpenter imagined for gay men, while "butterfly" might suggest European fairy lore as much as gay nature's emergence. Their appearance at the pueblo suggests a living spiritual tradition, but one troubled by the absence of any witnesses or participants apart from themselves. The image portrays an Indigenous social context for berdache in gay counterculturist claims, even as the appearance of that context only as static signs presents faggot shamans as, in effect, their *own* community. Marshaling Native culture as a cipher for minoritized sexuality omits any larger Native nation in which the dancers live or gain and transmit meaning. The only part of Native culture lived collectively is one that serves white gay men imagining minoritized Indigenous roots: Native nationality and sovereignty are not imagined, or even desired, in this appropriation.

Another Redwing image, "Untitled," more narrowly narrates gay nature by conjoining Indigenous Europe with Native America, while showing how such imaginaries mediated white gay men's inheritance of settler colonialism. Before a moon-illuminated forest, a nude and aroused Native man kneels before an obelisk on which sits the carved head of the European neo-pagan "horned god," sometimes imagined as Pan. Protruding at waist height from the obelisk is an erect phallus, on which the Native man's eyes are transfixed; he thrusts his erect penis forward in homoerotic homage and desire. This image complexly reverses white gay counterculturist discoveries of gay nature within Native culture. The Indigenous man's naked enrapture by the appearance of Pan marks his existence in a state of nature, and this as his first contact with nature's (and male sexuality's) European god. The scene reverses, and echoes, colonial representations of the disembarkation of colonists being met by Indigenous Americans who reverence their superiority and authority. Yet, by representing an *Indigenous* discovery of a European statue on redwood- and fir-studded land, the image establishes a global and transhistorical purview for European paganism, of which Native America is an example. That this man, absent any effeminate or religious trappings, recognizes the object of his submission and longing homoerotically suggests that berdache is not the only bridge for white gay men to claim a link to Native culture. Here, colonial narratives of indiscriminate sexuality echo with a twentieth-century genre of homoerotic cowboy–Indian and captivity narratives to project sexual freedom into the authentic Indigenous man whom white gay men desire. But, most important, the fantasy flips counterculturist white gay men's discovery of their nature

FAGGOT SHAMAN

POET
BUTTERFLY
DANCER

Jamal Redwing, "Faggot Shaman Poet Butterfly Dancer." Reprinted with permission of *RFD*.

within Native culture to suggest that their claim performs no history of encroachment or appropriation. In this image of original communion, white gay men address their inheritance of settlement by finding through gay nature a prior belonging to Native land, where histories of conquest are superseded by a more ancient and mutual desire.

The Spirituality Issue's quests for pagan indigeneity inspired debate in later issues reflecting divergent reader perspectives on gayness, spirituality, and settlement. Kelly Lindner of Pioche, Nevada, wrote that he remained interested in *RFD*—especially, he said wryly, if it helped him meet attractive "gay hippies"—but he had a "qualm" about

> your spiritual tone. You don't need to devote a whole issue to bring to the surface that you're all cultivating some ethereal home-brewed bullshit. I don't blame you. I got thoughts of my own. There's no need to go chasing after some crazy organized religion but there's also no need for you guys to constantly harp on your paganistic rituals and candle-burnings. Witchcraft ain't my trip and you guys seem to push it a bit too far. Keep your idealized solipsism a bit more to yourself![45]

Bill Holloway of Toronto later chastised Lindner for dismissing how contributors sought a "tribal connection," the absence of which he praised *RFD* for trying to address in its readers' "modern" and "western" lives:

> We have had no community, no tribe. Our only feelings of tribal connection have been through the family and through the abstract modern idolatries ... All of western society is in this state. No one has clear methods for communicating consciousness-raising experience. Your work in this area is extremely valuable.[46]

In kind, Tom Manes of Houston communicated his happiness that *RFD* affirmed that "just as there are alternatives to sexuality, there are also alternatives in spirituality."[47] Manes joined Holloway in countering Lindner's skepticism by calling on gay men to adapt "tribal" knowledges as "alternatives" to the "modern" cultures in the big cities where they and most other *RFD* readers lived.

The very thesis of back-to-the-land movement and non-Native desires for indigeneity were critiqued two issues later by "Arnold J. Cornbelt." Although the pseudonymous author admitted to originating on the West Coast and to having read *RFD* since 1974, he lampoons the journal in a crude sketch that parodies an *RFD* cover. Under the title "WHITE WEST-COAST GARABAGE" *[sic]*, captions such as "BUYING LAND IS EASY (IF YOU'RE RICH)" and "CITIES ARE O.K. TOO" bracket a man and woman posed as a hippie "American Gothic" in a field before their geodesic dome house. Near them, a four-legged creature marked "SAN-FRANCISCO SCENE" with a bee-hive coifed human head and feet in high heels pleads to the couple to "FEED ME!"[48] Cornbelt's critique of class-privileged expatriates from San Francisco claiming rural space also positions *RFD* close to the heteronormative roots of the back-to-the-land movement. But he also comments on Redwing's images:

> Issue #12 has showed me that whites can be Indians too! Although whites have murdered, raped, destroyed, starved, and cursed the Indian peoples to the ultimate, pages 8, 18, and 23 indicate they need only strip off their clothes, glue on a few chicken feathers, and dance around naked with a hard-on. Ta da! Instant Indian! What a wonderful world it is when ego-maniacal greedy white children can become all that their ancestors murdered in an instant.

Cornbelt's words prompted editor Candor Smoothstone to thank him facetiously for a "tacky" letter.[49] But by only briefly acknowledging Cornbelt's critique, Smoothstone glossed over the only direct comment on Redwing's images to appear in *RFD*. On setting it aside, *RFD* affirmed that it would present but leave unexamined white gay men's efforts to portray Native culture as a source of sexual liberation that also reconciled them to settlement by gaining belonging to Native culture and land.

Narratives in *RFD* tapped into conversations on gay indigeneity whose most widely circulated expression appeared in Arthur Evans's *Witchcraft and the Gay Counterculture*. Originally published serially in the more urban gay counterculturist journal *Fag Rag* (1975–76), his work was not cited directly in *RFD*'s Spirituality Issue, but, during these years, *RFD* contributors, including Evans, affirmed their shared intuition in the existence of an Indigenous gay nature. Evans first addressed this subject in 1975 in a short *RFD* article that announced his departure from graduate school "to look for land in the country and to begin a revolutionary new lifestyle." He reports:

> I had fallen back into the habit of scholarly reading . . . In the process, I had come across a lot of provocative material in history and anthropology having to do with Gay people. Much of this stuff deals with the people called "witches" in the Middle Ages. I was excited by these discoveries.[50]

Framing the material in these texts as "discoveries" thematically references gay liberation efforts to break homophobic silences to liberate truths and grant gayness a history. In the process, Evans regards these texts as repositories of facts rather than as an earlier era's interested readings, particularly when he cites ethnological or emancipationist texts to justify his desires for Indigenous gay nature.

In his book, Evans argues first that "nature people"—his euphemism for primitive or premodern—promise gay people liberation in their "sharp distinction to the Christian/industrial tradition: their love of sexuality":[51]

> The Indians who have been observed in the Americas; the myths that have survived in Europe; the artifacts that exist from all over the world—all attest to the *pleasure* of what the celebrants were doing . . . Gay people of both sexes were looked upon with religious awe, and sexual acts of every possible kind were associated with the most holy forms of religious expression. (109, 111)

This account hinges on Evans's "most famous example," berdache, as a model of "gay shamans" in ancient religions worldwide (101, 106). He invites embracing these histories as part of a "new socialism" in which modern subjects become the Indigenous people who inspire them, such that "a myriad number of autonomous tribes, small in population, growing like plants from the earth" will "[replace] industrial technology with people's technology" (154, 146). But amid entrenched "industrial patriarchy," such efforts will be "short-lived" unless people "tap into . . . the spiritual powers in nature and in ourselves" (148). Revolution will reinvigorate natural sexuality once gay people claim roles that demand to be reborn:

> If we are ever to rise up from the dead and regain our rightful place in nature . . . we will have to summon forth powers that have not been known since the days of the shamans . . . Let us invoke our friends, the banished and forbidden spirits of nature and self, as well as the ghost of Indian, wise-woman, faggot, Black sorcerer, and witch. They will hear our deepest call and come. Through us the spirits will speak . . . We look forward to regaining our ancient historical roles as medicine people, healers, prophets, shamans, and sorcerers. (133, 149, 154–55)

Evans argues that revolution will follow once white gay men are possessed by the spirits of "nature people," including the ghosts of Indians, or reincarnate those spirits as their own selves. White settler gay men here appropriate the ancestors of racial and national Others as their own subjectivities to justify or inspire revolutionary anticolonialism and sexual liberation.

Witchcraft and the Gay Counterculture was well received by its core audience, but I am interested in how it resonates with stories that already circulated among gay counterculturists. In 1975, a contributor to *RFD* named Carl showed how counterculturist claims derived not from singular sources but from intuitive inspiration by the origins they sought. Carl wrote that reading Evans's earliest serials in *Fag Rag* put words to a truth he had been waiting to recall. In a moment of studying medieval European dances, Carl's imagination was caught by seeing his sexuality reflected in the past:

> I notice the picture, a ring of fairies dancing in a circle. A few weeks later I am scribbling furiously delving into figures that I have danced for 15 years now: circles, reels, crosses. I am creating a mock-ethnology of Celtic dances. Surely these wonderful dances must have had their origin in some pre-Christian era. Without sources, without footnotes, without doubt I realize that the figures are celebrations of how ancient people loved each other. Sex is one kind of celebration of that, dance is another.[52]

Carl invokes Evans's historical and ethnological writing as conduits for his own intuition, as his "mock-ethnology" presents nothing so systematic while still evoking scientific authority. Indeed, the fact that Carl knows his ethnology to be mimetic does not reduce its utility: "I don't much care if it really happened, this culture he describes; I care only that what Arthur read has helped him to envision a better scheme of things" (31). The quests by Carl and Evans for sexual liberation by imagining indigeneity gain meaning by confirming what they already knew, or wished to know, about human nature. But rather than critique their manner of writing history, I wish to emphasize that claims by Evans, Carl, and contributors to *RFD* generated their personal, even spiritual, realizations in conversations—whether with one another, with real or imagined citations, or with the intuitions that these incite. Indeed, their conversations on Indigenous gay nature finally cite *themselves* as proof for their claims.

In a 1977 issue of *RFD*, Gary Phillips reflects on stories he heard that inform his gay identity:

> I make no pretense to being an anthropologist, but it seems to me that I recall being told that in many cultures the gay person is revered as witch-sacred. Folk knowledge often proves true, and I suspect that this is one of its successes.[53]

By arguing that folk knowledge has proven true, white gay men—citing counterculturist thought and affirming it in conversation—assert that an Indigenous gay nature comprises their sexual and spiritual heritage. In the early pages of *RFD*, a passage from European paganism to a global and transhistorical indigeneity answered white gay men's settler colonial inheritance by making them more like Indigenous people than the settlers they

otherwise represent. Making indigeneity their truth performed settler modernity by incorporating, embodying, and yet transcending indigeneity when
asserting their belonging on stolen land. In *RFD* and among its readers,
such realizations arose in conversations on an ancient and spiritual Indigenous gay nature, inspired by and inspiring of the object berdache.

Early issues of *RFD* presage and conditioned later conversations on
berdache, as we will see in chapter 4, which discusses how gay back-to-
the-land counterculturists were a historical backdrop to formation of the
Radical Faeries. In 1979, prominent Los Angeles gay activists decided to
promote insights of gay counterculturism more broadly and, as organizer
Harry Hay put it, "share our gay vision" while developing berdache and
other stories of queer indigeneity as "a resource for gay spirituality."[54] Their
work intersected other work on berdache, notably Hay, who as a collec-
tor of berdache literature consulted with Williams and Roscoe during their
research.[55] Roscoe in particular engaged gay counterculturist theses on
berdache, and his early research was inspired by his attending Radical Faerie
gatherings.[56] Roscoe's writing for anthropologists and Native communities was complemented by texts on gay spirituality. He describes how an
"archetypal basis for gay personality" can be found in stories of berdache,
which let gay men "*transform*" themselves from the strictures of a two-
gender system by learning the liberating place of "*third*-gender roles."[57]
While critical of judgments meted out on those who inspired him—Judy
Grahn, Mark Thompson, Arthur Evans, Harry Hay, and others—"for what
appears to be the crime of seeking truth outside of scholarly discourse,"
Roscoe defended his work to "make a history" for gay men and lesbians by
engaging knowledge that he took "back from fairy gatherings to later re-
examine, follow-up, substantiate, research, and test."[58] He says of those
encounters:

> Listening to the stories that gay men have to tell—and, we discovered, we
> all have remarkable stories to tell—it really became clear to me in the most
> definite way how much more is involved in being gay than simply having a
> homosexual orientation . . . Examining our lives as gay adults, we found more
> common ground in the special roles we often fulfill in interpersonal relation-
> ships, work, and families. The multidimensional model . . . really grew out of
> these dialogues with gay men, which have been going on at fairy gatherings
> for over ten years now. (245)

The significance of this account is not that Roscoe's writing on berdache
was inspired by the Radical Faeries—a fact that he widely noted—but

rather the *process* by which his work and that of other white gay counterculturists came to be linked. Here, Roscoe frames conversations with gay men at Radical Faerie gatherings as sites of knowledge production, where ideas learned elsewhere were brought for consideration before returning to broader debate. This recursive quality in Radical Faerie practice informed broader queer culture, politics, and knowledge with insights generated in gay counterculturist space. Roscoe also shows that the thinking space created by Radical Faeries was collective in that it invited each participant's historical or intuitive insights to spark those of others. Radical Faeries thus produced subjectivity similarly to the way earlier gay counterculturists did, and just as they in turn recalled earlier colonial, ethnological, and emancipationist tales of berdache. Gay counterculturist histories demonstrate how conversations on berdache and queer modernity are synchronic and diachronic. New insights refer to earlier claims of which they may or may not be aware but that they maintain and transform. Framing counterculturist conversations in this way also reveals that the boundary between academic and popular cultures is porous, if not a fiction that obscures how each produces knowledge for the other—indeed, *as* both at once. Finally, gay counterculturist histories suggest that if scholars saw a consonance between berdache and gay identity, their work followed white gay counterculturists who already saw in berdache a reflection of desires for an Indigenous gay nature. Apart from any citations, their intuitive and conversational affirmations mobilized berdache in sexual minority cultural politics. I agree with Roscoe that because of their commitments, *RFD* and the Radical Faeries remain vulnerable to ridicule by outsiders, and I engage their work seriously as a site where non-Native queer modernities reconcile to inheriting settlement. But while a sense of being on the fringe was important to gay counterculturists, I contend that they were never separate from non-Native queer modernities; indeed, they formed crucial sites for popularizing berdache as a resource for all queer non-Natives.

Native Negotiations: Displacing Berdache in Two-Spirit Organizing

By the 1990s, non-Native queer popularizations of berdache changed in response to Native queer and Two-Spirit activism. Native queer people in the United States and Canada represented Native histories and their lives in counterpoint to berdache, and instead proposed Two-Spirit identity. This section examines how, prior to Two-Spirit's emergence and in its wake, Native activists defined gender and sexuality discrepantly from non-Native queer modernities. Rather than a global and transhistorical nature reflected in berdache, Native activists embraced gender and sexual identities that critiqued settler colonialism and narrated Native culture for Native audiences whose solidarity transformed broader queer and Native politics. They engaged and fractured the colonial logics of non-Native conversations in anthropology and counterculturism and enacted a new Native politics within Two-Spirit identity.

Beginning in the 1970s, Native gay, lesbian, bisexual, and transgender people met in new networks formed in the wake of migration to cities that supported both urban Native and radical gender/sexual politics. While offering mutual support, they also asserted their belonging in Native and queer politics and in the histories of Native societies. Alongside Gay American Indians in the United States, groups that arose in the 1980s included American Indian Gays and Lesbians (AIGL) in Minneapolis, WeWah and BarCheeAmpe in New York City, and Nichiwakan in Winnipeg; in the late 1970s, Vancouver already hosted the Native Cultural Society, which brought Native people together in an annual drag ball and other activities. GAI also promoted Native queer people in the media and in Native and queer communities. GAI members set up booths at powwows and other Native community events (at times in the face of harassment); published testimonies in Native media; and directed Native health programs to address their experiences of AIDS.[59] GAI also sought to educate civic agencies and the broader gay and lesbian movement about their existence and their claim of a historical place in Native nations.[60] According to Randy Burns and Erna Pahe, GAI's visibility persuaded skeptical urban Indian organizations to later seek GAI out owing to its ties to media, government, and social movements.[61] Native queer activists increasingly kept in touch across great distances and periodically gathered at Native or queer activist events.

The identities promoted among early activists are reflected in *Living the Spirit*, which responded to burgeoning anthropological and counterculturist accounts of Native history as a first text "not just *about*... but *by* gay Indians."[62] In 1984, while anthropologists were conducting research on berdache, GAI formed its History Project "to collect information on our history and to make it available to the larger community." GAI announced the planned anthology in a 1987 ARGOH newsletter and invited ARGOH's help in securing a publisher.[63] *Living the Spirit* juxtaposes testimony, poetry, and interviews narrating Native activism with historical writing on berdache by Native writers. A reprint of "Tinselled Bucks," the 1975 article by Maurice Kenney (Mohawk), joined a feminist materialist essay by Midnight

Sun (Anishinaabe) on historical roles in social context.[64] Kenney in 1975 used berdache to name a role defined by male embodiment and homosexuality, whereas Midnight Sun in the 1980s cites feminist scholars to circumvent the object and discuss female embodiment while questioning the centrality of homosexuality. Yet both reject a transhistorical object by emphasizing variability among Native societies, which Kenney addresses to Native readers to inspire them to transform Native nations today and accept gender and sexual diversity.[65] Burns describes the significance of *Living the Spirit* in teaching Native queer people their "unique heritage as American Indians" while asserting that they come "from many different tribes" with "mutual respect for individual tribal customs and traditions."[66] Clyde Hall affirms this view and invites Native people to link traditions to everyday life by reimagining Native culture:

> Traditions need to be researched and revived. If traditions have been lost, then new ones should be borrowed from other tribes to create groups or societies for gay Indians that would function in the present. An example of this is the contemporary pow-wow that takes elements from many tribal groups and combines them into an exercise in modern Indian tradition and social structure . . . somehow, there should be a blending of the old with the new.[67]

In contrast to his experience of being raised on his people's land and taught traditions from a young age, Hall here also envisions identities for Native people with no tie to landed culture or tradition. Burns links all of these varied claims within a politics in which Native GLBTQ people claiming historical traditions as their "continuity" also organize to critique the effects of settler colonialism, in "poverty, poor education, and unemployment," racism in queer communities, and homophobia in Native communities.[68]

Contributors to *Living the Spirit* defined their lives and ties to Native tradition and colonial power in ways that contrasted with non-Native projections onto them of a primordial sexual nature. Yet this very distinction emerged as Native people engaged non-Native claims in conversation. We saw earlier that GAI highlighted its broad public profile by citing Judy Grahn's desire to romanticize GAI's activism as reflecting a primordial queer indigeneity. I argued that, rather than sharing Grahn's romanticism, GAI demonstrated a creative ability to adapt non-Native colonial desires to its own ends. *Living the Spirit* was assembled by GAI with the assistance of Will Roscoe, who approached GAI at the 1984 San Francisco Gay Pride festival with a proposal to collaborate that resulted in his being invited to edit the History Project's anthology.[69] Roscoe's writing for Native people focused on historical sources and on defending the integrity of Native cultures, while his extrapolations of a non-Native queer spirituality appeared in writing targeting interested non-Natives. These distinct projects surface in *Living the Spirit* when Roscoe's interpretation of Native activists incites them to speak in distinct voices.

For instance, in a 1985 interview with Erna Pahe in *Living the Spirit,* Roscoe solicits Pahe's life history with questions about her growing-up experiences and urban activism. He asks, "Do you see connections between what gay Indians do today and the traditional roles they may have had in the past?"[70] At the time, Roscoe was studying We'wha as a historical subject, but his interest in the *lhamana* as an interrupted past posed a break between gay Indian identities and "traditional roles." Pahe's response does not conform to his question but sets a distinctive trajectory. She first contrasts the "vocal" lives of Native people in GAI's generation to those of "the gay people that are fifty or sixty years old now." She describes them as having lived lives in Native communities that were consistent with their sense of self, and were recognized as such by others, as when one would

> just go in and start the fire and grind the corn and sit next to the women and laugh and joke ... The women encouraged that input from the males, because they could see that they tried so hard. But they didn't have to say anything about it. They didn't ask questions and that person or individual didn't try to make their stand known. It was done very quietly.

Her response to his question about a traditional "past" repositions tradition in the generation immediately prior to hers, among people she knows who faced historical constrictions of their lives. But she says that they remained sure of a distinct sense of self—indeed, choosing "to act it and play it to the hilt"—only with the support of comrades in contexts that prevented public "[speech] about what you were." Pahe thus does not describe queer Natives in any part of the twentieth century as posttraditional subjects who struggle to reach across modernity's break with Indigenous authenticity to feel "connections" to Native culture (110–11). Instead, for her, connections were never broken, because Native culture exists in the collective practices of survival and resistance that she describes. The only difference she acknowledges is a changed *political* reality: she and GAI can now proclaim what was earlier kept quiet. Against romantic appeals to tradition by non-Native queers, Pahe portrays queer Native life by displacing a tradition/modernity split, and in its place telling a story of Native *resistance* to colonial power *as* continuity between past and present. Pahe's words stand alongside those of Burns, Kenney, and Hall to frame Native writers in *Living the Spirit* not as icons of gay nature but as historical actors seeking a place within contemporary Native communities while holding non-Natives answerable to challenge the settler colonial power relations Native people still fight. Yet, the major insight I take from such narratives is their creative response to non-Native queer desires in conversation. GAI adapted the interests of interlocutors such as Grahn and Roscoe to announce the contrasting epistemologies and politics of Native queer activists, which defined their lives on terms that non-Natives were not invited to follow.

By the end of the 1980s, Native queer activists stepped up critique of anthropological and counterculturist popularizations of berdache. Native activists called berdache an erroneous colonial term that represented Native peoples in primordial and generalizing terms, while projecting masculinism and sexualization onto them. Such deliberations took place at a gathering of Native queer people sponsored by American Indian Gays and Lesbians in Minneapolis in 1988, which, in partnership with comrades in Canada, became an annual International Gathering of American Indian and First Nations Gays and Lesbians. At the 1990 gathering in Winnipeg, participants focused "on finding a new term for Native sexualities and gender diversity."[71] They decided to name their ties as Native queer people to Native national traditions and to one another with the term "Two-Spirit," which quickly spread as a new term to describe Native queer identities, communities, and activism.

Two-Spirit proposed to link traditions named in Native languages with the lives of Native GLBTQ people today. As a calque of a term from "Northern Algonquin . . . *niizh manitoag* (Two-Spirits)," which participants at the Winnipeg gathering defined as "the presence of both a masculine and a feminine spirit in one person," Two-Spirit in English referred at once to "gay, lesbian, transvestite, transsexual, transgender, drag queens, and butches, as well as *winkte, nádleeh,* and other appropriate tribal terms."[72] Two-Spirit enabled Native people to draw national traditions into transnational ties even as it affirmed gender and sexual diversity by rejecting the masculinism in berdache—which, according to Beverly Little Thunder (Standing Rock Lakota), was "meant to describe males, not me."[73] Some invoked Two-Spirit to resolve a separation from tribal identity, language, or society caused by racism and assimilation, as when Michael Red Earth (Sisseton Dakota) and Alex Wilson (Cree) recall how Two-Spirit identity helped them link childhood and adult life experiences, reconcile to their natal communities, and investigate how they might articulate their lives with their peoples' national traditions.[74] Persons affirmed by their communities within a traditional gendered, sexual, or spiritual role could claim Two-Spirit identity, although Wesley Thomas (Navajo) noted that in the Navajo nation, *nádleehi* would be unlikely to do so owing to Two-Spirit's negative translation in Diné language as well as the primacy of their traditional identity in national context.[75] But Native queer activists did not argue that Two-Spirit be translated into Native languages, given that its English usage was to affirm distinctive national traditions in new relationship. Two-Spirit thereby interrupted berdache and all generalizations of Native culture by facilitating identification that affirmed differences and fostered alliances. Even if Two-Spirit were applied in a generalizing fashion, this quality did not inhere in the term and remained opposed to its original purpose and use: Two-Spirit announced a Native identity that refused to be identical to or to be absorbed by berdache or any other gender or sexual identity defined on non-Native terms.

Two-Spirit identity rapidly reframed Native queer activism while deepening its interventions in Native and non-Native politics. Many Native queer organizations adopted the term, as in the work of WeWah and BarChee-Ampe and the Toronto organization Gays and Lesbians of the First Nations, which soon took the name 2-Spirited People of the 1st Nations, and later 2-Spirits.[76] The renamed annual International Two-Spirit Gathering also inspired many to join or form Two-Spirit groups where they lived. Some promoted Two-Spirit identity as a contribution to broader Native activism. WeWah and BarCheeAmpe's close ties to the New York City American Indian Community House made Two-Spirit identity part of urban Indian political discourse, including in activism leading to the 1992 quincentennial (discussed in chapter 3). In turn, Native queer people involved in Native health services related Two-Spirit histories to Native health, notably in HIV/AIDS organizing (discussed in chapter 6). All such projects were informed by the gendering of Two-Spirit, as Native lesbian and bisexual women and trans people joined Native gay and bisexual men in critiquing the masculinism of berdache and asserting Two-Spirit as an alliance-based term for them all. Native queer activists also distinguished Two-Spirit from berdache by joining academic allies to critique anthropology. Native and non-Native anthropologists who sought to shift scholarship on berdache joined Native activists in two conferences in 1993 and 1994, the proceedings of which were published in Sue-Ellen Jacobs, Wesley Thomas, and Sabine Lang's anthology *Two-Spirit People: Native American Gender Identity, Sexuality, and Spirituality* (1997). Although this book is noteworthy for recording a moment when anthropologists critiqued berdache in dialogue with Two-Spirit people, less well recognized (although the book recounts it) is the fact that the book records how Native activists questioned colonial knowledge production by presenting Two-Spirit as an Indigenous epistemology that methodologically performs decolonization.

In the early 1990s, Jacobs and Thomas met Lang, a German scholar sponsored by Walter Williams to conduct ethnography on berdache. In their work, including Thomas and Lang's visits to the Navajo nation and the International Two-Spirit Gathering, they affirmed a shared discomfort with anthropology's historical focus on the category berdache and "agreed with Two-Spirit friends that for too long discussions of Native American gender diversity and sexuality had taken place without benefit of shared discourse with Native Americans."[77] Thomas and Jacobs further noted that Native people were demanding that anthropologists recognize berdache as "insulting and part of the colonial discourse that continued to be used by select scholars who appropriate Indigenous people's lives," and that "Native people were talking about this issue long before non-Native academics noticed."[78] Jacobs further expressed her concern,

> if the recent non-Native interest in Native American sexuality and gender diversity was a phantasmagoric adventure of white homosexual males . . . who were either appropriating cultural elements from Native cultures (in a "new age" epistemological fashion) or imputing to Native cultures characteristics that would resolve their heartfelt desires to be recognized fully as productive and important members of their own society.[79]

The three scholars decided to ask anthropologists of berdache and Two-Spirit activists if they wished to meet during the 1992 AAA meetings in San Francisco to plan collaborative work. As soon as this idea was suggested, Gay American Indians and other Two-Spirit organizers took ownership. Jacobs reported that "GAI sent out a dinner invitation to all Native American anthropologists and non-Native anthropologists and others who had written about Native Americans (especially about the 'berdache') and who planned to attend the AAA meeting." GAI then brought a large contingent of local and visiting Native people to the meeting, where "the non-Native anthropologists were interrogated about their motives, interests, experiences, and ambitions in investigating Native American gender diversity and sexuality."[80] The meeting highlighted Native peoples' discomfort with use of berdache, including to describe their lives today. Encouraged by GAI, the anthropologists gained funds from the Wenner-Gren Foundation for a preconference and panel at the 1993 AAA meetings in Washington, D.C., titled "Revisiting the 'North American Berdache,'" as well as a follow-up conference at the Field Museum in Chicago in 1994. Jacobs says in her letter to participants:

> Word has been traveling among Native Americans in various regions of the U.S.A. and in Canada. We have each been contacted by individuals (some representing groups who want to attend our AAA session, at least) . . . Their desire and hope for new and useful research is clear and urgent.[81]

The bulk of available funds was distributed as travel stipends to Native activists who wished to attend. Participants in the first event received drafts of papers to be read by anthropologists at the AAA meetings, and the day was spent discussing first the papers and then topics of interest to attendees. The second event was organized to gather even more participants to address topics left unanswered. Talks by scholars and activists were recorded and their transcriptions along with prepared papers became the contents of *Two-Spirit People*.

Thus, the desire of anthropologists for new language was anticipated by Native people who already were organizing across the continent to change anthropology. Once the discipline's resources were gathered, Native activists adapted those resources to produce changes in anthropological knowledge production and to create new discursive spaces defined by their stakes in that process. Translating long-standing desires into demands shifted Native queer people from being objects of historically colonial knowledges to subjects of knowledge defined by a collective pursuit of decolonization.

The production of knowledge now shifted for lesbian and gay anthropologists. Native activists did not just displace the category "berdache," they also destabilized institutional practices of anthropology in relation to Native peoples as a key condition of the term's continued circulation. Native commentators in *Two-Spirit People* affirmed that they worked to decolonize the epistemologies and methodologies structuring knowledge about Native people. Terry Tafoya (Taos/Warm Springs) opposed a model of anthropology that presents Native people as in need of being "reminded by the anthropological Keeper of Knowledge" of the truth of their lives.[82] Beverly Little Thunder insisted that "anthropologists write about those of us who are alive now. And they must *listen* to us, hear us, and use our own words, not just their special anthropological language."[83] Here Little Thunder opposes both authenticating desires for Native history and cursory engagements with contemporary Native people and their differences from non-

Native expectations. Anguksuar Richard LaFortune (Yup'ik) emphasized that the observations offered by Native people "cannot represent any monolithic Native culture."[84] Tafoya affirmed both the multiplicity and the politicization of Native queer claims by arguing that to identify as Two-Spirit

> is to speak in what Cindy Patton has termed "dissident vernaculars," terms that move "away from the model of pristine scientific ideas which need 'translation' for people lacking in the dominant culture's language skills or concepts" and towards "meanings created by and in communities [that] are upsetting to the dominant culture precisely because speaking in one's own fashion is a means of resistance, a strengthening of the subculture that has created the new meaning."[85]

Evelyn Blackwood responded by recognizing that anthropology must critique its distanced determinations of Native truth, through which

> scholars wittingly or unwittingly codify categories that are always contested and achieved rather than natural and unchanging. As is clear from the Native authors in this book, anthropologists need to do less defining and universalizing and pay attention to what Two-Spirit people say about their lives.[86]

Thus, Native activist displacements of berdache promoted new bases for knowledge production in Native people's "own words." Their views hinged on a difference between berdache or any non-Native category and the function of Two-Spirit, which presented a distinctive logic and method for defining relations among gender, sexuality, and nationality for Native people.

Nevertheless, non-Natives could fail to recognize that, rather than being synonymous with all that berdache once named, the category Two-Spirit displaced the logic of berdache and opened all claims made through it to question. First, Two-Spirit held knowledge production accountable to anticolonialism, by rejecting the colonial conditions that made it possible to write at a distance from Native queer people's stakes in knowledge production. If non-Native scholars continued to do this, they remained part of the problem activists critiqued. Second, Two-Spirit challenged attempts to define a primordial role existing outside the time of settler modernity.[87] Despite invoking tradition, Two-Spirit fails to suggest the cultural authenticity proposed by colonial discourse, given that any such use confronts its purpose to name a link *among* diverse traditions and contemporary identities and activisms. Third, and interrelatedly, the definition of Two-Spirit within border-crossing networks evinces a transnationalism that displaces timeless uniformity *and* generic panindigenism. Two-Spirit recalls diverse

Native national histories as being potentially interconnected across differences that must be examined in the dialogic space Two-Spirit creates for Native queer people. None of these effects can be produced by a synonym of berdache, nor are they proposed to satisfy desires for primordial and universal Indigenous truth.

These distinctions are reinforced when Two-Spirit activists address non-Natives by critiquing the power of settler colonialism. For instance, non-Native queer critics may think Two-Spirit proposes a sex/gender binary—assimilated from colonial heteropatriarchy, or reflective of Native norms—that makes the term incapable of queer critique. Such claims already can be called into question by considering that if a sex/gender system exceeds two recognized genders, then these will produce power relations in multivariant relationships that will be incomprehensible to a critique of binary sex/gender. Yet Native queer and Two-Spirit critics already displace intimations of their recapitulation of heteronormativity by noting that this fails to learn *from* Two-Spirit activists that all queer claims are conditioned by settler colonialism. By locating Native queer people within tribally specific knowledges and anticolonial activism, Two-Spirit identity makes Native queer people unassimilable by queer critiques based on interpreting and naturalizing non-Natives in a settler society. Instead, non-Native queer critics may wish to join Native queer critics in discussing Two-Spirit by first evaluating settler colonialism as a condition of their conversations, and of their capacity to comprehend this term. Resituated this way, non-Native queer critics might understand that Native queer and Two-Spirit people already hold diverse opinions about the usefulness of Two-Spirit identity to their work, while still sharing an interest to displace settler colonialism in queer theory.[88] In this sense, the genealogical significance of Two-Spirit for queer studies is even greater than its specific claims, as it joins other Native queer critiques in locating settler colonialism as a condition of Native and non-Native knowledge production in conversation. Thus, Two-Spirit presents an Indigenous epistemology—rooted in Native traditions, articulating Native modernities—that challenges colonial knowledges, alters power relations with non-Natives, and incites new registers through which Native people can join and hold non-Natives accountable to work for Indigenous decolonization.

Two-Spirit activism fundamentally transformed conversations on berdache. SOLGA responded to critiques of anthropology's colonial legacies by shifting study of cultures as social units to processes of meaning making in histories of colonization, nationalism, migration, and economic and political globalization. Simultaneously, queer studies challenged lesbian/gay logics by focusing on the genealogical study of power relations producing sexual and gender marginality and normativity, including colonialism. These changes led to SOLGA changing its name in 2010 to the Association for Queer Anthropology and committing itself to examine sexuality and gender as relational to race, class, nationality, and disability within histories of colonization and globalization. Two-Spirit activism did not reduce the popularization of Native culture as a resource for non-Native gender and sexual liberations, but more critiques appeared of this practice, such as Towle and Morgan's critique of the citation of "third genders" in U.S. transgender politics. Gay men's and, more broadly, queer counterculturisms grew in this time precisely by adapting Two-Spirit identity and a resurgence of traditional knowledge to the Indigenous nature they sought. But Two-Spirit's redefinition of tradition as part of decolonial activism also lent a new and direct accountability to Native queer activists. In the process, non-Native queers became more adept at answering Native queer critiques by not doing what they once egregiously had done—projecting colonial discourse through berdache. However, they did not necessarily become any more adept at what few had done before: recognizing settler colonialism as a condition of their existence and of their relation to Native peoples and Native queer critiques.

Part II, "Movements," shifts from genealogies of non-Native and Native queer modernities to historical and ethnographic study of projects that they produced in the late twentieth century. The initial chapters contain an internal contrast, by portraying first how non-Native queer projects formed at a distance from Native queer and Two-Spirit people, which are then examined through the critical lens of concurrent Native activism. The final chapter focuses entirely on Native queer and Two-Spirit organizing that arose in the context of Native HIV/AIDS organizing. This section portrays movements that form not separately but within multiple interrelationships along lines of tension linking non-Native and Native queer modernities. The chapters address three qualities of colonial discourse in U.S. queer politics that are displaced by Native critiques: non-Native queer desires for *authentic culture, ancient roots,* and a *global purview.* By negotiating the cultural authenticity of queer politics, seeking ancestral ties on settled land, or projecting colonial desires on a global scale, non-Native queer cultures and politics negotiated their settler colonial heritance in relationship to the discrepant work of Native queer and Two-Spirit activists.

Part II **Movements**

Chapter 3   **Authentic Culture and Sexual Rights Contesting Citizenship in the Settler State**

SETTLER CITIZENSHIP—its acquisition and its contestation—conditions the relationality of non-Native and Native people within queer politics. Normative histories of U.S. queer politics locate freedom in the removal of state-sanctioned persecutions and the securing of state protection of sexual and gender diversity. This political progression arises within and elides an ongoing settler colonial situation, in which the state grants "freedoms" by incorporating diverse peoples under its rule, beginning with the colonial control of Native nations on Native lands. Whether markedly restricted or nominally universal, settler citizenship confers opportunity, liberty, and security by facilitating the colonial domestication or replacement of Native nationality. The white-supremacist terms of settler citizenship are transformed under a civil rights state into a project that nominally bars discrimination from citizenship while still regulating access by race, class, and nation as well as gender, sexuality, and disability. Nevertheless, white settler civilization remains citizenship's historical, cultural, and moral foundation, even as its conferral on Native peoples assimilates them as ethnic difference, creates them as wards of state management, or attempts to legislate them out of existence.[1]

Queer scholarship of citizenship can examine how queer "freedoms" become imaginable in the context of ongoing settler colonialism and Native resistance.[2] I argue in this chapter that queer narratives of cultural integrity inflected by "race" locate freedom in belonging to a settler nation. Scholars have noted that U.S. queer projects define their integrity by appealing to the cultural status of an ethnic group or to the legal status granted racial and national minorities, through "racial analogy."[3] However, they have not asked how these normatively white and *non-Native* queer routes to "race" play on indigeneity as a history or model of the authenticity they seek, while absenting Native people from the "racial" queerness that secures settler citizenship. In my analysis, "race" illuminates settler colonial definitions of queer cultural citizenship in two ways. First, narrating "race" invokes essentializing ideas of bounded sociality or authentic culture—including, colonial discourses on indigeneity—that, once included in or modeled by queerness, grant it the integrity to counter theories of perversion and defend group rights. Second, correlating queerness to "race" locates it in U.S. political discourses for managing social difference that function to occlude Native peoples: by assigning Natives as "race" a numerical insignificance or imminent disappearance that makes them tangential to "race" politics, and by erasing Native *nationality* as a project that could undercut state power, including a power to narrate citizenship in relation to "race." Queer people participate in this process by arguing that the "racial" qualities of their constituencies—multiracial in scope, or comparable to a racial group—should grant recognition as a social minority worthy of protection from injury and of full citizenship. As Wendy Brown suggests, each such claim reproduces whiteness as a condition of queers as "racial" and queers as citizens.[4] But I further argue that whiteness produces queers as *non-Native,* and their politics as a normatively white and non-Native claim of belonging to settler citizenship.

I interpret the formation of U. S. queer politics as a project of settler citizenship by reference to Elizabeth Povinelli's analysis of *liberal settler multiculturalism.*[5] My reading resituates queer and critical race scholarship on histories and processes of U.S. citizenship in a critique of white-supremacist settler colonialism. In the late twentieth century, a civil rights era answered historic racial and national discrimination by conferring citizenship, which then produced modes of multiculturalism increasingly contested by neoliberal post–civil rights critiques.[6] Povinelli interprets such social relations in the context of settler colonialism, in which the settler state regulates freedoms by producing liberal subjects of rights, who articulate multicultural governance by adjudicating race differences in a manner that delegitimatizes Indigenous claims on national integrity. I interpret liberal settler multiculturalism and its neoliberal contestation in the United States as contexts in which queers sought their own "racial" integrity in white, non-Native, and settler colonial form. Queers tracked paths to settler citizenship by incorporating and transcending indigeneity to attain settler modernity. That journey could be contested by the very proposal of racial analogy, if it placed the whiteness of its proponents in sharp relief, or marked queers of color as negotiating queer politics distinctly. Nevertheless, narratives of queer citizenship as "racial" already sought to absorb queers of color into a normatively white, non-Native, and settler colonial project, a process that even queer of color critiques did not entirely question. The most direct displacements of liberal settler multiculturalism and its conditioning of queer politics arose in Native queer and Two-Spirit activism. During the early 1990s, the New York City Two-Spirit organization WeWah and BarChee-Ampe mobilized queer of color coalitions in critiquing white-supremacist settler colonialism under Native leadership and while pursuing Indigenous decolonization. Their work demonstrates how Native queer activists and allied queers of color identified and challenged the colonial formation of U.S. queer projects while imagining a queer politics that could directly displace the colonial power and rule of a settler state.

Gay American History and Gay American Indians

In 1976, Jonathan Katz announced a new generation of gay and lesbian activism when he defended gay and lesbian culture as worthy of national inclusion. The "American focus" of his landmark book *Gay American History* sought to address "the influence of a particular national setting on the historical forms of homosexuality found within it."[7] Katz's argument indexes a shift in U.S. sexual politics in the 1970s. Research for his book began in 1971 amid the universalizing theories of sexual liberation characteristic of gay liberation and lesbian feminism. Yet, by mid-decade, a minoritizing defense of civil rights informed activists and scholars first inspired in the earlier moment—as was Katz, who first conceived his project while participating in New York City's Gay Activists Alliance (GAA). The book promotes minority cultural identity to counter the individuating and pathologizing effects of phobic theories of homosexuality, as its first words proclaim:

> We have been the silent minority, the silenced minority—invisible women, invisible men . . . Our existence as a long-oppressed, long-resistant social group was not explored. We remained an unknown people, our character defamed . . . That time is over. The people of the shadows have seen the light; Gay people are coming out—and moving on—to organized action against an oppressive society. (1)

Katz then traces his claim on "the existence of homosexuals as a people with our own history, traditions, and culture" (7) to a general political moment in the United States of "radical social change in which each group, starting from a sense of its own particular oppression, is struggling for the democratic control of that society in which all work, live, and try to love" (9).

Katz assembles archival records within chapters that proclaim a developmental narrative, progressing from the first two chapters, titled "Trouble: 1566–1966" and "Treatment: 1884–1974," to the concluding chapters, "Resistance: 1859–1972" and "Love: 1779–1932." These themes describe experiences of gay men and lesbians throughout the history of the United States and the prior British colonies, while the book highlights race, class, nation, and gender differences among them despite the overrepresentation of Anglo men in archival records. Katz interrupts this thematic progression to insert two chapters that address distinct groups. Chapter 3, "Passing Women: 1782–1920," addresses "the recent women's liberation and Lesbian-feminist movements" by questioning masculinist histories and making lesbians and gay men "equal in quality and quantity" in his book (2). He does not highlight race in a comparable chapter responding to critiques by people of color of white gay and lesbian racism, although people of color are referenced from time to time. But while race receives no special attention, nation and culture do in chapter 4, "Native Americans/Gay Americans: 1528–1976." This chapter does not respond to Native critiques of non-Native gays and lesbians—although such a critique does appear in sources it reprints, as we will see—but focuses instead on collating colonial anthropological reports of the histories of Native cultures. Native people's appearance here marks their absence in the rest of the book—that is, from histories of the United States. Native people differ in this book from non-Native people of color, who do appear (sporadically) in the text as evidence of multiracial diversity in U.S. society. Thus, a key effect of the chapter is to frame the subjects, topics, and audiences of the rest of the book—the subjects of "Gay America"—as non-Natives. Even when highlighted in a narrative of gender and sexual diversity, Native people are bracketed by a distinctive *national temporality* into the culturally authentic Native prehistory of the historical modernity of the "America" that supplants them. Although this book was lauded by gay and lesbian anthropologists as a first collection of rare colonial accounts of berdache, its popularization of Native peoples in a "denial of coevalness" established "Gay Americans" as non-Native inheritors of settler colonialism who adopt knowledge of Native culture as part of a primordial gay and American history.

Katz offers his representation of Native Americans *as* a form of anticolonialism for gay and lesbian politics. He argues that colonial violence transformed Native societies, using the language of progressive alliance politics:

the Christianization of Native Americans and the colonial appropriation of the continent by white, Western "civilization" included the attempt by the conquerors to eliminate various traditional forms of Indian homosexuality—as part of their attempt to destroy that Native culture which might fuel resistance—a form of cultural genocide. (284)

These words at first may appear to evoke Native feminist and queer critiques, but the argument that actually drives how the book narrates its evidence is the recovery of Native tradition for non-Native gay liberation:

The existence of homosexuality among the people who originally inhabited the United States will no doubt hold a certain special fascination for those Lesbians and Gay men who are today beginning to *repossess* the national and world history of *their people*—part of the struggle for social change and to win control over their own lives. (284; emphasis added)

The anticolonialism Katz offers to gays and lesbians naturalizes settlement so well that it appropriates Native history as a former *and* renewed possession of non-Natives. Native peoples in fact are not those "who originally inhabited the United States" given that the settler state exists in violation of the prior and sustained sovereignty of Native nations. But this implicit naturalization of settlement then permits contrasting Native people as "original" inhabitants of the United States to "Lesbians and Gay men" as its present inhabitants, whereby the latter as non-Natives appear to be related to, yet distinct from Natives. Racial and national analogies frame gay men and lesbians *as* a people in "struggle to win control over their own lives" while simultaneously authorizing them to take from peoples to whom they, as non-Natives do *not* belong the sexual and gender liberation they desire. Their incorporation of Native culture as part of their history displaces Native gay men and lesbians from a modern politics that would try to "include" them, but first displaces them from modern subjectivity. Shifting lesbians and gay men from the pathology of "homosexuality" to the integrity of a "people" lets them adopt the trappings of Indigenous authenticity as part of the integrity they require to claim rights. Making gay men and lesbians analogous to racialized or Native peoples defines them as white subjects not otherwise racialized or indigenized in a settler society, albeit now with a capacity to include Native people and people of color in a "peoplehood" that whites can represent. The logic of white settler colonialism is at work when racial analogy lets gay men and lesbians adopt Indigenous cultural authenticity, in a settler narrative, as if it were the origin of gay America. Katz locates Native people as primordial to help non-Natives secure settler citizenship. The performance of settler modernity remains compatible with believing in their anticolonialism, as non-Native gay men and lesbians can portray Native culture as something they adopt and defend as they seek their own freedom as settler citizens.

Katz's chapter "Native Americans/Gay Americans" closes by breaking from anthropological narrative to republish accounts by Native gay men and lesbians: a 1965 interview with Elmer Gage (Mohave) in *One Magazine* and a 1976 interview in the *Advocate* with GAI's leaders Barbara Cameron and Randy Burns. Katz's project is concluding even as contemporary Native gay men and lesbians are beginning to explain their lives to interested non-Natives. In these interviews, non-Natives defined sexual subjectivity and politics by adapting Native activist claims to their own. Yet the Native gays and lesbians being interviewed displaced settler desires and defined their lives on discrepant terms.

One's "rare interview" in 1965 with a "homosexual Native American," in interviewer Bob Waltrip's words, contrasts non-Native homophile activism with Gage's identity in Mohave society. The interview appeared six years after *One* published Dorr Legg's account of berdache as evidence of sexual inversion, and five years after *Mattachine Review* published Omer Stewart's review of the anthropology of berdache.[8] Unlike either text, Waltrip frames Gage not so much through the object berdache as in a tone reminiscent of Kent Mackenzie's 1961 film *The Exiles*, in which a muckraking critique of settler stereotypes of Indians portrays Native people as tragically impoverished by lost authenticity. Nevertheless, Gage displaces Waltrip's reading by narrating the normalcy of his life struggles and their mediation by his secure location within Mohave kinship and religion. When Waltrip invites Gage to describe his life as embattled, Gage speaks instead of the household he and his elderly aunt, who he calls his grandmother, keep on Mohave territory, where his leasing of land to agricultural firms lets him care for her while participating in Mohave cultural practices. He participates as a Bird Dancer in local ceremonies in addition to producing beadwork, taught to him by his "grandmother" at a young age; as she interjects during the interview, "He was interested."[9] Gage mentions his longing for a partner, but he deflects Waltrip's suggestion that one could be found in an urban gay community by relating the recognition he receives in Mohave community, from early sexual experiences with other boys to seeing the very Mohave men who tease him about their ongoing sexual friendships.

His account echoes early-twentieth-century stories told by Mohave and non-Native writers about the lives of *hwame*, a term Gage does not use but that resonates with the gendering of his upbringing, his relationships, and his commitment to religious practice.[10] Waltrip, apparently ignorant of these potential connections, presses Gage to discuss his life as being more difficult than that of gays in the city. Gage responds that although urban gay life is accessible to him, he chooses the value of his life in Mohave community. Gage defies Waltrip's opposition of reservation/poverty/conservative tradition from urban/wealth/liberal modernity by narrating a facility within Mohave life with capital, migration, and modernity that he prefers. Without asserting an authentic past—he even repeats Waltrip to call his life "typically American"—Gage deflects non-Native desires even as he adapts their interests to assert a place in U.S. society based on Mohave survival.

In the final interview reprinted by Katz, Cameron and Burns announce the founding of Gay American Indians one year prior to the publication of *Gay American History*.[11] Both identify themselves as urban, pantribal activists who challenge colonial legacies in Native people's lives and seek dialogue with Native gay men and lesbians across the country. Cameron succinctly states how their work differs from that of the non-Native gay and lesbian movement: "We were first and foremost a group for *each other* . . . Bringing together gay Indians is our most important current task." Burns explains that GAI organizes by raising awareness in Native communities of the "trampled traditions of our people" in which "Gay people were respected parts of the tribes" (333). Cameron locates this within a broader critique of settler society by Native gay men and lesbians. Asked by interviewer Dean Gengle of her reaction to the U.S. Bicentennial, she says:

> Angry. . . It's ridiculous. What should Indians celebrate? Two-hundred years of broken promises, land theft, genocide and rape? It is one thing to talk about "celebration" and another to look at the little Vietnam the government has going in South Dakota. We're going to be demonstrating in Philadelphia in '76. There are plans for demonstrations at Mount Rushmore. Gay Indians will be there. (334)

Despite Gengle's interest in portraying a gay group for Native people, Cameron and Burns frame GAI as a *Native* organization that commits Native gay men and lesbians to broader Native activism for decolonization. They cite Native histories of gender and sexuality not to invite ties to non-Natives but to support each other as Native gay men and lesbians while convincing Native communities of their belonging so they can join in working for decolonization. They call on non-Native gay men and lesbians to support them on these terms, which would locate non-Natives as allies in a struggle to challenge settler society.

Gengle nevertheless ends by framing GAI for the *Advocate* in terms that persisted in gay and lesbian media for years: "If they do succeed in reasserting the wisdom of native American tribes concerning gay people, all of us will benefit" (ibid.). As the final words of the chapter "Native Americans/Gay Americans," Gengle hails an "all of us" who adopt Native "wisdom," repeating Katz, who addresses "Gay Americans" as non-Natives who need Native history to achieve their own freedom. Native stories politicize a gay and lesbian minority whose internal racial diversity is bound by culturally authentic Native roots that echo in claims on multicultural settler citizenship. In the wake of this book, stories of Native peoples as part of gay "history" would echo within U.S. sexual minority claim on liberal settler multiculturalism and justify claiming sexual minority cultural authenticity and settler citizenship as non-Native acts.

Yet the very distinctions addressed here reveal the formation of non-Native and Native queer modernities in conversation. Claims on Native history that naturalize gay men and lesbians as non-Native appear *simultaneously* with Native gay and lesbian critiques of non-Native appropriations. Popular gay media quoted Native gay men and lesbians as telling non-Natives that they are seeking to renew their place within their nations by leading efforts for decolonization. Yet, in non-Native media, that plain speech always appeared askew, always outside the necessary interpretive frame. I am highlighting Native gay and lesbian claims because they show, ironically, that their announcements of a refusal to be colonized are precisely what non-Natives appropriated as a basis for their own pursuit of settler citizenship. As in Grahn's witnessing of the GAI poster, encountering Native gay men and lesbians who assert their distinctions triggered a whole chain of associations for non-Natives that already defined liberated sexual minorities on normatively white settler terms. Thus, in these encounters, both Native and non-Native gay men and lesbians narrated divergent politics precisely by engaging one another. They also demonstrate that from the inception of cultural appropriation in late-twentieth-century sexual minority politics, a critique interrupting it appeared in non-Native narratives. Whether admitted or not, non-Native gay and lesbian claims on Native histories have remained interdependent with the decolonizing critiques of Native gay and lesbian activists. From this point forward, non-Native appropriations of Native activist work would arise in conversation, making future claims answerable to the degree to which they ignored or engaged their linked history.

Race and Coalition in the National Gay and Lesbian Task Force

Theories of the trope of Native disappearance suggest that absenting Native people from a story tells a story of settler colonialism. Just as claiming Native peoples as history portrayed sexual minority politics as non-Native, the national stakes of Native peoples readily disappear when sexual minority politics seeks fulfillment through settler citizenship. The 1973 founding of the National Gay Task Force (NGTF) and its growth into the National Gay and Lesbian Task Force (NGLTF) indicate how critically engaging normatively white queer politics to pursue multiracial and antiracist work readily naturalizes settler citizenship as a horizon of freedom and distances from Native queer critiques. Progressive antiracist coalitions such as those formed by NGLTF consistently challenged the racial and sexual boundaries of U.S. citizenship, but in ways that permitted its settler formation to remain intact.

NGLTF has been a significant national group in U.S. gay and lesbian civil rights activism, as it set up the country's first national gay lobby and, after the rise of the Human Rights Campaign (HRC), the only one to consistently pursue multiracial and antiracist coalition politics. Under Director Urvashi Vaid and the influence of the policy institute she founded, NGLTF during the 1990s focused on coordinating grassroots activism around racial and economic justice agendas related to immigration, welfare, and citizenship. The HRC, in contrast, has promoted homonationalism by focusing on fund-raising from a middle- to high-income constituency while promoting national integration of sexual minorities through such themes as gay marriage, patriotism, and military service.[12] If we interpret homonationalism as a colonial project, HRC is exemplary of the settler formation of U.S. queer modernities. But however satisfying such a reading might be to HRC's critics, it does little to explain how the lives, theories, and activism of more politically progressive queers also reflect a desire to gain rights in the settler state. In fact, NGLTF historically promoted multiracial coalitions precisely to link sexual minorities across racial differences in common pursuit of liberal settler multiculturalism. The group's history is a testimony to how settlement can be naturalized even within progressive trajectories of multiracial civil rights politics.

The National Gay Task Force presented itself as representative of gay and lesbian diversity and identified as accountable to grassroots organizing, despite its degree of accountability remaining open to criticism. After activists in 1973 successfully reversed the American Psychiatric Association (APA) designation of homosexuality as mental illness, NGTF sought to coordinate future national activism that would defy individuating theories of pathology by defending the integrity of a social minority with evidence from science, history, and culture. In the collected NGLTF papers, records from the time of the APA protests include a paper by Judd Marmor delivered at a 1973 psychiatric convention, which marshals anthropological accounts of berdache and Indigenous gender and sexuality as justification for gay and lesbian civil rights.[13] In the wake of the protests' success, NGTF members staffed educational booths at annual APA meetings. Photographic records portray their tables set before posters with photos of people participating in family and work roles, and all arrayed under a banner proclaiming "We Are Everywhere." The apparent whiteness of the figures in the poster and the booth staff conveys an image of a white "we" for science to affirm as representative of U.S. society. Using a Gay Liberation Front (GLF) slogan to portray a sexual minority as being everywhere in modern society also echoes a universalizing suggestion that sexual diversity exists everywhere in human life. Yet if efforts to establish legitimacy as a minority hinge on incorporating Indigenous evidence, once won, it appears to transcend that difference with the reweighted value of claiming white settler citizenship.

The presumptive white constituency of NGTF's sexual minority civil rights efforts fractured in the face of gender and racial criticism. Women staff members critiqued gender inequality and formed a Lesbian Caucus in response to the normalizing of gay male issues. Their feminist intention to liberate a multiracial constituency invested radical white women with a power to advocate for all women, regardless of race. In the late 1970s, recognition of the paucity of staff of color at NGTF led lesbians and gay men of color within the organization and from allied groups to press for an integrated race, class, gender, and sexuality analysis in activism. They won support from NGTF to cosponsor a first Conference of Third World Lesbians and Gays in Washington, D.C., in 1979. Autonomously organized by activists of color, the event inspired a spate of early 1980s organizing by gay men and lesbians of color separately from organizations run by white progressives. Meanwhile, the Lesbian Caucus persuaded NGTF to change its name to NGLTF, and the organization supported leading roles by activists of color linked to antisexist, multiracial, and cross-class politics. This history shows that progressive gay and lesbian politics negotiated its white origins—at first primarily masculinist, but ultimately in a more feminist form—by attempting to be inclusive of gender and race differences in a historically white political model and space.

NGLTF became a leading force in sexual rights activism by calling for coalition work across sexuality, gender, class, and race, as Urvashi Vaid explains in her book *Virtual Equality: The Mainstreaming of Gay and Lesbian Liberation* (1995). She cited gay, lesbian, and AIDS activism among people of color when she called on NGLTF to confront its historical whiteness, even as she promoted NGLTF as a solution if it helped lead broader sexual, racial, and economic justice activism to gain rights in the state. She traces the racial formation of gay and lesbian politics to three successive historical moments. She critiques initial gains by "organizing around individual identity" as problematic for having proposed a unified "culture" that neglects differences, and then "diversity politics or multiculturalism" as problematic for its tokenism and resulting minor change. Finally, she lauds a present moment of "forging coalitions within the gay movement as well as between gay people and straight allies," in which movements break from identity politics to find common ground across differences. Vaid claims that such coalitions will be effective only if they are led by groups like NGLTF, rather than by smaller, local, or more specific groups. Dismayed by what she calls a "stunning lack of interaction across racial lines" in national activism, she admits that "I find myself torn about the question of race-specific versus multiracial organizing" (291). While noting that "'integration' could pose . . . a possible lessening of visibility, priority, and empowerment," she suggests that "race-specific" organizing ultimately may be responsible for reproducing whiteness:

> At the risk of offending colleagues whom I admire enormously, without whose work in the racial minority AIDS and gay organizations we would not have visibility and empowerment that allows me to even make this statement, I believe that race-based methods of organizing unaccountably maintain the status quo on racial prejudice. Our work within single-race organizations must be augmented by the presence of a multiracial movement in order to become fully effective. (292)

Vaid does not advocate abandoning organizing by people of color, but she does promote "the mainstreaming of gay and lesbian liberation" by investing national groups with the power to unify more specific agendas. For her, making sexual rights politics *coherent*—gathering constituents across their differences for collective recognition—is desirable because it produces a group status that the liberal state can recognize. By defending coalitions, Vaid complicates political efforts to enforce unified identity, but her solution ensures the influence of national leaders who receive the power to speak for coalitions when securing state recognition for their diverse membership.

Native activists place Vaid's model and the power of the settler state to grant freedom in question. Vaid does not examine the state's colonial interest in determining freedom for those it rules, or announcing its magnanimity when it confers recognition. She does not address the national interests of Native peoples, and only cites Native activists twice as examples of activism by queers of color, mistaking them for a racial/ethnic minority in a multiracial society (90, 289–90). These elisions are important not because they might be fixed by more inclusion, but because they indicate that Vaid and the NGLTF naturalize liberal settler multiculturalism as their horizon of freedom, one that is displaced by anticolonial Native activism. Gay American Indians problematized white sexual minority politics on the national and transnational grounds of Native sovereignty. Cameron and Burns represented their work as convincing *Native* nations to accept gay men and lesbians so that their constituencies could jointly challenge settler colonialism. By honoring tradition and defying colonial heteropatriarchy, Native lesbian and gay activists sought their own liberation by freeing their *peoples* from colonial control. The national and transnational scope of their efforts provided a context for non-Natives to ally not with a Native sexual minority but as common critics of colonial heteropatriarchy joined across nationality to challenge the settler state. The resulting coalitions would displace the state's colonial apparatus as a horizon of freedom not only for sovereign Native peoples but also for non-Natives, who now could define their queer politics in opposition to the incorporative power of the settler state.

The models of NGLTF and Native activism produced contrasting results. In the 1990s, NGLTF responded to a backlash against civil rights activism by creating a new policy institute under Vaid's directorship. Two of its early reports model how queer of color activism troubled whiteness and national inclusion as premises of sexual minority politics. NGLTF's survey of black pride, *Say It Loud, I'm Black and Proud* (2000), portrayed the distance from white queer politics felt by black pride participants as a reflection of their primary efforts to get black communities to embrace differences and address social and political issues of common concern. Rafael Diaz and George Ayala's *Social Discrimination and Health: The Case of Latino*

Gay Men and HIV Risk (2000) argued that homophobia, racism, and anti-immigrant backlash must be addressed as social determinants of health among Latino gay men. In both reports, researchers stressed that the well-being and survival of queer people required jettisoning "inclusion" as the narrative of sexual politics and organizing instead from the distinct needs of queers of color within communities of color. Such work reflects theories among Native queer activists about the conditioning of sexuality and gender by national, racial, and economic power, yet it still falls short of recognizing settler colonialism as a condition of all these processes. The institute's reports on racism and immigration never addressed indigeneity or decolonization.

Although it lacked any similar organization to support Native queer activist research, such issues were addressed in Native AIDS organizing. For instance, Gilbert Deschamps (Ojibwe) assembled material on the colonial histories and anticolonial resistance of Two-Spirit people in *We Are Part of a Tradition* for the Toronto AIDS organization 2-Spirits. University of Washington Professor Karina Walters (Choctaw) drew National Institutes of Health (NIH) funding for the Honor Project, an Indigenous research project examining gender, sexuality, and HIV risk for Two-Spirit people. These and many other works traced Native queer people's political traditions and struggles for decolonization. In principle, they could align with the antiracist activist scholarship of queers of color, but in the 1990s, in the absence of any questioning of incorporation into the power of a settler state, these links did not form within the NGLTF. The NGLTF policy institute produced some of the best work to emerge from antiracist queer politics in its era. But without a critique of settler colonialism that could address the needs of Native queer activists, its work naturalized the settler state as a horizon of queer freedom.

Later in this chapter I explore how non-Native queer politics could shift in response to this legacy, but first I discuss how U.S. queer activists engaged liberal settler multiculturalism in the 1990s by naturalizing their diversity in response to neoliberal post–civil rights politics, in a way that still persists today in homonormative and progressive antiracist queer politics. An ethnographic study of social practices demonstrated to me that the normalization of whiteness in queer multiculturalism was disrupted by the antiracist work of queers of color, but so long as that occurred within the framework of state responsibility to a "public," the settler colonial context of civic battles over race and sexuality and of queer projects remained undisturbed. I ask now what goes missing in queer radicalism when the settler colonial conditions of racial and sexual power are naturalized, even as a new homonormative politics reinforces neoliberal agendas and further naturalizes settler citizenship.

Queer Multiracialism and Post–Civil Rights Politics

During the 1990s, from my base in Santa Cruz County, I participated in San Francisco Bay Area queer activism that took place at a distance from Native queer politics. Their deliberations over the racial composition and stakes of queer politics were mediated by a discourse on culture in which white queer politics engaged "race" by articulating liberal multiculturalism in two ways. First, white queers sought to perform antiracism by announcing queer racial diversity, but establishing the commonalities to link them reestablished whiteness at their center. Second, white queer progressives adapted antiracism by presenting themselves *as* a form of diversity analogous to race, yet, in so doing, they displaced queers of color and set up a conflict over the putative "diversity" of whiteness. Alliances led by queer activists of color challenged queer appeals to cultural authenticity and multiracial inclusion and modeled alternative forms of queer and antiracist activism. But the conjuncture of queer politics of "race" and culture with post–civil rights shifts in the terms of state recognition produced political conundrums that illuminated their conditioning by the settler state.

Queer politics in Santa Cruz County was shaped by the regional social geography of transnational labor migration in the information technology, agricultural, and service industries and in higher education. A white/ Anglo majority and Chicano/Latino minority defined this region, along with much smaller African American and Asian American communities, alongside the Ohlone Costanoan tribes who asserted their survival against erasure by the legacies of the Spanish missions and Anglo conquest. This largely rural region of small cities was defined by the contrast between the Santa Cruz city region of "North County" and the "South County" region around the city of Watsonville. The counterculturist reputation of Santa Cruz was belied by its white middle-class majority that included generations of University of California graduates and Silicon Valley homeowners. South County's working-class Chicano/a and Latino/a communities remained defined by white/Anglo agricultural businessmen with minority political power as well as their role as a historical epicenter of radical activism in the United Farm Workers and Chicano/a arts movement. Chicano/a and Latino/a queer networks existed, but rarely achieved leadership in white, middle-class North

County institutions that assumed the role of representing queer Santa Cruz. North County queer politics also split between a downtown community center and student organizing at the University of California campus, where the racialization of regional queer activism was marked by queer students of color who organized separately. I offer an account of activism in the North County region, where I lived, worked, and studied during the 1990s, to trace how normative modes of racializing queer politics powerfully shaped this region and transformed over time.

Queer Whiteness and the Question of Culture

Long before my research began, I encountered Santa Cruz queer politics through public education on its racial formation, at a time when critiquing racism marked whiteness in local queer politics. While strolling downtown one morning in 1991, soon after moving to Santa Cruz, my eye suddenly was caught by a flyer on a telephone pole with a large portrait of a pale, conventionally handsome young man, lips parted and brow tensed, next to a text that said, "As a member of the gay community, I am affected by racism everyday." Bemused, I scanned the text and moved on, only to see a series of such posters, each offering critique of racism by people presenting as white lesbians or gay men. I later learned that these were the work of local art activists Brian Hull and Robin White. In *Going Public: A Folk Art Project*, White photographed fifteen area residents who identified as white members of queer communities and Hull edited their thoughts on racism as public statements.

This campaign was a response to struggles over racism at the Santa Cruz Lesbian, Gay, Bisexual, and Transgender Community Center. Founded in 1988 as the Lesbian and Gay Community Center, the organization changed its name in 1989. Demands by activists of color had led the new center to invite people of color onto its board, and during its first year the center was shaken by conflict over racism. This conflict was recalled in a local LGBT news magazine by Brian Tate Anderson—known locally as Gryphon Blackswan—a black gay critic of queer politics who commented on his participation in a recent antiracism workshop:

> I learned the workshop had arisen from the Lesbian/Gay Community Center's failed efforts to diversify its board. In a fast forward replay of the saga of affirmative action in corporate America, recruitment succeeded admirably followed by disaster. As the new colored folk tried to make real the welcome they were extended, they ran into depressingly familiar difficulties and eventually

resigned. A common exit comment was their belief that the board needed to address its own racism. The surprise is, they did! The workshops were a direct outgrowth of that process.[14]

In the same issue, Hull and White explained that their project responded to the workshops with a white antiracist effort to "go public" with calls for change in queer communities. Hull praised how "the posters got people talking and thinking" and "transformed the landscape I live in . . . Seeing them made it a little easier to breathe."[15] Yet, he admitted that the project's introspective nature left open the question of how it would create change. Hull named this among the things he "didn't like about this project":

> (a) There was little context for most of the people who read the posters on the street. I imagined some people thinking, "Just who are all these white people talking about racism? And why are there only white people, anyway?" (b) The project did not in any way work to make basic needs (housing, literacy, health care, employment) more accessible and abundant. At some point the posters felt frivolous. One could think, "When are they going to stop talking about it and actually do something?" (c) The posters were ripped down at an alarming rate.

The posters apparently elicited both racist and homophobic responses from some viewers. Hull admits that the focus on white queer self-reflection had been removed from a local context of struggles at the community center and accountability to queers of color, given that white speakers appeared to discuss racism only among themselves. He also wonders if talk about racism lets white people off the hook of actually "doing something." His words may be a criticism of the popularity of diversity trainings as a bureaucratic response to racism. While his argument is sensitive to structural inequalities, it also invites a transformation of consciousness among white queers that could lead to new politics. Although the artists created this project to promote antiracism, I regard it as a textual reflection on queer whiteness that its narrators variously contest and reinscribe.

The narrator of the poster "The Women Left Angry and Most Likely Disgusted With Us" reflects on the founding of Santa Cruz Queer Nation, where those gathered faced a critique of their race and class formation and their incapacity to engage it. The narrative reads:

> At the first ever QUEER NATION meeting in Santa Cruz there was a proposal to have our first action at the Boardwalk. As I recall, the idea was that we would march down there as a group and do a kiss-in or whatever. At that point, two

Chicana women raised their hands and said if we were going to march down to the Boardwalk, they wanted to know what we, as a mostly white group, were going to do about the tension we would cause marching through a pre-dominantly Hispanic community. How were we going to address the issues of concern in that community, such as AIDS, outreach to Hispanic gays, racism, etc. Well, the response of the group was to not respond at all. No one in the room addressed their concerns and the discussion continued as if the two women had not spoken at all. The women left angry and most likely disgusted with us.[16]

The speakers invoked by the narrator arrive as potential participants to invite a multiracial, cross-class queer politics under Chicano/a and Latino/a leadership. Yet they leave after the group fails to recognize why queer activism in Beach Flats must engage the community's concerns. The narrator implies that whiteness so defined Queer Nation's radicalism as to make the group incapable of a response. Of course, calling the group "mostly white" indicates that this testimony cannot speak for other queers of color in the room. Was their silence a critical witnessing of whiteness in this space? Did they also leave after the women spoke, unnoticed by the narrator? These questions are left unanswered by the poster, as the narrator's and editors' efforts to focus on white racism necessarily occlude the more complex racialization of Queer Nation. The narrator's intention "to combat and resist racism in my gay community" models the project's purpose to turn reflection into antiracist action. Yet even this statement asserts a relationship to community that potentially leaves open a problem raised by the speakers at Queer Nation: that proposing or desiring an inclusive queer community belies the fact that right now, multiple and divergent communities exist. Here I want to affirm the narrator's use of "my" as meaningful. With a Chicano/a and Latino/a queer community in the next neighborhood, per-haps the narrator's "gay community" never was inclusive but rather was based on whiteness. If it conflates its formation with queerness, then doing antiracism in that space could simply give it new opportunities to assert itself as a necessary center of queer politics. What, then, would happen to the claim of Chicano/a and Latino/a queers from another community that self-reflection should lead to relationships across differences? What if white queers displacing their hegemony are not to be antiracist in a queer domain, but antiracist in all white-supremacist domains: representing no longer a marginality that includes race difference, but a specific and power-ful location within ongoing relations of racism?

As a member of the gay community, I am affected by racism everyday.

By creating a lack of communication and interaction, racism divides my community. Racism hinders us from moving forth on political issues. If the groups in my community could interact and communicate with each other, we could strive for liberation. With a strong coalition comes solidarity; with solidarity comes power.

Even though some racism is overt, I believe most of it exists on a covert level. An example of covert racism is the myth of Columbus discovering America. It is still being taught. Television typically portrays Blacks as drug abusers or convicts. So most people don't even realize they are racist.

11/15

Going Public: A Folk Art Project (11 of 15). Courtesy of Robin White and Bryan Hull.

Compared to the tone of this poster, the first one I saw in Santa Cruz— "As a member of the gay community, I am affected by racism everyday"— optimistically portrays white queer antiracism as a force for change. Yet its route to white antiracism also reflects certain qualities of queer whiteness by presuming that a shared queer culture undergirds and will be fulfilled by including differences. The poster text reads:

> By creating a lack of communication and interaction, racism divides my community. Racism hinders us from moving forth on political issues. If the groups in my community could interact and communicate with each other, we could strive for liberation. With a strong coalition comes solidarity; with solidarity comes power.[17]

This testimony succinctly portrays two distinct yet ultimately compatible accounts of race and queerness: imagining them apart, analogically; or imagining all differences of race to be incorporated by queerness. The narrator opens by arguing that an extant group, *the* gay community, carries an inclusive integrity only secondarily troubled by racism. But his next claims define community only in the terms of distinct (racialized?) groups lacking unity. His last claim suggests resolution if various groups appeal to solidarity. Here his words reflect a paradox in normatively white queer politics: despite being motivated by ideals of inclusion, only disparate groups appear to exist amid an unrealized imaginary of unity. Calling for solidarity might seem useful to create change, but even this rests on a desire to believe that "my community" possesses a multiracial integrity that racism only interrupts. Here, even alliance work among white queers and queers of color can sustain a belief that its purpose is to become not many but "one." This resolution of queer racism would grant antiracist white queers a return to desired "community," rather than ask how racialization conditions their enduring interest to discover "one."

The narrator marks the discursive and institutional contexts of white queer antiracism by examining racism on a "covert" level. He says narratives such as "the myth of Columbus discovering America" ("It is still being taught") mean that "most people don't even realize they are racist." Here, his self-reflexive *and* social analysis shifts racism from prejudice to a normalization of white culture. But he also situates racism and antiracism within the horizon of a white *settler* society. Referring to Columbus's discovery as a "myth" recognizes that the logic of elimination proposes that Europeans arrive on empty land *(terra nullius)* and justifies erasing and replacing Native peoples. Yet framing this as "racism" also naturalizes the settler state and its society as the contexts to address it (presumably, by being "antiracist") while "race" displaces "nation" as an analytics through which this power can be contested. To do that would require the narrator marking himself not only as white, and racist, but also as a non-Native inheritor of settler colonization who participates in state agendas to settle Native lands, control Native peoples, and eliminate Native nationality as a difference that can disrupt settler rule. Liberal settler multiculturalism repositions conflicts over nationality as "race" to protect the settler state from critique. My point is not that critiquing racism is in competition with critiquing settler colonialism. Rather, white supremacy and settler colonialism are interdependent and must be theorized together, particularly if settler states define "race"—including, through antiracism—to occlude an illegitimacy that would be exposed by assertions of Indigenous nationality.

My reading of *Going Public* suggests that white queer antiracist narratives elicited deeper issues in need of critique if white queer antiracism is to proceed: namely, white queer desires to resolve racism by reasserting that queerness is an integral, if diverse, social or cultural group; and naturalizing the horizon of the white settler state and its liberal multiculturalism as the context in which queers resolve conflict over difference. I now turn to cases that arose after *Going Public*, in which queer responses to liberal multiculturalism newly marked their racialization for critique.

Queer Diversity and Queer of Color Mobilizations

Topics raised by *Going Public* continued in the 1990s in debates about the racial formation of Santa Cruz queer politics in the context of "the community center." The downtown LGBT Community Center was soon joined by a new institution for queer students at the nearby university. Each center discussed the racialization of queer culture and politics against the backdrop of state recognition. Yet queer subjects of "race" in Santa Cruz were narrated not as subjects of the state but as part of a queer "community," and especially in relationship to its "center." Heeding Miranda Joseph's call to question "the romance of community" as deferring critique of the production of queers for state and economic management, I ask how institutionalizing queer "community" articulated "race" within the horizon of liberal multiculturalism.[18] Like Joseph, my ethnographic stories note how creative work marked contradictions in communities.The compatibility of queer multiracialism with whiteness was displaced by queers of color who allied in pursuit of what I call a "decentering" politics, which also reflected work by queers of color across the United States.[19] The contrast in their methods reached a flash point in 1999–2000 during a neoliberal backlash against queer and antiracist appeals to the state, in the form of California Propositions 21 and 22 (discussed later in this chapter). This crisis exposed limits in each project's capacity to critique the power confronting them.

(DE)CENTERING COMMUNITY

After years of student activism, the first state-funded LGBT Student Resource Center was formed at the university campus in 1994, a sign of state recognition of LGBT people as a social minority deserving antidiscrimination and institutional support. This located them within a logic formerly based on race, as university support for minority groups had previously funded only the Ethnic Student Resource Centers for African American, Chicano/a and Latino/a, Asian American, and Native American students, with the last group defined as an ethnic minority rather than as constituting a multiplicity of national differences. The granting of a resource center indicated that queer students had "arrived" as legitimate participants in public education through a multicultural logic of racial analogy. Yet, granting this to the predominantly white networks that had organized queer activism positioned them as an equivalent to communities of color, which occluded the ongoing efforts of queer students of color in the Ethnic Student Resource Centers and the LGBT center to offer alternatives to white queer narratives of queer multiracialism.

In 1995, students responded by forming a new affinity group, Queers of Color, which formed ties with the Ethnic Student Resource Center directors and with faculty of color whom they invited to be allies. Queers of Color extended its organizing to the many locations where students of color gathered, including off-campus networks with regional youth. Queers of Color used the LGBT center to do this initial work, but on a path that did not conform to and went beyond the center's scope. The center celebrated its first African American History Month in 2000 by documenting black queer history and addressing racism in queer communities. New educational activism in queer, racial/ethnic, and feminist spaces on campus analyzed intersectionality and multiple identities, including in a discussion series, "Intersections of Oppressions," on such topics as "racism and homophobia" and "white privilege." Queers of Color members also took these messages to system-wide programs for students of color where they challenged heterosexism within antiracism.

Queers of Color also questioned the ways whiteness permeated the languages, networks, and politics of queer identities at the center. During spring 2000, a longtime Queers of Color organizer and I reflected on institutional memory while standing in the center's lounge surveying decorations recently hung for the center's first Asian American/Pacific Islander History Month. "I wish there could be images of queers of color up all year round," he said, his eyes glancing at the LGBT social-service posters and magazines around us depicting athletic young white men and women. I recalled a winter morning that year when I noted that a wall of the center recently covered with photographs, posters, and commentaries on black queer history had been replaced at the end of Black History Month with three paintings of abstracted pink female and male nudes. More than a desire for "representation," I understood his comment and my recollections as a recognition that normative whiteness still informed both the center's "everyday" practices *and* recent efforts through representation to achieve "inclusion" by portraying queers of color amid the continuation of unmarked norms.

The normativity of queer "inclusion" was evoked by a project that culminated the center's efforts to embrace racial/ethnic diversity: the creation by students and staff of a mural on the exterior of the center building. Titled "lesbian gay bisexual transgender queer allies," the mural's rectangular border states "welcome" in a number of languages—including those requested by some student members as their native languages—while a rainbow flag floats behind human silhouettes colored gray to beige dancing in a circle. The links among the figures vary, as one's hand melds with the next, while a third does not touch the fourth. Thus, together the many images mark forms of difference in proximity, language, and color; but they simultaneously appear as variations on a larger, linking principle. Students of color at the center helped conceive and produce the mural, and many remarked to me their sense that redefining the center as a multiracial and multicultural space gave them pleasure, relief, and a desire for renewed activism. Nevertheless, representation of queers of color as diversifying elements at the LGBT center was not identical to the historical work of Queers of Color to make it a node within broader work. The group's formation at that center was important, in that, unlike the separated Ethnic Student Resource Center, students of color could argue that all their racial and national identities were recognizable here, as was their queerness. Nevertheless, after years of work making them equally visible in the Ethnic Student Resource Centers and as a distinct group, Queers of Color *decentered* the LGBT center as an origin of their work *and* its projects of "inclusion" to position them within its domain. They actively utilized the LGBT center as a space with multiple entries and exits, but not one that contained all that they were. In this sense, Queers of Color did not represent queer "diversity" because they challenged the notion that their differences could or should appear first as diversifying evidence of some more fundamental, and inclusive, principle. Visually, decentering models might take many forms, but they likely would trouble the image of a circle dance. Queers of Color in fact succeeded in the 1990s in marking the normatively white "culture" of queer multiracialism by promoting a discrepant multiracialism in their decentered and decentering alliance politics.

CENTERING "DIVERSITY"

Racism and whiteness already represented historical concerns of the downtown Santa Cruz LGBT Community Center. Its conflict over race posed an unresolved legacy for the volunteer organization. With a potentially multiracial constituency, yet no affinity group for people of color, the center's leadership, volunteer base, and facilitators remained predominantly—and, in some cases, entirely—white. During my participation in the center from 1994 to 1998, whiteness remained a problem that leaders sought to solve by learning how to serve and represent the multiracial scope of regional communities. Efforts included inviting volunteers to attend antiracism training, ensuring that the annual pride celebration contained Spanish-language translation of its program, and publication in its newspaper of a bilingual edition with columns in Spanish that were distributed across South and North counties. These efforts produced some new ties, particularly after a South County Latino gay men's group advertised with the center. But the efforts all took place within a social geography that separated South County by twenty miles from the predominantly white queer networks of North County, where even sustained self-reflexive critiques of their own homogeneity did not substantially alter the situation.

Years of work on a shoestring budget left the center in 1999 facing the possibility of having to close, and the directors sent out a call in local LGBT media for assistance in the crisis. After a meeting drew a host of volunteers, a new board of directors convened and sought to save the center through reorganization. The board now included a larger proportion of white gay businessmen, a constituency that had been less evident in the previous decade of grassroots activism led by radical dykes and bi and transwomen as well as queer-identified gay men. The new cochairs worked in the Silicon Valley information technology industries, and one had previously helped organize another regional group, Hi-Tech Gays. The board's combined agenda of fiscal responsibility and growth included seeking corporate and foundation funds to re-create the center as a nonprofit leader in regional politics and social services. The board also immediately determined that its plans for growth would be aided by taking a new name, The Diversity Center. While the older mission was retained—as was the subtitle, "The LGBT Community Center of Santa Cruz County"—this new branding presented "diversity" as the key contribution that the center and its constituents would advertise to the public they wished to inform while gaining financial security and civic recognition.

The most immediate result of this change was a rejuvenation of the center's activities. The previously underutilized center offices now teemed with life, as rare open hours burgeoned into a seven-day schedule accommodating a plethora of new affinity groups, including a men's group, a women's group, game night, film night, women's film afternoon, coming out group, and two transgender and trans-allied groups. By the time of the center's first annual report in 2000, the new board touted new activities alongside ful-fillment of all its former duties, while active fund-raising was keeping cash flow for the first time in four digits and had raised trust money to almost fifteen thousand dollars.[20] Thus, despite the seeming backgrounding of the center's constituents in the subtitle of the new name, the center appeared not only to have increased participation by its various constituents but also to have gained more institutional staying power than ever before.

This very "success" led the board to confront unfinished business, as its annual report announced a decision to form its newest committee: Diversity Outreach. The board noted that both it and the many groups now using the center were predominantly or entirely white, and it asked why more people of color were not coming to the revitalized center. It reflected on the pos-sibility that its identity named a contradiction: promoting LGBT people *as* "diversity" insufficiently names the "diversity" the board wished to present. Amid the popularization of "diversity" as multiculturalism's object, the reference to sexuality or gender remained conditioned by making queers analogous to racial/ethnic minorities.[21] If queer "diversity" was claimed by whites with no history of antiracism, it effectively used a logic suggestive of racial minoritization to occlude their whiteness so they would be viewed only in terms of their oppression as queers. The Diversity Outreach commit-tee acknowledged that this ruse had been exposed, albeit by the very nor-mative logic that it embraced. In this year when Queers of Color energized university activism, the downtown center board invited one of the group's members to chair Diversity Outreach. This recognition of local leadership also served as a reminder that members of Queers of Color had not worked at the downtown center until they were hired to address its "diversity." The committee gained foundation funds to support diversity programs, specifi-cally antiracism training for the board by diversity training professionals. Few others were privy to the event, but stories circulated afterwards that recalled the event that had first split the center board a decade earlier. The training appears to have been taken seriously by this predominantly white group, even as board members of color questioned the manner in which race and racism were presented by the trainers. But without a mandate to carry this event forward, the Diversity Outreach coordinator stayed on to gather resources on antiracism for the center library before departing, and the committee itself disbanded.

My story now turns to a moment when political configurations revealed their limits—in struggles over sexuality and race around Propositions 21 and 22. These voter-initiated electoral propositions elicited a post–civil rights political struggle over conflicting narratives of queerness and "race" in each center.

NEGOTIATING ALLIANCE

In winter 2000, Californians faced two ballot propositions that purported to protect the individual liberty of citizens from the violent insurgence or special rights of racialized and sexualized subjects. Proposition 21, a "tough-on-crime" law, would expand state power to try teenagers as adults by criminalizing "gang"-associated dress styles and graffiti while opening youth so profiled to charges of life imprisonment under the California "three strikes" law. Proposition 22 would amend the state constitution to define marriage as a union between a man and woman. Together, the initiatives reflected the neoliberalism of a post–civil rights era in which the state must protect citizens from an alleged threat by insurgent groups empowered by state-approved multiculturalism. Both initiatives defined white heteronormative citizenship, by assigning hypermasculine violence to youth of color, men and women, with overtones of nativism if "gangs" were linked to migration; and by inviting communities of color to perceive same-sex marriage as an agenda of wealthy whites using race and class privilege to incite perversion.

This racialization and sexualization of political debate highlighted tensions in Santa Cruz queer politics. At the Diversity Center, study of diversity was eclipsed by responding to Proposition 22. An ad hoc group of local activists, including former city politicians and center organizers, initiated a regional campaign to oppose 22. Their calls for fund-raising and proposals of organizing strategies—house parties, phone banks, Democratic Party door hangers on election day—demonstrated their political experience. At the first two meetings at the Diversity Center, each attended by one to two dozen volunteers, the initial organizing strategy did not seriously address Proposition 21. Organizers did remind volunteers that 22 was not the only hateful item on the ballot and that they should encourage opposition to 21. But the phone-banking script suggested discussing 21 if time allowed and if doing so did not jeopardize opposition to 22. This circumvented the racialization of both propositions, as became clear at the first meeting when a tense dialogue on tactics led one organizer to cut off debate by interjecting, "We are not going to do outreach to South County!" I thought that this person, as a South County resident and longtime regional activist, might be referring

to a recent struggle when the county's only Latino high-school superinten-
dent resisted a challenge to antigay harassment of South County students.
But we also learned at the meeting that the Yes on 22 committee was funding a growing South County campaign in Latino/a working-class districts
through door-to-door voter registration. When no comparable counter-
effort was proposed, there was a sense of resignation among those present,
whom I perceived to be white/Anglo with no representatives from South
County Latino/a queer networks. In this case, a North County response
to 22 was limited to a white queer politics that consigned working-class
Latinos/as to conservative mobilization by focusing on rallying the white
middle-class vote in defense of queer rights. This looked less like a strategy
than a default recognition of the lack of relationships among white/Anglo
and Latino/a queers—*even* in South County—despite regional legacies of
white queers seeking a desired multiracial "community." It implied a perception of Latino/a communities as irremediably homophobic, which then
justified white queers not crossing race/class divides and returning to the
white middle class as the proper home for defending their nominally multiracial vision of queer politics.

From my North County location at the university, I joined activists to
reach voters countywide with messages opposing both 21 and 22. The earliest student coalition explained the common roots of 21 and 22 as a conservative backlash against marginalized groups by legislating Christian Right
values and restricting civil liberties. They initially framed those affected by
21 and 22 as separate—adult same-sex couples, police-profiled youth—
but linked as mutual targets of backlash. This message shifted somewhat
once the student coalition was joined by members of Queers of Color, who
had already been stressing the interdependence of race, gender, and sexuality in queer communities and communities of color. One event reflecting this
analysis was a poetry slam to raise awareness about 21 and 22, sponsored
by the alliance against 21/22 and Queers of Color, among others. The event
drew students to a dining hall where, encircled by an array of campaign
tables, an audience gathered by a small stage for a spoken word event. One
poet read a set of poems proclaiming her radically queer gender and her
black feminist consciousness. Her poems invoked how, as a butch boy dyke
walking in public with a girlfriend she might never be able to marry, she
already knew her vulnerability to both homophobic violence and police
brutality even prior to Propositions 21 or 22. Another poet evoked anti-
Asian racism and police harassment as recurrent experiences that questioned his sense of manhood. Yet he then decried a retreat into masculinist

posturing in defense against racist and state violence, which would hold him aloof from other men and prevent him finding the empowerment and love that could follow queering manhood. As artists and activists, students named their multiple positionalities as targeted for control by hegemonic culture and state power, and offered this as an analysis to draw the audience into relationship and a new mobilization. Their work complicated the model of fighting 21 and 22 as distinct issues linked through coalition. In contrast, by embodying intersections that even "coalitions" tend to imagine as separate, queer students of color challenged a logic of analogy, inclusion, or unity that would absorb their differences in a transformative vision of political action.

These tantalizing visions of another kind of politics were not taken up broadly in the few weeks before California voters approved Propositions 21 and 22, even though a majority in Santa Cruz County rejected both. In a moment when defining queers analogically to racial minorities secured civic participation and professionalization, no North County queer politics critiqued how racialization and sexualization shaped neoliberal contestation of liberal multiculturalism apart from the decentering work of queers of color. The creators of *Going Public* had admitted that they lacked a public context to reflect and mobilize to create the change they sought. The arrival of "diversity" later provided a context by eliding whiteness while professionalizing queers as "racial." Queers of Color responded like Policy Institute contributors by disturbing beliefs that queers share a culture or necessarily cohere as a diversified whole. Meanwhile, white middle-class liberalism at the downtown center racialized Chicanos/as and Latinos/as as a bloc that was potentially dangerous to queers, after a decade of addressing the racism that Chicano/a and Latino/a queers had identified by offering inclusion as a solution. Yet the Diversity Center did shift in the decade following these events, as its accountability to Chicano/a and Latino/a queer organizations drew on their leadership: from the group Conexiones hosting events in South County and North County, including "the first linguistically accessible Transgender Day of Remembrance in Watsonville," to an alliance with Latinas y Lesbianas y Aliadas, a regional group that in 2009 organized the first Watsonville Dyke March.[22] Moreover, the distinctive work of Queers of Color in the campus center gained new importance after its 2002 renaming in memory of Professor Lionel Cantú, whose scholarship on Mexican queer migrations complicates national, economic, racial, gendered, and sexual borders and invites a decentering analysis into the center's work.[23] Yet, in the end, to locate how Chicano/a and Latino/a queers engaged these events within analysis of "race" elides not only their diverse racial/ethnic identities but also their complex relationships to "nation." The transnationalism of migrant and immigrant communities intersects the history of Anglo conquest of Mexico that racialized mestizo communities, and the prior and ongoing deployment of *mestizaje* to attempt to erase the Ohlone/Costanoan peoples on whose lands these struggles took place. While I did not hear indigeneity raised in engagements of Chicano/a and Latino/a queers with the Santa Cruz community centers, both the racialization of their relation to indigeneity and its possible reclaiming are crucial to a history of Chicano/a and Latino/a queer politics, and bear potential to center both nationality and indigeneity in queer studies.

I now turn to queer of color alliances that foregrounded indigeneity and Native queer leadership in the 1990s by critiquing liberal multiculturalism as a colonial project that naturalizes settlement.

Challenging Settler Multiculturalism: Two-Spirit Activism and Queer of Color Alliances

Whether northern California queer activists challenged or reproduced whiteness, their struggles resolved by debating "race" within the horizon of the setter state. In this section, I cross geographic distances to ask how queer activism shifted once it confronted its relationship to the settler state, in the work of New York City's WeWah and BarCheeAmpe. From its founding in 1989, WeWah and BarCheeAmpe brought together Native queer people to challenge settler colonialism and defend Native peoples within pantribal alliances. The group drew non-Native queers of color into antiracist queer alliances committed to Native decolonization. Their work showed that queer politics of race, culture, or citizenship will fail to explain their condition unless they theorize settler colonialism, as Native activists did by challenging liberal multiculturalism as a method for naturalizing settlement.

WeWah and BarCheeAmpe formed at a time of growing Native queer and AIDS activism in the United States and Canada. Over the preceding decade, Gay American Indians and *Living the Spirit* had been joined by a proliferation of organizations from American Indian Gays and Lesbians in Minneapolis (AIGL) to Gays and Lesbians of the First Nations in Toronto, in addition to WeWah and BarCheeAmpe. In 1987, Native queer activists from the United States met in Washington, D.C., for the March for Lesbian and Gay Rights, where they camped on the Mall, held a sunrise ceremony for participants, and had a contingent in the march.[24] In 1988,

AIGL brought together Native GLBT people for the first of a series of international gatherings. At the third one, in Winnipeg in 1990, Two-Spirit identity was defined. Toronto organizers quickly adapted Two-Spirit identity by renaming themselves 2-Spirited People of the 1st Nations (later, 2-Spirits) and also committing themselves to serve Native people affected by HIV/AIDS. WeWah and BarCheeAmpe formed in 1989 and remained active into the 1990s, while being succeeded later in the decade by the current New York City group, North East Two-Spirit Society. Founded by Leota Lone Dog (Lakota), Curtis Harris (San Carlos Apache), and Ben Geboe (Yankton Sioux), the group benefited from the experience of Harris and Nic Billey (Choctaw), leaders of the HIV/AIDS Project at New York City's American Indian Community House (AICH).[25] In early writings, WeWah and BarCheeAmpe thank AICH director Rosemary Richmond "for her unfailing support and open door policy here at the Community House."[26]

WeWah and BarCheeAmpe presented a model of Two-Spirit organizing that arose prior to the contemporary definition of Two-Spirit identity. The group promoted indigenist identity for Native queer people by affirming gender and sexual diversity in their nations and through pantribal ties, as indicated by the group's identification with two historical persons: We'wha and Bar Chee Ampe. A flyer announcing the group's formation explains its relationship to its namesakes. The text asserts that "We'wha (1849–1896) was an important member of his tribe," the Zuni nation, for having the "*lhamana* status—*an individual who bridged the roles of women and men.*" Quoting colonial observers, it states that We'wha "has been described as . . . 'that man of enormous strength who lived a woman's daily life in woman's dress, but remained a power in his Pueblo's gravest councils.'"[27] It explains that We'wha visited Washington, D.C., as a guest of Matilda Coxe Stevenson, and that "he demonstrated weaving at the Smithsonian and helped Stevenson document Zuni culture" and "called on Speaker of the House Jon Carlisle and President Grover Cleveland."[28] The flyer then cites historical reports by frontiersmen about Bar Chee Ampe (Crow), also known as Pine Leaf or Woman Chief, who "could rival any of the young men" and who "became a warrior . . . leading her own war parties." One historical report says that "the Indians seemed to be proud of her and sung forth her praise in songs composed by them after each of her brave deeds," even as she finally supported four wives. These passages situate We'wha and Bar Chee Ampe as historical figures in traditional roles that remain accessible to Native people today, a point reinforced by the flyer's introduction. After opening with the statement, "We are Indian Gays and Lesbians living in New York. We are the present voices of all our ancestors who would today be called Gay and Lesbian," the group lists more than one hundred names in Indigenous languages for roles that they name as "our ancestors who would today be called Gay and Lesbian."

WeWah and BarCheeAmpe asserted traditional belonging for Native queer people in Native communities by linking them to tribally specific roles, even while reaching across differences to imagine pantribal alliance. The flyer is consistent with concurrent Native activism in using terms linked to sexuality to name roles the flyer defines by gender. While *gay* and *lesbian* must not be read here in a non-Native register as inaccessible to transgender Native people, the use of pronouns and terms does not name their specific stakes in identifying with We'wha or Bar Chee Ampe. The group offers distinctly Native grounds for sexual and gender diversity that do not derive from any non-Native queer history, identity, or politics. It also asserts traditional ties on national *and* transnational terms that reinforce one another. WeWah and BarCheeAmpe thus anticipated Two-Spirit identity by asserting that inheriting the legacies of historical figures recognized Native queer people as belonging in Native communities and traditions. Although other groups also made this claim, WeWah and BarCheeAmpe did so with a name that invoked historical and traditional figures. The belonging the group claimed for Native queer people was not a form of acceptance for a marginal or minority group, but of honored tribal leaders who acted in defense of their nations. The group thus offered Native queer people ancestral ties not just to gender and sexual diversity but to national responsibility and leadership. Native languages and histories presented an epistemology for Native queer and Two-Spirit organizing when WeWah and BarCheeAmpe required Natives *and* non-Natives to pronounce tribally specific names and recall their stories as a condition of relating to their work. In retrospect, the group's decision to embrace Two-Spirit identity *without* changing its name makes sense, for the national *and* transnational logics announced in Two-Spirit identity already, and literally, defined this group's indigenist and decolonial work.

In articles published in its journal, *Buffalo Hide* (1990–92), WeWah and BarCheeAmpe members situated Native queer and Two-Spirit activists as responsible to broader Native struggles for decolonization that challenged the power of the settler state. Addressing legacies of Two-Spirit activism in the North East Two-Spirit Society, WeWah and BarCheeAmpe member Kent Lebsock and NE2SS elder wrote that "the purpose" of such work is to make a comfortable, safe space for two-spirit people to talk about our unique issues and provide a nurturing resource to our own folks. But, as members of our New York City community, as well as members of our nations, we attempt to discipline ourselves to the reality that we, as two-spirit people, cannot live in a shell . . . The issues faced by two-spirit people cannot be limited to "gay" activism. We are part of communities and nations, and that is to whom we owe our loyalty and our responsibility. Sovereignty, treaties, environment, sacred sites, cultural revival and language preservation must be folded into all of our other work.[29]

All these qualities are apparent in writings in *Buffalo Hide*, from calls to support land claims, to oppose legal challenges to tribal sovereignty, to critique cultural appropriation, and to renew traditional knowledge, teaching, and leadership as foundations for Native nations today.

The commitment of Two-Spirit organizing to broader work for decolonization was advanced when WeWah and BarCheeAmpe helped to inspire the New York City queer of color coalition, the Cairos Collective. As Vaid noted, increased organizing by queers of color in racial/ethnic and national groups gave rise to new efforts to form alliances in the 1990s. Yet, unlike the cases Vaid notes—where Native people appeared marginally or not at all—WeWah and BarCheeAmpe defined the early work of the Cairos Collective, particularly in its news magazine *COLORLife!* The first issue thanks "Curtis Harris, Ben Geboe, the members of WeWah and BarCheeAmpe: Native Two Spirits in New York and Rosemary Richmond, executive director of the American Indian Community House in New York for your invaluable support in helping us launch this project."[30] The first editorial theorizes queer of color alliance politics in relation to Native queer critiques of political inclusion in a settler society. Saying that "the American Dream is a lie. There has never been a 'melting pot,'" the collective writes:

> many of us will never pledge allegiance to the United States flag because of the atrocities and genocide perpetrated against many People of Color by the U.S. government, because of the stolen land and destruction of the earth over the last five centuries that continues to this day. . . . We dedicate COLORLife in recognition of 500 years of the survival and resistance of the first nations and to the continued, principled struggle of People of Color in a deeply racist society.

By saying that "many of us" (and hence not all members) agree, room remained for queers of color to take up varied relationships to the state. For instance, a subsequent statement—"we have yet to see multiracial, multicultural democracy in this country"—leaves open the possibility that readers might wish to seek freedom by participating in "democracy in this country." Yet the editorial then situates all such aspirations within

> the centuries-old tradition, much of it handed down orally from generation to generation, of documenting the ongoing fight for freedom, justice, and dignity for People of Color—especially lesbians, gay men, Two Spirits, transsexuals, and bisexuals of color. COLORLife reaffirms our allegiance first to our ancestors, our tribes, and our cultures. We uphold values that are life-affirming, stressing cooperation over competition, respect and responsibility to ourselves, to one another, our families, our communities and the earth before we pledge allegiance to any flag or government.

Here, a vision of liberation for queers of color draws from ancestors and their freedom struggles, and locates allegiance in such ties rather than in the settler state or its nationalism. If this claim could be translated as a commitment to nation, then nation here can be distinguished from any government that claims to represent itself as a nation to queers of color. Peoples and nations come before their representatives, just as representatives gain allegiance only by speaking from generational ties in which the political stakes of queers of color appear. The collective suggests that colonialism, racism, and heterosexism can be opposed by queers of color through forms of national resistance, in which governmental power is displaced by genealogies and alliances. In turn, nations are redefined as being led by queers of color, and hence, as perhaps altered radically from any currently observable governmental form. In turn, ties to ancestors and their struggles are not theorized by queers of color along separatist lines, but in relation to national resistance, so that gestures to family and ancestry invoke ties within and between nations that are cultural, political, and open to new alignments.

In this context, WeWah and BarCheeAmpe aligned queer of color mobilizations with Two-Spirit politics. The first article in *COLORLife*'s inaugural issue, "Role Model," reprints profiles of Bar Chee Ampe and We'wha from the flyer mentioned earlier. A second article titled "What Are Two Spirits?" continues:

> We use this term because it is culturally relevant to us. As Two Spirits we are members of our Tribes, families and communities. We prefer to use this term because the titles "lesbian" and "gay" mean belonging to a white segment of white culture. Though we have gratitude to the white lesbian and gay communities who have done work to secure a safe space in mainstream culture

for homosexual lifestyles and issues, we find it most important for us to identify and remain a part of our specific communities. Therefore, as Two-Spirits
we are Native first.[31]

The article states that, "in today's world, we suffer from the same homophobia as everyone else," and that they intend "to assume our place among
our people—the First Nations of Turtle Island" (4). These statements up the
stakes for queers of color seeking antiracist queer politics as they suggest
that whiteness and settler colonization are naturalized in sexual and gender
identities. Asserting that *lesbian* and *gay* "mean belonging to a white seg-
ment of white culture" locates this comment on racialization within the
national distinctions to which Native people lay claim. In this light, I retro-
actively read the use of *gay* and *lesbian* by WeWah and BarCheeAmpe as one
that challenged white and colonial registers by making the words signify the
lives of Native people grounded in cultural tradition. Nevertheless, by 1990,
Two-Spirit identity let the group no longer have to prioritize such appropriations. Thus, while writings by WeWah and BarCheeAmpe in *COLORLife!*
did present Two-Spirit people as role models for non-Native queers of color,
this did not invite their absorption into non-Native people's lives. Rather,
they demonstrated that Native peoples resist white-supremacist settler colonization, oppose colonial theft of Native culture, and define solidarity as a
relationship across national differences. For instance, when the collective
described its work as for "LGBTST people of color"—a phrase inherited by its
successor, the Audre Lorde Project—it could seem to invoke the liberal multicultural logic of inclusion within sexual minority politics. But in the model
of WeWah and BarCheeAmpe, with Two-Spirit people representing *nations*
distinct from *all* non-Natives on Native land, "LGBTST" challenges multiculturalism: for, whereas "LGBT" may potentially be shared by any members,
"TS" cannot be, regardless of how anticolonial non-Natives might become.
Native activism represented in *COLORLife!* thus positioned non-Natives as
needing to challenge all colonial legacies in a white settler society, including
any desires to absorb Native culture, if they wished to ally with Two-Spirit
people.

Asserting Native distinctions within queer of color alliances strongly
informed WeWah and BarCheeAmpe's call to the collective in 1991–92 to
protest the incipient quincentennial. Writing in *Buffalo Hide*, it stated:

> As we approach the 500th anniversary of one of the events that radically
> changed the history of the American continents . . . we as lesbian and gay/
> two spirited people of color can . . . develop a clear analysis of our political unity

and why it is important for us to struggle in solidarity with each other... we can use this time to plan observances that will help to educate our communities about the survival and resistances in response to the half-millennium of oppression that we are now unmasking. Each of us needs to ask some questions about the meaning of the Quincentenary—a period of 500 years—and then discuss why we need to have our own perspective, as people of color and lesbians and gay men.[32]

The statement concluded with a call to interested people to contact the group, which was taken up in the next issue of *COLORLife!* when Curtis Harris joined members of the Cairos Collective in considering how they could challenge settler colonialism. Writing jointly, Mariana Romo-Carmona, Lidell Jackson, and Curtis Harris examine their responsibilities as Latino/a, African American, and Native queers to address the quincentennial by aligning with Native struggles for collective survival, resurgence, and sovereignty.[33] WeWah and BarCheeAmpe organized a Two-Spirit contingent to lead the New York City Pride march in 1991 that denounced the quincentennial by calling all queers to join them in questioning the power of the settler state on Native lands.

With the Cairos Collective, WeWah and BarCheeAmpe countered the normative production of U.S. queer politics as multiracial by forming alliances with queers of color where "race" did *not* eclipse "nation." Challenging settler colonialism located all their engagements as transnational alliances across national differences. Their work disrupts histories of U.S. queer of color alliances that append Native queer people as a racial group or ignore Native participation altogether. In sharp contrast, New York City queer of color coalitions formed by being radicalized by Two-Spirit activists who led them in challenging settler colonialism as being at the root of institutionalized racism on stolen land and as a proper target of antiracist and anticolonial queer critique. They thereby located queer whiteness within the *settler* logics of liberal multiculturalism that colonize Native peoples while potentially co-opting activism by people of color into the multiracial project of a settler state. Importantly, this work *distinguished* queers of color from white queers by marking their distinct positions under white-supremacist settler colonialism. This model of organizing called queers of color to interrogate their inheritance of settler colonial power, by allying with Native people in studying their distinct experiences of racism, capitalism, imperialism, and heteropatriarchy in a white settler society.[34]

The Cairos Collective demonstrated a unique capacity for solidarity among Native queer people and queers of color, which suggests that they will not take identical paths as white queers when challenging settler colonialism. White queers were not part of the collective because they are not the targets of the conquest and the racism that "queers" peoples of color and Indigenous peoples outside the norms of white settler society. Heteronomativity defines all queers as problematic to the racial norms of white settler society, but white queers retain a capacity to redefine whiteness in queer form and on that basis claim national belonging. The Cairos Collective thus modeled a politics with which white queers could ally, but not one to which they intrinsically belonged. The queer politics modeled by the collective called all queer people to account by first committing to practice antiracism and anticolonialism. White queers who aspire to participate can recognize their specific non-Native formation in a white settler society as a primary condition of their lives. WeWah and BarCheeAmpe and the Cairos Collective thus model how antiracist and anticolonial queer politics might develop: in alliances led by Native queer and Two-Spirit people across differences of "race" and nation in opposition to settler colonialism.

Chapter 4   Ancient Roots through Settled Land

Imagining Indigeneity and Place among Radical Faeries

SETTLER CITIZENSHIP OFFERS QUEER POLITICS normatively non-Native belonging to a settler nation. Yet non-Natives also resolve their settler colonial inheritance by creating queer cultures that make the land their medium for liberating sexuality and gender. Gay and lesbian counter-culturists in back-to-the-land collectives across the United States and Canada inspired broader circulation of their rural practices. One of their enduring legacies is the Radical Faeries. Radical Faeries apply back-to-the-land principles to a mobile practice that made retreat to rural space a conduit for urban and itinerant people to realize portable truths. Radical Faerie culture privileged rural retreat as a means for non-Native gay men to liberate an Indigenous gay nature and integrate it in their everyday lives. Most accounts of Radical Faerie culture examine its gender and sexual radicalism, but apart from Povinelli few do more than note its traversals of colonial discourses—notably, the colonial and masculinist object berdache—or how this informs gendered and sexual practices.[1] My account locates Radical Faerie narratives of indigeneity within material practices articulating settled land, which mediate Radical Faeries' diverse racialization as non-Natives negotiating their relationship to settlement and Native peoples.

At the first "Spiritual Conference of Radical Faeries," held over a summer weekend in 1979, leaders in Los Angeles gay organizing led more than two hundred primarily urban gay men to a rented retreat in the Arizona desert to realize the ancient spiritual roots of being gay. At that and later gatherings, a few dozen to a few hundred gay men briefly removed to spaces coded as rural or natural to liberate gay subjectivity. The Radical Faerie founders argued that gay men historically received honor in societies they read as Indigenous, which they adapted to promote self-love and social acceptance.[2] Radical Faerie networks then formed in the urban regions where most lived in order to sustain their culture between gatherings, in part by

127

raising funds to buy rural land as sanctuaries that could host gatherings in perpetuity. Although white gay men from urban middle-class gay communities became their core constituents, Radical Faeries always attracted a wider array of people. Gatherings included a sizable minority of rural men, among them many urban expatriates, while a "no one turned away for lack of funds" policy welcomed people across class differences with poor or itinerant people supported by the resources of wealthier ones. Women and bisexual men at times visited gatherings and sanctuaries or identified as Radical Faeries, even while recognizing that Radical Faerie culture had formed to reflect gay men's lives.[3] Gay men of color participated by playing on and in primitivist narratives of queerness while studying their ancestral histories of sexual and gender diversity. Yet, on joining, all were promised a global and transhistorical gay nature by addressing non-Natives as inheritors of Native culture on Native land. By making rural space invoke Native Americans and, by extension, all Indigenous peoples through the world and time, gatherings created queers as non-Native seekers of Indigenous truth, while sanctuaries grounded their desires in negotiating non-Native occupation of settled land.[4]

My reading of Radical Faeries derives from a long familiarity that was resituated by ethnography. I first met them in predominantly white circles of urban California queer politics in the 1980s, when their writings were prominent in gay studies and their participation inflected queer Left networks and AIDS activism. Those whom I met were white gay men for whom Radical Faerie culture made their activism sharper, their spirituality gay-centered, and their gender a bit more blurred. I found that I and many other white gay male critics of urban capitalism, religious heterosexism, and U.S. imperialism shared the experience of being invited by Radical Faeries to find a natural home in their communities. I declined these invitations because of my initial ambivalence and later critique of what I understood to be their racial and colonial formation as a network of white gay men who appropriated Native culture to enliven their sexual subjectivities. Yet, on examining the colonial and racial formation of U.S. queer politics, I learned that the forthright addressing of these topics by Radical Faeries made it necessary for me to engage them. I finally accepted invitations to participate by agreeing to do so as an ethnographer. My ethical responsibility to experience and understand the situated practices in which I participated on their own terms complicated the relative simplicity of distanced criticism and generated, in its place, the critically reflexive account I provide here. My ethnographic account centers my experiences as a subject interpellated by Radical Faerie culture to explain, reflectively, what I had been called to be. If Radical Faeries met me first as an outsider, over time many read me as a potential member or, at least, an old friend. Some affirmed my self-positioning as an ethnographer while playfully arguing that this must be deflecting some deeper desire on my part to identify as a Radical Faerie. I never assumed this identity as my own, but by participating I learned some of the power of Radical Faerie culture to interpellate white U.S. gay men as non-Native inheritors of indigeneity on settled land and thereby resolve their queer and settler formation.

My ethnographic account portrays the way Radical Faeries produce queer subjects by creatively deploying rurality and mobility in the context of settlement. Notably, this resolves racialized exclusions of white queers from sexual modernity by claiming roots in Native authenticity that appear to resolve contradictions in their non-Native inheritance of settlement. My account emphasizes how this normative practice shifts once Radical Faeries engage Native Two-Spirit people, a proximity not present in Povinelli's account. Povinelli investigates how Radical Faeries in the United States and Indigenous people in Australia mutually and disparately negotiate the "autological subject" and its constraints by a "genealogical society."[5] I examine Radical Faeries in the United States as non-Natives living in power-laden relationships to Native American peoples, cultures, and lands, and Native queer and Two-Spirit people in particular, mediated by the colonial desires producing modern queer subjectivity as non-Native—for them, especially through the colonial object berdache. This mutually constituting relationship within a single settler colonial situation produces linked negotiations of queer modernities with distinct implications and effects. At times, Radical Faeries are criticized by Native queer people for adapting Two-Spirit people's lives and claims to a non-Native imaginary of indigeneity. If this resonates with Indigenous women who repudiate white feminists as imperialist appropriators of Indigenous spirituality, as often Native queer and Two-Spirit people hold Radical Faeries to a closer relationship by educating them with distinctive understandings of how queerness, indigeneity, and settler colonialism shape their interrelated lives.[6] I attended to such critical engagements from the location of ethnography, which replaced the distancing effects of constructing Radical Faeries as an object by closely analyzing their creative production of what Indigenous observers critiqued or transformed. Tracing Radical Faeries' negotiation of their racialized relationships of settler colonialism led me to notice how engaging Radical Faerie culture has been adapted by Native queer and Two-Spirit people to their work for decolonization. My story presents encounters among Radical Faeries and Native gay men as further evidence of the relationality of non-Native and Native queer modernities within power-laden conversations, which Native queer and Two-Spirit people nevertheless negotiate discrepantly.

Imagining Home

During the late 1990s, I accompanied Radical Faeries to various gatherings and sanctuaries, in particular the Nomenus Wolf Creek sanctuary in southern Oregon and the Short Mountain sanctuary in central Tennessee.[7] The tiny town of Wolf Creek is located off Interstate 5 in the valley of its namesake river, where since 1987 the San Francisco–based organization Nomenus has owned land nearby to host gatherings. On my first visit, I turned onto a private drive off the valley's public road and crossed a small bridge over the creek to park in a clearing at the edge of a wide meadow. As I began walking along a path toward the sanctuary's common buildings, hidden behind trees in the distance, in the late afternoon light I suddenly noticed a slender archway loom over my head. On either side of the path stood a tall, thin pole and between, decorated with colorful fabrics, hung a string of letters woven from twigs announcing "WELCOME HOME." I recall being bemused by the meanings resonating in this welcome that I sensed were directed at me. What does it mean to arrive somewhere one has never before been and be welcomed home? For, if "home" signifies a site of origin, then true home would be found nowhere but there. But if home is where the heart is, then its sentimental promise—perhaps, of original and eternal intersubjective belonging—becomes portable; requiring no certain recollected person or place, home may be discovered anew. This latter framing seemed to explain my Wolf Creek welcome; friends had assured me that on arrival I would feel that I belonged. Yet the specificity of the sign standing at this site demands a more complex accounting. Can home be eminently portable, producible wherever comrades assemble, yet still link profoundly to one particular site? Could one site in fact originate the innumerable analogous places and times where future home may be found, all of which become available on arrival there? Radical Faeries produce these effects by coming home to sanctuaries, where myriad qualities of Indigenous gay nature are recalled through intimacy with "the land." Radical Faeries invest sites of rural gay collectives with desires that seem inaccessible in urban life, where land seems to

"Welcome Home" archway at Nomenus Wolf Creek Sanctuary. Photograph by author.

have been made inauthentic by modernity. Framing the sanctuary as natural and Indigenous ground privileges it as a space to discover an ultimately portable Indigenous gay nature, which can sustain Radical Faeries while they are living far off in space and time from gathering on the land.

The sexual, racial, and national homecomings Radical Faeries sought through land reflect early U.S. gay liberation and lesbian feminist projects, in which white lesbian and gay politics was grounded in revolutionary opposition to racism, capitalism, and imperialism by enacting self-exile from privilege. Historians insist that studies of their racial or national form account for how they pursued radically multi-issue sexual politics.[8] I agree, by asking how that multi-issue radicalism articulated desires to reject the racial, economic, national, or global power that accrued to them, and to materialize this rejection by relocating to homes based in democratic socialism, anarchism, or counterculturism. Belief that removing white U.S. gay men or lesbians to spaces coded as communal, antiauthoritarian, or premodern would interrupt their power was the very means by which such spaces fostered modernist sexual politics animated by colonial discourses. In their racial, economic, or national homogeneity, they imagined themselves as allies to peoples of color and colonized peoples worldwide, but their desire to also emulate or even embody the oppressed whom they knew they were not translated into their ruralist, naturist, and primitivist projects.

Radical Faeries inherited the material legacies of this cultural production by white U.S. gender and sexual radicals. The anticapitalist collectivism of early gay liberationists at times adapted back-to-the-land practices, as when land at Short Mountain was purchased in 1973 as a safe house for gays and lesbians by a North Carolina Weather Underground cell, which on disbanding passed the land to Milo Pyne, who created a gathering site for gay and lesbian counterculturists in the South.[9] The early 1970s also saw lesbian feminists adapt women's back-to-the-land projects to new radical politics. Lesbians who split from gay liberation over masculinism helped redefine women's liberation around a universalizing communion of lesbian feminism, which new rural women's communes modeled. The sexual politics of rural separatism also saw lesbian-feminist cultivation of a women's spirituality based in European pagan and indigenous antitheses to patriarchal religion.[10] By the mid-1970s, collectivist gay men inspired by lesbian feminists formed rural collectives on principles of radical sexual politics, separatism, and feminist paganism, and by applying lesbian feminism's universalizing gestures to gay men. For instance, the gay men's collective at Magdalen Farm adopted Maoist principles and brought gay men together through rural gatherings, including the 1976 "Faggots and Class Struggle" conference.[11] Participants in rural gay men's projects also pursued counterculturist imaginaries of primordial roots for revolutionary gay culture, as when Arthur Evans, in *Witchcraft and the Gay Counterculture,* tied feminist paganism to colonial ethnology to propose "gay shamanism" as a nature honored by Native Americans, ancient Europeans, and all "nature peoples" that radical gay men now renewed.

When Radical Faeries formed in 1979, they adapted gay and lesbian efforts to find a home in opposition to modernity, even as they altered back-to-the-land practice to serve an urban desire for temporary retreat. They framed the country and primitivity as repositories of an ancient authenticity long sought by urban subjects of metropolitan societies. Gatherings granted participants a new affinity with differences defined by place, race, class, and nation that let them feel more rural and Indigenous than they felt in everyday life. Although some Radical Faeries critiqued normative gay culture, all at first identified as subjects of that culture who chose rural mobility out of a self-critical rejection of certain terms of modern sexuality and then returned to their everyday lives to call on their comrades to follow. The work of cofounder Harry Hay, later extended by Will Roscoe, Bradley Rose, and Randy Conner, emphasized "gay shamanism" as a natural, shared basis for defining gay men's lives in a modern society.[12] Such claims were not embraced by all Radical Faeries; some questioned if the culture or community they created was normatively white, anti-intellectual, or appropriative, although the rarity of such critiques left Hay's legacy intact.[13] Yet such diverse opinions remained compatible with retreat to rural gatherings and sanctuaries as a method for finding a sense of authentic belonging to gay subjectivity and community.

I contend that Radical Faeries discovered homecoming in four interlinked ways. First, home appears in the context of back-to-the-land movements. Although rural gay collectives predate Radical Faerie culture, Radical Faeries adopted and sustain them. The original gay collective at Short Mountain was the first such group to host a Radical Faerie gathering, and their land and community prospered in the 1980s by benefiting from persistent enthusiasm for the Radical Faeries even as other rural gay collectives faded away. For instance, the old Magdalen Farm and later Creekland site at Wolf Creek was sold by its owner, the last member of the original gay collective to live there, and was purchased in 1986 by Nomenus members from across the West Coast to create a Radical Faerie sanctuary. Second, Radical Faeries sustained their sense of shared belonging in the reader-written journal *RFD*, which was inherited from rural gay collectives and functioned as a de facto Radical Faerie journal. In these ways, Radical Faeries grounded otherwise mobile and multi-sited practices in a landed infrastructure that granted them a deeper sense of history and integrity.

Third, home is elicited by a sense of history in the land that may be felt upon arrival. The sanctuaries at Wolf Creek and Short Mountain are suffused with signs set out by caretakers that invoke distant yet sustained communion. Wolf Creek's eighty acres surround a rectangular meadow interwoven by paths; on one long side runs the namesake creek's ravine, bordered by Garden House (a common house) and the Barn (kitchen with storeroom), and beyond them the meadow's low slope leads to a forested ridge. Short Mountain's two hundred forested acres of mostly uninhabited gullies surround a ridge-top meadow, hosting a kitchen and dining building, barn, gazebo, and bathhouse, from which paths radiate across the land. Each space evokes its history as a locus for gathering generations of gay men and friends, from a drag closet of playful attire accumulated over the years to small libraries of gay and counterculturist literature; paths dotted with small cabins and old campsites that pass by small groves, altars, or statues memorializing Radical Faeries and others who died of AIDS. The materiality of each space evokes the sexual, spiritual, and communal pursuits of a multigenerational constituency that are key to the site's continuity. In those contexts, homecoming appears again when re-creating that sense of life on the land at gatherings. Major Faerie gatherings link small groups of residents to up to hundreds of visitors for days or weeks at a time, where gatherers cook, repair buildings, and host performances and rituals and discussion circles, with food cooked by the gatherers from food purchased with advance registration fees. Sanctuary gatherings create a functioning community that the land could never sustain, but that still recall a vision of rural collectivism as their model of belonging. Only a few residents live on the land, and even they moved there from somewhere else, but sanctuary gatherings act to welcome visitors home.

And, fourth, homecoming appears through the sanctuary as a site holding out hope that these qualities will be sustained even when Radical Faeries live far from them in space and time; for the people gathering at Radical Faerie sanctuaries *are* the urban and modern queers seeking the rural, natural, and Indigenous in order to resolve their inheritance of settler colonialism. My consideration of their racial and national formation and its relationship to indigeneity, including to Native gay men, follows the paths I took after passing under the welcome arch.

Gathering Subjectivity

Gathering enacts the central metaphor and practice through which Radical Faeries fashion rural, natural, and Indigenous roots for a modern queer liberation. Although the rarity of gathering community frequently defines accounts of Radical Faerie culture, its rural spatiality and temporality generate a portable subjectivity that references its origin long after the gathering ends. Gatherings assemble not merely their participants but the very methods of subject formation that participants take away as a potential to be realized. The rural space of gatherings nurtures the Indigenous nature participants seek, even as gatherings privilege tales of Native American cultures as quintessential indigeneity. Gatherings thus welcome gay men home to themselves and to a world of sexual truth by fashioning Radical Faeries from an eclectic assembly of desires, enacted here as a performative map they may realize and then take with them wherever they go.

Gatherings appear to liberate gender and sexuality thanks to the inspiration of rural space. Early gatherings cited Harry Hay when cultivating effeminacy and sexual libertinism as authentic to gay subjectivity. Hay wrote near the time of the first gathering that heteronormative culture recognizes gay nature in the appellation "sissy," which he asked gay men to reclaim and thus shed "the ugly green frog skin of Hetero-male imitation . . . to reveal the beautiful Fairy Prince hidden beneath."[14] Gatherings reflected this antiassimilationist path to gay sensibility by promoting drag—while eschewing passing in favor of "genderfuck" juxtapositions that troubled normative gender—and by inviting sexual exploration, whether in the form of a "gathering boyfriend" (or more than one) or, on occasion, in more collective venues for sexual play. A mood of sexual possibility at gatherings belies the fact that sex usually does not occur in plain view, even as stories circulate that sexuality here is freed from expectations of privacy, coupling, or monogamy. Yet, from the start, such practices accrued meaning from a rural or natural context that appeared to go beyond their urban expression. Faerie genderfuck regularly undermines urbane drag imagery of hyper femininity in a parody of the putatively unrefined or abnormal genders and sexualities of the rural working class. Articulating discourses that would frame them as being unable to differentiate proper sex, gatherers perform "trashy" housewives and cowhands to mock and indulge degeneracy as a way of countering "civilized" restrictions. Radical Faeries also parody their efforts to take up rural life by effeminizing its tasks of clearing hay, harvesting trees, or maintaining cabins, as when one year Wolf Creek gatherers donned eclectic drag outfits for a day's work under the hot sun burying electrical wire between the Barn and the Garden House. Sexuality at gatherings also gets represented as unencumbered by civilizational propriety owing to having arisen in a natural, and hence freed, state. Such readings overlap a relationship between dress and nudity at gatherings. If urban gay cultures sexualize nudity at beaches, gyms, and bathhouses while extolling a limited range of beauty based on consumption, gatherings foster nudity as a form of dress that presents and celebrates the body "as it is." Radical Faeries thus resemble naturists by rejecting the shaming concealment of the body, but they apply this to foster eroticism, in that unreconstructed bodies will more effectively link gay men in natural communion. The gathering thus promises participants a homecoming to self and community in uniquely rural or natural settings for freeing sexuality and gender.

Gatherings further define gay liberation in a spirituality assembled from global and transhistorical evidence of indigeneity. The first gathering hosted rituals that mixed quasi-Indigenous rituals with gay translations of feminist neo-paganism to honor gay men's effeminate ties to the land, as in the "mud ritual" that immersed gay men in the earth as an inspiration for ecstatic communion.[15] During the 1980s, gatherings proliferated by taking place near in time to major neo-pagan holidays, such as the spring celebration Beltane. Here, the procreative metaphor of the maypole inseminating a fecund earth could be reframed to celebrate a natural gay sexuality emerging from Gaian roots. At gatherings throughout the year, spontaneous rituals were interspersed with recurrent ones such as Donald Engstrom's Queer God ritual, which combines chant, meditation, and touch to incite gay nature while invoking ancient Greek, European pagan, and Native American cultures as inspirations for gay shamanism.[16] The gay spirituality produced in gathering rituals codes an array of ancient cultures as evidence of indigenized sexuality and spirituality. Yet its transcendence of racial or national borders repeatedly analogizes ancient paganisms in Europe and America, portraying indigeneity as invoking the Native American cultures Radical Faeries first tapped and the land where gatherings arose, even as European paganism remains foregrounded as a properly racialized basis for white people to claim indigenized ties to Native Americans. Yet despite the perception that adopting European neo-paganism keeps white members of settler societies from appropriating Native culture, neo-paganism itself is reinvented by them to gain a relationship to Native land and culture that does not feel like the conquest that they know they inherit. Gatherings thus offer belonging to sexual truth via Indigenous sexuality and spirituality, but one that in its U.S. origination specifically articulates white desires for Indigenous European and Native American roots.

Beyond tales of gay shamanism, non-Native imaginaries of Native culture are naturalized most thoroughly at gatherings through the ritual of heart circle. Heart circle is the only ritual to have occurred at all historical Radical Fairie gatherings, and it has come to embody the gathering's meaning and intended effects. The practice seats participants in a circle, where they speak "from the heart"—privileging words about feelings while passing an object known as a talisman, which grants the holder a right to speak and obligates others to listen until it is relinquished. Heart circle structures everyday life at gatherings: the morning call to circle announces the day's first event, and all others occur around it, none preempting it. Some heart circles I attended lasted one to two hours, others could approach four, or continue through the day, so long as speakers carried the group's attention until someone made an uncontested suggestion to close. Heart circle makes emotional speech, deep listening, and collective conversation central to Radical Faerie subjectivity while setting these as the tone for everyday life at gatherings. Heart circle's ties of authentic gayness to emotionality

affirm effeminacy as a strength, even as they invite gay men into a nurturing solidarity that Harry Hay described as a "circle of loving companions," where their experiences are mirrored by what he termed "subject–
subject consciousness."[17] Yet these qualities rest more deeply on tying
liberated gay subjectivity to indigeneity. Radical Faeries created heart circle
from a similar source as other non-Native counterculturists, who in the
1970s promoted the adoption of "council process" as a mode of intentional
speech they described as having derived from consensus practices in Native
American societies. Despite the existence of other consensus methodologies,
council process received unique authentication by ascribing an Indigenous
origin to the equality or collectivism that non-Natives desired. The Radical
Faeries' invention of heart circle from council process then tied an indigenization of truthful speech to emotionality, in some reflection of civilizational correlations of emotionality with both femininity and primitivity.[18]
Heart circle thus addresses non-Native gay men with indigenized tools for
emotional communion as a means to realize an Indigenous sexual nature.

Taken together, the quotidian practices of gatherings performatively constitute Radical Faerie subjectivity, as work, play, and ritual welcome participants into a global and transhistorical Indigenous gay nature. I saw this
effect at a gathering at Short Mountain in 1995, when vistas afforded by
the sanctuary's central knoll portrayed Radical Faerie subjectivity bringing
gay men home to one another by bringing the world home to them. Under
the afternoon sun, I sat with more than forty gatherers spread lazily across
the grassy knoll. Many had begun the morning outdoors in heart circle, and
as the participants huddled for warmth and companionship, the clouds that
had defined this gathering opened into sunlight. After circle many stayed to
revel in the weather, and kitchen helpers prepared a lunch that people coming to the knoll brought to share. A growing group sprawled across the grass
in varied forms of drag and nudity and sustained the circle's sense of connection. At this center of the commons, the group could watch as the day's
events, previously announced in circle, began. Across the knoll, people naked
or wearing yellow fabric entered the bathhouse for a Santeria-inspired ritual
celebrating the Yoruba goddess Oshun, led by a shaven-headed, androgy-
nous faerie as priest/ess of the ceremony. Others passed by on their way to
the common buildings, reminding us that a discussion was about to begin
on the Mayan calendar, a form recently popularized among rural and itinerant people who sought timekeeping alternatives for lives lived "off the grid."
The assembly on the knoll continued unbroken until a strong chant arose
behind the common buildings, and, amid a repeated phrase "Purple hands

of healing, faggot god, faerie god," a group of twenty or more began strolling down the hill toward us, chanting to the beat of their steps. Thus commenced the gathering's Queer God ritual, with participants weaving around the group on the knoll to sit in the gazebo on our opposite side. The structure stood just far enough away that we could see their ritual commence without it interrupting our interactions, which continued for the rest of the afternoon.

The activity on the knoll that day performed a key gathering promise, of emotional communion, even as it became a vantage from which the gathering could be seen to have successfully assembled a global and transhistorical array of gay truths to ground our emotional bond. For if this gathering welcomed participants home to ourselves or each other, it was to discover belonging in a remarkably small world. In the bathhouse one could meet Caribbean indigeneity and the African diaspora; on the hilltop, the ancient Maya; in the Gazebo, a gay refashioning of the ancient Greek, Celtic, and Native American. "Above," lunch came from a hilltop kitchen run by a rural collective, while "behind," at the start of the day, circlers had been promised a link to inner truth through indigenized ritual. We in the group did not join the events that transpired around us, even as their participants joined only one: but our vantage modeled the gathering's assembly of them all as complementary routes to shared nature. Our interactions might disappear from an account of gatherings that focused on ritual activity. But if, in Harry Hay's words or Edward Carpenter's legacy, "a circle of loving companions" is the supportive envelope for the spiritual liberation of gayness, then the performance of a world of gay culture around the knoll that day produced Radical Faeries as gay men who love themselves and one another because they know they are already loved by a world of sexual and spiritual truth, ready to be known at any time once tapped in this space. Our vantage thus revealed the gathering to act as a crucible, melding eclectic knowledges into a tableau of global and transhistorical journeys that embrace Radical Faeries with their sense of home.

Rural gatherings perform such effects whether they are held at retreat centers, wilderness camps, or sanctuaries. But my story's location at a sanctuary reveals qualities that I now must pursue. By forming a portable identity that frees subjects and objects from ties to time or place, gatherings beg a question about the arrival that began my tale: for the sign at Wolf Creek welcomes Radical Faeries home perpetually to *that* place, even when no one is gathered to witness it. While sanctuaries may appear as naturalized backdrops to the activity of gathering, they differ from camps or retreats

in that their permanent possession creates them as repositories of historical communion. A promise that the qualities of gathering continue year-
round at sanctuaries may be recalled by Radical Faeries on their dispersal,
and sought or rediscovered on their return.

Materializing Sanctuary

Like gathering, sanctuary is a crucial metaphor and practice Radical
Faeries use to fashion modern sexuality in mobile relationship to place. Yet
if gatherings use rural spaces to assemble diverse routes to realization that
disperse with their participants, sanctuaries ground all such realizations
at one site. In name and practice, sanctuaries offer Radical Faeries refuge
from an embattled life while making rural land into a medium for renewing
spirituality at its landed source. Sanctuaries drew such qualities in their
U.S. contexts of origin by linking rural land not to a generic indigeneity,
but a specific one through which non-Native gay men could take refuge on
originally Native American land. Yet, despite being a legacy of an earlier
era, the creation of sanctuaries amid the growth of Radical Faerie community transpired in the specific period when U.S. gay men first experienced the HIV/AIDS epidemic. During the 1980s and after, Radical Faeries
used gatherings at sanctuaries to mediate their experience of the epidemic,
including by making sanctuary lands sites of memorials to Radical Faeries
who had died of AIDS. Linking Radical Faeries memorialized at sanctuaries to gatherers seeking gay nature created radical faerie community in an
indigenized relation to settled land that simultaneously healed the trauma
of epidemic and the inheritance of conquest for non-Native gay men.

When acquiring rural land as sanctuaries, Radical Faeries in the United
States tied the gathering's itinerant practices and global imaginaries to histories of settlement. Yet if Radical Faeries acquired originally Indigenous land
with the anticolonial intention to tap its heritage—in a counterculturist
legacy Philip Deloria read as normative to histories of Indian impersonation—they argued uniquely that, unlike straight non-Natives, their ties
to indigeneity were a birthright of being gay.[19] Radical Faeries also adapted
a prior generation's rural hideaways as sites not for removal but for ease
of commute from the urban regions where most lived. Thus, if sanctuaries
promised belonging to the land, no matter how much they resembled set-
tlements, they functioned as sites of transit. If movement was manifested
in the arrival, departure, and return of travelers, it also was referenced in
the spatial and temporal scales of Indigenous gay nature that travelers to
the sanctuary sought to traverse. To adapt James Clifford's formulation,

sanctuaries materialized as simultaneous sites of dwelling *and* traveling.[20] Arrival at the Wolf Creek welcome arch acted as a passage to further travels of body and spirit. Yet, as a structure fashioned from the land and emplaced there, the arch framed dwelling at the sanctuary as a practice of mobility, where the accreted memories of generations of travels became uniquely available at this one site. Histories of settlement thus inform the sanctuary's promise of safe haven, but its invitation to non-Natives to articulate Indigenous land shifted their occupation into movement, and back again, as methods to link Radical Faeries to the integrity of an embattled community, as well as to sure knowledge of an original and permanent ubiquity in all imaginable human worlds.

The promise of sanctuaries became acute during the mounting impact on gay men of HIV/AIDS. The promise of indigenized refuge and sanctification answered displacements caused by the epidemic for the white men from urban middle-class gay communities that were the Radical Faeries' core constituents. Histories of AIDS tell of a rapid destabilization of social and cultural institutions that precipitated crises of belonging, as gay men confronted death in the face of exclusion from phobic familial or religious homes and from national belonging.[21] Yet, if these crises were the effects of homophobia, they were conditioned by the racial, economic, and national structuring of home, community, and nation. AIDS activism often developed among queer people of color apart from the norms of white and urban middle-class AIDS projects, while challenging heterosexism in communities of color as a new cadre of community leaders addressed race, sexuality, gender, and health.[22] Their efforts show that crises of identity, community, or spirituality among gay men with HIV/AIDS negotiated sexual, racial, and national belonging, such that whiteness, urban class privilege, or appeals to citizenship conditioned narratives of gay community institutions being disrupted or renewed. Radical Faeries responded to AIDS by answering white, middle-class, or urban desires for rural, natural, or indigenous solutions to a crisis of displacement from belonging. The culture of rural gatherings can be reinterpreted in this light, as can its materialization at sanctuaries, where memorializing struggles with the epidemic grounded a new, and yet ancestral, collective belonging by indigenizing non-Natives and their relationship to settled land.

Gatherings fostered solidarity by recalling and sustaining sexual cultures that were threatened by the epidemic. Celebrating drag and public sex defied the increased pathologizing of urban gay cultural forms by promoting them as conduits to a healing gay nature that could mend shattered bonds with new community. Indeed, Radical Faerie culture already promoted qualities that would appear in primary and secondary HIV prevention education, as it sought to break social isolation among gay men by encouraging strong community identification and emotional communication while supporting self-care and care for others. Heart circle specifically invited gay men to articulate feelings related to illness, death, loss, or survival; to receive aid from comrades sharing their struggle; and to strengthen shared identity by tracing their personal stories to common roots. These qualities spoke to people who otherwise might never have approached a counterculturist space, but who found in heart circle or other Radical Faerie practices a means to communicate needs and receive support in crisis. At one Wolf Creek gathering, a man experiencing the early stages of AIDS spoke of attending this, his first gathering as part of recovering from caring for his lover, who suffered from multiple AIDS-related illnesses. He came to the gathering taxed from managing their welfare with little support, and I recall that he remained wary of neo-pagan ritual, with which he was unfamiliar. But in heart circle he spoke with gratitude for the support that he had received, in spoken affirmations from the group and after circle, he stated that he wished he had known that connections like this were available to him, for he did not know how he could have gone on without it. For him, the emotional intentionality modeled by heart circle mediated a line between despair and survival, including as it specifically addressed grief. A longtime practitioner and old friend once put it to me in this way, early in my time among Radical Faeries:

> one thing that would be very faerie—one thing that is a very advanced faerie kind of interaction that could happen—is for you, when you're in a space of profound grief, or knowing that you need to get in touch with some really raw and difficult stuff, that you could call me, as a faerie, and say, I need to work through some difficult things, and to have me support you and stand with you through that vulnerable space.

I received these words when my struggle with the AIDS-related illness of a friend of my own was intensifying, and I felt the value of his words entirely apart from their reflections on Radical Faerie culture. I also recognized in them something that heart circle participants might offer someone dealing with grief: complete attention, followed by affirmation by a loving community. Indeed, his words distinguished Radical Faeries from other people precisely in their knowledge of how to bond by forthrightly facing grief—at an "advanced" level that, perhaps, comes from many experiences of heart circle and the connections it had forged among Radical Faeries during the epidemic. Emotional communication within or beyond heart circle thus appeared as both an emblem and a crucial tool of the natural, reliable, and enduring solidarity promised by Radical Faerie subjectivity and solidarity during the AIDS crisis.

Desires for indigeneity among Radical Faeries addressed HIV/AIDS by grounding gay subjectivity and culture in emotional communion. This specifically informed Radical Faerie spirituality's answer to the religious embattlement of gay men facing death or survival. Attacks on gay men by the Christian Right linked homosexuality to disease and divine punishment at the moment when some gay men were seeking religious or spiritual support. By this time, Radical Faeries were a fully realized movement affirming gay men's spiritual worth: rather than gay sexuality being equated with sin or harm, it was a carnal and spiritual path to truth. The fact that the truth being realized was indigenized also rendered moot religious rejection of Christian gay men, for, in the legacy of feminist neo-paganism, gay sexual nature derived from ancient cultures preceding the patriarchal and colonial force of European Christian conquest. This bypassed claims of Christian conservatives to represent America by granting non-Native gay men a greater belonging to this land via their inherent alignment as indigenized pagan queers with Native histories. These qualities resonated when gatherings and sanctuaries offered to protect gay men from endangerment in a heteronormative society through the resource of queer Indigenous nature.

The indigenization of Radical Faerie culture became especially evident as gatherings took place at sanctuaries increasingly marked by memories of AIDS. Nowhere was this more apparent than in establishing sanctuary memorials to Radical Faeries who had died of AIDS. In the scattering of ashes and in ritual remembrances, lost friends became one with the spiritual powers of Indigenous land. Memorials and their rituals then drew Radical Faeries back to sanctuaries as privileged sites of pilgrimage, to sanctify the memory of those who had passed while making this activity key to renewing their collective nature, solidarity, and survival. As emplacements, sanctuaries sustained these qualities over the long periods when most Radical Faeries did not travel to experience them, making them crucial sites of cathexis where gay men could be assured that their nature and its integrity was maintained.

Memorials dotted the landscapes of sanctuaries I visited, teaching gatherers about the inheritance of present and future community. At one Wolf Creek gathering, while strolling a footpath behind the Barn I unexpectedly found myself before a large altar resting near the base of a big oak tree.

Boxes and planks covered with colorful fabrics ensconced photographs, toy figures, costume jewelry, note cards in Ziploc bags, and metal religious statues honoring a longtime Radical Faerie who had died recently from AIDS. At Short Mountain, many times I strolled from the central knoll along a wooded escarpment to a shaded clearing housing the sanctuary's memorial grove. Amid the many objects placed on the ground—personal mementos, small cairns of stones, fronds, and flowers—one rock, carefully tended and placed for ease of viewing, announced the anonymously carved message: "UNION. This place is dedicated to our holding together. 1985." This proclamation of solidarity against dissolution in the first years of the epidemic echoed when I met it in 1995 in a space long nurtured by the Short Mountain community.

Sanctuary gatherings also could include rituals in which participants experienced memorials as key sites maintaining community. At one Wolf Creek gathering, at the annual processional, gatherers circumambulated the meadow and visited each memorial site. In the afternoon twilight, a group of forty began the circuit to the beat of African and South Asian drums. The group first visited the land's oldest memorial, the pendulum, where a tripod suspended a stone under which for years the ashes of friends had been scattered. After some time, we walked a few hundred feet farther to a memorial garden planted originally by Oskrr, a longtime resident now deceased. At both sites, huddled in the evening chill, members of the group invoked Indigenous, pagan, and Radical Faerie spirits of the land, and told stories recalling old friends in moments of fun, sadness, or rage. The ritual concluded as the group walked under the stars around the meadow's far side to the Barn and tent, where a kitchen crew had laid out dinner. The processional linked participants by not presuming shared history or identity but narrating it, with memories of absent people joining invocations of a deeper spiritual context in a material union with the land where gatherers renewed their ties in community.

I observed sanctuary memorials cohere a dispersed constituency at the creation of the Wolf Creek bridge memorial. In early 1995, rains had swelled the creek and toppled the sanctuary's only access bridge. The organization Nomenus was emerging from a period when major gatherings had not occurred, although the most recent one was well attended. Nomenus leaders promoted raising funds to replace the bridge by establishing a memorial supported by donations in the names of Radical Faeries who had passed away. Many donations came in, including from old-time members who had not participated since the sanctuary's founding in the 1980s. Building the bridge joined with other efforts to enliven Nomenus and led to hundreds attending subsequent gatherings, in particular the 1996 midsummer gathering when the memorial was built. Its design and construction were led by a Radical Faerie who at the time spent part of the year in India following his chosen spiritual practices. Implementing a plan to fashion a cairn from hefty stones in the creek bed, the designer recruited people early in the gathering to carry stones up the short ravine and assemble them near the bridge. The stones encased a colorful central plaque fashioned by a Radical Faerie artist on which were inscribed names of people who had died, including, but not limited to, those for whom memorial donations had been received. During the gathering, as people visited the construction site or wandered past to or from their campsites, the artist invited them to leave items recalling absent friends that would be embedded in the mortar.

One day late in the gathering, scores of gatherers met to dedicate the memorial. Volunteers assembled the group on the far side of the new bridge, and then led us single file across the creek, while a young man softly played songs on his guitar. On stepping onto the land, each person received a red ochre mark on the forehead, which the artist had requested to sanctify our act as what he understood as a form of *puja*. The group then gathered to sit or stand around the cairn, its candle-lit central basin filled with water and flowers, the bright colors joining the plaque and embedded objects in reflection of the eclectic attire worn by this otherwise somber group. During a silent period before the leaders invited people to speak, many present wept singly or in small groups holding each other. Then, one after another, people rose to tell stories about those memorialized on the stone and others. Many repeated a theme that those who had passed were still present in the gathering's play of gender and desire, and they exhorted everyone to sustain and grow this community by drawing strength from their memory. Some speakers praised a power they sensed in the memorial, fashioned as it was of rocks from this land, while bonded to spiritual truths that they welcomed from other places. As silence returned, the leaders finally closed the ritual and led the group to dinner to share in the community whose roots had been renewed in this place.

In this scene and others, grappling with epidemic brought Radical Faeries home, when memorials and their collective ritualization materialized the sanctuary's promise of sacred refuge in Indigenous sexual nature. Memorials made Radical Faeries and sanctuary land one: in scatterings of ashes; by building memorials from the stuff of the land, which were then invested with local and world-traveling spiritualities; by making these memorials privileged sites for the memory of lost comrades; and by recognizing their place in a spiritual pantheon made proper to Indigenous land. Memorials dotting the landscape thus embodied a multigenerational community's union with rural, natural, and Indigenous truth. Recalling memorials focused an otherwise dispersed and mobile constituency on its ties to land in a way that assured their future communion. If that ever felt under threat, memorials became a means to invite pilgrimage to renew an ancestral community's survival and sustain this space that promised a home even in their absence. Memorials demonstrate how sanctuaries grounded dispersed constituencies and their mobile quests for Indigenous nature in eternal spiritual communion through originally Indigenous land.

Troubling Homecoming

The potentially fractious diversity of Radical Faeries is mediated by gathering subjectivity and its materialization at sanctuaries. Radical Faeries of color have argued that scenes like the ones I portrayed are racialized by the naturalization of whiteness in the global cultural diversity they invoke. Particularizing pagan Europe as a history inspired by Native America produces a white settler imaginary of counterculturism. Yet, if Radical Faeries of color as racialized non-Natives trouble this vision, they also negotiate their own inheritance of a relationship to settlement on Native land. Their critiques of whiteness and efforts to decolonize racialized sexuality still can employ colonial discourses on indigeneity that naturalize settlement when pursuing their liberation through Radical Faerie culture.

I open my troubling of Radical Faerie culture with an episode that, in its anomaly, was crucial to the day that I and others spent on the Short Mountain knoll. Not long after the Queer God ritual—the last of many quests for gay spirituality that we saw being led by white gay men—I and those near me noticed a lone figure emerge from the Barn. Arms undulating, the figure crouched and stepped slowly toward us, slowly revealing itself to be a naked person painted luminously blue through which glowed deep brown skin. Those near me recognized our comrade Genie, and looked bemused as he edged by our group with a fierce grin, all the while raising and waving his blue (and brown) arms above our seated heads, only to pass us by and disappear down the knoll into the forest, alone.

Many of us knew Genie as the only African American resident of Short Mountain at the time, and one of two black participants whom I knew to be at this gathering of more than two hundred people. An urban-based artist, Genie had relocated to the sanctuary, where he lived in a cabin decorated with his paintings and other art, including pieces crafted from materials on the land. I gathered from talking to him that he enjoyed his time at Short Mountain but that he did not consider Radical Faerie identity to be primary or that he had to retain it if he were to leave the land. He rarely hesitated to speak if he thought something required comment. For that reason, I interpreted his passage across the knoll to reflect an artistic playfulness and a pointed awareness of his location at this gathering. He performed gathering subjectivity by perhaps ritually invoking a spirit or blessing within Radical Faerie spirituality. Yet he also creased the flow of the day's otherwise collective events. His was the only solo performance that day, and the only one not led by a white person. He also did not invite anyone to join him, but left witnesses to ponder his offering. I knew that Genie regularly rejected projections onto him of African cultural authenticity, despite his personal interest in the ancestral roots of his queer spirituality. His performance thus stood out from ones that proclaimed an authentic racial or national location for gay nature. Genie conjured himself in a color divested of queer primitivity's racial spectrum, but its multiple tones of blue and brown ultimately revealed quantitatively more color, which remained differently framed than any other performance.

I hold this image in mind to tease out three critical readings of the locations of Radical Faeries of color. I contend that queer people of color negotiate Radical Faerie culture by marking and displacing whiteness, and furthermore that they explore sexual and spiritual possibilities by creatively adapting the primitivism in circulation around them in ways that displace normatively white desires for cultural authenticity. Yet I also suggest that continuing to link queerness to primitivity invests Radical Faeries of color in a unique inheritance of a settler colonial relationship to Native peoples and land.

Radical Faeries of color regularly remarked on the racialization of space at rural gatherings, as well as in urban Faerie circles. An extended account of this topic in the San Francisco region and at Wolf Creek appeared in a 1992 essay by Gryphon Blackswan, a longtime member of the Santa Cruz Radical Faerie circle. Blackswan told of the end of his time as a Wolf Creek resident after incidents of harassment by town residents whose targeting of him as a black gay man led him to "flee physical attack, vehicular intimidation and the general terror which had come to be my daily life in rural southern Oregon."[23] His comment reveals that if Radical Faerie promises of rural sanctuary do not entirely protect gay men from homophobia, they do not even name the potential intersections of homophobia with racism faced by gay men of color. The white gay founders of Short Mountain and Wolf Creek fought stereotypes of the homophobic hinterlands, but neither arose in explicit challenge to the normative whiteness or sustained legacies of antiblack and anti-Native racism in rural central Tennessee and the southern Cascades. If queers of color visited these regions, they were confronted with new contexts to experience racial violence that Radical Faerie culture, as a project of gender and sexual liberation, was not equipped to address. Blackswan framed his retreat from Wolf Creek back to urban California as a critique of white queer complicity with racism, as the title of his essay suggests: "It's a Shame We Don't Have More People of Color Participating." On his return, he felt a "sense of abandonment by the community of faeries I lived with":

> As I tried to emerge from my aloof solitude and began to explore queer Santa Cruz I was treated to a hero's welcome by the local faeries and found a deeply loving community. But . . . and it's a big reservation! I found a white community repeatedly assuring me "It's a shame . . ." My reflexive fear response left me distant and unwilling to engage. (27)

Blackswan suggests that white Radical Faeries expressed a desire to live in multiracial space, while deflecting responsibility for forming a white space that produces the absence they regret. Blackswan continues:

> I can see now what prevents queers with a strong ethnic identity from joining with faggots and dykes. Generally, to do so means to lose some or all of the support for dealing with the recurring presence of racism in this culture. If white queers can't support their rainbow-hued sisters and brothers when we face racism, we will either remain where we do get support, or move like pastel phantoms through queer life. What's more, if we can't tell you when we smell racism in your attitudes, we won't let you get close enough to hurt us. It's only common sense. (28)

Echoing queer of color critiques of queer whiteness in the United States and Canada at this time, Blackswan intimated that it *is* a shame if people of color avoid a camaraderie they otherwise might seek because white queers fail to act as antiracist allies.

Radical Faeries of color later gathered to foster ally work at a 1999 gathering at Short Mountain by forming Faeries of All Colors Together (FACT).[24] FACT facilitated discussions, writing, and public actions at rural gatherings and among Radical Faeries in New York City. A key theme was that racism and classism shaped cities and rural regions to preclude working-class and urban people of color from finding their way to Radical Faerie culture.

FACT's analysis remained committed to Radical Faerie culture. Named similarly to the interracial gay organization Men of All Colors Together (MACT), FACT echoed MACT's position that racial inclusion in gay space allows camaraderie to heal racism among men of color and white men. In this model, racism manifests in people of color being constrained from participating in Radical Faerie culture, not in the culture facilitating racialized colonial discourses. FACT fostered antiracism precisely by affirming loving solidarity as a means for queer people to cross racial differences in realization of a shared sexual and spiritual nature. Critically engaging racialization among Radical Faeries thus highlights the racial implications of primitivism. If white Radical Faeries seek cultural authenticity through European neo-paganism or a generic queer indigeneity, they tend not to recognize the racism in primitivist and sexualized objectifications of people of color. Yet, conversely, Genie, Blackswan, and members of FACT among other queers of color adapt Radical Faerie primitivism to address their experiences of heterosexism and racism, along two routes. First, playing on and in queer primitivism exposes the colonial discourses projected upon them as queers of color, albeit while being unable to control how their performances are consumed in normatively white space. Second, they also invest in Radical Faerie culture to achieve a distinctive sexual and spiritual decolonization, such that their adaptation of a white settler queer primitivism may sustain its settler colonial logics in their lives.

Reflecting on the first route, one evening at Short Mountain a few days after the day on the knoll, I was sitting with a handful of others awaiting dinner in the Library. This room in the land's original house embodied a counterculturist homestead, with old wooden carpentry lining cozy bookshelved nooks packed with antiquated texts and cushioned chairs illuminated by lamps. I sat reading amid murmurs around me that invoked gathering culture: the leader of the Queer God ritual speaking with friends about the suffering of another from AIDS; beside me, the second self-identified African American man whom I knew to be at the gathering, besides Genie, chatting with a white friend about people in the city where they lived. Into the room walked one of the three cisgender women, and the only woman of color whom I knew to be at this gathering. Hips cocked, she stood and raised a serving tray with an arch smile, announcing "Appetizers?" The hungry gatherers responded with gratitude over the cubes of tofu in tamari and sesame oil she had prepared. As she moved about the room I was in awe of her proud performance of Radical Faerie culture: the metallic glitter and bright pastel body paint decorating her body contrasted with her brown face and shoulders, while her bare chest marked her difference from the many hairy chests and male genitalia visible at the gathering. Nevertheless, her partial nudity performed the self-love that Radical Faerie culture invites for the body. I read her choice of silky pantaloons as an effort by a South Asian woman to act in and against Orientalist imagery of Asian female sensuality, just as camping up a racialized domestic role became a means to assert her authority in Radical Faerie space while simultaneously performing egalitarian communalism. My reverie was shaken as she approached the two men nearest me. The white one took her in with appreciation and a glad smile and, leaning in to get a snack, softly said, "Oh! I feel like I'm in some exotic restaurant!" For a second it seemed that his mock belief in her play on the alien servant role would slide. But she paused, and looked down at him; and his friend paused, mouth open as if unsure what to say. But then she moved on, as at least some of us noted how the speaker's "joke"—or sincere reflection—marked a power within which everyone busily played, but that in this case seemed to make her play serve his.

This moment reminds me of the dilemmas in spaces that queerly perform racial and colonial discourses. My account implicitly invokes José Esteban Muñoz theorizing disidentification for queers of color as a mode of troubling false choices between separatism and assimilation by critically engaging the terms of dominant discourses.[25] I am reminded of Jana Braziel's reading of the drag performance of Dréd/Mildred Gerestant as portrayed in Gabriel Baur's *Venus Boyz* (2001).[26] Braziel rejects readings of Dréd's performance as either a celebratory liberation of black masculinity or a recirculation of racial stereotype for a white gaze. For Braziel, Dréd's performance critically inhabits blaxpolitation imagery of black masculinities to force white audiences to confront their racialized desires while exceeding them by manifesting desires for gender-queer black subjectivity. I read the scene in the Library similarly, except that here the primitivism that Radical Faeries promote as a route to freedom leaves queers of color open to projections of its racism. For Genie, as in the Library, practicing gathering subjectivity led to exhibiting the naked body, but precisely by defying a white naturist belief that the unclothed body is emptied of social meaning: by creatively using color and comportment to force audiences to consider the racialization of skin and the capacity to performatively rearticulate it. Neither scene performed an authentic primitivity, but rather adapted colonial stereotypes for critical witnessing by white Radical Faeries, as well as by *themselves* and by one another as queers of color.

Of course, the flip side to primitivism as hegemony for Radical Faeries of color is its ability to be adapted to their own liberation, as suggested by oral accounts of people of color participating in Radical Faerie culture from its earliest years. While Radical Faeries of color often critique white racism, they have tended not to regard the route to Indigenous gay nature through European neo-paganism as inherently oppressive. That model presumes Indigenous sexualities and spiritualities as primal to all queers, so that a distinctive form analogous to berdache will appear in every person's cultural or racial heritage. Radical Faeries of color can adapt this model to find roles that are unique to their heritage while still linked to a general Radical Faerie principle. For instance, in 1990 Henry Holmes profiled Radical Faerie culture in the black gay and lesbian magazine *BLK*, and called it a space where black gay men can explore the spiritual qualities of being gay and argue for their embrace in black communities.[27] In another essay, "Searching for My Gay Spiritual Roots," Blackberri says that "as an African-American gay man, I have no desire to embrace cultural, spiritual, or religious roots that are not my own. I have sought out my ancient roots and I am proud of my discovery."[28] He says that his roots are not drawn from, nor should they be claimed by, anyone who does not share his heritage. Yet even this defense of cultural specificity, in the context of Radical Faerie culture, is premised on belief in a universal Indigenous queer nature. Even if Radical Faeries agree only to perform roles that are "racially appropriate" to them, any such performance will affirm the belief inspired by imaginaries of berdache that a common Indigenous nature runs through them. Here, antiracism in the form of a critique of cultural appropriation is compatible with white settler queer primitivism defining white queers and queers of color as non-Natives discovering their truths by imagining Native American and, by extrapolation, their own Indigenous roots. Of course, if men of color like Holmes and Blackberri use Radical Faerie culture to assert their belonging to *another* community—for them, the black community—they differ from white gay men who claim their primordial European or global Indigenous heritage to belong only to the Radical Faeries. In this sense, gay men of color may be positioned less like white gay men and more like Native gay and Two-Spirit men who wish to achieve belonging to Native nations. But if gay men of color identify with the white settler queer primitivism of Radical Faerie identity, then their racial and sexual liberations may track the routes of white colonial desires.

This possibility returns in Blackswan's account, after he finds renewed homecoming through Radical Faerie community and Native American spirituality. After withdrawing for a time from the Radical Faeries, he was drawn out again by attending a sweat lodge. He does not say who hosted this lodge, and it is not described as a Radical Faerie activity, but the apparent absence of Native people, its mixed-gender composition, and its therapeutic use for emotional communication mark it as a non-Native practice. The ritual allowed him to purge accumulated stress and achieve a powerful resolution:

> As the bile and sulfur poured forth . . . one brave white woman silenced all the participants urging me to trust them, aborted their efforts to deflect the discussion into the safety of abstraction, and waved away all hands seeking to soothe my savage breast. With a level gaze she chanted "I hear you," as decades of bitter pain and flaming anger erupted from me.[29]

The moment ends with her simply holding him and repeating, "I hear you, I hear you" (27). Having "unleashed my demons," Blackswan says the experience inspired him to renew his ties to the communities he had left, including by returning to join the Radical Faerie caretakers at Wolf Creek. He ends by recalling that "I had a wonderful time with my faerie brothers and left feeling even more hopeful" (28).

Blackswan's account locates Native America as a spiritual and emotional medium he traverses as a black gay man to heal racism and heterosexism so that he can rejoin a non-Native community that emulates Native spirituality. Scholars of the historical interdependence of Native Americans and African Americans argue that efforts to recall it infuse black subjectivities quite distinctly from white desires for Native roots, and should inform how we read narratives like Blackswan's that do not explicitly state any tie to Native heritage.[30] Yet, by attempting to form ties from within an apparently white appropriation of Native spirituality, Blackswan's healing from racism and his experience of white antiracism are enabled by perpetuating the frame of white settler colonial desires. His return to Wolf Creek finally suggests that his journey is mediated by the sanctuary's promise of healing through ties to Native land. With the myth of protection and communion at the sanctuary already disturbed, Blackswan never lives there permanently again. Thus, with the landed ritual of the sweat lodge as a trigger, his visit to Wolf Creek seems less a wish to rejoin Radical Faerie community than a desire to access the *sanctuary*'s landed method of linking non-Native queers to Indigenous gay nature. Although he ends by warning that racism remains a deal breaker, his use of Native ritual to affirm shared Indigenous roots does connect non-Natives across race to make indigeneity a condition of their mutual liberation. Critiquing whiteness and healing racism remain compatible with naturalizing settlement among queers of color if their goal is to join a queer modernity that locates the Indigenous peoples of the lands where they live in the past so as to let them realize a non-Native future of liberation.

Negotiating Friendship

Radical Faerie efforts to realize Indigenous gay nature transformed during the 1990s when they increasingly sought to collaborate with Native gay and Two-Spirit men. I now trace how such ties grew in the 1990s in relationship to Two-Spirit organizing. Native gay men were increasingly cultivating spiritual leadership as Two-Spirit people in Native communities, and Radical Faeries sought to learn from them. Some Native gay and Two-Spirit men found it useful to hold Radical Faeries responsible to their independent work to renew traditional spirituality in their nations. At times, the intimacy of their exchanges could appear to be attempts to indigenize Radical Faeries or to locate Two-Spirit spirituality within a non-Native queer spirituality movement. Yet Native gay and Two-Spirit men answered invitations to collaborate with Radical Faeries by clarifying their differences and then applying that work to pursuing their leadership as Two-Spirit people in Native communities pursuing forms of decolonization. Their very proximities can be read as signs of non-Native and Native queer modernities forming distinctly in relationship, in particular by conversation on the terms and implications of their "friendship."

I have experienced Radical Faerie space as not only predominantly white but distinctly non-Native. On those occasions when I met Native people, I heard them identify not as Radical Faeries so much as old friends of Radical Faerie community. Similarly, I understood Radical Faeries who seek ties to Native gay and Two-Spirit men not to be asking that they join and claim a Radical Faerie identity, but that they interact precisely as a *difference* that Radical Faeries desire. Maintaining the specificity of Two-Spirit (correlated here to berdache) sustains the focal point around which all global and transhistorical extrapolations of gay nature are made—a function that would be lost if Two-Spirit, among all other evidences of indigeneity, did not remain *different from* the amalgamated identity of a Radical Faerie. I observed this reinforcement of difference when Radical Faeries described their ties to Native gay men in the language of friendship, which suggests that they cross a meaningful difference in order to enter into relationship. And Native gay and Two-Spirit men who interacted with Radical Faeries invoked friendship, differently; friendship was a way that they affirmed how non-Natives have supported them while still holding them accountable to work for Indigenous decolonization. The logic of friendship placed Radical Faeries and Native gay men in conversation, but its meanings and effects differed for each group. Importantly, their friendship interactions increasingly brought Radical Faeries to admit their non-Native locations in a settler society and to hold themselves responsible to Native people as critics of colonialism.

During the late 1990s, the stories of friendship I witnessed most among Native gay men and Radical Faeries referenced Harry Hay. Will Roscoe, Walter Williams, Sue-Ellen Jacobs, and other non-Native scholars recognized Hay's collection of anthropological and sexual minority writing on berdache as a key resource for their work. When communicating with Native gay men about Radical Faeries, I often witnessed gestures of respect for Hay, as well as for scholars such as Jacobs or Lakota anthropologist Beatrice Medicine, for the years in which they attended to the historical knowledge Native queer people later reclaimed at a time when racism and heterosexism left them with few allies. At times I heard Native gay men also cite a story linking their affirmations of Hay's friendship to a moment in his youth when he met the Shoshone and Paiute religious prophet Wovoka. I also heard this story from Radical Faeries, with somewhat different implications, after it appeared in Will Roscoe's 1996 collection of Hay's writings, *Radically Gay: Gay Liberation in the Words of Its Founder.* Its opening chapter, "How Did He Know?" describes how as a young man Hay lived one summer in Nevada near a Shoshone and Paiute gathering, which he felt drawn to visit. On arrival, participants at the gathering brought him to be introduced to Wovoka, who spoke with him for some time and then touched him on the forehead, saying "You will be a friend." The implications drawn from this story by Radical Faeries included that Wovoka had recognized Hay as a Two-Spirit person, and that this granted all Radical Faeries permission to recognize themselves as comparable or even equivalent to Two-Spirit people. In contrast, when I heard Native gay men tell this story—one that was apparently known to them before Roscoe's book—their statements of deep respect for Wovoka and his leadership affirmed Hay as important to their work to recall Two-Spirit traditions and reestablish their own belonging as Native people within their nations. Wovoka's affirmation of Hay's friendship indicated to them that his acts would benefit *Native* people, not non-Natives—and not that the latter were therefore authorized to adopt Native culture. The multiple retellings of this story mark the nonidentical locations and stakes of Radical Faeries and Native gay and Two-Spirit men, even as the retellings surfaced precisely in discussing their mutual relationship to Hay.

Both mutual ties and distinctions appear when Native gay men communicate with non-Native proponents of queer spirituality. For instance, Mark Thompson's *Gay Soul* (1994), a collection of interviews with fifteen white theorists of gay spirituality includes an interview Thompson specifically sought with Clyde M. Hall, founding GAI member and contributor to *Living the Spirit*. As a chronicler of Radical Faerie culture, Thompson learned in the early 1990s that Hall was among the Native gay and Two-Spirit men studying traditional religion and accepting forms of spiritual leadership in their nations. Hall's autobiographical writing tells how during his time with GAI he remained linked to the Shoshone-Bannock reservation where he was raised, and where he returned to work as a tribal magistrate during the 1980s. His participation in Native queer community inspired him to come out back home and integrate a Two-Spirit identity specific to Shoshone culture into his participation in Shoshone community. This included receiving from his aunt the authority to renew and lead the Shoshone Naraya dance.[31] The Naraya had not been danced since the 1930s. With renewed interest in traditional religion in the 1970s during the heyday of the American Indian Movement (AIM), the dance keepers introduced Hall and other Shoshone youth to the dance, only to retire it once again. In the 1990s, Hall accepted responsibility to renew and lead the Naraya in his Shoshone community and as a means to link Shoshone and other Native peoples in the Great Basin and beyond.[32] Hall presented the Naraya as "A Dance for All Peoples" that could grow by placing Native people of many nations and non-Natives under the direction of its Shoshone leaders. Religious leadership brought Hall new visibility among Native queer people in Two-Spirit organizing. Some affirmed his work as renewing traditional spiritual leadership or Two-Spirit people, while others criticized him for allowing non-Natives to participate and questioned if this marketed Native culture for non-Native consumption.[33] Hall's work also drew attention from non-Native gay men, and led Thompson to include Hall in his profiles of leaders of gay spirituality.

In the interview with Hall, Thompson's questions promote themes common to non-Native queer spirituality movements, which Hall engages while offering alternative viewpoints reflecting the perspectives of Native people.

Thompson invites Hall to tell his life story by choosing words that clearly condition what Hall will say within a set of assumptions: that a gay social minority exists in all human societies; that it expresses a spirituality all gay men must learn if they wish to know their true selves; and that the "social constructionism" promoted by academics is inimical to this truth.[34] Without directly contradicting any of Thompson's assumptions, Hall deflects the directions Thompson sets out by beginning his answers in other places and arriving at distinct conclusions. Hall's recollections of his life repeatedly reference the effects on Shoshone and other Native peoples of living in a settler colonial situation: growing up with extended family on the reservation; facing white racism, and its internalization in his life and among other Native gay men; and overcoming this by "having a connection with . . . pride in oneself," which Hall traces to support by his family, GAI, and recognized leadership in Shoshone community (123). At several points, Thompson asks Hall to explain how gay Shoshone people on the reservation live distinctive lives—implying that he wants to hear about how they might perform a traditional gay role. Hall responds by situating Shoshone gay men's lives in contemporary social conditions, notably in struggles with self-acceptance. He suggests that Shoshone gay men and lesbians might connect to unique roles in Shoshone religion, but if they did so they would not all be taking a single role or path (ibid.). By the end of the interview, Hall has stated that traditional roles existed for masculine women and feminine men in Shoshone culture, and that these persons had access to distinctive forms of spiritual insight (125). But his words do not directly validate Thompson's efforts to propose and generalize a universal gay nature for non-Natives. Rather, all his responses situate Shoshone people's experiences specifically within the distinctive contexts of Shoshone national culture and their struggles amid ongoing colonization.

This contrasting effect is particularly apparent when Hall replies to Thompson's final question, "What can non-Indian gay men learn from gay Indian traditions or beliefs that would be of most value to them?":

> The most important thing is survival. Survival as a community. Survival in a spiritual sense, individually and collectively. Indian people, of course, were devastated a hundred years ago by diseases and warfare. At one point we were called the vanishing American. But we're still here. And that's what gay men have to think about, what with AIDS, political unrest, and fighting for basic rights. Spirit willing we as gay people will still be here a hundred years from now, and we will look back at what we've done to make it. (130)

Gay Indians appear here not as "traditions" or "beliefs" (in Thompson's words) but as constituents of Native peoples who survived and still resist colonization. The lesson for non-Native gay men is taught by Native peoples *collectively*, and by Native gay men as members of their nations. Hall further indicates that the issues facing non-Native gay men today also are faced by him, except that he locates the AIDS crisis and New Right homophobia as qualities of a *settler colonial* society that created health inequalities and political backlash in ways that distinctly confront Native and non-Native gay men. His words allow for flexibility in the pronoun *we*, which first references "Indian people" collectively ("we're still here") and only subsequently invokes "we as gay people" needing to survive in a time when "we will look back at what we've done to make it." The link Hall finally offers "Indian people" and "gay people" is a lesson in survival: Natives who survived a genocide brought by non-Natives remain to educate non-Native gay men in surviving their endangerment by studying settler colonialism and Native resistance. His responses to Thompson's effort to place Native gay men within a global and transnational gay spirituality are neither primordial nor authenticating, but historicizing. These distinctions arise in an attempt to converse within a space of mutual regard and potential friendship. In this exchange, non-Native gay men adapt the words of Native gay men to their desires for Indigenous nature, while Native gay men engage those desires by inviting non-Native gay men into new accountability in their work for decolonization.

The difference among historicizing tales of Native survival and colonial desires for Indigenous truth informed how Radical Faeries and Two-Spirit people interacted in the 1990s. I first met Native gay men seeking out Radical Faeries with an offer of religious leadership in 1999. Near the winter solstice, the Santa Cruz Radical Faerie circle invited Marten, an old friend of some members, to join them for a few days to reconnect. Marten had lived nearby before returning to work with his tribal community, yet some local Radical Faeries said that he had faced homophobia there. Recently, he had asked friends for help in affirming his sense of spiritual belonging to his culture by creating space for him to practice his religious leadership. Arrangements were made for him to lead a sweat lodge for Radical Faeries and friends. The evening event drew nearly forty people to one participant's property outside town. As I drove up to the oak-crowned knolls of the land owned by our host, I saw in the twilight dozens of Radical Faeries dressed in varieties of working professional or hippie attire. Some cleared a circle on level ground below the house's hilltop perch, where a lodge was being built on a frame of staked branches, and a fire was stoked by Marten and the assistant he had chosen for this task, Jorge, a guest who lived on the host's property. As night fell, Marten called on those gathered to stand in a circle. Marten asked Jorge to bless the ceremony in the name of his Central American Indigenous ancestors. Those few not joining the sweat, myself included, took supporting roles that ranged from guarding the lodge entrance to cooking and preparing for dinner in the house. After the ritual ended, participants retired to the house to drink water and eat; some brought out drums for a spontaneous jam session. As I moved through this crowd, it struck me that the event had lifted Marten's spirits, even as it clearly inspired many Radical Faeries. Some spoke about how this retreat into Native religion had bonded them together or brought them closer to a sense of gay nature. One spoke his hope that the local Radical Faeries would honor what Marten had shared by hosting another time a "faerie lodge" as a new method to explore gay spirituality. The idea circulated enough in conversation that some people went home that night thinking that Marten's departure might not mean this would be the last such event they would enjoy.

The evening's end highlighted the ease with which Radical Faeries—in each case, white gay men—casually appropriated Native cultural and, specifically, religious practices as routes to discovering their own Indigenous gay nature. This was compatible with, and depended on, Marten's occupying the distinct social location of a Two-Spirit man within an extant Native American community. Yet Marten also asserted this distinction, differently, by having approached Radical Faeries not as one of them, but as their friend, and with the purpose of defying homophobia by reaffirming his connection to the traditions of his people and his religious leadership as a Two-Spirit person. He did this through the traveling ritual form of the sweat lodge, which already linked to his tribe on the Great Basin's edge through long-standing routes of cultural exchange, even as it had gained renewed significance in its recent circulation within pantribal Native religious and health movements. Marten's role as a spiritual leader and the tools he used to practice it announced historical, not primordial, ties among Native peoples. In turn, the pantribal qualities of the ritual enabled him to form a connection with Jorge and affirm each other's Indigenous heritage across Jorge's potential exclusion from this when racialized as Latino. Marten thus negotiated Radical Faerie interests in him toward his own ends, even if his choosing to do so presented Radical Faeries with an opportunity to turn his interests toward theirs. Marten made Radical Faerie desires a context for negotiating his marginality as a Native gay man in Native society by attempting to hold non-Native gay men responsible to his traditional religious leadership while drawing other gay men of Indigenous American heritage into shared roles.

Near the end of my research, friendships among Radical Faeries and Native gay men nurtured collaborations that were situated by assertions of Native sovereignty. For example, when Harry Hay in his advanced age received recognitions from people who long had held him in respect, they included a public gesture from Clyde Hall. In honor of Hay's life and work, Hall offered to lead the Naraya with other Shoshone and Native dance leaders at the Wolf Creek sanctuary in 1999. This event was not advertised as a Radical Faerie gathering; those who attended were admitted on Hall's approval. Despite my involvement with Radical Faeries in California, I and others heard nothing about the Naraya being danced at Wolf Creek until after it had happened. Even then, I was struck by how little we were told: casual references seemed thirdhand, or arose only while discussing other topics. I found this especially surprising given the event's significance as, to my knowledge, the first time a Radical Faerie sanctuary had hosted Two-Spirit people in a religious ceremony currently practiced within a Native nation. Given that this could represent for Radical Faeries a fulfillment of what so many desired, something seemed to have shifted in its narration. I heard that the dance leaders had stated that the dance was not being given to Radical Faeries to practice or to inspire any other invention. By joining, participants respected the Shoshone and other Native dance leaders by honoring the dance as sacred and not for discussion or repetition outside of that space. As a result, for the first time, I heard among Radical Faeries an articulate silence about a quality of Native culture that they desired. I also noticed increased discussion among Radical Faeries about their being non-Natives who bore a responsibility to Native people not to usurp Native culture. This sharply contrasted with the ongoing practice of gathering, which still promised Radical Faeries access to Indigenous gay nature by adopting anything anyone met and shared that suggested it. Similarly, identifying as non-Natives responsible to Native people did not stop Radical Faeries from desiring to experience Native culture; if anything, being invited to participate and accepting this invitation affirmed that desire. But these Radical Faerie qualities did arise on new terms: as acts by non-Natives accountable to Native people asserting sovereignty over Native culture within the power relations of a settler colonial society. Whether or not Radical Faeries recognized its implications, their call to accountability positioned them in a new relationship to life on Native land. From a naturalized non-Native formation pursuing colonial desires through theses of Native disappearance and transcendence, Radical Faeries became a project marked as non-Native in a settler society that needed to situate its definitions of Native culture in relation to Native interlocutors. I am not suggesting that Radical Faerie cultural practices changed fundamentally. Rather, these moments appear to be signs of a potential epistemic shift, in relation to which present and future accounts may ask to what extent a responsibility to Native work for decolonization leads to troubling colonial desires for queerness, modernity, or indigeneity or to denaturalizing the relationship of Radical Faeries to settlement.

I recount these events to emphasize that whatever relationships or effects they denote arose when Radical Faeries and Native gay men negotiated their nonidentical work within conversations on "friendship." While Radical Faerie culture views Two-Spirit as a primordial and desired cultural difference, Native gay men differentiate themselves by grounding their lives in the defense of Native nations and the pursuit of decolonization, even in their closest and most "friendly" interactions with Radical Faeries. Holding Radical Faeries accountable to this does nothing necessarily to address or question the colonial desires motivating their relationship or shaping their work with Native gay men. Nevertheless, whatever other effects were produced by their interactions, they arose when Native gay and Two-Spirit men pursued traditional leadership as Two-Spirit people in their nations and in broader Native alliances. In this context, even Marten's and Hall's efforts to contact Radical Faeries announced their prior and primary adherence to a responsibility as Two-Spirit men to the survival and decolonization of Native communities. This divergence in the grounding, articulation, and effects of Radical Faerie and Two-Spirit practices marks their meetings as moments in larger conversations articulating non-Native and Native queer subjects within the power relations of ongoing settler colonialism.

Chapter 5 Global Desires and Transnational Solidarity
Negotiating Indigeneity among the Worlds of Queer Politics

SETTLER COLONIALISM CONDITIONS THE GLOBAL PROJECTIONS of U.S. queer modernities. In the context of white settler society, queer projects propose a global scope by naturalizing their inheritance of settlement and then projecting a desired indigeneity worldwide. This configuration of settler colonial and global power is informed by queer theories of coloniality and globalization, but the specificity of settler colonialism has not yet been theorized. Scholars have portrayed Western queer projects as a (neo)colonial globalizing force dominating local sexualities, or postcolonial queers as distinctly engaging colonial legacies and Western politics without being assimilated.[1] Transnational feminist and queer diasporic critics trace how local creativity and global constraints cause colonial complicities to be inherent to queer postcoloniality even while inciting critical agency.[2] These readings meaningfully inform an account of settler colonialism and queer modernities while being resituated. The biopolitics of settler colonialism results from global political and economic processes, which displace Native peoples in diasporas on Native lands, and form a transnational proving ground *within* settler societies to produce a white settler state for imperial projection abroad. In this context, non-Native queer modernities reconcile to settlement by incorporating Native history as aspects of a general primitivity, while transcending this through settler citizenship's civilizational advancements. These acts grant non-Native queers a global purview, by projecting them along the twinned global scales of primitive roots and civilizational futures, all of which return them to negotiating their settler colonial inheritance of Native culture and land. Native critics recognize queer globalisms as settler colonial projects. Making indigeneity a cipher for the global hegemonies of borderless subjects positions Native peoples in the past so that settlers can inherit a globalized world in which settler colonialism remains naturalized. In contrast, Native queer activists formed movements along

161

linked national *and* transnational routes that draw Natives and non-Natives into solidarities amid the power relations of settler colonialism and the globalizations that it conditions.

The formation of U.S. queer projects as simultaneous arbiters of colonial and global power is explained by Jasbir Puar's critique of homonationalism. Puar indicates that U.S. queer subjects marshal the civilizational project of national whiteness to project (neo)colonial rule over queered subjects and populations worldwide, in an analysis anticipated and affirmed by the work of Jacqui Alexander and Katie King.[3] Such work inspires my efforts to mark homonationalism as a settler colonial project, within an analysis that scholars can pursue in at least two directions. In one, we may ask how U.S. queer projections of national whiteness perform settler colonialism, by making human rights, tourism, or the media global arenas to assert or protect queer embrace by the settler state, or to form relationships to queer subjects worldwide that recapitulate colonial logics. I am interested in such accounts, but I wish to complement such theories of civilizational queer globalism in another direction by examining globalism's appearance within primitivity. U.S. queer modernities become homonationalist in the horizon of settler politics by adapting the oppositionality of indigeneity to argue queer belonging to sexual modernity and settler citizenship. In this process, "civilizationalism" and "primitivism" are complementary inflections of colonial modernity and its globalism. Colonial modernity may be critiqued by targeting its civilizational commitments, but its processes will not cease so long as commitments to primitivity remain unexamined. Queers can align with primitivism when asserting progressive or radical opposition to homonationalism as conservatism. But in an analysis of settler colonialism, this also arises within the political horizon of a settler society. When acting as settlers, queer radicals produce homonationalist effects as readily as the political conservatives they oppose.

I examine the homonationalist implications of queer radicalism by adapting Chela Sandoval's reading of late-modern globalization as having destabilized the modernist foundations of "First World citizens subjects," once a postmodern economy detaches culture from essence in new modes of circulation.[4] In this context, as Philip Deloria also explains, indigeneity circulates among counterculturists as a site of political oppositionality.[5] Deloria indicates that settler primitivism already permits liberating indigeneity from specificity to let settlers reconcile to settlement. Sandoval locates this in the power relations of late-modern globalization, where queer primitivists become homonationalist by pursuing a globalism that leaves their settler formation unexamined. Their politics of primitivity then generally grants modern queers a means to engage the power relations of globalization by reconciling to inheriting settlement. I explain multiple histories of white settler queer primitivism as modes of globalizing U.S. queer modernities. I then articulate them with the decolonial work of diasporic queers of color, whose creative engagements with national and global queer liberations engage white settler queer primitivism, and raise the question of how they disrupt or reinstate its settler colonial logic. Transnational Native queer and Two-Spirit activism clarifies this question by articulating queer politics of primitivity so as to displace its settler colonial logic, while inviting potential queer allies across national locations into transnational solidarity with Native queer people.

Settler Globalism and Queer Primitivism

Radical Faeries in the City

The reputation of Radical Faeries as icons of queer primitivism hinges on their appearance as a radical fringe to queer projects that border on assimilation within a heteronormative society. Radical Faeries launch this critique from their distinctive proximity to rural communalism. Up to now I have read their rural ties as the meaningful center of a shared culture, but their desires for rural emplacement read more complexly—for Radical Faeries and the queer spaces they intersect—once they are known to have originated in cities. After 1979, a dispersal of participants from the first gathering generated regional networks in or near the urban centers where most participants lived. Here, "faerie circles" planned future gatherings, and over time many acquired sanctuary lands to support them.[6] Planning gatherings and managing sanctuaries from afar sustained Radical Faerie culture over the long periods when most participants lived far away from rural life. As a result, a critical mass of practitioners from the inception of Radical Faerie culture experienced it primarily as an urban phenomenon. In the process, Radical Faeries in cities have acted much like other queer primitivists: as conduits for the urban queer constituencies from which they are drawn and in which they live to discover a queer indigeneity that— I now emphasize—also projects a global purview for their queer cultures and politics.

While practicing ethnography with Radical Faeries in the San Francisco area, I came to see how participants' urban lives made sense amid stories of a rural base. Radical Faerie narratives suggest that authentic gay nature realized at rural gatherings is endangered by an inauthenticity in urban life. In cities, Radical Faeries endeavor to sustain a shared experience understood to be properly realized far away, even while they extol any success at creating it in a context that appears inimical to it. But if they do succeed, then the culture they create becomes, in fact, a product of urban life, completing a circle from its original urban imagining. Radical Faerie subjectivity thus is defined by perpetual deferrals of its creation of "rural" culture within and for urban space, without requiring rural retreat. Urban queers tap into Radical Faerie identity to discover all that the rural appears to signify as a route to realizing queer nature. On this basis, I understand Radical Faerie subjectivity to produce subjects in a state of perpetual transit along the spatial and temporal scales of modern sexuality, which seeks lost origins for its own progress. Those scales also describe a globalized world of primitive sexual and gender differences, just as among Radical Faeries in the United States they reference Native roots in relation to which queer worlds are being imagined.

In large and small cities of the San Francisco Bay Area, I met Radical Faerie community in the work of creating the ethos of rural gathering within and for urban life. Radical Faerie culture manifested whenever participants met one another or their friends in everyday life. I often ran across gay men whom I knew from gatherings or urban circles in accidental meetings while walking the streets or shopping at markets, or on being invited to lunch or dinner by local groups of friends. Common experience with Radical Faerie culture also linked many gay men I knew in shared households or employment. Radical Faeries often brought each other and friends out to experience urban queer culture, from drag productions to new independent films. Each summer in Santa Cruz in the mid-1990s, a fluctuating network of gay men who knew one another from Radical Faerie contexts reconnected at a weekly gay men's beach volleyball event advertised in local queer media. In San Francisco's Castro district, a gay man friendly to Radical Faeries outfitted his house as a space for sex parties, and Radical Faeries from the region were among those who regularly attended or hosted events. On my first visit to this space, I was struck by being welcomed at the door by two twenty-something men sporting brightly dyed punk haircuts, whom up to then I had known only from gatherings in Tennessee, but who, it turned out, lived nearby. The first floor of this house brought me not to a space for sex but to well-lit areas for conversation, near the kitchen vegetable-and-dip tray and patio hot tub, where a talkative crowd introduced me to local Radical Faeries, some of whom I did not yet know.

In cities around the Bay Area, I found Radical Faeries among the invitees to annual garden parties hosted at the homes of well-connected gay men. My first invitations to such events came not from any prior link to their hosts but from gay men I knew from Radical Faerie contexts. Their invitations were one of my key means to be introduced to gay men prominent in regional business, electoral politics, and nonprofit organizing whom I otherwise might not have known, and whose work crucially informed my accounts of queer politics in Santa Cruz and the San Francisco Bay Area more broadly.

The participation of Radical Faeries in urban queer communities included taking roles in joint activism and investing them with Radical Faerie values. I knew many Radical Faeries who worked as social-service professionals in city or county health departments, or as businessmen or entrepreneurs, and who took public leadership roles in local queer activism. Although their participation was not dissimilar from that of their colleagues, theirs reflected Radical Faerie culture if they critiqued normative qualities of urban life or promoted ancient or natural spirituality as an alternative. Such claims grew in the late 1990s when one regional faerie circle received funds to host a summer camp for queer youth. Framed by HIV and suicide prevention models that fostered self-esteem, the hosts presented Radical Faerie culture as a way to cultivate a healing queer identity by living in harmony with nature, practicing emotional communication, and exploring queer spirituality. Because the camp required sponsors to gain insurance coverage through the local LGBT community center, sponsoring the faerie camp turned this particular faerie circle from what had been an ad hoc friendship network into one of the community center's formal 501c3 affiliate organizations authorized to provide urban social services. In these and more ways, Radical Faeries created their culture and community throughout the seasons of the year as constitutive parts of urban queer organizing, and at times as key representatives.

All such public work rested, however, on urban faerie circles sustaining intimate community among gay men and their friends. Urban faerie circles formed an infrastructure that recalled and shared the qualities of rural gathering—self-love, friendship, mutual aid, and natural spirituality. Yet doing so in urban space also enabled others to meet Radical Faerie culture for the first time while enmeshed in urban life. Heart circle notably served this role in the Bay Area. When Radical Faeries told me of their difficulty in sustaining the culture of gatherings year-round, I regularly heard a wish for more regular practice of heart circle. Heart circle functioned like a portable gathering, and more than any other factor I found that its practice shifted faerie circles from being relatively dissociated networks into cohesive groups grounded in common work to change themselves and society. Regular practice of heart circle in the city affected how gay men lived Radical Faerie identity, if this made rural retreat unnecessary to experience the culture's heart. Newcomers to urban heart circles sometimes later claimed Radical Faerie identity by naming their interest to attend rural gatherings. Yet, others I met were satisfied to have found in urban community the center or full extent of their Radical Faerie identification. Certainly, in relation to a two-hour weekday evening heart circle in the living room of an urban house, rural gatherings carried a far greater capacity for spatial and temporal displacement of urban gay men into an indigenized rural communalism and its promised encounter with queer nature. Yet the very success of regular heart circle in sustaining the sensibility associated with rural gathering over long periods of time in urban life let both old-timers and newcomers realize, or even entirely locate, their experience of Radical Faerie culture in the city. In this light, faerie circles indicate that, despite suggestions that they only echo rural retreat, the experience promised by the Radical Faerie founders ultimately did not require it. If the ethos of rural gathering can arise apart from rural space, then even it can appear to be a formulation of urban life. On this basis, I understand Radical Faerie rural imaginaries and their practice to be constituted by urban desires, apropos not so much to the rural sites where they transpire or that they invoke as to the urban spaces where they were proposed and are sustained. By arguing that the city interrupts an experience that, in fact, urban conditions produce, Radical Faeries occlude their own formation within urban queer communities and simultaneously motivate their perpetual retreat to rural, natural, and Indigenous sources to realize queer nature.

I have explained Radical Faerie culture as a method to produce modern queers as transhistorical and global subjects by reconciling them to inheriting settlement.[7] Yet, when read as a product of urban queer life, Radical Faerie globalism appears less as the countercultural fringe of their common reputation and more as a primary and constitutive expression of the primitivist *and* globalist desires endemic within the everyday political and cultural practice of U.S. queer modernities. After all, Radical Faeries *are* the modern queer subjects who benefit from Radical Faerie culture—alongside all who tap into, learn from, or pass through their activities without identifying with them. Just as strongly Faerie-identified gay men participated fully in urban queer life without naming a subcultural identity, other participants in queer cultures and politics could recognize Radical Faerie culture as part of the diversity of queer communities. Without requiring that participants assume, or even fully comprehend, theories of Indigenous queer nature, Radical Faerie culture attracts a generic belief that something substantive underlies queer subjectivity and that Radical Faeries are among its arbiters. If observers or friends ever accept Radical Faerie education in mediating modern sexuality with rural, natural, or Indigenous truth, they bear no responsibility for explaining their desires so long as self-identified Radical Faeries appear to be its proper, "subcultural" subjects. Thus, rather than reading them as a social fringe, I understand them as positioned within queer communities, but their primitivism to be just far enough "outside" queer modernities (while, obviously, produced *inside* them) that Radical Faerie culture then can grant queers solace, from time to time, in knowing that an Indigenous nature actually underlies the progressive modernism driving queer politics.

Although my thoughts on the politics of queer primitivism extend beyond the Radical Faeries, I first considered its political usage by witnessing how Radical Faeries participated in Santa Cruz queer politics in 1999. As we saw in chapter 3, this was a period of reckoning with race at the downtown Santa Cruz LGBT Community Center, as a shift from grassroots organizing to foundation-funded social services elicited a reevaluation of the center's historical whiteness. Even after it was renamed the Diversity Center, struggles over race, class, and citizenship continued to embroil Santa Cruz city politics more broadly. A new city council majority led by a slate of progressive white male councilors recently had come under criticism for their proposed solution to a fiscal crisis. Their support for the Santa Cruz Beach Boardwalk's expansion would have allowed redevelopment of the Chicano/a and Latino/a working-class neighborhood of Beach Flats—the same neighborhood through which Queer Nation Santa Cruz first marched. Activists locally and countywide scrutinized this contradiction in the council's image as a force for inclusion of marginalized people. During this conflict, two council members (one from this progressive slate) were recognized for their support for LGBT civil rights by being invited to be grand marshals of the 1999 pride parade, whose theme that year was "Celebrate Diversity." At the pride parade, I noted this alliance among progressive leaders of two historically white institutions facing crises over their racialization and commitment to "diversity" in other than name only. As the parade marched through downtown Santa Cruz to a festival near the county government building, I also thought about these issues in relation to the participation of Radical Faeries, which inflected the event's civilizational appeals to queer citizenship with queer primitivity.

I stood that day in a sidewalk crowd near the center of downtown, shaded by the trees near one of the city's two gay bars, and opposite an upscale natural foods market. Many contingents calmly marched by in casual business dress holding banners and signs representing social-service agencies or LGBT affinity groups; these received sporadic bouts of applause from the spectators. They were interspersed at times with slightly more raucous crowds of school-based student groups. In this array, I and others who stood near me began to hear the unusual echoes of drums before we could see their players. After queries of, "What is that?" word began spreading: "It's the faeries!" Behind a group of orderly walkers, we saw twenty to thirty people holding hands and skipping in a long, meandering line up the street toward us. They appeared to be a group of men, most bare-chested, a colorful few in skirts or festooned with scarves, jewelry, headdresses, face paint, or bells. Their pace increased to the beat of *djembes* and tablas being played behind them, and punctuated from time to time with ululations. Behind their line appeared similarly attired drummers seated in the back of a pedaled rickshaw, which I recognized as an import from Southeast Asia now decorated in bright colors and an eclectic mélange of images, statuary, and organic objects intimating neo-pagan and Buddhist spirituality. After nearly an hour of staid marching and soft applause, I sensed the heightened energy around me in the broad smiles being shared by witnesses and the many photographs being snapped. As the only contingent to eschew the seeming transparency of signs and slogans, the group invited its own interpretation. I asked people around me how the dancers appeared to them, and one remarked that they were communicating "the joy of being gay." Another near me spontaneously announced, "They sure know how to have fun!" Later that afternoon I ran into an old friend, a white woman professional active in local lesbian and bisexual organizing. On rushing up to see me, her years of honoring Radical Faeries as men who publicly critiqued sexism and homophobia echoed in her excited words: "Weren't the faeries fabulous?!" Here she echoed a Radical Faerie marching chant heard at a prior generation of ACT-UP marches and pride parades, with syllables punctuated by staccato claps: "fae-ries are fab-u-lous . . . faeriesarefabulous!"

Indeed, the Radical Faerie contingent that year was a fabulous alternative to the parade's civilizational appeals to civic recognition. Yet my interest here is in how the image they presented to onlookers functioned as *part* of the celebrated progress of modern queer politics. I recognized many old friends and acquaintances among the contingent's dancers, but participants in civic politics and queer activism in this small city also would have recognized many dancers from those contexts. The group never named themselves "Radical Faeries," but had this read onto them by witnesses with prior knowledge of their not-unexpected appearance within the diversity of local queer community. That so many participants should depart wildly from an orderly march marked an awareness that in this space, queer cultural citizenship can be affirmed through more than civilizational performance. Santa Cruz, like San Francisco, differs from most U.S. cities in its civic embrace of counterculturism; but the scene carries a deeper implication. We see here that invoking primitivism in queer cultural citizenship practices can buttress progressive claims on queer modernity, as one guise that its representatives may assume when appealing for recognition. By performing global cultural ephemera and Indigenous queer nature, queer primitivism makes normatively white communities appear more culturally diverse than if they were only represented by the performance of civilizational achievement. Homonormative politics struggles to edit drag, S/M, and public sex out of the publicity surrounding gay rights, as at pride parades. Gender and sexual radicals may think they win this battle if they sustain an unapologetic public presence. But as part of Pride 1999's progressive effort to celebrate "diversity," Radical Faeries appeared less as a protest of modernist claims on cultural citizenship and more as their primitivist complement and affirmation.

I knew that this year, and in the years immediately before and after it, the Santa Cruz Faerie circle increased its participation in pride events to raise its profile as a contributor to local queer civic and cultural life. With changing themes each year, the group worked to validate their integrity: by acknowledging participants, many of them major local figures, in the guise of their primary identity; by showing that their culture was sustained by a closely knit circle; and by inviting onlookers to witness the pleasure and freedom granted by Radical Faerie culture. These sentiments did not differ markedly from participants' everyday participation in local queer life. Thus, the politics of primitivity for Radical Faeries appeared simply to fulfill a thesis of Radical Faerie culture: inviting not just gay men, but all queer people, to seek out and be liberated by their Indigenous queer nature. Thus, I read Radical Faerie participation at Pride 1999 as a familiar sentiment— grounding queer modernities in queer primitivity—being inadvertently, or inevitably, caught up in the racial and national contours of queer citizenship practices. Radical Faeries participated just as queer activists and the government in which they sought belonging struggled with the whiteness of their progressive politics while trying to assure of their own diversity. Pride organizers called on people to celebrate diversity, and announced that they supported multiculturalism even as they positioned queer culture as a form of diversity. Their claim on citizenship then informed a city council whose image as a protector of diversity needed reinforcement. At the parade, the council accepted appreciation from a predominantly white queer constituency, while celebrating the city as diverse in a way that did not challenge its policies in Chicano/a and Latino/a communities. Whiteness in queer politics and civic government thus was sustained by presuming their own diversity. In this context, the Radical Faeries' presence, however fleeting, was absorbed into a message that queers celebrate diversity. Whether their performance was meant to be or was perceived as "fringe," it became inserted in this moment into the political norms of a white settler society. Radical Faeries presented a rare group that truly did "celebrate" diversity, in the primitivity they offered modern queer subjects to appreciate or adopt. Their performance then informed queer and broader civic desires for a multicultural modernity that was challenged by their normative whiteness, but perhaps ameliorated by this reminder that, after all, "we are everywhere." Celebrating queer diversity through primitivity invited witnesses to excavate deep pasts and cross distant borders in hopes of confirming roots on this land that also promise present and future forms of national and global belonging.

Queer Primitivist Globalizations

Beyond the work of any particular subculture, U.S. queer cultural politics in the 1990s engaged primitivism as a leading edge of queer radicalism. I witnessed this amid the established appeal of San Francisco to counterculturists. European neo-paganism had gained local legitimacy after decades of work by Starhawk's Reclaiming Collective, among other regional institutions. Vibrant art scenes drew on pagan themes to transform a late-1980s San Francisco beach gathering into the annual Nevada desert extravaganza Burning Man with its tens of thousands of celebrants.[8] A local confluence of radical sex and body modification scenes in the late 1980s inspired journalists to proclaim the era of "modern primitives," which soon seemed to command a global scope.[9] None of these formations contradicted San

Francisco's status as a global finance capital or destination for the world's rich and famous; indeed, counterculturisms of many kinds augmented the city's founding myth of Gold Rush frontier bohemianism that let it lead settler modernity by incorporating and managing the wild edge of civilization. Queer primitivists informed this space, whether they arose here or were drawn as migrants, by mobilizing primitivism as a form of queer radicalism wherein non-Natives applied their inheritance of indigeneity to incite queer liberation "at home" and throughout a globalized world. If their queering of embodiment or desire gained recognition or affirmation in queer theory, then primitivism and its globalism constituted the cutting edge of queer modernities serving non-Natives within the naturalized context of a settler society.

In the 1990s, visitors seeking San Francisco's libertinism might have encountered one of the Castro district's largest annual events at the time: the Halloween Party sponsored by the Sisters of Perpetual Indulgence. Founded to raise funds for HIV/AIDS services, the event celebrated drag and sexuality at a nighttime street fair and costume party. In 1994, local artists addressed increased homophobic and transphobic violence during the event by mobilizing art activism. "HomoHex" was formed by Keith Hennessy, cofounder of the queer arts collective 848 Community Space, and by Jack Davis, associate of 848 and a practitioner in Reclaiming Collective. As a public form of contact improvisation and neo-pagan ritual invoking those lost to AIDS, HomoHex would re-create the Halloween Party as a challenge to heteropatriarchy and pandemic. Hennessy described Homo-Hex participants as "body-based and polydisciplined life artists" who

> come primarily from the urban cliques of radical faeries, performance/dance artists, anarchopagans, and queer sex activists. We act and write and pray from our specific bodies, and from the communal body. We . . . embrace queer and feminist leadership, pagan rituals, consensual explorations of power, and dance-based trainings in intentional touch . . . We are protesting and praying and performing, simultaneously, as we have always done.[10]

At the 1994 Halloween Party, nearly one hundred people marched through crowds on Market Street chanting, "Dyke Sex! Fag Sex! We're here to throw a HomoHex! WHEE!" (14). Part of the group linked arms in a circle and edged back the crowd to create a space where performers/celebrants stripped off their clothes and leaders proclaimed the establishment of a sacred circle. As Davis recalls:

> There is wild drumming, mad dancing with kissing, pelvic humping, whole body hugging, naked bodies thrown into the air . . . There are hundreds of people watching us. There are untold numbers of ancestors present. We are worshipping in the old way: naked, doing sex play outdoors, near midnight on Halloween. We are queer witches and this is how we pray. (16)

Here Davis strongly echoes Evans's *Witchcraft and the Gay Counterculture,* which projected sexual spirituality onto all "nature peoples" while locating U.S. queers within a European legacy of "queer witches" as sources of liberation. Hennessy further asserts that with AIDS having "instigated a more developed consciousness in relation to death," the neo-pagan rituals of Samhein (Halloween) allow queers to recall and "gain strength" by connecting to loved ones lost to the epidemic (15). At HomoHex, queer feminists turned a night when the worlds of the living and the dead collide into a site where primitivist spirituality performed queer politics, by mobilizing the dishonored dead to empower survivors of collective trauma in renewing their defiance of heteronormative violence and their achievement of a primal queer liberation.

Public approbations of queer primitivism like HomoHex circulated in San Francisco during this time in the manner Sandoval described, as a postmodern market of primitivist consumption. As exemplified by the Radical Faeries, queer primitivism broadly informed public queer cultures, in bookstores, workshops, performances, and in community, civic, and health organizations. For instance, regional queer feminist women's sexual cultures responding to antiporn feminism embraced primitivism as a route to sexual agency, by welcoming performers like Annie Sprinkle, whose "Sluts and Goddesses" workshops narrated a world of sexual and spiritual possibility for "exploring the different sexual personalities inside yourself, and accepting them."[11] Gay men inspired by globalist visions of sexual agency formed spaces to learn safe and spiritual sex, as when Joseph Kramer's Oakland-based Body Electric School of Massage taught sexual and spiritual healing by linking cultural knowledges from around the world. Workshops like Sprinkle's and Kramer's became available at local marketplaces like Good Vibrations, a woman-centered erotica store in San Francisco and Berkeley founded by sexual health writer Joani Blank, and known for hosting free and fee-based events promoting sexual exploration. Texts by these and other persons and groups popularized their themes, as when books by Radical Faeries on gay spirituality were promoted as resources for queer communities to realize their potential. One local project in wide circulation published the work of Randy Connor, David Hatfield Sparks, and Mariya Sparks as *Cassell's Encyclopedia of Queer Myth, Symbol, and Spirit* (1997), in a compendium of references to queer primitivist texts and other literary and scholarly sources that purportedly recorded the existence of a global and transhistorical queer spirituality. Such knowledges and practices circulated primitivism to remake First World citizen-subjects as modern queers liberated by grounding borderless lives in primal truths.

Queer primitivism in San Francisco overlapped in the 1990s with the rise of the phenomenon of "modern primitives." At a time of increasing primitivist cultural activity such as piercing, tattooing, and body modification, V. Vale and Andrea Juno, writing from San Francisco in 1989, defined it as the cultural moment of the "modern primitive." They projected a uniformity across disparate activities that led them and many practitioners to recognize the qualities of a movement. In his study of modern primitives, Daniel Rosenblatt observes that "if tattooing, piercing, and scarification were not already grouped together, they certainly became so after Vale and Juno's book." He notes that

> The title *Modern Primitives* makes a double assertion. First, by calling people who practice body modification "primitive," it reflects a claim that what people are doing today in San Francisco and elsewhere bears some relation to things that non-Western or "primitive" people have "always done." Second, by calling them "modern," it asserts that they are on the cutting edge (so to speak) of our own or the world's history.[12]

The spatial relationship Rosenblatt frames links the placeless, past worlds of primitives to the modern site of San Francisco, representing here the West that transcends primitivity as well as the West (or "left") Coast whose frontier proximity in space *and* time to indigeneity facilitates recovering primitivity. Yet this formulation also denotes a white racialization of modernity and primitivity within a settler society. For Vale and Juno, the modern primitive body is a legibly modern body whose achievement of primitivity is remarkable because this body appears not to have been racialized as primitive prior to its modification. Modification then appears as a modern adaptation of "traditions" of modification by improving on their skill while gathering more of them than any single tradition ever knew. We are not surprised, then, to encounter the iconic modern primitive body as white, although in San Francisco (and not only there) whiteness as a product of settlement is known to inherit Native American indigeneity and all to which it might link. This normative whiteness of modern primitives obscured the distinctive participation of people of color. For instance, Vale and Juno portray the Japanese teachers of Don Ed Hardy as racialized *and* modified representatives of local tradition that modern primitives now adapt. Yet people of color in modern primitive communities such as Tina Portillo and Gryphon Blackswan challenged such terms by making body modification assert and contradict their racialization as primitive, notably by juxtaposing diverse markers of primitivity that displaced the overdetermination of their bodies within a white gaze.[13] Nevertheless, the complexity and marginality of their efforts indicates that whiteness remained naturalized within the iconic freedom of the modern primitive to assign primitive meaning to a body previously empty of it, which potentially let it represent *all* primitive meanings at once. In its San Francisco origins, the modern primitive economy of cultural difference caused the Indigenous inheritance of white settlers to perform not a distinctive Native root but a primitive diversity to which that root offered access, making white modern primitives both quantitatively and qualitatively more Indigenous than any specific Indigenous life could be.

Although Vale and Juno did not focus on gay or lesbian practitioners, modern primitive culture drew from long-standing uses of primitivism to blur embodiment and pleasure in San Francisco gay male and queer radical sex scenes. Building from BDSM (bondage and discipline, sadism and masochism) and leather sex subcultures of mid-twentieth-century San Francisco, gay radical sex practitioners in the 1970s cited gay counterculturism to proclaim a grounding in primitivism. Geoff Mains, in his 1984 book *Urban Aboriginals: A Celebration of Leathersexuality,* frames BDSM and other sexual scenes among gay men as a "tribal society" where spatial concentrations of gay eroticism produce spiritual transformation.[14] He cites the work of Margaret Mead and Ruth Benedict as evidence that gender-segregated ritual spaces and shamanic practices in primitive societies reappear in modern gay cultures that perform them as their nature (160–63). Yet he also describes leathermen as demonstrating the "fraternity, equality, liberty, and humility" of a modern and egalitarian national brotherhood, as men "not apart from but of the very blood of civilization"; indeed, "urbane and savage in the same breath, they are animal and human in the same stroke" (179). Here, sexually radical gay men act as "a bridge between two worlds" by embodying the liminality of modernity and a primitivity indicative of white settlers and modern queers (162, 180–81). Radical sex cultures increasingly blurred gender and sexual boundaries to become more "queer," as reflected in Mark Thompson's 1991 collection *Leatherfolk: Radical Sex, People, Politics, and Practice.* Reflecting recent reassertions of radical sex by lesbian and trans practitioners as queer feminist methods for modifying embodiment and pleasure, *Leatherfolk* under Thompson's guidance nevertheless emphasizes a Radical Faerie trajectory of reclaiming primitive "third genders" as a primal nature to liberate modern queers. Yet the text's contributors suggest that by blurring gender and sexuality, radical sex transforms narrower theories of gay nature into queer liberations that exceed preconceived boundaries of embodiment and desire.

Modern primitive culture in San Francisco grew through ties to queer radical sex culture, notably in the premier regional network of Black Leather Wings (BLW). BLW is profiled in *Leatherfolk* as a pangendered and pansexual radical sex fellowship based in San Francisco with members from across the United States. Formed as an affinity group of Radical Faeries, in 1989 it was disinvited from Wolf Creek after a heart circle process determined that BDSM was violence and threatened Radical Faerie community. BLW became an independent San Francisco group that nevertheless adapted Radical Faerie methods of rural retreat and heart circle to radical sex practice as methods to tap queer people's Indigenous spiritual nature. Committed practitioners sustained BLW in local play parties, while annual retreats drew sixty to one hundred people, many of them casual participants who carried what they learned back to regional and national queer communities. When I first met BLW, their retreat occurred at Saratoga Springs, a center founded in 1871 on Pomo land at a site promoted as once used by the Pomo "for peacemaking and healing...the valley still resonates with this energy, which enhances the experiences of all who come."[15]

Soon after its formation, BLW formed a close relationship with a key figure among modern primitives, Fakir Musafar. Vale and Juno profile Musafar as an icon within their largely heteronormative framing of the movement; yet *Leatherfolk* also profiled Musafar as having found in BLW a space where he could queer his embodiment by using body modification to blur boundaries of male and female, while encouraging his interest to discover the spiritual roots of his practices.[16] Musafar grew up under the given name Roland Loomis in a white village on Lakota land in South Dakota. From a young age he explored masochistic practices, from corsets to genital constraints, although he took particular inspiration from pictures of "primitive people" in *National Geographic* and stories of Lakota religious ritual, especially the Sun Dance—a practice he and other non-Natives later reenacted, as recorded in *Leatherfolk*.[17] He took the name "Fakir Musafar" from a nineteenth-century Persian man known in U.S. body modification communities for living adorned with pierced hooks and beads. Musafar relocated to the San Francisco region, where he worked by day as an investment banker, choosing not to take tattoos or piercings that could be seen outside business dress, and used his resources to travel to learn about and collect instruments of body modification from religious practitioners worldwide. His fame in regional fetish communities often brought him invitations to lead their rituals, which raised the profile of BLW once he began attending their retreats. In the year when I met BLW, Musafar had introduced a number of practices to their repertoire, including a structured activity based on his study of Hindu ritual in which decorative ornaments are affixed to the torso and face and ritually danced. BLW adopted this practice as "the ball dance," and the day devoted to it formed their rural retreat's major collective event.

Musafar's modern primitive practice converges with queer primitivism, as he taps BLW's spiritual resources to queer his embodiment, while BLW adapts his global journeys to sustain the primitivist desires of queer radicalism. Musafar's story suggests that settler subjects discover their desired Native American indigeneity simultaneously with its global extrapolations. As an icon of modern primitives, he performed the modern primitive as a subject who forms and returns to a relationship to settlement by traversing global scales of primitivity within global economics of cultural appropriation and transformation. Yet this globalist primitivism becomes meaningful only on its return to the settler spaces where its amalgamations of indigeneity ground modern settlers in their roots on Native land. Effectively, in a settler context, the global is accessible from the ground of everyday life: global imaginaries are settler imaginaries, projecting Native Americans within globalist claims for reconciliation to settlement. Queer primitivism thus performs a mobility across time and space, making the world available to subjects in transit between the modernity and primitivity defining the lives of settlers on Native land.

The broad inculcation of queer primitivism as political, cultural, and theoretical radicalism in the 1990s affirms that U.S. queer modernities traverse primitivity as a route to modern subjectivity. While queer primitivists, Radical Faeries, and radical sex practitioners clearly present themselves as subcultures opposed to homonormativity and its national embrace, they remain ciphers of the sexual modernity performed even by the queers they critique. Their primitivism oscillates with the civilizationalism that they target to produce settler subjects, whose liberation depends on forming a relationship to the indigeneity they appear to inherit and supplant on stolen land. Queer primitivists are the modern subjects who turn primitivity into a resource for progressive change in a settler society. In this light, radical arenas of U.S. queer politics and queer theory should be reinterpreted as sites that produce settler subjects and their globalist projections. To what degree have queer theories of radical sex or body modification invested in primitivity to perform postmodernity—in Sandoval's or Deloria's sense— as the act of modern settlers negotiating a colonial inheritance? How is queer radicalism produced by settler colonialism to articulate Native American indigeneity and its globalist and primitivist extrapolations as inspiration? My reading complements critiques of homonationalism by suggesting that homonationalism arises not just in civilizational alignments of queers with empire, but also in primitivist critiques of heteronormativity *and* homonormativity that make a settler relationship to indigeneity constitutive of queer radicalism.

Globalism, Transnationalism, and Decolonization

Diasporic queers of color and Native queers also engage the settler formation of globalism in queer modernities. Diasporic queer of color critiques examine how colonial histories inform their traversal and disturbance of nationality in postcolonial and imperial states. But the efficacy of such critiques depends on the degree to which they theorize settler colonialism and the relationship of diasporic queers of color to Native queer people. Native queer critiques disrupt queer globalism precisely by locating settler colonialism as its origin and context on stolen land. These critiques also distinctly engage white settler queer primitivism. I now ask how queer primitivist globalism inflects diasporic queer of color critiques in ways that may affirm rather than challenge settlement. Chicano/a queer theories in particular mark the porousness among Native and non-Native queer identities, even as their traversals of white settler queer primitivism potentially replicate a colonial relationship to Native queer and Two-Spirit people. Chicano/a queers and non-Native queers of color can join Two-Spirit people in allied relationship to transnational Indigenous movements for decolonization. In particular, Two-Spirit activists negotiate white settler queer primitivism as a key form of colonial discourse that has attempted to define their histories and purpose for settler societies and the colonial world they engage.

By holding its globalist gestures accountable to the national and transnational locations of Two-Spirit people, they denaturalize settler colonialism as a condition of theories and practices of queer modernity, and they inspire new transnational alliances.

Queer Diasporas and Indigenous Solidarity

The globalism of U.S. queer modernities has been disrupted by queers of color theorizing diaspora. Some work valorizes queers of color as having this effect, an implication questioned by Puar who locates diasporic queers of color in multiple mediations by homonationalism.[18] One such thread implies that diasporic cultural practices by queers of color disrupt colonialism and its legacies. Centering settler colonialism raises the stakes in making such a claim. A focus in queer diasporic scholarship on recent globalizations and migrations has framed colonization through the lens of the postcolonial, in which nationalisms, migration, and global governance sustain colonization's "afterlife."[19] Yet a troubling effect of the assertion that today colonization is everywhere is that scholars do not place colonization itself under study or specify its forms. One result is to elide settler colonialism as needing no afterlife because its primary form never ended. As a result, and as Indigenous feminist and queer critics argue, queer diasporic accounts of "colonialism" tend not to explain the colonial formation of settler societies, or the locations of diasporic queers of color within them as non-Natives in relation to Native peoples.

Articulations of diasporic queers of color with U.S. settler colonialism can be elicited from current scholarship. Martin Manalansan explains that diasporic Filipino gay men challenge their colonial locations as racially premodern in relation to U.S. queer modernities by destabilizing "a monolithic gay identity," in a "counter-narrative to the prevailing view of the immigrant route as a movement away from tradition in the homeland and toward an assimilated modern life in the land of settlement."[20] When Manalansan affirms "an alternative form of modernity" formed by Filipinos negotiating legacies of U.S. colonization, he invites asking how this relates in "the land of settlement" to white settler rule relocating and marginalizing Filipinos as occupants of Native American and Kanaka Maoli lands.[21] Interpreting how Filipino gay men claim transnational identities in relation to Native queer diasporas on stolen land could clarify how they perform queer modernities that, by defying U.S. colonial modernity, also open all its settler colonial power to question.

Juana Rodriguez deepens such themes by tracing how "queer Latinidad" troubles U.S. colonial power by evaluating settler colonialism. In her account, the San Francisco queer Latino/a AIDS organization Proyecto Contra SIDA Por Vida defines queer Latino/a diasporas as anticolonial when its members transpose the European conquest of the Americas as a metaphor for the U.S. colonial relationship to Latin America. In doing so, Rodriguez relates, Proyecto invokes Latino/a and specifically Chicano/a queer identifications with indigeneity.[22] Longtime Proyecto organizer Ricardo Bracho wrote in its mission statement, "queremos romper el silencio y repression among our pueblos who for 500 years have been colonized/catholocized/de-eroticized." Here Bracho evokes his co-imagining with Cherríe Moraga of a "queer Aztlán," in which claiming erotic belonging to Indigenous heritage defies Chicano/a internalizations of white supremacy and colonial discourse while invoking, in Moraga's words, "a Chicano homeland that could embrace *all* its people, including its jotería."[23] Rodriguez explains that Proyecto's mission and art projects portray queer Latinos/as as mestizo/a and encourage embracing indigeneity as part of an antiracist and anticolonial queer diasporic consciousness that rejects U.S. whiteness as colonial. Yet the words and images Rodriguez examines do not name the relationship of queer Latino/a indigeneity to the colonial situations of Native nations in the United States or Latin America today. She thus suggests potential ties and sustained differences among anticolonial theories of queer Latino/a indigeneity and the relationship among indigeneity, settler colonization, and queerness for Native nations.

Chicana feminist and queer theorists have plied the tensions in such ties, notably when examining the work of Gloria Anzaldúa as well as Moraga and Bracho as performing what Emma Perez calls a "decolonial imaginary."[24] This work defies the violences of conquest that forcibly amalgamated Indigenous peoples with Europeans, subjugated mestizos as a racialized caste, and established Western civilizationalism and its colonial, racialist, and heteropatriarchal logics of domination. Reaffirming ancestral indigeneity allows not only renewed Indigenous Chicano/a identification but also potential alliances with Native peoples who survived conquest by maintaining national differences. In particular, many ties exist between a Chicano/a queer decolonial imaginary and Native American Two-Spirit identity, as attested by Two-Spirit people who take inspiration in their decolonial work from that of Anzaldúa. Mindful of these interconnections, I deepen their discussion by considering how Anzaldúa's Chicana queer claims on indigeneity historically engaged white settler queer primitivism. By reflecting on these engagements in her later work, Anzaldúa opens to question the degree to which doing so extended or troubled the globalist and white settler logics of queer primitivism. I have argued that globalism in white settler queer primitivism obscures its subjects' locations in settler colonialism, and that these must be marked in relation to Two-Spirit people to accountably form transnational alliance. My reading of Anzaldúa in relation to this is shaped by two concerns: my demonstration that Two-Spirit people intimately engaged white queer colonial desires to produce discrepant, decolonial ends; and the fact that white-supremacist settler colonialism genocidally locates Chicanos/as and other mixed-blood Native peoples outside authentic indigeneity precisely to block their claims on Indigenous heritage—perhaps because such claims trouble the primacy of state-authenticated indigeneity when determining who can claim to be Native. With this in mind, I navigate between the possibility of reading Anzaldúa as recapitulating or disturbing white settler queer primitivism to end on the crucial question: how Chicano/a queers and Native American Two-Spirit people are now, or can become, aligned in the space of transnational solidarity committed to mutual decolonizations.

Anzaldúa's work has been subject to many critiques of its adaptations of colonial discourse on indigeneity. The observation that she adapts colonial discourse is less interesting to me than an explication of the ends to which this adaptation leads. I push other scholars' critiques to ask: along what *national* horizons in a settler colonial society do Anzaldúa's engagements with colonial discourse travel, and how does this block or engender *alliances* with contemporary Native peoples, including Two-Spirit people as members of their nations? Sheila Marie Contreras reads Anzaldúa's adaptations of race essentialism and primitivism in *mestizaje* by noting that "certain features of the primitive have changed surprisingly little in the migration from Anglo and European textual projects to a Chicana indigenist manifesto," as when Anzaldúa cites "a colonial and anthropological archive" that "reproduce(s) the convention of anthropology and modern primitivism."[25] The important point is not that Anzaldúa cites narratives of primitivity legible in colonial texts, but whether or not her use also tracks the globalist epistemology of anthropology that amalgamates Indigenous differences as the "primitivity" needed for "modern" subjects to consume to know their own roots. Contreras further notes that "whether primitivist borrowings are viewed in terms of artistic invention, spiritual reconstitution, or social transformation, they always promote quite consciously a critique of Western norms, as does Anzaldúa.[26] She here affirms Philip Deloria's observation that in the United States, settler formulations of primitivism as opposition define the normative formation of white settler subjects of the civilizational West, and that this route to subjectivity must be displaced if invoking primitivism will act to destabilize, rather than restabilize, settler colonialism. Maria Saldaña-Portillo argues that Anzaldúa's play on *mestizaje* recapitulates revolutionary nationalism and its racialization in Mexico:

> What Anzaldúa does not recognize . . . is that her very focus on the Aztec female deities is an effect of the PRI's [Partido Revolucionario Institucional] statist policies to resuscitate, through state-funded documentation, this particular, defunct Mexican Indian culture and history to the exclusion of dozens of living indigenous cultures.[27]

Linking Saldaña-Portillo and Deloria (through Contreras), we might ask to what degree Anzaldúa's vision of Chicano/a queer indigeneity or, in Moraga and Bracho's terms, a "queer Aztlán" defines this decolonial nationality in a manner that disrupts or repeats the national horizons of U.S. American or Mexican settler colonialism.

These critiques can be complicated by articulating them with the theoretical insights of women of color feminism that Anzaldúa also inspired. Anzaldúa offered "la conciencia de la mestiza" as a de-essentializing theory of Chicana subjectivity, echoing what Alarcón described for "the theoretical subjects of *This Bridge Called My Back*" as "consciousness as a site of multiple voicings."[28] Sandoval, in *Methodology of the Oppressed*, cites mestiza consciousness and interlinked theories in her claim that U.S./Third World feminists "differentially" traversed modernist oppositional movements to create decolonial feminist and queer projects. Yet, if Anzaldúa inspired women of color feminism to critically inhabit and cross colonial borders and open their contingency to change, her work may be pressed by certain other implications. Sandoval's account of a postmodern economy of cultural difference invites asking whether Anzaldúa has portrayed Chicano/a queer indigeneity by facilitating or troubling globalist logics of indigeneity and methods for their circulation. In turn, the alliance politics of U.S./Third World feminism—in Chandra Mohanty's words, to create "a political constituency, not a biological or even a sociological one," from "a *common context of struggle*"—troubles any feminist claims on a universality not situated by historically contingent struggle.[29] Read together, Mohanty and Sandoval place in question whether globalist imaginaries of indigeneity—if or when they appear in Anzaldúa's work—interrupt, or may be altered to enable, alliance among Chicano/a queers and Native American Two-Spirit people, whose activism defies globalism by situating national differences in transnational alliances.

These considerations inform my reading of Anzaldúa's traversal of white settler queer primitivisms in the San Francisco contexts of my stories, as explained in her foreword for Conner, Sparks, and Sparks's *Cassel's Encyclopedia of Queer Myth, Symbol, and Ritual*. Here Anzaldúa cites a quotidian history that she shared with Conner and David Sparks in the early 1980s "when we were all living on Noe Street in San Francisco":

> I remember a night in the winter of 1980 . . . shoving a note under Randy and David's door, asking "Is there a Queer spirituality?" My question led us to many discussions over *lattes* at Café Flore. As I read *The Encyclopedia of Queer Myth, Symbol, and Ritual,* I feel a sense of belonging to a vast community of *jotos,* "queers," who participate in the sacred and mythic dimensions of life. Again and again, I see parts of myself reflected in many of its narratives and symbols.[30]

She reflects on her personal reading of the array of accounts the authors present:

> Like one who is starving, once I tasted such articles as "Shamanism," "Tlazeolteotl," and "Xochiquetzal," and other kernels of Aztlán (the mythical homeland of the ancient peoples of Mexico), I quickly lapped up the Queer stories of cultures beyond my own. (vii)

Anzaldúa situates her relationship to the text and her claims in the national and cultural specificities of Chicana indigeneity. But her praise shows how the text arouses in her a desire, framed here by hunger and consumption, to incorporate into herself "cultures beyond my own." As a global and trans-historical compendium of apparently culturally specific and authentic queer spiritualities, the *Encyclopedia* adapts the colonial epistemology of metropolitan universalism, even as that form appears to be countered by promoting indigeneity. Objectivism in the colonial encyclopedia can be reinforced when an array of writers transmit their narrow expertise. That style is adapted by the *Encyclopedia* with all entries being written by the three coeditors, who then weave a singular story through a form that, by marking differences, invites readers to discover relationships written into the text. Thus, not unlike Arthur Evans's "discovery" of gay shamanism by studying sexological and emancipationist texts oriented around berdache, Anzaldúa appears to read the *Encyclopedia* not as a story of queer indigeneity prepared for her to find, but as a signpost to a prior, interior knowledge whose recollection the text incites.

My first reading of these passages suggests that the *Encyclopedia* and Anzaldúa traverse normative routes for late-modern U.S. queer subjects to consume queer indigeneity, in which citing cultural specificity leads to globalist amalgamations of indigeneity that free newly indigenized queer subjects from complicity in practicing settler colonialism. Yet I immediately question this reading by recalling that Anzaldúa's relationship to the text is marked by the hunger of a queer feminist Chicana critic defying white supremacy *and* settler colonialism by reaffirming her Indigenous heritage on lands her peoples traversed prior to conquest. White-supremacist settler colonialism already racializes and indigenizes Anzaldúa *across* a normative relationality to white settler subjects who consume indigeneity as difference. How, exactly, do their vastly distinct locations then similarly, or differently, articulate white settler queer primitivism? I contend that Anzaldúa's pursuit of her own decolonization as a queer Chicana retains its integrity, even though her contribution to this book also makes her decolonial work compatible with, or inspirational of, white settler consumption of indigeneity.

This effect becomes apparent in the globalist implications of Anzaldúa's inviting *Encyclopedia* readers to link her claims and those in the book to "spiritual *mestizaje*":

> For a "postcolonial" *mestiza* like myself, any single way is not "the" way. A spiritual *mestizaje* weaves together beliefs and practices from many cultures, perhaps including elements of Shamanism, Buddhism, Christianity, Santeria, and other traditions. Spiritual *mestizaje* involves the crossing of borders, incessant metamorphosis. It is a spirituality that nurtures the ability to wear someone else's skin, its central myth being shapeshifting. In its disturbance of traditional boundaries of gender and desire and its narratives of metamorphosis—as amply presented here—as well as in its traversing of cultural and historical borders, Queer Spirit qualifies as a kind of spiritual *mestizaje*. (Ibid.)

In a Chicana queer decolonial imaginary, *mestizaje*'s "shapeshifting" invokes what Anzaldúa elsewhere calls "nagualismo—a type of Mexican indigenous shamanism where a person becomes an animal, becomes a different person."[31] Her account of "spiritual *mestizaje*" thus resonates with her other work to locate Chicana heritage in Mexican indigeneity. Read in that frame, saying that "Queer Spirit qualifies as a kind of spiritual *mestizaje*" might perform a Chicana queer indigenist appropriation of prior white queer primitivist appropriations within queer spirituality movements. But read near her reminiscences in the *Encyclopedia*, this passage reminds us that in 1980 Anzaldúa, like Conner and Sparks, already envisioned "a Queer spirituality" broader than any specific Indigenous heritage and, perhaps, global in scope. In the intervening time, the *Encyclopedia* arose to market a globalist vision of queer indigeneity in the era of modern primitives and growing white queer primitivist movements, which became an immediate audience. I in no way presume that such a book cannot be rearticulated by Native American, Chicano/a, and other queer people of color in discrepant, decolonial ways, as I suggested by questioning any sense that Anzaldúa's consumption of globalist narratives must produce identical ends as white queer readings. But the concurrent popularization of U.S. queer primitivism *as* radicalism *and* diversity requires asking what it means for Anzaldúa to promote "spiritual *mestizaje*"—its purpose being "to wear someone else's skin"—as a resource in a queer spirituality movement still defined by white settler colonial desires. I will say more on this later, but this narrative act differs from Clyde Hall and other leaders of the Naraya inviting Radical Faeries to join a Shoshone and pantribal religious practice, while requiring non-Natives not to repeat it outside interpersonal and landed relationships to Shoshone people. As I argued, such ties are troubled if they do not necessarily alter or if they even extend the colonial desires that lead Radical Faeries to participate. These grounded relationships differ from Anzaldúa's broadcasting of "spiritual *mestizaje*" in a globalist *Encyclopedia* without stating how this does, or does not, provide non-Chicano/a or non-Indigenous people a new resource for their primitivism, or indeed how Chicano/a or other Indigenous queer people should respond. Absent such statements, Anzaldúa appears to be centering the critical work of Chicano/a queer decolonial imaginaries within a globalist queer spirituality movement, which could be interpreted as either confirming or disrupting its logic. I raise these questions because I hope that examining them will inform how we understand Anzaldúa's work not only to be engaging colonial discourses, but also to be modeling possibilities for alliance within the national and global horizons of settler societies or the national and transnational spaces of Two-Spirit organizing.

The possibility that Anzaldúa imagines Chicana queer indigeneity outside a relationship to Native peoples structures Saldaña-Portillo's critique. Recognizing that Anzaldúa "undoes the artificial duality of a border" and its "material violence," she argues that "Anzaldúa could proceed to resituate the Chicana/o as mestizo, the Mexican as mestizo, and the Indian as

Mexican within a transnational frame that would address the unequal power relations among such positionalities."[32] But instead,

Anzaldúa quickly slips back in to the conventional usage of mestizaje, constructing Chicanas/os in the borderlands as the "us" against the Anglo "them" [and] rallies mestizaje to access an indigenous ancestry that legitimates a prior claim to the Southwest . . . ignoring the contemporary Native American inhabitants of the Southwest and their very different mytho-genealogies. (281)

She continues: "Mestizaje is once again deployed to produce a biological tie with pre-Aztec Indians rather than a political tie with contemporary U.S. Native Americans or Mexican Indians" (282). Arguing against "the condition of possibility for Chicana/o nostalgia over our indigenous subjectivity" being "the rarefication of indigenous peoples as past," she suggests that

mestizaje is incapable of suturing together the heterogeneous positionalities of "Mexican," "Indian," and "Chicana/o" that coexist in the United Sates, or, more importantly, of offering effective *political* subjectivity to those represented by these positionalities. (279)

Saldaña-Portillo asks here if the political locations of Anzaldúa's theory in the United States incite a settler colonial relationship to Native peoples, if Chicano/a queer indigeneity is envisioned outside accountable relationship to Native nations on the lands where it is imagined. Yet she further suggests that the political danger of primitivism lies in letting Anzaldúa reclaim an indigeneity always in the past of the Chicano/a queer modernity she asserts. In this light, Anzaldúa's queer modernity remains Indigenous, but within the United States it also may code as non-Native if it is deployed across a difference from Native Americans or, indeed, the distinctive lives and politics of Native American Two-Spirit people.

As I have noted, productive engagements with Anzaldúa's work by Native American Two-Spirit people show that no absolute disjuncture can be detected between them. I raise the possibility of a difference in response to calls by Native queer and Two-Spirit activists that queer alliances commit to Indigenous decolonization, and that Chicano/a and Latino/a queers respond. One model appeared in activism surrounding the 1992 quincentennial by WeWah and BarCheeAmpe and the Cairos Collective, as recalled in *COLORLife!*. Mariana Romo-Carmona reflected there on her "responsibility as a Latina lesbian, a Chilean immigrant, a Mestiza living in the U.S." to organize for social change relevant "not only to myself, but to those who survived and resisted ... Knowing it or not, they gave me a future."[33] She names a responsibility to resist her assimilation into a colonial culture, given that "the mestizos, the product of the mixing of African, Native, and European, are in a constant battle of allegiance that attempts to make us forget two parts of our origins and make us remember only one." She then positions this affirmation of mixed heritage as nonidentical to her commitment to ally with WeWah and BarCheeAmpe and other contemporary Indigenous movements:

> We Latinos and Latinas, while we exoticize our roots, the basis of our music, medicine, and spirituality, still answer to the names given by the conqueror. This is the time to step back and examine what has been the cost of our survival. We are a new people, it's true, but our older brothers and sisters still inhabit these continents. The Mapuche, Aymara, Quechua, Araucano of the Southern cone of America still maintain their languages and their sovereignty. It is time to step back and accept leadership from all our people, beginning with those who have been the most silenced and have the most to say. (12)

Romo-Carmona's position honors her Indigenous heritage and the kinship it grants her to contemporary Indigenous peoples, although in doing so she is mindful not to, in her own word, "exoticize" it. But while recognizing mestizo heritage and its creation of Latinos/as as "a new people," she locates "the cost of our survival" in the embattled differences that sovereign Indigenous nations today struggle to sustain: when "in the Americas, Native people are still marginalized ... I recognize the importance of my solidarity with the struggles of all Native peoples and all People of Color" (11). In principle, Romo-Carmona's position does not differ from Anzaldúa's or from Chicano/a queer theories that seek decolonization for *all* people of Indigenous descent. But she reads indigeneity not as distant in time (primordial) or generic in scope (globalist) but as a multiplicity of contemporary national locations on the lands where she was raised and now broadly travels. For her, these locations first must be negotiated across their contemporary national and transnational distinctions, in forms of alliance, prior to and as a context for her consideration of the personal meaning of her own Indigenous heritage. Saldaña-Portillo also invokes these relationships by contrasting the "biological" logic of *mestizaje* to the invitation to relationship offered by the Indigenous activism of the Zapatistas, which she says is defined "not simply on biology but on the rigorous practice of thoroughly modern cultural, linguistic, social, religious, and political forms that constitute one as indigenous."[34] She accepts from the

Zapatistas an "offer" of "nonbiological forms of culture that are not only shared among a practicing community of indigenous people but hold the possibility of an alternative model of democratic practices of revolutionary subjection" (287).

The alliance work of Native American Two-Spirit people has invited ties with Chicano/a and Latino/a queers from within Indigenous transnationalisms that cross their interlinked yet nonidentical locations in white settler societies. Yet Two-Spirit activism suggests that the decolonial work of Chicano/a and Latino/a queers reimagining indigeneity, while necessarily traversing colonial discourses, also may articulate a colonial relationship to Native peoples if they do not deliberate their landed relationships across their differences. Queer diasporic critiques more broadly can learn from such relationships that theorizing queer mobility or displacement without articulating their relationship to settler colonialism and Native peoples will extend colonial power. In their stead, Two-Spirit movements already model forms of transnational alliance politics that potentially link Chicano/a and Latino/a queers, diasporic queers of color, and all queer people in a settler society in pursuing the decolonization of gender and sexuality.

Two-Spirit Transnationalisms and Indigenous Decolonization

If queer globalism in the United States projects a settler politics by naturalizing its settler colonial conditions, then Native queer and Two-Spirit activism disrupts queer globalism—in civilizational or primitivist form—by locating it in the national and transnational work of Native peoples denaturalizing settlement and pursuing decolonization. In those instances when Native queer and Two-Spirit projects engage queer primitivism, their adaptations also attempt to disrupt its globalism by positioning it within settler colonial relationships to Native nations and calling this to account. Two-Spirit identity arose by positioning Native queer people within Native nations and transnational Native alliances. Their disruptions of globalist imaginaries of queer indigeneity also called all non-Natives to ally with them in transnational work to challenge settler colonialism. Native queer and Two-Spirit movements thus incite a queer politics that disrupts colonial *and* global power, including by articulating critiques of global power in transnational Indigenous activism more broadly.

When Native queer people in the United States and Canada proposed Two-Spirit identity in 1990, their histories already exemplified Native responses to the transnational conditions of settler colonialism and decolonization. Native peoples and, specifically, radical Native movements for decolonization have been burdened by the perception of being problematically tied to place. In an early moment of postcolonial studies, non-Native European and North American scholars positioned Native peoples as being in conflict with postcoloniality, which represented a transnationalism that breaks modernist ties to nation and land.[35] Yet, against equations of indigeneity with fixity, Native studies scholars show that Native people formed multiple transnationalisms: in relations among Native societies, and in mutual or divergent engagements with settler societies and colonial modernity.[36] Settler colonialism itself functioned as a transnational power relation, as its impositions on Native peoples through genocidal displacements engendered diasporas and multiple experiences of Native history and identity. But relationship to land and peoplehood also fostered old and new transnationalisms among Native people, both prior to and subsequent to colonization. Furthermore, because colonial borders were modernist in logic and practice, Native anticolonialism places their logic in question. Amid calls to embrace nationality on settler terms, theorists of Indigenous governance challenge the colonial modernism of the nation-state form and reassert Indigenous epistemologies for the relatedness of peoples and land.[37] Against this background, scholars in Native studies call for the study of globalization as articulating settler colonialism. For some, contemporary law, politics, economics, and culture hinge on who counts as Indigenous and what role they will play in a globalizing world. Here they note the work of global Indigenous movements to challenge international law, global economics, environmentalism, and global health with assertions of Indigenous sovereignty.[38] In light of all such work, the transnational practices of Native peoples can be read as destabilizing the nation-state prior to and coincident with the appearance of global governance and economic globalization, even as they continue to question the nation-state form as a method for decolonization.[39]

All these implications are present in the historical work of Native queer activism, and specifically in the form of Two-Spirit organizing. Two-Spirit organizers join other Native people in marking the inherent transnationalism of Native experiences of colonization and resistance and their critical impact on theories of globalization and transnationalism. Native queer and Two-Spirit people confronted these histories in the border-crossing mobility of their encounters within urban centers of Native migration, even while retaining links to their counterparts in rural, reservation, and reserve communities. The formation of Gay American Indians in an urban space defined by Native diasporas performed the work of Native migrants to create urban communities as what Renya Ramirez theorized as "hubs" that help sustain ties to their nations and lands. While Randy Burns maintained ties with his Paiute family and community on their Nevada reservation lands, as did Barbara Cameron with Lakota people in the upper Midwest and across the continent, as leaders of Gay American Indians their identities also became linked beyond Lakota or Paiute nationality to the transnational activism their work inspired. The crucial role of pantribal work in Native queer and Two-Spirit activism must not discount or appear to erase its sustained relationships to multiple Native nations and lands. Nevertheless, non-Native queers consistently projected a global and transhistorical indigeneity of their imagining onto Native queer and Two-Spirit people that they did not request. Even repeated criticism in Native community circles of Two-Spirit activism as an indelibly "urban" phenomenon distant from rural, reservation, or reserve realities fails to ascertain that "urban" people created it precisely as expressions of their sustained ties to communities and lands that first and perpetually distanced *them* from belonging.[40] Blithe characterizations of Native queer and Two-Spirit activism as "urban" should be questioned until the participants' relationships between diaspora and landedness are explained. Thus, despite the perceptions of academics or activists, non-Natives or Natives that Two-Spirit identity invites a pan-Indigenous blurring of Native nationality, in fact Native queer activism, including Two-Spirit organizing, arose as pantribal and transnational alliances among Native peoples sustaining relationships to many nations. Indeed, as is evident in assertions by Burns and Hall and their adaptations of research on Native history cited in *Living the Spirit*, Gay American Indians linked Native national histories in a new language that did not erase their differences but invited their alliance. Hall's contribution is particularly indicative of comparisons of national traditions enabling new ties. He foregrounded the Shoshone traditions that defined his personal and familial understanding of self and social role. But he also invited Native queer people in diaspora to think across national histories, so those whose communities had lost knowledge of social roles could learn from others, or—along the model of the powwow—use tradition to invent new forms precisely for pantribal work. In Hall's formulation, gestures to nationality enable thinking transnationally, just as the national is *reimaginable* by thinking transnationally. Hall thus joined Midnight Sun, Maurice Kenney, and other contributors to *Living the Spirit* in arguing that Native queer activism will be guided not by universal claims but by proposing situated ties among Native nations, taking note of their distinct methods of kinship, economics, politics, and religion and their historical and contemporary national relationships.

The compatibility of national specificity with ties across differences also was modeled at the 1988 formation of WeWah and BarCheeAmpe. The flyer announcing the group's formation narrated it not as a uniform project, but as a relationship among situated lives, in its long listing of names in Indigenous languages of historical roles indicating gender and sexual diversity. Accompanying this list, WeWah and BarCheeAmpe made no statement that all the names should mean one thing: the list's existence simply proposes a relationship. Determining that relationship became the work of the Native people who joined, as their specific differences entered relationship. The group's name also was a constant reminder of these stakes. Rather than collapsing the lives of We'wha and Bar Chee Ampe into a singular or distinctly contemporary term, WeWah and BarCheeAmpe pronounced their names in Indigenous languages so that witnesses must inquire about them and their national contexts to even understand what the group represented. WeWah and BarCheeAmpe was one of the first Native gay and lesbian organizations after 1990 to begin using the term "Two-Spirit." Yet the group maintained its commitments to the landed struggles of various Native nations and to the formation of alliances among them and with non-Natives to challenge settler colonialism, all of which WeWah and BarChee-Ampe represented as Two-Spirit activism. WeWah and BarCheeAmpe thus exemplifies how the activism that led to proposing Two-Spirit identity, *and* the organizing that was revitalized in its wake, arose precisely from alliances across the differences of Native people representing varied national heritages. I invoke this model of Native queer and Two-Spirit activism in my application to it of the term "transnational," which crosses but does not erase the national fields it arises from, moves beyond, and returns to engage. In their historical formation, Native queer and Two-Spirit activists defied and destabilized a globalist power to collapse Native differences into primitivism or panindigeneity.

Gathering across differences produced Two-Spirit as a transnational category defined by dialogue across differences. In the United States during the 1980s, Native queer activists communicated across distances between local groups in urban and rural regions. Many recall the efforts to gather a Native contingent at the 1987 March on Washington for Lesbian and Gay Rights. At this, one of their first transcontinental meetings, participants reflected on their aspirations to meet again apart from the space of non-Native gay and lesbian activism, and affirm how their work originated in efforts to engage Native nations. American Indian Gays and Lesbians then organized in 1988 a continental gathering of Native gays and lesbians in Minneapolis, led by AIGL founders Anguksuar Richard LaFortune (Yupik), Lee Staples (Ojibwe), and Sharon Day (Ojibwe), among others. Participants examined Native histories of gender and sexual diversity and their own lives, in conversations later excerpted in Mona Smith's film *Honored by the Moon*. AIGL's second gathering in 1989 drew participants from Manitoba, who proposed that they host the third, Winnipeg gathering as the "International Gathering of American Indian and First Nations Gays and Lesbians." This gathering formed the space where participants sought to develop new language that could bring them together across national, geographic, and cultural differences, while still linking them to historical roles within their nations. This border-crossing space produced the term "Two-Spirit," which reflected its transnational production within and for dialogue among Native peoples. Rather than having been proposed in mailing lists or published texts, it arose to describe people who met to talk and develop a relationship after traveling great distances and despite differences of nationality, geography, and identity. Two-Spirit then contextualized and sustained this conversational relationship. The term inherited the logic of the gathering—a cohort of Native people in transnational movement—so that its capacity to cross borders originated from work to link and sustain differences gathered in relationship. Two-Spirit affirmed these qualities when it spread from among its originators through their urban, rural, reservation and reserve communities. If it quickly enlivened the pantribalism of urban Native activism, its slower percolation within rural, reservation, and reserve spaces marks its negotiation of historical local terms and their physical distance from the Native queer communities to which they nevertheless were linked. Despite later ties of the term to its urban or coastal expression, at its origin, Two-Spirit identity spread from the center of the continent through constituencies that bridged varied locations as a method to link Native peoples in transnational alliance across sustained differences.

In light of this reading, the national and transnational commitments of Two-Spirit identity *methodologically* disrupted the globalism within the colonial discourses that formerly defined Native gender and sexuality. Two-Spirit displaced the only term to have described Native queer people and their gendered and sexual histories: the colonial object berdache. The object had consigned them to a culturally authentic past aligned with colonial heteropatriarchal expectations of primitivity, which its promoters creatively adapted as a premise or tool of non-Native queer liberation. Non-Natives in those conversations engaged Two-Spirit as a Native term into which they could transpose their investments in berdache, or that they would critique for failing to meet their desire to do so. Yet, even misreading Two-Spirit as a continuation of berdache is a sign that Native queer people live amid colonial discourses and necessarily traverse them when making activist critiques. The decolonial logic of Two-Spirit identity meant to traverse and displace the primitivism in berdache, by countering its ubiquity and exceeding its logic while claiming a renewal of subjugated Indigenous knowledge. When non-Natives mistook Two-Spirit as replacing berdache, they failed to notice that Native activists had replaced the globalism and primitivism of berdache with Two-Spirit's situatedness within national and transnational alliances. If the new term ever led Native queer people to make timeless or universal claims, this followed a prior effect of disrupting colonial discourse and emphasizing Native differences so that they may be crossed. No universalizing claim can constrain the continued capacity of Two-Spirit identity to open up assertions of common meaning by reminding of the sustained differences that it attempts to place in relationship.

Two-Spirit projects that engaged white settler queer primitivisms proposed relationships with them that directly mediated colonial and globalist desires. Two-Spirit people achieved these effects by positioning non-Native queers within the transnational power relations of settler colonialism that they must oppose, while supporting Two-Spirit efforts to revitalize the cultural traditions of Native peoples. In the case of the Naraya, one might debate the effects of the efforts by leaders to make non-Native queers accountable, but any such debate should note that those efforts arose in the context of an intertribal renewal of Native traditional culture and national alliances that proposed to alter settler society, including by teaching non-Natives through Native culture that they were told not to appropriate. Such ties differ from those that Anzaldúa invited among the non-Native and predominantly white queer readers of the *Encyclopedia*. By enunciating Chicano/a queer indigeneity within a conversation defining white settler queer primitivism, and situating spiritual *mestizaje* as a quality non-Natives might adapt to satisfy their desires for a relationship to indigeneity, Anzaldúa's writing in the *Encyclopedia* extended the globalist effects of queer primitivism and its settler colonial relationship to the cultures of Native peoples in the United States and worldwide. Yet her Chicana queer decolonial imaginary could engage Two-Spirit claims by locating them within an alliance as people of Indigenous heritage across nonidentical locations in the power relations of settler colonialism. In this sense, Anzaldúa's desires resemble those of Native American queer people for whom genocide has so erased cultural traditions that only the border-crossing scope of Two-Spirit identity provides relief. But in doing so, Two-Spirit identity differs from spiritual *mestizaje* by referencing sustained national spaces that are linked within the situated transnationalisms of a contemporary politics of alliance. Indeed, national locations—and, within them, familial ties—for Hall and other Two-Spirit Shoshone leaders explain why they teach the Naraya, just as the historical purpose of the dance to produce pantribal relationships among Native nations is maintained by Hall, even as he extends this to non-Natives. If this positions him in a fraught relationship to queer primitivists, that effect is located within a prior alliance politics among Native peoples wherein the Shoshone histories of the Naraya invite ties among distinct Native nations. Non-Native participants then examine their basis for relationship to Shoshone religion, which they do not adopt as their own, even if some translate their experience into primitivist or globalist terms. The question remains open whether the practice of Native religion can be a means for disrupting the colonial desires of non-Natives. But the question also remains open as to how Chicano/a queers and Native Two Spirit people will reclaim indigeneity together within transnational relationships, and whether, had this structured her words in the *Encyclopedia*, Anzaldúa would have addressed queer primitivists differently.

Two-Spirit activists enact political movement that disrupts the settler colonial effects of queer globalism. They correctly identify that non-Native queer people seek to be global subjects to evade confronting their inheritance of settler colonialism, just as their use of colonial discourses dislocates Native cultures to become analogues in a global array of queer indigeneity that defies situated analysis. Queer non-Natives then may perceive themselves as citizens of the world to the extent that they do not examine the settler colonial power structuring their lives and granting them global spaces of imagination and movement to satisfy colonial desires. By asserting linked national and transnational activisms, Two-Spirit people situated non-Native queer cultures and politics as, already, transnational projects on Native lands. Holding them accountable to confronting settler colonialism blocks globalism's capacity to evade or disguise that power. Two-Spirit activism thus models a decolonizing and transnational queer politics that can disrupt the settler colonial conditions of queer globalism, including by calling on non-Natives to challenge their locations within these power relations and to ally with Native queer and Two-Spirit people's work for decolonization. Two-Spirit's transnationalism has acted as a method to challenge settler colonialism that leads Native activists into the broadening transnational ties of global Indigenous alliances. I now examine these effects in the historical and ongoing growth of Indigenous AIDS organizing.

Chapter 6

"Together We Are Stronger"
Decolonizing Gender and Sexuality in
Transnational Native AIDS Organizing

THE CONTRAST OF U.S. QUEER PROJECTS that invest in settler institutions and discourses and the work of Native queer and Two-Spirit activists is made stark by Native activist commitments to the collective sovereignty and decolonization of Native peoples. Whereas homonationalism produces queer integration into settler citizenship and union with Native lands by naturalizing settlement, Native queer activists lead Native peoples to challenge settler colonialism, the very formation homonationalism reinforces. Native activists thus resemble queers of color who lead communities of color in antiheteropatriarchal struggles against racism and imperialism that challenge the power of the state. But when Native queer activists defend Native nations, they uniquely contest the naturalization of settler colonial rule while locating all non-Natives in accountable relationship. In turn, by engaging Native peoples in diasporas caused by colonization, Native queer and Two-Spirit movements model transnational modes of naming and defending Native sovereignty. All these themes imbue the participation of Native queer and Two-Spirit activists in Native American and global Indigenous AIDS organizing. Responding to HIV/AIDS in Native communities was a key context in which Two-Spirit identity first circulated in North America. Addressing Two-Spirit people in Native AIDS organizing then marked Native peoples' experiences of colonial governance over sexuality, gender, and health, and framed acceptance of Two-Spirit people as a decolonial mode of traditional healing in Native communities. Similar arguments shaped Indigenous AIDS activisms crossing the Americas and the Pacific and inflected global alliance in which Two-Spirit people play a leadership role. Identifying colonial heteropatriarchy as a danger to Indigenous health led Native AIDS organizers to target and critique the biopolitics of settler colonialism in state and global health governance.

I locate the promotion of Two-Spirit identity in Native AIDS organizing within broader Native activist promotions of indigenist and decolonial approaches to health, which I shorthand as the pursuit of *health sovereignty*. Here I invoke *sovereignty* to refer to establishing Indigenous epistemologies and methodologies as bases of Indigenous governance and of Indigenous peoples' relationship to colonial power, which they displace. Native health activists pursue health sovereignty when they promote the decolonization of consciousness and social life among Native people as a basis for asserting cultural, economic, and political control over the conditions and methods of health.[1] Native AIDS organizers pursued this work by challenging colonial power over Native peoples and its internalization among them. While the biopolitics of settler state and global health operate by requiring the participation of Native people, Native health activists engage that power more complexly than simply considering their participation in state or global health programs to be a form of co-optation. Kevin Bruyneel argues that colonial formations of sovereignty are shifted by Indigenous peoples' self-determining demands for relationship with state or global power, which create a "third space" for Native sovereignty that is neither total removal from settler states nor assimilation by their power. For Bruyneel, asserting sovereignty is, to use Chadwick Allen's term, a critically (post) colonial act in that it creatively navigates the ongoing activity of settler colonialism with disruptive effects.[2] Taiaiake Alfred counters the power of settler sovereignty by asserting Indigenous governance, while warning that "sovereignty" as a Western and colonial category marks a position inside rather than beyond the logic of settler rule.[3] Yet Andrea Smith locates settler sovereignty's disruption in efforts by Indigenous feminists to reject the heteropatriarchal nation-state form and to invite all Indigenous peoples into alliance-based identifications and movements, within Native nations and transnational movements.[4] Indeed, the colonization Native AIDS activists challenge includes the internalization of heteropatriarchy, and the naturalization of sexism, homophobia, and transphobia as traditional to Native peoples. Native AIDS activists thereby mark the destruction of colonial heteropatriarchy—as a condition of the biopolitics of settler colonialism, and of the complicity of Native communities in its reproduction—as a primary condition of health for *all* members of Native nations. Both Two-Spirit and Native AIDS organizing formed to defend Native nations within transnational alliances that sought to change the border-crossing power of settler colonization. Whereas "sovereignty" tends to invoke Native peoples as distinct from one another or from settler society, transnational Native activists reimagine sovereignty not as inherent in a state—as in the Western sovereignty theorized by Giorgio Agamben and critiqued by Alfred—but as a capacity of Native peoples across differences *and* interrelationships to assert autonomy from colonial rule. Thus, differently from Alfred's questioning of the term but with similar effect, Indigenous feminist, queer, and AIDS activists displace settler theories of sovereignty by asserting forms of decolonization.

In this light, I use the term "health sovereignty" to refer to a broad array of conditions that disrupt settler colonial control over life, notably in the relation of living beings to land, the water and food it provides, and all its economic and social uses and political management. Asserting Native sovereignty over the *conditions* and methods of health potentially disrupts the entire institutional apparatus of settler colonization. But in the context of fighting AIDS and the genocidal legacies of disease for Indigenous people, calls for health sovereignty specifically challenge the biopolitics of settler colonialism that presumes Indigenous peoples are destined to die. Thus, when Native queer and Two-Spirit activists argue for their inclusion in Native nations while fighting AIDS to save themselves and Native peoples, they defy the biopolitics of settler colonialism both as a colonial heteropatriarchal targeting of queerness and as a genocidal logic that produces death for Indigenous peoples. Both a specific and general subjection of Native people to genocide is challenged when Native queer and Two-Spirit people in AIDS organizing disrupt Western sovereignty with Indigenous modes of governance and alliance and thereby disrupt the power to adjudicate the boundaries of life within settler colonialism.

Indigenous Methodologies in HIV/AIDS Organizing

From the early years of the epidemic's effects in Native communities, Native AIDS activists joined with Native scholars in centering theory of the colonial conditions of AIDS in Native people's lives. Irene Vernon in *Killing Us Quietly: Native Americans and HIV/AIDS* introduces the crisis in the context of histories of colonization: "the devastating impact of introduced diseases on Native Americans" followed by occupation made diseases "even more lethal when combined with grossly inadequate or total lack of health care."[5] In the United States, the National Alliance of State and Territorial AIDS Directors (NASTAD) framed Native people's experiences of the epidemic by the historical legacies of "Removal, Reservations, Allotment and Assimilation, and Elimination," which contained or broke apart Native communities, and forced assimilation into settler society through boarding schools, incarceration, adoption, and relocation. The authority retained by the U.S. federal government to control Native identity and community—as in the terms of tribal recognition, or termination—also controlled access to services set by treaty or trust obligations.[6] Federal obligations led to sporadic health services before the establishment of the Indian Health Service (IHS), which health activists also recognize as being undermined by inadequate funding in relation to need, even as access to its services is limited by its primary establishment in rural or reservation locations and its restricted use to federally recognized tribal members.[7] Even as the material conditions of conquest set health-care disparities, they conditioned subjectivity. Engaging the work of Bonnie and Eduardo Duran, Karina Walters asks how Native people encounter the epidemic in relation to the personal and collective effects of "historical trauma," as legacies of war, displacement, disease, and the denigration or erasure of Indigenous identity have created forms of marginalization that produce and predict poor health.[8] Shared knowledge and experience of trauma then inform how Native people negotiate health services, as when Bonnie Duran and Walters observe that "the use of disease as a strategy of colonization, a history of unethical research practice, and ongoing substandard medical treatment has left many [Native] individuals and communities distrustful."[9] Native AIDS organizers established interventions in concert with such analysis. The National Native American AIDS Prevention Center (NNAAPC) in the United States cites the work of Walters and Simoni to conclude that "many health problems among Native people can be directly attributed to 'their colonized status and to associated forms of environmental, institutional, and interpersonal discrimination'": not only because "racism makes it difficult for many Native people to access assistance from legal and social service agencies," but also because "oppression in conjunction with the chronic stresses linked with discrimination may lead to more physical and mental health problems among minority groups."[10]

Native people in the United States and Canada responded to HIV/AIDS by creating new knowledge and services in urban and rural contexts and on reservations and reserves that answered health disparities by enhancing Native control over health. Organizers engaged the colonial context of health care by adapting the material resources of treaty and trust obligations and external federal funds to create Native-centered health care. While Native health workers on or near reservations and reserves and in rural areas worked with tribal/band councils, federal agencies, and regional Native health organizations, urban workers addressed limited services by forming Native health organizations, at times linked to urban Native community centers. In the process, some urban Native organizations sought to access federal funds and also shape countrywide agendas by lobbying federal policies and distributing resources to rural areas.[11] But across their varied constituencies, Native AIDS organizers recognized that the colonial conditions of the epidemic presented a crisis not only of material resources but of knowledge. Native people's experiences of HIV/AIDS remained nearly invisible in medical literature until Native activists and allied scholars investigated them. Deeply mindful of the colonial power institutionalized within research, Native organizers and researchers linked HIV/AIDS services to the creation of new knowledge under Native control that could address Native understandings of health, health care, and disease. Recent Native research on Native people's experiences of HIV/AIDS has been modeled by the Honor Project, a multiyear NIH-funded study based in the United States and coordinated by Karina Walters, which is producing an extensive and varied portrait of Native people's experiences of trauma and health. Long-standing efforts to assert and control Native knowledge are also reflected in the Canadian Aboriginal AIDS Network's *Aboriginal Strategy on HIV/ AIDS in Canada*, which in 2003 proposed a Canada-wide coordination of Native AIDS programs — sharing models and resources, developing service capacity, and lobbying agencies and governments for resources — guided by the philosophy of Ownership, Control, Access, and Possession, or OCAP, when pursuing research on health. Such work displaces colonial methods of research to enhance control by the Native communities under study of knowledge production.

Multiple local and border-crossing modes of Native AIDS organizing arose in the United States and Canada. At times, health services formed to support longitudinal studies. After its 1987 founding, NNAAPC became the first recipient of U.S. CARE Act funds supporting long-term HIV/AIDS research and service provision by and for Native Americans, and founded the Ahalaya Project in Oklahoma. By "[consolidating] access to medical, mental health, spiritual, social, emergency, and educational services," Ahalaya presented a profile "built on cultural, spiritual, and traditional healing dimensions" that fostered indigenist identity and traditional healing.[12] The data NNAAPC collected was revisited at the 2003 "Gathering Our Wisdom" research and policy summit when participants argued against Native HIV education based on "disease prevention" rather than "wellness" and argued that "culturally appropriate care and treatment" for Native people should develop tools for "maintaining mental/emotional/physical/spiritual balance."[13] Regional

Native AIDS projects also promoted culture-based health services from an early date. The Indigenous People's Task Force (former Minnesota American Indian AIDS Task Force) formed in 1987 to coordinate HIV/AIDS education and health care for Native people in Minnesota. Under the leadership of founding director Sharon Day, the task force has centered access for clients living with or affected by HIV/AIDS on methods of traditional healing, and has fostered creative modes of HIV/AIDS education. For instance, the task force–based peer education troupe Ogitchidag Gikinooamaagad Players produces performances based in storytelling to transmit HIV/AIDS information to Native audiences.[14] In all such work, Native AIDS organizers adapted available resources, including federal funds, to create health education and health care that offered alternatives to the institutional and cultural form of non-Native medical management. Their focusing on Native cultural traditions for clients to adapt fostered indigenist identifications as decolonial contexts for working with illness and enhancing health.

Early Native AIDS organizers utilized visual and other creative media to promote decolonial and indigenist identity as a mode of wellness and healing for Native people. I now compare a small set of high-profile media by NNAAPC and the Indigenous People's Task Force that show how imaginative representations countered AIDS stigma—including by foregrounding Native women—while inviting Native people affected by HIV/AIDS to see themselves as central to the strength and survival of Native communities. In 1988, NNAAPC presented one of its first major prevention education projects, *We Owe It to Ourselves and to Our Children*, as a large-format booklet on natural-fiber paper together with a video presentation and storytelling packets. Made for small-group presentations, these texts invited audiences to connect to Native cultural traditions in a form the writers described as "subtle and beautiful . . . to diffuse the embarrassment associated with STD's," even as "images and legends" invited readers to "think not only of themselves" but also "of generations to follow."[15] The text opens by juxtaposing photographs of natural spaces with a nineteenth-century photograph of a Pima mother holding an infant, next to a narrative of motherhood as a theme of multigenerational interconnection. The booklet's midpoint then shifts to address health, with two large pages containing scattered text set against a thin interleaf, where statements about STDs and phrases such as "My doctor says it could make it hard for me to get pregnant" and "I AM AFRAID" are juxtaposed against resolutions such as "I just said, *you don't mind using these, do you?* AND HE DIDN'T," and "I WAS AFRAID." By then closing with STD and testing information set against the opening images, the text directs readers to health knowledge by shifting fear of disease, sexuality, or power to recall historical ties while centering motherhood as a metaphor of survival. In messages also reinforced in the video by codesigners Cathy Kodama and Terry Tafoya, *We Owe It to Ourselves and to Our Children* calls on Native people confronting AIDS to adopt indigenist identity and a sense of shared responsibility for collective survival as a basis for making healthy decisions.

In concert and contrast, an early video produced by the Minnesota American Indian AIDS Task Force, *Her Giveaway* (1988), directs Native audiences confronting the epidemic to relate to a specific life that challenges normalized boundaries of tradition and community belonging.[16] The video primarily presents first-person interviews with Carole LeFavor, who speaks frankly about her identity as a lesbian, her IV drug use, and her survival as a Native person living with HIV. Her story challenges the invisibility and stigma faced by Native lesbians and IDUs (intravenous drug users). Her narration of her struggles before and after her HIV diagnosis is interspersed with images and music evoking her spoken ties to indigenist identity and spirituality. She says, "Living the life of a spiritual person is the most important thing any of us can do, whether we're experiencing severe illness or wonderful health." LeFavor's narrative challenges stigmas by foregrounding Native lesbians and gay men, including by focusing on lesbian experiences, even while representing IV drug use by Native people and focusing on a journey to drug use by a Native woman and lesbian. Task force director Sharon Day (quoted by Andrea Rush) explains that *Her Giveaway* was designed to break through forms of "denial," such as "'that we don't practice homosexuality,' or that 'American Indians do not use IV drugs.'" Day also notes the need to challenge even more denials surrounding AIDS, by observing that at the time of the video's production, "many of the materials focusing on Native Americans do not discuss the groups most at risk: gay and bisexual men," and that "Not being able to say those words or put them into print does a disservice to the community."[17] Yet *Her Giveaway*, framed as a gift freely given to Native audiences, let LeFavor represent Native women's relationships to HIV/AIDS, and to Native community or spirituality, without centering either heterosexuality or motherhood, even while it urged strong ties for lesbians and IV drug users to Native familial, spiritual, and political solidarity.

Across their distinctions, *Her Giveaway* and *We Owe It to Ourselves and to Our Children* show early Native AIDS activist media using storytelling to evoke indigenist identity and decolonial renewal of traditional spirituality as a basis for health, as well as to link Native people across differences of sexuality, gender, drug use, and health status to challenge the epidemic. An example of these qualities being addressed to healing for persons living with HIV/AIDS appears in a text by Tom Lidot, first produced in 1991 for the Indian Health Council, and reissued by NNAAPC in 2003 as *Creating a Vision for Living with HIV in the Circle of Life*. Lidot described the revised text as "the only culture-based curriculum designed for Native people who are HIV-positive."[18] He opens it by saying that it

> provides a framework of Native teachings that encourage the reader to embrace the lessons of living with HIV/AIDS and to create a vision of living in beauty, health, wellness and balance. It is also a workbook that provides an interactive structure, allowing the individual to pause and reflect on the material. The workbook sections prompt the reader to dig deeply into their personal experiences and to write down ideas and revelations that have occurred as a result of the text and visualizations. (i)

Through the central image of the circle of life, the booklet graphically narrates a pantribal mode of Native spirituality linking personal health, community, and the surrounding world, in prose set against colorful photographic backgrounds of natural spaces and icons. In sections reminding readers to accept life experiences, release fear, reduce stress, and foster wellness, the text directs them to the historical and collective teachings of "elders and ancestors" so as "to draw upon this strength as we face the challenges of living with HIV" (24). A theme of connection to all life, and especially to Native communities, invites Native readers facing marginalization while living with HIV/AIDS to form bonds with other Native people in new and purposeful relationship ("You are part of the solution that helps our community successfully deal with the challenges HIV/AIDS brings") and the text closes with the reminder, "Our Ancestors are standing beside you" (23, 47). Against fears or experiences of rejection in Native communities owing to HIV status or other stigma, it exhorts readers to take up a promised and needed place as leaders of Native communities' struggles with AIDS—not as outsiders intervening, but as fulfillers of proper roles that are invited and affirmed by elders and ancestors. This text locates physical, mental, and spiritual self-care for Native people living with HIV/AIDS in collective Native identity and action in response to the AIDS crisis.

These texts indicate how, at the end of the first decade of the AIDS epidemic, Native AIDS organizers created high-profile media that theorized the colonial conditions of Native people's experiences of HIV/AIDS by inciting decolonial and indigenist identities and solidarities. They reflected the view that the marginality of Native people from good health attended on material and cultural legacies of colonization, but they also put that view into practice, by promoting identities for overturning stigma and inspiring solidarity across the differences of gender, sexuality, and drug use that AIDS highlighted among Native people. Contributions by Native people living with HIV/AIDS thus became crucial not just to their personal healing but to the survival of Native communities. Enacting these decolonial and indigenist reflections would interrupt the colonial conditions of health and bring Native people together across differences in solidarity to fight AIDS.

Decolonizing Gender and Sexuality, Redefining Collectivity

Two-Spirit identity and other assertions of traditional gender and sexual diversity presented Native AIDS activism with theories and methods for the *collective* decolonization of Native peoples. Native queer and Two-Spirit activists often were key to creating Native AIDS projects. These projects differed from early AIDS groups in the United States and Canada in the indigenist and decolonial nature of Native queer and Two-Spirit activist efforts to reclaim traditional gender and sexuality while marking settler colonization as a condition of their own and their communities' vulnerability to AIDS. Against those power relations, Native AIDS organizers situated respect for Two-Spirit people and traditional gender and sexual diversity as methods of personal and collective healing in Native communities and conditions for asserting health sovereignty.

Native AIDS organizing arose historically in close relation to Native queer and Two-Spirit activism. During the 1980s, Gay American Indians in San Francisco, the Native Cultural Society in Vancouver, and American Indian Gays and Lesbians in Minneapolis formed cultural spaces that respected and supported Native GLBTQ people even as they educated non-Native and Native people about their existence. These and similar groups played key roles in forming the first Native AIDS organizations or in staffing their programs—so much so that, over time, many local AIDS programs became key spaces for linking Native queer people in community. Their participation also infused early AIDS organizing with a forthright addressing of sexuality and gender diversity in Native communities. As a result, Native HIV/AIDS education increasingly affirmed a traditional basis for gender and sexual diversity and traced stigma associated with sexuality, gender, and AIDS to colonization.[19]

Many examples exist of Native AIDS organizing being grounded in renewing tradition and fostering solidarity under the leadership of Native GLBTQ people. In 1988, WeWah and BarCheeAmpe was co-organized by Curtis Harris and Nic Billey, who worked in the HIV/AIDS Project at the American Indian Community House. The group's invocation of We'wha and Bar Chee Ampe reflected ties to tradition already promoted at the Community House and encouraged by its HIV/AIDS Project, which organizers described as providing

> peer counseling, support groups, skills building workshops, and sexually transmitted disease education. These culturally appropriate services are also based in the traditions and spirituality of the "urban" American Indian/Native American/Alaska Native.[20]

In Minneapolis, the Minnesota American Indian AIDS Task Force was founded nearly simultaneously with American Indian Gays and Lesbians (AIGL), which then shared staff and programs. One of the task force's first HIV/AIDS education videos, Mona Smith's *Honored by the Moon*, recorded people at the first International Native GLBT gathering (1988) discussing their ties to traditional spirituality. By placing AIDS in the background, this video testifies to a recognition that challenging sexual stigma and honoring traditional belonging would promote health for Native people in the AIDS crisis.

Such efforts to realize acceptance energized Native GLBTQ people's desires for new language to communicate and directly informed the first international gatherings under the direction of AIGL and its Winnipeg allies, and the adoption in 1990 of Two-Spirit identity. The term's adoption initiated its circulation in rural and reservation contexts where many participants lived, although it did not translate as quickly among them, whether because of the term's local silencing of gender or sexual diversity or the presence of local categories that did not appear to require translation. Two-Spirit more quickly informed urban Native queer activist communities, whose prior efforts to link multiple histories in border-crossing narratives found in it a pantribal language that still could be adapted to describe particular Native traditions. This is the context in which Two-Spirit's rapid inspiration of urban Native queer activism also informed their AIDS activism. For instance, Darcy Albert recounts how the Toronto group Gays and Lesbians of the First Nations was formed in 1989 to address the fact that "a number of people from our community had already been infected or affected by HIV/AIDS, and there were some who had already died of AIDS related illnesses."[21] In this context, members changed their name to 2-Spirit People of the 1st Nations—and, later, to 2-Spirits—while growing into Canada's largest urban Native AIDS organization.[22] Two-Spirit identity also galvanized WeWah and BarCheeAmpe's efforts in one of its first major events to host the first North American conference on Native GLBTQ people and AIDS, "Two-Spirits and HIV," in 1991.[23] Hosted by the Community House, the event drew Native AIDS organizers from across the United States and Canada to discuss HIV/AIDS and Two-Spirit identity, only one year after the term's adoption. Such work recognized Two-Spirit identity as an effective means to assert the community belonging of Native GLBTQ people that Native AIDS organizers had long promoted.

The deepened knowledge of tradition that Two-Spirit identity promised did not end homophobia and transphobia. Native GLBTQ people still faced rejection by Native organizations and governments, but their marginality also resulted from more subtle forms of silencing.[24] Ron Rowell, cofounder and former director of NNAAPC, responded in 1995 to persistent homophobia in Native AIDS programs by convening a National Leadership Development Workgroup of Native gay and bisexual men. He was prompted to do so by a recognition that "the majority of the Native American community-based HIV-prevention programs have focused on the general population" despite the fact that gay, bisexual, and Two-Spirit men continued to be the majority of HIV and AIDS diagnoses.[25] Rowell noted that

> NNAAPC's strategy has been to train community organizers and educators through a series of week long workshops . . . Participants would divide into small groups [and] choose a target population . . . Over the [past] seven years . . . no more than three small groups chose to target gay men. When questioned, those who did not choose to target gay/bisexual men would commonly say, "We don't know of any people like that in our community," or "I would not be comfortable working with gay men because of my religious beliefs."[26]

Rowell concluded that NNAAPC's efforts to serve Native gay and bisexual men had to confront two "problems in our own strategy": a commitment to Native community self-determination "had not applied that lesson to subpopulations" and had let Native gay and bisexual men remain marginal "despite traditional teachings in many tribes that do not condemn homosexuality"; and given that health staff "in Native America . . . only seldom include gay men," NNAAPC's support for existing programs rather than advocacy for new ones "circumscribed who will be at the table" (5).

After convening in 1995, the workgroup concluded that "the failure of Native American HIV-prevention programs in most of the country to address the needs of gay/bisexual/Two-Spirit men is a direct result of the absence of such men," and argued for an AIDS organizing agenda based on the involvement of "Native American gay/bisexual/Two-Spirit men . . . at every level of HIV prevention in Native American communities," including by affirming that "recovering the traditional respect for the unique contributions these members of our tribal families will play a critical role in developing healthy Native American communities."[27] The workgroup then gave rise to the Pathmakers Project, which to the end of the decade gathered Native activists and scholars while broadening to form a Two-Spirit network that included Native women and, in 1998, addressed the erasure of Native lesbians from HIV/AIDS education for Native women or Two-Spirited men.[28] NNAAPC then developed a new curriculum for Native AIDS educators, *Addressing Two-Spirits in the American Indian, Alaska Native, and Native Hawaiian Communities* (2002), which used the term "Two-Spirit" to describe Native women and men across varied identities and histories, and then qualified its address to Two-Spirit men as a function of targeting MSM (men who have sex with men) HIV prevention.[29] This reflects a problem with focusing on Two-Spirit in AIDS organizing: it can remove the very visibility it grants Native women after years in which they were erased by other colonial terms for Native gender and sexuality, like berdache. While Native lesbians forthrightly entered AIDS projects that focused on Two-Spirit to address needs among Native MSM and Native women, these gendered implications remain in tension and invite ongoing reflection.

In this curriculum, and in programs promoted in its wake, NNAAPC explicitly recognized gender and sexual diversity within Native communities, although here as an indigenist and decolonial effort to assert collective Native health sovereignty that Native queer and Two-Spirit people would not just join or benefit from, but lead. A dynamic example of this—and of certain limits to it—appears in media activism by Native AIDS organizations directed at Native health workers and clients. NNAAPC responded in 2006 by producing the poster and video campaign "Together We Are Stronger," a set of four posters and one video public-service announcement targeting NNAAPC's constituencies of Alaska Natives, American Indians, and Native Hawaiians.[30] The campaign portrayed Native GLBTQ people within Native communities by arguing that their participation strengthens collective Native responses to AIDS. Each poster repeats the phrases "We are brothers & sisters. We are sons & daughters. We are uncles & aunts. We are friends. We are co-workers," which then leads to subjects identifying as Native ("We are Native"). The statement "And we are gay"—or, in the Kanaka Maoli/Native Hawaiian poster, *mahu*—then concludes the "many things" that "Native" can mean. A doubled resonance in the pronoun "We" might refer to the many identities of the subjects of the poster or, more broadly, to Native communities as a whole, suggesting their interdependence in one voice.

With Native health workers and clients as their primary audience, the posters do not use the term "Two-Spirit," perhaps reflecting common perceptions of it in 2006 as a recent or urban term. The Alaska Native and American Indian posters use *gay*, perhaps similarly to its use by Gay American Indians to invoke lesbian, bisexual, and trans Native people as well as Native gay men. Nevertheless, claims that echo the traditional belonging asserted by Two-Spirit identity structure the campaign. This appears in the two Hawaiian posters, which address *mahu* with the respect cultivated by Kanaka Maoli queer and AIDS activists who reassert this traditional gender identity in Hawaiian society. The message is reinforced when the poster in English is printed simultaneously in the Hawaiian language, with Hawaiian words overlapping the two subjects who dress in a gender presentation for Kanaka Maoli space.

The portrayal of nationally specific tradition also imbues the video public-service announcement profiling Kurt Begaye, an NNAAPC staff person and organizer of Navajo AIDS programs. Begaye relates in English and Navajo his unique personal qualities, including his clan affiliations and heritage. His narration of his many personal relationships in English—following the English script of the poster series—is intercut by a brief fade to black, after which he is portrayed against the backdrop of the landscape of Navajo territory while narrating in the Navajo language his relationship to family and place. The video thus introduces him in a narrative register as a person named in ways that still could be imbued by exclusion, while ending in a register that suggests he is not separable from a grounding in traditional belonging and that such belonging cannot be questioned. For a skeptical viewer, fearful of the implications of accepting GLBTQ people into Native community, the first part presents a challenge to join in work for social change, a temporal narrative that the second subverts by suggesting that no "change" need take place for the life of this Native gay man to be affirmed within the collective inheritance of the Navajo people. The campaign thus makes implicit and explicit statements that rejecting GLBTQ people from Native communities is a nontraditional act that must be placed under greater scrutiny in response to the crisis of AIDS. It portrays Native

We are many things.

We are brothers & sisters.
We are sons & daughters.
We are uncles & aunts.
We are friends.
We are co-workers.
We are Native.

And we are gay.

Our community is stronger *together*.
For more information, and to hear the stories of other
Native gay, lesbian, bisexual, and transgender individuals, please log onto www.nnaapc.org.

THE NATIONAL NATIVE AMERICAN AIDS PREVENTION CENTER

"Together We Are Stronger." Advertisement for National Native American AIDS
Prevention Center.

GLBTQ people in AIDS organizing performing leadership while grounded
in tradition and thereby calls on traditionalist Native viewers to respect and
follow them.

Crucially, amid all such exhortations of acceptance, the campaign makes
its titular claim by linking its address to the present with future work, concluding: "Our community is stronger *together.*" This assertion, implicit in
earlier Native AIDS organizing, here invokes the struggles Native peoples
must fight as strengthened by the participation of Native queer people. Certainly, in responding to a health crisis, the struggle requiring strength is
fighting all social conditions that exacerbate the spread of HIV. Yet, in light
of long-standing work by health activists to build decolonial and indigenist
approaches to prevention of and living with HIV/AIDS, the strength to be
gained may be an enhanced decolonization of Native culture and politics,
by a rejection of homophobia and transphobia and a renewal of the traditional knowledge that Native queer and Two-Spirit people recall. "Together
We Are Stronger" thus answers past struggles in Native health care by
arguing that centering gender and sexual diversity enhances the capacity of Native communities to challenge colonial conditions shaping their
health. Strengthening those communities will be a result of bridging dif-

ferences—of nationality, gender, sexuality, and all HIV-stigmatized practices—to foster collective work for health.

Without needing to mention the category Two-Spirit, then, "Together We Are Stronger" represented a response by a major Native AIDS organization to historical implications of Two-Spirit organizing—its epistemology, and methodology, of identity and social change in Native communities. Native queer and Two-Spirit people benefited from Native AIDS activist efforts to promote their lives through assertions of traditional belonging. This transpired not merely as the acceptance of marginalized persons, but as a mode of healing their lives *and* those of all Native people by correctly identifying the harm caused by colonial heteropatriarchy to kinship, tradition, and solidarity. When grounded in a broader assertion of collective control over the conditions of health, this activism challenged the rule of the settler state by mobilizing Indigenous knowledge and health responses. Such organizing bore broader implications within national and transnational politics. The very mobility and globalization of HIV/AIDS, as well as the transnationalism of Native activism, led Native people to respond to AIDS within and beyond the borders of settler states.

Global AIDS and Indigenous Transnationalisms

Two-Spirit and Native AIDS movements in the United States and Canada participated in and helped inspire global AIDS movements in which Indigenous queer people lead efforts for Indigenous decolonization. While attending to matters within Native nations or settler states, activists theorized how AIDS similarly affected Indigenous peoples worldwide and used this knowledge to critique global health governance by articulating Indigenous sovereignty on a global scale. Indigenous AIDS organizers thus model a decolonizing politics of sexuality, gender, and health with a potential to challenge the biopolitics of settler colonialism globally.

North American histories of Native AIDS organizing already map the activist routes of Indigenous transnationalisms. Norms of health governance in the settler state link Native nations across geographic and cultural differences. NNAAPC formed after a network of Native queer and AIDS activists accessed federal funds to address unmet needs among Native people affected by AIDS. The organization thereby became responsible to fund Native health services that the federal government did not need to run but could influence. Nevertheless, it also enabled Native activists to undertake local organizing that otherwise might not have happened, while linking

Native people to produce new methods for addressing AIDS and negotiating the power of the settler state. NNAAPC shows that state efforts to control Native peoples also created opportunities for Native people to collaborate in new ways.

An example of the diversity and potential alliances among Native peoples joined by AIDS activism became clear when NNAAPC followed its mandate to coordinate Native North Americans with Kanaka Maoli in Hawai'i. NNAAPC's origination on the continent made Two-Spirit a key category of analysis that entered broader dialogue when engaging Kanaka Maoli AIDS activists. Traditional Hawaiian gender and sexual diversity and its renewal has been central to the contributions of Kanaka Maoli GLBTQ people to work for Hawaiian sovereignty.[31] Leaders in Kanaka Maoli AIDS activism include self-identified *mahu* activists presenting a traditional role while defending communities. Yet distinctions between their work and Two-Spirit organizing were evidenced by the NNAAPC curriculum *Addressing Two-Spirits*, which only discusses Native American gender and sexual diversity. NNAAPC workshops taught the curriculum to organizers from tribal or nonprofit agencies from across the United States, including Alaska and Hawai'i. At a 2002 workshop in Minneapolis, representatives from such programs included many who identified as Two-Spirit, in addition to one contingent from Hawai'i with two members who identified as *mahu*. Participants' discussion of the definition of Two-Spirit evoked points of commonality and distinction, including when one in the Hawaiian delegation said how she understood Two-Spirit to describe her life, even though her identity remained *mahu*. She noted that life as *mahu* in Hawaiian contexts aligned more with transgender identity on the continent than with the lesbian or gay identities that Native American Two Spirit people commonly claimed. Here, Two-Spirit's North American pantribalism met its geographic specificity—and potential governmentality as part of the mandate of a state-funded health initiative—when Kanaka Maoli partners had to argue the distinctions of Hawaiian culture. Yet their engagement also demonstrated an intention to pursue alliance in defining traditions of gender and sexual diversity in the space facilitated by NNAAPC, albeit not necessarily by amalgamating *mahu* within Two-Spirit identity. Structures facilitated by the state thus simultaneously facilitated Indigenous transnationalism and marked certain limits within it, even while the exchanges engendered there affirmed commitments to decolonization that went beyond this space and continued to inspire border-crossing AIDS activism.

Indigenous AIDS organizers beyond North America centrally pursued the recollection of histories of gender and sexual diversity. Conversations at the NNAAPC workshop noted the ties that *mahu* activists were forming with Samoan AIDS activists in Samoa and Hawai'i who identified and worked in *fa'afafine* social networks. Samoan activists participated in forming the Pacific Sexual Diversity Network (PSDN) with Indigenous AIDS organizers from Fiji, Tonga, Vanuatu, Cook Islands, and Papua New Guinea, many of whom practiced what they defended as traditional nonheteronormative social roles. Initially funded by UNAIDS, PSDN aligned with the Australian Federation of AIDS Organizations as a regional network coordinating AIDS programs organized locally by Pacific Islanders, and emphasizing men who have sex with men and transgender women. Concurrently, as examined by Maori scholar and HIV/AIDS researcher Clive Aspin, AIDS organizers aligned with Maori queer politics promoted the term *takatapui* in Aotearoa New Zealand to name traditional recognition of same-sex and transgender partnerships in Maori societies. Aspin argues that this work models to Maori people and Indigenous peoples worldwide the fact that promoting "health and well-being" in Indigenous communities, especially in the era of AIDS, rests on the decolonization of gender and sexuality.[32] Among many more examples, these suggest the resonances among Indigenous Pacific and Native American AIDS activists, as well as the continued mediation of state and global health funding as forms of governance amid prior and ongoing efforts by Indigenous queer people and allies in Indigenous communities to fight AIDS and the social conditions that facilitate it.

A global shift in Indigenous AIDS organizing followed local and regional efforts to send representatives to pursue Indigenous agendas at international health conferences, especially the biennial International AIDS Conference (IAC). This conference of the International AIDS Society has, since 1985, offered a venue where medical researchers join AIDS service organizations, governments, and pharmaceutical corporations to define knowledge and coordinate responses to AIDS. The authority of this conference was heightened after its early targeting by AIDS activists, as traced by Cindy Patton, when ACT-UP's "stings" at the 1993 Berlin IAC demanded accountability, and received increased accessibility for local and international activists to engage the conference.[33] These were the contexts where Indigenous AIDS activists first met at the IAC. Barbara Cameron attended the Berlin meetings as NNAAPC's official representative. She reflected afterwards on her unplanned encounters during this trip with Indigenous people, including

Native American expatriates living in Berlin who helped delegates form a sense of transnational Indigenous community outside the conference, even as Indigenous delegates from around the world held daily meetings at the conference to support their participation.[34] Rodney Junga-Williams, a Narunga-Kaurna and Adelaide Plains activist in Indigenous Australian AIDS organizing, wrote of his travel to Berlin as "the first Aboriginal gay man living with HIV to speak" at the IAC: "like other nungas I went looking and found other Indigenous people from the U.S.A., Canada and New Zealand and we stuck together throughout the event. As a group of people we weren't that many but we were very vocal."[35] He is referring to Indigenous delegates' efforts to write a statement for the closing session, which called on international agencies to challenge colonial legacies that make Indigenous peoples vulnerable to AIDS and to recognize the autonomy and self-determination of Indigenous nations. From their earliest shared engagements with global health institutions, Indigenous AIDS activists acted to hold those institutions accountable to transnational assertions of sovereignty by Indigenous peoples over the local, global, and national conditions of health.

Political theorists increasingly bracket a distinctive arena of recent historical politics as "transnational activism," indexing the rise of nongovernmental organizations (NGOs) as players in the power relations of states and international agencies. Margaret Keck and Kathryn Sikkink examine a distinctive method in such activism, "the boomerang effect," in which political actors who cannot achieve change in states call on NGOs or international agencies at global policy arenas to place pressure on their issue and thereby broker decisions with states.[36] Feminist theorists also interpret this activist method as a mode of global governmentality when it integrates nongovernmental organizing into international law as a normative site for managing subjects and rights. Inderpal Grewal explains that feminists in transnational activism challenge formal exclusion from national or international law only to find that women privileged by nation, class, and race in global arenas gain authority to speak on behalf of others while being recruited to manage an NGO-ization of social movements.[37] Transnational activism thus produces a governmental site to legitimate the international laws that states define to regulate social change, even as citizens in dominant states are mobilized to impose hegemonic power relations in the name of advocacy. Yet feminist scholars attentive to the pervasion of these power relations also note that the structures they produce remain adaptable on the margins by the very targets they mean to control. As Anna Tsing explains in *Friction* (2005), when local actors in Indonesia encounter global power not just through global economies or governmental agencies, but also in transnational activism such as environmentalism or feminism, engaging them with discrepant local stakes exposes global power to critique while inciting unpredictable actions that may trouble its effects. One effect could be to engage the circuits of global power by asserting sovereignty *from* their global and borderless authority as a basis for relationship with their power. While engagements with global power may co-opt radical intentions, zones of friction merit study of their potential to produce unexpected relationships and effects.

I am interested in how Indigenous AIDS activist involvement in global politics disturbs the naturalization of settler colonialism within global governance, while facilitating the imagining of transnational Indigenous alliances that exceed global systems and model the alternatives of Indigenous governance. For Indigenous peoples responding to the AIDS epidemic, the biopolitics of settler colonialism predicts their elimination and ensures their regulation. Its globalization then naturalizes their definition and management by "independent" states without regard for their inherent sovereignty. When these power relations coalesce in global health governance, the "participation" of Indigenous people is not in question: the power of biopolitics ensures that this will occur regardless of whether they choose to engage it. In this context, I am interested in how Indigenous AIDS activists rooted in the defense of national sovereignty and the formation of transnational Indigenous alliances addressed global health arenas with discrepant stakes. As activists accountable before and after this participation to projects that exceed the power of the global and seek to destroy its settler colonial formation, they exhibit a critical edge that bears frictive possibilities for decolonial work amid the pressures of the AIDS pandemic and its settler colonial and international management in a globalizing world.

Global actions by Indigenous AIDS activists have arisen largely as interventions into the IAC by holding the organization and its stakeholders accountable to Indigenous demands for health sovereignty. In response to alliances formed at the Berlin IAC and after, Indigenous AIDS activists in Canada and Mexico mobilized Indigenous participants at the IAC within existing activist ties crossing the Americas and the Pacific. Their first event was held prior to the 1996 IAC in Vancouver, in the form of an International Indigenous People's Summit. The British Columbia Native AIDS organization Healing Our Spirits hosted this off-site preconference to link Indigenous delegates from around the world with British Columbia Native activists and others traveling from across Canada and the United States. Because the summit model is external to the IAC, it readily connected local and regional Indigenous people as key constituencies of the work it coordinated with regional Indigenous AIDS organizations and Indigenous delegates from around the world. Later summits repeated this model of linking regional activists with international delegates in an autonomous space. The 2008 Mexico City summit was led by Zapoteca *muxhe* organizer Amaranta Gómez and Indigenous activists from across Mexico and Latin America, while the 2006 Toronto summit was hosted by the Toronto Native AIDS organization 2-Spirits and by the Ontario Aboriginal HIV/AIDS Strategy. Summit events thus arose in relation to the IAC and the global circuits of people, capital, and government it creates by forming spaces for collaboration—not at the conference, but nearby—where hosts and visitors linked multiple struggles in growing networks.

Such work shaped how organizers at the 2006 Toronto summit drafted this network's first statement of shared values in a form that would draw the attention of the IAC, states, and global institutions. Composed as an international policy document, *The Toronto Charter: Indigenous People's Action Plan on HIV/AIDS 2006* asserted sovereignty over health for all Indigenous peoples. Activists from North America and the Pacific spent two years composing the charter, which demanded that states and global institutions answer Indigenous demands to control the conditions and methods of health. I interpret the charter by inspiration of Robert Warrior's analysis of the 1881 Osage Constitution, which he says presents a creative Indigenous adaptation of U.S. constitutional law that responded to a changing colonial situation by setting indigenist terms for negotiating sovereign relationships.[38] In the narrative form of public policy, the charter demands that settler states and international agencies become accountable to the authority of Indigenous peoples to define and manage health from within modes of Indigenous governance. In the two years prior to the 2006 IAC, summit organizers traveled to prepare the text "at a session of the United Nations Permanent Forum on Indigenous Issues and in numerous cities in Australia, Canada, New Zealand, and the United States," and submitted drafts to Indigenous AIDS organizations worldwide for feedback.[39] The final text was printed as a poster and announced at the Toronto conference as a form of media activism and an intervention into policies governing Indigenous people and AIDS.

The charter opens as "a call to action" to the states, international bodies, and nongovernmental agencies that control "the provision of HIV/AIDS services for Indigenous Peoples around the world" to recognize the "devastating effect" of AIDS on Indigenous peoples. Marginalization within settler states produces a "range of socio-cultural factors that place Indigenous Peoples at increased risk of HIV/AIDS," such that "in some countries, Indigenous Peoples have disproportionately higher rates of HIV infection than non-Indigenous people." The charter resituates this reality by asserting Indigenous peoples' "inherent rights . . . to control all aspects of their lives, including their health" and "to determine their own health priorities." This assertion of a sovereign relationship to settler societies also centers Indigenous control over the conditions and methods of health. When the charter calls on settler states to fulfill obligations to the Indigenous peoples whose lands they occupy, it marks colonial rule as a force that Indigenous demands can shift. The text asserts that "governments are responsible for ensuring" that Indigenous people will experience "a state of health that is at least equal to that of other people" and sets the terms of such health care in such qualities as "access to their own languages" and addressing the "physical, social, mental, emotional and spiritual dimensions" of health, while "[communicating] information about the prevention and treatment of HIV/AIDS that is relative to the reality in which Indigenous Peoples live." These statements admit that, all demands for autonomy aside, Indigenous peoples experience settler colonialism as the source of the conditions of poor health that now require intervention. Thus, to the extent that Indigenous communities are so marginalized from good health and Indigenous governance that only state health institutions can offer care, the very agencies that created poor health within a colonial biopolitics to produce social control will continue to manage health for Indigenous peoples. Yet the charter insists that such changes will not be a prerogative of settler states, but will respond to the authority asserted by Indigenous people to define the conditions and methods of their health despite ongoing colonial occupation, including Indigenous control over the production of knowledge. The charter asserts that "governments must be committed to consulting with Indigenous Peoples in order to ensure that health programmes meet the needs of Indigenous Peoples," and that "it is essential that HIV/AIDS data on indigenous peoples be collected in a manner that is [determined] by Indigenous Peoples themselves." Governments then will "ensure the central participation of Indigenous Peoples in all programmes related to the prevention of HIV and programmes for the care and support of Indigenous Peoples living with HIV/AIDS" and will provide "resources to Indigenous Peoples to design, develop and implement HIV/AIDS programmes . . . so that Indigenous communities can respond." This last statement acknowledges that organizations such as NNAAPC or the Canadian Aboriginal AIDS Network (CAAN) are not common, and that their ability to support local Native projects that precede and exceed their state funding remains one model within state health governance that Indigenous AIDS activists can accept for its track record of being open to critical adaptation. Finally, all these calls to transform the practices of settler states are framed by a demand that international agencies "monitor and take action against any States whose persistent policies and activities fail to acknowledge and support the integration of this Charter into State policies relating to HIV/AIDS," while ensuring that the "participation of Indigenous Peoples in United Nations forums is strengthened so their views are fairly represented." These statements put settler states on notice in international arenas that they are sites of colonial rule of Indigenous peoples, while they also show how the UN Permanent Forum on Indigenous Issues joins other sites that Indigenous activists already engage to make their interventions on international platforms while holding national *and* international law accountable to addressing settler colonialism.

The Toronto Charter is a critical intervention within the still-hegemonic colonial terms organizing state and global governance of health and, as a result, Indigenous peoples. The charter's language does not model Indigenous governance, but it does tactically open possibilities for discourse that may facilitate the more radical and decolonial ends that Indigenous AIDS activists envision and seek. It never directly names gender or sexuality, but an implication that sovereignty attends on the assertion of Indigenous knowledge reflects activist efforts to ground the defense of gender and sexual diversity in the protection of Indigenous communities from AIDS.

Although the charter only alludes to such work, its announcement at the 2006 Toronto IAC performed it. During the conference, Indigenous delegates invited delegates and Toronto-area residents to a press event at the IAC-designated Indigenous people's pavilion where Indigenous delegates joined local Native AIDS activists, including many Native queer and Two-Spirit people, to hear the charter read before global and Indigenous media. Organizers announced the charter as a first statement by an international alliance of Indigenous AIDS activists; they read key portions, and called for a response from the society and governments, before distributing the poster to attendees. The framing of this photograph suggests how activists adapted the visuality of international conference space to act on the boundaries of global power. We see here a space where global agencies officially recognize Indigenous peoples, but, at the same time, a public space within

Launch of *The Toronto Charter* (formally known as *The Toronto Charter: The Indigenous Peoples' Action Plan on HIV/AIDS*) at the XVI International AIDS Conference, 2006. Photograph by Michael Costello. Courtesy of Australian Federation of AIDS Organizations.

the settler state that Indigenous peoples contest along its border with the power of global health. On the left side of the frame is the convention center passage to the conference where registered delegates enter, but on the right side of the frame are open public gates to downtown Toronto. This event pursued media activism by calling on global corporate and independent media at the conference to cover the novelty of an Indigenous AIDS protest, while creating a historic event for recording by Indigenous media representatives and activists' own organizations. While the press event called attention to Indigenous AIDS activist interventions at the conference, the event was not in fact designed as a presentation to the IAC's stakeholders, none of whom attended it. In this sense, the significance of this event is less that it should have received a formal response from global health managers than that it succeeded in performatively *imagining* health sovereignty by demonstrating that Indigenous AIDS activists do constitute a global alliance that can demand control over the conditions of health by Indigenous peoples worldwide.

One other image in this photograph stands out in the background: it is a flag that the San Francisco Bay Area American Indian Two-Spirits, which more than a decade earlier succeeded Gay American Indians, gave to the Toronto organization 2-Spirits for their use in the Toronto pride parade. The flag's symbolism, which includes a medicine wheel and other images, asserts an Indigenous difference overlaid on, yet incompletely absorbed by, the queer "diversity" represented by the rainbow flag. Indeed, this flag announces the identity Two-Spirit, which represents a unique location within the colonial histories of sexuality and gender, to which all non-Native queer people in the background are accountable. But the flag's appearance at this event is also a reminder that *The Toronto Charter* never mentioned Two-Spirit or any other indigenist claim on gender or sexuality. "Together We Are Stronger" intimated those claims by calling Indigenous people to challenge heteronormativity's colonial roots and affirm relationship across differences. The charter, by contrast, specifically addressed as its audience *non*-Indigenous arbiters of *colonial* power—and not to educate them in Indigenous culture but to demand that they make way for Indigenous people to decide how their cultures will be engaged. At the IAC, the charter's announcement linked Indigenous AIDS activists who live as Two-Spirit, *mahu, muxhe, fa'afafine,* and *takatapui,* as well as people identified as GLBT or queer. Without collapsing their differences, they crossed many sites for Indigenous queer stakes to lead a new movement for the health of their own and all Indigenous communities. This is the work of a transnational Indigenous politics of gender and sexuality, and it arose when AIDS redefined kinship and solidarity to link Indigenous people across differences in pursuit of the decolonization of health.

Challenging Colonial Biopolitics

The decolonial sexual politics of Indigenous AIDS organizing indicates that critiquing colonial heteropatriarchy challenges settler colonialism in state and global governance while mobilizing new movement for decolonization. In the process, Indigenous AIDS organizing opens the colonial biopolitics of modern sexuality and global health to critique. Activists' efforts to traverse health systems mark their potential co-optation even as their pursuit of Indigenous decolonization invites those systems' disruption.

Global health governance is a key arena of the continued activity of colonial biopolitics and its naturalization. Cindy Patton explains that colonialism conditions the biopolitics of global health in the circulation of two "thought-styles" that structured World Health Organization efforts to manage public health, including the AIDS pandemic.[40] The first she traces to the discipline of tropical medicine as it historically studied the effects of disease on the traveling European body. For Patton, *tropical* thought-styles define a normatively European human body as endangered by movement through geographies of disease inhabited by tropical bodies. In this narrative, disease is localized, while the subject of disease travels. She contrasts this to the *epidemiological* thought-style extrapolated from the rationalizing scientific method of public health. Here, disease agents travel along vectors to create nodes of illness whose chains of relationship must be diagnosed by epidemiologists. Within epidemiology, the subject of disease may be local, but diseases are mobile, as researchers and research must be. For Patton, both narratives sustain a colonial legacy, in the racial and civilizational reading of tropical zones of inexorable disease, or in the seemingly deracialized and civilizational imagining of a world united by disease as well as by the positionless mobility of researchers and their universal claims to knowledge. With their different spatializations, Patton argues, "these two major scientific thought-styles... were competing ways of claiming the mantle of neutrality that invoking science affords."[41] In her analysis, colonial discourses and institutional practices are sustained when populations marked by disease become the focus of global health governance.

In addressing the contrast of Africa and Asia to Europe or "the West" in global health, Patton does not specify the locations within her narratives of Indigenous peoples. Indigenous peoples appear specifically within the *settler* colonial biopolitics of global health as populations destined for elimination by the arrival of colonial modernity. Tropical thought otherwise might seem helpful to explain colonial accounts of Indigenous peoples as essentially localized. But while colonial medicine narrated Asia and Africa as hardier in relation to disease than the European body, Indigenous Americans and Pacific Islanders were narrated as excessively vulnerable to disease and inevitably disappearing in the wake of colonial modernity's expansion. Global health narratives may rest easily in the settler colonial legacy by portraying genocidal diseases among Indigenous peoples as non-human and bereft of agency, thereby performing and naturalizing the discourses as well as institutional practices of settler colonization that predict Indigenous elimination. Narratives of Indigenous peoples' constitutive isolation—geographic, temporal, cultural, *and* biological—code with narratives of elimination to frame their encounter with HIV/AIDS. A failure of global health programs to stem the epidemic in Africa or Asia can be explained by tropicalizing those regions as sites of permanently entrenched disease. But those same programs' failure to address HIV/AIDS among Indigenous peoples can appear as an effect of those peoples' naturalized marginality—too isolated to be served—conjoined with their vulnerability to change (i.e., to death) by "contact," in an inevitable march to extinction that even modern public-health programs cannot stop. Such narratives were recalled in Canada in 2009 amid public-health responses to the H1N1 epidemic, after federal agencies delivered to rural northern Native communities vaccine and face masks accompanied by unmandated body bags. Outraged community health leaders deplored this as a sign that the very agencies charged with protecting them had given up and were being readied for their deaths. Here, an epidemiological reading that public-health measures cannot prevent epidemic in rural northern Native communities appears as the rationalizing logic of a settler colonial biopolitics. Moreover, the very settler health systems that "manage" Indigenous health amid continued narration of the biopolitics of settler colonialism participate in establishing the authority of global health programs that then set protocols and fund procedures through which settler states, as "independent" states serving their "populations," manage the localization of pandemic. State and international health governance thus becomes a medium for the simultaneously settler colonial *and* global biopolitics contextualizing the relationship of Indigenous peoples to disease and health.

This book has argued that recollections and reimaginings of Native knowledges of gender and sexuality and their promotion within and as Native activism mark and destabilize the biopolitics of settler colonialism, notably in the form of settler sexuality. As Indigenous AIDS activists traversed their subjection within state and global health governance, their actions denaturalized the ongoing practice of settler colonialism and its animation of knowledge claims about Indigenous people. Addressing HIV/AIDS, and the stigmas and marginalizations that would prevent this, Indigenous AIDS activists adapted available resources in ways meant not to result in co-opting their decolonial aspirations for health sovereignty. As Taiaiake Alfred and Glen Coulthard observe, co-optation readily arises by aligning Indigenous "sovereignty" with "recognition."[42] Activists at the Toronto IAC convened at the Indigenous pavilion designated by the IAC's policy of including, and thus containing, critical constituencies. But the intervention activists brought already went beyond the "recognition" their acts were granted by the IAC or global institutions. As in Joanne Barker's critique of "recognition" as an end point of sovereignty activism, *The Toronto Charter* does not hinge on state or global institutions recognizing Indigenous sovereignty, although members may interpret it that way.[43] The charter announces that Indigenous peoples already know and practice an inherent sovereignty in politics, culture, and health regardless of whether settler state or global institutions recognize it. On this basis, they demand responsible engagement from institutions exerting power over Indigenous health by making them accountable to Indigenous control over its conditions and methods. This knowledge that Indigenous sovereignty never disappeared and cannot be removed already inflected AIDS activist promotion of Indigenous epistemologies and methodologies as bases for health—largely because of their being grounded in the antiheteropatriarchal legacies of Native queer and Two-Spirit activists asserting their traditional belonging within and leadership of Native decolonization struggles. Deployed against state and global health management, such claims simultaneously interrupt logics of subjectification and population control in colonial biopolitics. Thus, while this effect can be read throughout the history of Indigenous health activism, the unique foregrounding in Indigenous AIDS activism of gender and sexual diversity already marked settler state and global power as colonial through their heteropatriarchal formation. Indigenous AIDS activism thus centers Indigenous epistemologies that dare to imagine and assert autonomy from biopolitical control by proposing the decolonization of gender and sexuality and the pursuit of sovereignty over health.

I highlight these possibilities precisely because scholars of the AIDS pandemic, and specifically within Native communities, know that health programs, AIDS activism, and their amalgamation readily normalize sexual, gendered, and Indigenous identities and require critical vigilance.[44] The history of Two-Spirit identity within Native AIDS organizing is a crucial case in point. Brian Joseph Gilley explains how Two-Spirit identity became useful to Native AIDS organizations because its pantribalism facilitated claims compatible with the needs of Native health promotion in urban Native communities.[45] Of course, even here, Two-Spirit identity remained tied to tribal specificity, as when WeWah and BarCheeAmpe emphasized national differences so as to link them in alliance. Yet Two-Spirit's pantribalism readily appears generic rather than an allying of sovereign differences—and productive of colonial governance rather than displacing of it—if health programs in the mode of liberal multiculturalism produce "culturally appropriate" health care by citing the term to define an object of Native sexual deviance for management.[46] As noted earlier, the very history of promoting Two-Spirit identity to challenge erasure of Native gay and bisexual men from Native health projects led to its problematic association with male embodiment and same-sex sexuality, even for Native organizers and health scholars who know the term's broader meaning.[47] Two-Spirit identity was defined by the diversely gendered participants of the Third International Gathering to supplant masculinist bias in the object berdache and to no longer marginalize Native lesbian and bisexual women and trans people. That Native AIDS activism could deploy the term against this very intention is a poignant example of the insidious convergence of the need Sharon Day and Ron Rowell noted at an early date to address Native male same-sex sexuality, and the interests of colonial health governance to define Indigenous and racialized bodies by their practice of health-endangering male sexual deviance, precisely by portraying them through the seemingly noncontrolling population marker of cultural specificity.

Whether or how colonial governance appears within public health citations of Two-Spirit is something that practitioners and scholars of Native AIDS organizing investigate. I raise the issue because my argument in this chapter has taken two critical directions when evaluating the defense of gender and sexual diversity as tradition in Native communities defended by AIDS activists. The first was a historical view emphasizing the local arenas, contingent relationships, and tactical activist projects that linked Native queer/Two-Spirit and AIDS activisms. Their convergence preceded and exceeds any potential adoption of them within colonial governance. Distinctive intellectual histories of decolonizing thought and movement therefore constitute, and resonate within, the legacies of Native queer/Two-Spirit and AIDS activisms. Resituating current practices within an accountable relationship to this heritage, without any guarantee, remains capable of interrupting any attempt to absorb them into new modes of colonial governance within liberal settler multiculturalism or global public health.

The second critical direction of my analysis has evaluated these activist histories to tell a story that merits attention in *non*-Native queer and AIDS activisms, where it demonstrates the impact of Native activists on power relations in settler societies. Unlike non-Native projects in these areas, Native AIDS activism directly denaturalized settler colonialism as a condition of sexuality, gender, and HIV/AIDS, and of queer and AIDS movements. When Native activists face their potential complicities in colonial power and its reproduction, these are important because they persist despite Native activists' having *already denaturalized settler colonialism* in ways that *non*-Native queer and AIDS activists have barely begun to imagine. Comparisons of how colonial power conditions various non-Native and Native queer or AIDS activisms will illuminate their degrees of commonality or distinction.

But my book indicates that at any point where such comparisons might be made, their usefulness will be interrupted if non-Natives who seek them do not first disrupt how settler colonialism conditions their relationship to Native peoples and their thoughts and actions in that relationship.

My argument also addresses Native AIDS organizers by asserting that a critical potential in their work already exceeds that which is offered by AIDS organizing that aligns with or is absorbed within normative models of state or global health governance. Recalling and asserting subjugated Indigenous knowledges and transnational alliances in pursuit of health sovereignty shatters the logics of the biopolitics of settler colonialism and colonial heteropatriarchy. In the process, centering Indigenous queer people as leaders defending their nations undermines sexism, homophobia, and transphobia while centering HIV/AIDS, gender, and sexuality in Indigenous struggles for decolonization. Countering assertions that would place Indigenous peoples as being anterior to modernity or eliminated by disease and conquest, Indigenous AIDS activists redefine health as a practice of decolonization that can restore Indigenous governance.

Epilogue

THE BIOPOLITICS OF SETTLER COLONIALISM continues to attempt to eliminate Native nations as a difference that can disturb the finality of settlement, precisely by regulating them within a state of exception. As Taiaiake Alfred notes, an illusory sovereignty may be transposed onto Native nations that remains contained by the normative power of Western sovereignty as settler colonialism. When Native people fight the AIDS pandemic and its conditioning by heteropatriarchy in Native nations and settler societies, they confront the biopolitics of settler colonialism within global health: in knowledges of disease that facilitate global governance determined by settler states and their allies for ongoing rule of Native peoples and lands. Yet Andrea Smith's portrayal of Native feminists decolonizing heteropatriarchal leadership in Native nations and challenging settler rule highlights Native activists' capacity to form "unlikely alliances," which may describe how Native AIDS activists traverse colonial definitions of sovereignty to assert control over health while respecting queer Native leadership in work for decolonization. As they practice survival in the face of pervasive death and, at times, a failure of leadership within Native nations, Native AIDS activists intervene in spaces managing the biopolitics of settler colonialism and global health by troubling its logics, inspiring broader action, and demonstrating their capacity to think beyond the national and heteropatriarchal terms of settler colonialism.

Their work also addresses the globalization of the biopolitics of settler colonialism. I write this book at a time Sherene Razack defines by the "eviction" of Muslims from Western law into a state of exception.[1] Razack recognizes that in Canada and the United States this follows those states naturalizing their formation by white settler conquest. On this basis, we may note that when Prime Minister Steven Harper differentiates Canada from other G20 members in possessing "no colonial history," or when President

George W. Bush targets Iraq as part of an "axis of evil," we can ask how their embodiment of Western law as a noncolonizing project that naturally recognizes primitive targets for civilizational conquest is not a legacy but an enactment of the power of a white settler state. How does settler colonization of Native peoples naturalize white settler states as arbiters of Western law that places Muslims and Islam in a state of exception? As Jennifer Denetdale asks, how does this then compel Native peoples or any racialized subjects of white settler rule to participate?[2] And, as Judith Butler and Dana Olwan ask, how does this condition the restriction of speech in the United States and Canada criticizing the Israeli state's racialized settlement of Palestinian territory—notably, if Palestinians and Indigenous Americans name similar experiences of racism and settler colonialism and join in solidarity?[3] We must ask how the biopolitics of settler colonialism in the Americas creates resonances among these processes that also inform queer studies. Narratives protecting Western citizenship from mobile "savages" and "terrorists" justify projecting military power to contain and displace subject populations and to control their lands. Thickly gendered narratives justify heteropatriarchal conquest and civilizing of perverse, barbaric manhood and abjected, voiceless womanhood within a new moral order. Queers within a white settler state then become modern through homonationalist participation in colonial and imperial rule that awards citizenship for defending the state and educating subject peoples in civilizational values, including sexual modernity. If these comments evoke Afghanistan, Iraq, Palestine, or Guantánamo Bay, each readily transposes onto the past *and* present rule of white settler societies over Native peoples, and onto investments by non-Native or Native people to dismiss them by progressing into a heteropatriarchal civilizational future "at home" and "abroad."

As Butler, Puar, Smith, and a broad range of queer studies scholars point out, these matters constitute the conditions of the field and its necessary concern, and failing to address them will naturalize settlement once again in the worlds queer studies examines.[4] The critical models of Native queer and Two-Spirit activists, Indigenous feminist and queer theorists, and allied projects call on non-Native queer people to new action to challenge settler colonialism in the settler state and global arenas. Non-Native queers can evaluate their work by the degree to which it troubles settler colonialism while being held accountable to Native queer and Two-Spirit activists and allied critics.

Having questioned desires to belong to the settler state or to possess Native history, non-Native queers can consider the groundlessness that follows critiquing settlement as a condition of their existence. My words here are inspired in part by theories of emplacement and mobility in queer migration and diaspora studies. Critically engaging histories of colonial, national, and racial violence and their survival has engendered mobile and transformative modes of decolonization for queers of color in diaspora.[5] Such work links to Indigenous queer decolonizations of Indigenous nations by acting from within mobile alliances. I invoke groundlessness to invite new theory to displace settler imaginaries among queer non-Natives. By detaching from colonial desires to belong to stolen land, the settler state, or their projections into global possibilities, queer non-Natives can release imaginaries of indigeneity that formed to resolve the contradictions of settlers possessing stolen land and Native peoples' pasts and futures. White-supremacist settler colonization in North America has produced distinct relationships to Indigenous heritage for people seeking this in any region, or indeed in multiple locations at once. Without attempting to define or contain so many experiences, I consider an image that perhaps can help us imagine what must take place for us to be able to connect in this place across our differences. In the space that opens up when non-Natives release attachments to place, while Native people contest how place might be known or controlled, a possibility of allied work for decolonization grows.

Among many routes such work might take, I return to where this project began: engaging conversations as the spaces between non-Native and Native queer people that shift when made accountable to Native queer and Two-Spirit people's pursuit of decolonization for their nations. I recall the difference once I engaged Native queer and Two-Spirit people on these terms. I learned for the first time about Native politics and, consequently, about myself without my life being central, and with the conditions creating my life being displaced. I experienced a decentering of non-Native interests in conversation with Native people as a prerequisite for accountable alliance. Among the many threads in Native studies examining alliance, I invoke one that raises the stakes for theorizing alliance as conversation through an image by Lisa Brooks, when she likens critical dialogues by Native scholars in Native studies to conversation at the kitchen table. Tracing this image to Joy Harjo, Brooks describes Native literary criticism as having arisen in the form of dialogues across communities that recalled to her mind family reunions and community meetings where Native people gather around the kitchen table to cook, eat, tell stories, and argue politics.[6] At one point, Brooks offers this image to remind her readers of what many Native literary critics say sabotaged Elvira Pulitano's attempt to theorize Native American literature: Pulitano's self-recognition as a non-Native scholar who lived far from any dialogue with the Native writers and communities she was examining.[7] This location let her represent their works in ways entirely out of sync with the stakes brought to those works by Native writers and readers, including scholars in Native studies. But Brooks then says of Pulitano, "if she had brought her work to the kitchen table . . . she certainly would have become aware of those implications."[8] In such a literal or imagined space, Pulitano's work could have become a site of struggle, teased or argued over; or, Brooks says, she might have been left alone until she prepared something in the kitchen that could be shared. Whatever Pulitano were to say while working in that space of Native dialogue, it would certainly remain *hers*, to share and also to be responsible for in any subsequent debate. Brooks ends by observing that Pulitano needed her claims to be deliberated in Native space not to serve Native people: "you see," she says, "I am advocating that she should have come to the kitchen table not for our sake, but her own."

When I think back to when I first was invited to adopt Native culture as queer history, I recall feeling a sharp, and surprising desire to accept, which I nevertheless experienced at a certain distance, as if this were someone else's feeling transposed onto my own. Perhaps my response was owing to the concurrent presence of a stronger and, it seemed, more proximal feeling, of queasiness; which grew more disturbing as friends and communities tried to compel me to join practices that I somehow knew to be deeply problematic. Surrounding all these feelings, I also recall an awareness that in retrospect I would call skepticism; for I also recognized that to accept what was being offered would not result in my forming any relationships with Native people. Queer non-Natives in the late-twentieth-century United States regularly found everyday speech, activist agendas, and historical and anthropological writing that invited them to form a relationship with indigeneity *at a sustained distance*. For some queer non-Natives, this made no difference if they found indigeneity more useful to them in the form of history. Yet, for others, accepting Native history only stoked a hunger to possess more. Native history was easy to consume, prepackaged in settler narratives; yet no degree of consumption placed non-Natives in greater relationship with queer Native people, or indeed *any* Native people, across the distances of geography, community, and politics that already divided them. With the benefit of reflection on these processes, I now think I understand some of the desires of non-Native queers to find themselves in Native religion, to form multiracial, global movements that incorporate Native people, or to define Native truth: they desire to be even closer to

Native people than adopting Native culture as their own history satisfies. I fear that their desires will perform the coloniality that initiated them if they include, or join, Native people after being motivated to adopt Native culture as queer history.

These are not the motivations to enter relationship that Brooks invites. Her image of the kitchen table evokes a spatial and interpersonal metaphor of the dynamics of conversation. And yet, this space remains distinct from the conversations this book traced. My analysis shows that non-Native and Native queer people have entered into conversation as a normative effect of settler colonialism. Their "conversations" constitute them in power-laden discursive and institutional relationships, whether they wish this or not. In this analysis, conversation is not something that can be sought out, as if it were not already taking place; nor can it be absolutely refused. Yet, critically engaging such a conversational relationship to challenge its colonial formation has defined the survival work and activism of Native queer and Two-Spirit people; and this book too has contributed to troubling that formation as a non-Native queer response to the model of Native activists. Critically participating in and displacing the conversations that condition non-Native and Native queer modernities can occur now, from within ongoing relationships that we learn to engage differently. Doing so may incite new dialogues among Native and non-Native people. But non-Natives likely will *not* find these dialogues taking place at the kitchen table. The conversations that already powerfully constitute them *are* the settler colonial power relations that Native queer and Two-Spirit people displace by gathering at the kitchen table of Two-Spirit organizing, and all forms of queer Native belonging within Native communities. All normative modes through which non-Native and Native queer people *appear* to be in conversation must be disrupted for dialogue to occur from the decolonizing stakes of Native queer and Two-Spirit activists. My experience has taught me that if this disruption occurs, it might follow non-Native queers first critiquing settler colonialism in the power-laden conversations that already constrain them. Their critical work will mark them as accountable to Native queer and Two-Spirit activism, and they may be drawn into collaborations with Native people who work with them in the fraught spaces of a settler colonial society. Such collaborations must be sufficient for non-Native queers who wish to act as allies to Native decolonization struggles. No greater proximity to Native cultural space is necessary, nor necessarily helpful for them to desire. If non-Natives ever do get invited to work or talk around the kitchen table, that will follow, and depend on, their having demonstrated a prior and sustained commitment to start and end their day *elsewhere*, in the normatively non-Native spaces where they pursue the work of unsettling settler colonialism.

Given the lack of commitment to Indigenous decolonization struggles in queer politics, clearly there is work to be done. This book's critique focused on denaturalizing settler colonialism, but not to posit this as an end. It would be all too easy for non-Natives to merely unthink their relationship to settler colonialism rather than act in relationship to others in struggle. This book argued instead that denaturalizing settler colonialism will displace any project that grounds queer life within the state, institutions, cultures, histories, or futures of a settler society. Any such project will be opened to critique and transformation once settler colonialism is denaturalized. What happens after such radical change will be something we learn in practice. Returning to struggle in the power-laden spaces constituted by settler colonialism holds queer activism and scholarship responsible to the critical models of Native queer and Two-Spirit people, whose self-determining transformations of colonial knowledges and power relations create conditions for non-Native and Native people to form allied work for Indigenous decolonization.

Acknowledgments

I WRITE WITH RESPECT FOR ALL among whom I have lived while preparing this book. My primary work took place on the lands of the Ohlone, Dakota, and Mohawk peoples: near the bluff where Santa Cruz Mission housed forcibly relocated Ohlone people; near the confluence of the Mississippi and Minnesota rivers, the spiritual homeland of the Dakota people and the site of memorials to internees at the Pike Island concentration camp established after the Dakota War of 1862; and near Tyendinega Mohawk territory on land subsequently taken by the United Empire Loyalists. Naming these storied places and their nations reminds of my responsibility to act in response to not only them but all ongoing struggles by Native peoples on lands that, however much they might have changed, remain Indigenous.

Among many constituencies to whom I am responsible, I acknowledge first the Native queer and Two-Spirit organizers whose work I discuss: American Indian Gays and Lesbians (Minneapolis), Bay Area American Indian Two-Spirits (San Francisco), Canadian Aboriginal AIDS Network (Vancouver), Gay American Indians (San Francisco), Healing Our Spirit (Vancouver), Indigenous People's Task Force (Minneapolis), International Indigenous People's Summit (Toronto 2006; Mexico City 2008), International Two-Spirit Gathering, National Native American AIDS Prevention Center (Denver), Ontario Aboriginal AIDS Strategy, 2-Spirits (Toronto), and WeWah and BarCheeAmpe (New York City). I thank those historical and current members and Native scholars of their work who engaged my thinking and, at times, provided crucial feedback that significantly shifted my ideas and writing: Randy Burns, Sharon Day, Clyde M. Hall, Ken Harper, Anguksuar Richard LaFortune, Kent Lebsock, Nick Metcalf, Yvonne Davis, Wesley Thomas, Irene Vernon, and Art Zoccole.

My response to Native queer and Two-Spirit organizing benefited from a remarkable moment in Native studies when Indigenous feminist and queer scholarship highlighted gender and sexuality and Native and non-Native scholars in response forged the intellectual and political ferment in which this book took shape. For their leadership and our dialogues I thank Chadwick Allen, Clive Aspin, Jennifer Nez Denetdale, Qwo-Li Driskill, Michelle Erai, Chris Finley, Brian Joseph Gilley, Mishuana Goeman, Jodi Byrd, Lisa Kahaleole Hall, Sharon Holland, Daniel Heath Justice, J. Kehaulani Kauanui, Dan Taulapapa McMullin, Mark Rifkin, Bethany Schneider, David Shorter, Audra Simpson, Andrea Smith, and Lisa Tatonetti. I thank all organizers of the Native American and Indigenous Studies Association for creating a dynamic space for Indigenous scholars and Indigenous knowledge production, where my work received indispensable critique in its final years of preparation. I thank Michelle Erai and Mishuana Goeman in particular for helping me compose the title of the book.

I acknowledge the scholars and activists whose antiracist engagements with queer politics sparked the critical thinking that led to this book. Among my scholarly interlocutors I give deep thanks to Roderick Ferguson, Gayatri Gopinath, Eithne Luibhéid, Martin F. Manalansan IV, Kevin Mumford, José Esteban Muñoz, Juana Maria Rodriguez, and Nayan Shah for the inspiration their work continues to offer. For our activist and scholarly collaborations in California I thank organizers of the University of California, Santa Cruz student group Queers of Color and Rhane Alexander, Kai Azada, Richard Baldwin, Meliza Bañales, Catalina Berumen, K. C. Bly, Clara Brandt, Scottie Brookie, Aaron Brown, Jorge Bru, Robert Imada, Mark Krikava, Kwai Lam, Susan Nilsson, Sharon Papo, and Corey Tax.

For their many years of engagement in my work I thank the members of the Radical Faerie circles of Santa Cruz and San Francisco, the organization Nomenus, and the residents of Short Mountain Sanctuary (Tennessee) and Wolf Creek Sanctuary (Oregon). For assistance in research I thank Deb Abbot and students and staff at the UCSC Lionel Cantú LGBTI Resource Center, as well as directors and staff at the Santa Cruz LGBT Community Center (1988–99) and The Diversity Center (since 1999).

I am grateful for financial support from the UCSC Graduate Division and Department of Anthropology; Macalester College; the Mellon Foundation; and the Faculty of Arts and Sciences and Department of Gender Studies at Queen's University. I am grateful to the Phil Zwickler Memorial Foundation for receipt of two Zwickler Research Grants to study at the Human Sexuality Collection of the Cornell University Library, where Brenda Marston offered invaluable assistance. I received archival research support at the Gay and Lesbian Historical Society of Northern California; the Canadian Gay and Lesbian Archives; and the Tretter Collection at the University of Minnesota. I especially thank Jean Tretter for his help and Anguksuar Richard LaFortune and Randy Burns for their public donations to the Tretter Collection's Two-Spirit Archive.

This project originated as a dissertation at the University of California, Santa Cruz, where my advisers Anna Tsing, Lisa Rofel, and Gayle Rubin provided invaluable guidance. For assistance in my home departments of anthropology and women's studies and in linked departments I thank Bettina Aptheker, Nancy Chen, James Clifford, Michael Cowan, Donna Haraway, Ann Kingsolver, Paul Ortiz, Nancy Stoller, and Patricia Zavella. Many colleagues in Santa Cruz, Minneapolis/St. Paul, and beyond gave crucial scholarly engagement. For a lovely writing group I thank Bianet Castellanos, Kale Fajardo, Karen Ho, Hoon Song, and David Valentine. Deep thanks also to Anna Lorraine Anderson, Darshan Campos, Beth Cleary, Ulrika Dahl, Aureliano DeSoto, John L. Jackson, Debra Klein, Ellen Lewin, Adriana Garriga Lopez, Tera Martin, Lance McCready, Karen Nakamura, Joan Ostrove, Peter Rachleff, Lena Sawyer, Omise'eke Natasha Tinsley, Deb Vargas, Michelle Wright, and Cynthia Wu.

For invitations to share my work, I thank Marc Schachter, Robin Weigman, and Karen Krahulik of the departments of Women's Studies and Romance Studies and the Sexuality Studies Program at Duke University; at the University of Minnesota, Twin Cities, William Beeman, Karen Ho, and David Valentine in the Department of Anthropology, Jigna Desai in the Department of Gender, Women, and Sexuality Studies, and Kevin Murphy and Anna Clark of the Global Sexualities Research Group; William Leap and the organizers of Lavender Languages and Linguistics; Theresa McCarthy and the Haudenosaunee Native American Studies Research Workshop at Buffalo University; and Ann Kingsolver and Drue Barker for inviting me to present the inaugural Alice Bee Kasakoff Lecture in Native American and Gender Studies sponsored by the anthropology and women's studies departments at the University of South Carolina.

I am thrilled to finish this book with faculty and graduate students of the Department of Gender Studies and Graduate Program in Cultural Studies at Queen's University and with staff and community at the Four Directions Aboriginal Students Centre. I thank Janice Brant, Paul Carl, Dia da Costa, Richard Day, Karen Dubinsky, Terrie Easter-Sheen, Janice Helland, Janice Hill, Margaret Little, Emily MacGillivray, Sam McKegney, Katherine McKittrick, Dana Olwan, Ishita Pande, Sarita Srivistava, and Dana Wesley for supporting and informing my work.

I could not have asked for a more enthusiastic, patient, and critically engaged team than the editors and production staff at the University of Minnesota Press. I am deeply grateful to Richard Morrison and Jason Weidemann for their sustained support. I offer my lasting thanks to the First Peoples publication initiative and the Mellon Foundation for sponsoring this book, and to Natasha Varner and Abby Mogollón for all their work. I also thank Nadia Myre for use of her beautiful visual art in the cover design.

Friendship, love, and mindfulness kept me and my work going. I offer my lasting gratitude to Kerry and David Avilla, Jerry Burg, Richard Gomen, London Elise, K'Lyn and Phil Matthews, Robert W. and Bonnie Morgensen, Mike and Shannon Morgensen, Eric Reed, Michelle Rosenthal, Cy Sugita, and Katherine Thanas. A special thank you goes to my old friends Rev and Alexander, without whom I certainly never would have finished. Most of all, I thank my mother, Lyn Lauria, for life, leadership, and boundless support.

Notes

Preface

1. Razack, "Introduction: When Place Becomes Race."
2. King, *Theory in Its Feminist Travels*.
3. Smith, *Native Americans and the Christian Right*.
4. "Cisgender," synonymous with "non-transgender," also indicates the privilege that accrues in a transphobic society to persons whose gender assignment at birth and gender identity match.
5. See, for example, Pratt, "Identity: Skin Blood Heart"; Visweswaran, *Fictions of Feminist Ethnography*.
6. I received this training within joint doctoral study in the departments of anthropology and women's studies at the University of California, Santa Cruz. Texts from this context that reflect the methodologies I invoke include Alexander and Mohanty, "Introduction: Genealogies, Legacies, Movements"; Bérubé, "How Gay Stays White and What Kind of White It Stays"; Frankenberg, *White Women, Race Matters*; Gluck et al., "Whose Feminism, Whose History?"; Luibhéid, *Entry Denied*; Martin and Mohanty, "Feminist Politics"; Mohanty, "Cartographies of Struggle"; Trinh, *Woman, Native, Other*; Zavella, "Feminist Insider Dilemmas." Notably, transnational feminist critics highlight inequalities that persist despite desire for feminist collaboration, and they call for forthright engagement in those sustained power relations. See Alexander and Mohanty, "Introduction"; Desai et al., "Disavowed Legacies and Honorable Thievery."
7. The identities of persons referenced only in ethnographic stories have been concealed, at times by use of a pseudonym or composite characterization. The names of major organizations referenced in ethnographic stories have not been changed.

Introduction

1. I use "Native" and "Indigenous" interchangeably as terms of collective identity across sustained national differences, and, at times, as normative locations within settler colonial law or society. In reference to the United States I emphasize "Native," which also invites the common comparative term "non-Native." I use "Indigenous"

to reference its preferential use for identity, or when gesturing beyond contemporary U.S. politics, whether to refer to other eras or to locations or relationships that go beyond the United States.

2. Smith, *Decolonizing Methodologies;* Warrior, *Tribal Secrets.*

3. Wolfe, "Structure and Event," 103.

4. Smith, *Native Americans and the Christian Right.*

5. Smith, "Queer Theory and Native Studies," 42–44.

6. Driskill et al., eds., *Queer Indigenous Studies;* Justice and Cox, eds., *Queering Native Literature;* Justice, Rifkin, and Schneider, eds., *Sexuality, Nationality, Indigeneity.*

7. Duggan, *The Twilight of Equality;* Murphy, Ruiz, and Serlin, eds., *Queer Futures;* Puar, *Terrorist Assemblages.*

8. Puar, *Terrorist Assemblages,* 11, 24.

9. See Morgensen, "Settler Homonationalism."

10. I redefine Robert Young's formulation to name a recursive relationship of settler subjects to inheriting and transcending indigeneity, as also examined by Philip Deloria and Renée Bergland (Bergland, *The National Uncanny;* Deloria, *Playing Indian;* Young, *Colonial Desire*).

11. Butler, *Precarious Life;* Butler, "The Question of Social Transformation"; Foucault, *The History of Sexuality: Volume 1.*

12. Tsing, *Friction.*

13. King, *Theory in Its Feminist Travels.*

14. Grahn, *Another Mother Tongue.* The book received the 1985 American Library Association's Stonewall Book Prize.

15. Ibid., 71–72.

16. Ibid., 72.

17. Bergland, *The National Uncanny.*

18. Grahn, *Another Mother Tongue,* 105.

19. Katz, *Gay American History,* 333 (emphasis in the original), original publication: Gengle, "Reclaiming the Old New World."

20. Gay American Indians and Roscoe, *Living the Spirit.*

21. Midnight Sun, "Sex/Gender Systems in Native North America"; Kenney, "Tinselled Bucks"; Hall, "Children of Grandmother Moon"; Pahe, "Speaking Up."

22. Hall, "Children of Grandmother Moon," 104.

23. Ramirez, *Native Hubs.*

24. Burns, "Preface," 4–5.

25. Hall, "Children of Grandmother Moon," 97, 101, 99.

26. Given more space, a productive reading could examine Grahn's *Another Mother Tongue,* Allen's *The Sacred Hoop,* and the relationship Allen and Grahn shared prior to their writing. Grahn references this when recalling the home invasion of the house she and Allen shared, and their response by joining lesbian-feminist comrades in spiritual ritual. Grahn portrays this ritual as evincing Allen's relationship

to Laguna Pueblo—a relationship to land she does not grant to the others—in contrast to the borderless lesbian spirituality of non-Native participants.

27. Allen, "Some Like Indians Endure," in Gay American Indians and Roscoe, *Living the Spirit*, 9.

28. Weaver, *That the People Might Live*; Tatonetti, "The Emergence and Importance of Queer American Indian Literature."

29. Chrystos, "Today Was a Bad Day like TB."

30. See Roscoe, *Queer Spirits*; Roscoe, *The Zuni Man-Woman*; Roscoe, "The Geography of Gender."

31. In addition to *Living the Spirit* and *The Sacred Hoop*, see Brant, *A Gathering of Spirit*; Chrystos, *Dream On*; Jacobs, Thomas, and Lang, eds., *Two-Spirit People*.

32. On San Francisco Bay Area histories of sexual minority and queer community, see Boyd, *Wide-Open Town*; Stryker and Buskirk, eds., *Gay by the Bay*. On histories of Bay Area American Indian communities, see Intertribal Friendship House, *Urban Voices*; Ramirez, *Native Hubs*. Despite repeated return to Bay Area locations, this book ultimately displaces regionalism by examining border-crossing projects that condition any local activity. "San Francisco Bay Area" in this book also will refer to the North Bay counties of Sonoma and Napa and to the Monterey Bay counties of Santa Cruz and Monterey because they are interlinked with the economic, political and cultural life of the Bay Area proper.

33. Towle and Morgan, "Romancing the Transgender Native"; Jacobs, "Is the 'North American Berdache' Merely a Phantom in the Imagination of Western Social Scientists?" Further use of *berdache* to define transgender subjects appears in Cromwell, *Transmen and FTM's*. Mark Rifkin examines Feinberg's interpretations of berdache in Rifkin, *When Did Indians Become Straight?*.

34. Den Ouden, *Beyond Conquest*, 40.

35. Wolfe, "Structure and Event."

36. See, for example, Kauanui, *Hawaiian Blood*; Lawrence, *"Real" Indians and Others*.

37. O'Brien, *Firsting and Lasting*.

38. Turner, *This Is Not a Peace Pipe*; Lawrence, *"Real" Indians and Others*.

39. Alfred, *Peace, Power, Righteousness*; Brooks, *The Common Pot*; Deloria, *Indians in Unexpected Places*; Denetdale, *Reclaiming Navajo History*; Warrior, *The People and the Word*; Wilson, *Remember This!*.

40. Hobsbawm and Ranger, eds., *The Invention of Tradition*; Horsman, *Race and Manifest Destiny*.

41. Cox, *Muting White Noise*.

42. See Hardt and Negri, *Empire*; Wallerstein, *World-Systems Analysis*; Wolf, *Europe and the People without History*; and Wynter, *We Must Learn to Sit Down Together and Talk about a Little Culture*.

43. Lowery, *Lumbee Indians in the Jim Crow South*; Miles and Holland, eds., *Crossing Waters, Crossing Worlds*; Naylor, *African Cherokees in Indian Territory*.

44. Lawrence and Dua, "Decolonizing Antiracism"; Trask, "Settlers of Color and 'Immigrant' Hegemony."

45. Sharma and Wright, "Decolonizing Resistance, Challenging Colonial States."

46. See Alfred, *Wasa'se*; Brooks, *The Common Pot*; Bruyneel, *The Third Space of Sovereignty*; Smith, *Native Americans and the Christian Right*.

47. Lawrence acknowledges this critique in Amadahy and Lawrence, "Indigenous Peoples and Black People in Canada."

48. Fujikane and Okamura, eds., *Asian Settler Colonialism*. I invoke here efforts by Dana Olwan and the organization Incite! Women of Color Against Violence. See Olwan, "Between Settlement and Indigeneity"; http://www.incite-national.org.

49. Lawrence, *"Real" Indians and Others*; Lowery, *Lumbee Indians in the Jim Crow South*.

50. Saldaña-Portillo, *The Revolutionary Imagination in Latin America and the Age of Development*.

51. Even as I ask how inheriting settler colonialism produces non-Natives, I learn from Native critiques of colonial, racial, imperial, and heteropatriarchal power in Native communities. See Alfred, *Peace, Power, Righteousness*; Denetdale, "Securing Navajo National Boundaries."

52. Smith, *Native Americans and the Christian Right*.

53. Driskill et al., "The Revolution Is for Everyone."

54. See the work of Coalición de Derechos Humanos: www.derechoshumanosaz.net; O'ohdham Solidarity Across Borders Collective: oodhamsolidarity.blogspot.com; accessed September 30, 2010.

55. Pratt, *Imperial Eyes*.

56. Hartman, *Scenes of Subjection*; Issac, *American Tropics*; Luibhéid, *Entry Denied*. See also Fajardo, "Transportation," Tinsley, "Black Atlantic, Queer Atlantic."

57. Smith, *Conquest*, 10, 139.

58. Anderson, *A Recognition of Being*; Lawrence, *"Real" Indians and Others*; Lawrence and Anderson, eds., *Strong Women Stories*; Finley, "Decolonizing the Queer Native Body." On Indigenous feminist thought and women's movements, see Goeman and Denetdale, eds., "Native Feminisms"; Green, ed., *Making Space for Indigenous Feminism*; Suzack et al., eds., *Indigenous Women and Feminism*.

59. See Driskill et al., eds., *Queer Indigenous Studies*; Justice and Cox, eds., *Queering Native Literature, Indigenizing Queer Theory*; Justice, Rifkin, and Schneider, eds., *Sexuality, Nationality, Indigeneity*.

60. Finley, "Decolonizing the Queer Native Body"; Miranda, "Extermination of the *Joyas*"; Rifkin, *When Did Indians Become Straight?*.

61. Driskill, "Stolen from Our Bodies."

62. Anguksuar, "A Postcolonial Colonial Perspective."

63. Smith, "Queer Theory and Native Studies," 59; Driskill, "Doubleweaving Two-Spirit Critiques," 76, 78.

64. Smith, "Queer Theory and Native Studies," 48.

65. Ibid., 54.

66. Driskill, "Doubleweaving Two-Spirit Critiques," 77.

67. Povinelli, *The Empire of Love*, 4.

68. Smith, *Native Americans and the Christian Right*, 271, 275.

69. Sandoval, *Methodology of the Oppressed*.

70. Muñoz, *Disidentifications*.

71. See Boellstorff, *The Gay Archipelago*; Rofel, *Desiring China*.

1. The Biopolitics of Settler Sexuality and Queer Modernities

1. Achille Mbembe, "Necropolitics."

2. Morgensen, "The Biopolitics of Settler Colonialism."

3. I call berdache a colonial object to reference its colonial genealogy and Native queer critiques of its use (explored in chapter 2). Although Jacobs, Thomas, and Lang propose using the specific formulation "'berdache' [sic]" to mark this quality (see Jacobs, Thomas, and Lang, "Introduction"), I investigate it not by bracketing it outside common speech but by marking its circulation as an object of colonial thought. In my usage, *berdache* never describes Native culture; it only describes a colonial imaginary of indigeneity.

4. Wolfe, *Settler Colonialism and the Transformation of Anthropology*.

5. Foucault, *The Birth of Biopolitics*; Foucault, *Discipline and Punish*; Foucault, Senellart, and Ewad, *Security, Territory, Population*.

6. Agamben, *Homo Sacer*; Agamben, *State of Exception*.

7. Rifkin, "Indigenizing Agamben," 94. On the location of Indigenous peoples in the state of exception under white settler colonization, see also Thobani, *Exalted Subjects*.

8. Stoler, *Carnal Knowledge and Imperial Power*; Stoler, *Race and the Education of Desire*.

9. Foucault, *The History of Sexuality: Volume 1*; Stoler, *Carnal Knowledge and Imperial Power*, 144.

10. Stoler, *Carnal Knowledge and Imperial Power*, 156; Stoler, *Race and the Education of Desire*, 190.

11. The introductory chapter to Stoler, *Carnal Knowledge and Imperial Power*, provides a useful review.

12. Stoler, *Race and the Education of Desire*, 83.

13. See Hartman, *Scenes of Subjection*.

14. Goldberg, "Sodomy in the New World," 4, 6–7.

15. See Laqueur, *Making Sex*.

16. Behrend-Martinez, "Manhood and the Neutered Body in Early Modern Spain"; Shepard, *Meanings of Manhood in Early Modern England*.

17. Tortorici, "'Heran Todos Putos,'" 35, 41.

18. See, for example, Little, *Abraham in Arms;* Plane, *Colonial Intimacies.*

19. See, for example, Child, *Boarding School Seasons;* Warrior, *The People and the Word.*

20. Roscoe, *Changing Ones,* 31.

21. Williams, *The Spirit and the Flesh,* 179.

22. Roscoe, *Changing Ones,* 35.

23. Ibid., 36.

24. Williams, *The Spirit and the Flesh,* 183.

25. Ferguson, *Aberrations in Black* and "Of Our Normative Strivings"; Luibhéid, *Entry Denied.* See also Carter, *The Heart of Whiteness;* Eng, *Racial Castration;* Shah, "Between 'Oriental Depravity' and 'Natural Degenerates.'"

26. Somerville, *Queering the Color Line.*

27. Mumford, *Interzones;* Johnson and Henderson, eds., *Black Queer Studies.*

28. Terry, *An American Obsession.*

29. See Adam, *The Rise of a Gay and Lesbian Movement;* D'Emilio, *Sexual Politics, Sexual Communities.*

30. Bederman, *Manliness and Civilization;* Gustav-Wrathall, *Take the Young Stranger by the Hand."*

31. Kennedy, *Ulrichs;* Steakley, "Per Scientiam ad Justitiam." Oosterhuis portrays Krafft-Ebing and Karl Westphal as developing theories of "contrary sexual feeling" in response to Ulrichs's invitations, while readers of *Psychopathia Sexualis* wrote to Krafft-Ebing to invite or suggest their own diagnosis (Oosterhuis, *Stepchildren of Nature*).

32. For the frequency of historical citations of berdache, see Roscoe, "Bibliography of Berdache and Alternative Gender Roles among Native North American Indians."

33. Krafft-Ebing, *Psychopathia Sexualis;* Ellis, *Studies in the Psychology of Sex;* Seligmann, "Sexual Inversion among Primitive Races"; Karsch-Haack, "Uranismus oder Päderastie und Tribadie bei den Naturvölkern."

34. See Seligmann, "Sexual Inversion among Primitive Races," 12; Ellis, *Studies in the Psychology of Sex,* 16–17, 23.

35. Carpenter, *Intermediate Types among Primitive Folk;* Carpenter, *The Intermediate Sex.*

36. See Brickman, *Aboriginal Populations in the Mind;* Torgovnick, *Gone Primitive.*

37. Hay, *Radically Gay.*

38. Hay, "A Separate People Whose Time Has Come"; Thompson, "This Gay Tribe."

39. Stewart, "Homosexuality among American Indians and Other Native Peoples"; Carpenter, "Selected Insights."

40. Miranda, "The Extermination of the *Joyas* "; Driskill, "Shaking Our Shells"; Driskill, *Walking with Ghosts.*

41. Smith, *Decolonizing Methodologies.* I draw this connotation in Smith's term from Driskill (Driskill et al., "Introduction").

42. Gilley, *Becoming Two-Spirit.*
43. Foucault, *The History of Sexuality: Volume 1.*
44. Pratt, *Imperial Eyes*, 6–7.

2. Conversations on Berdache

1. I refer here not to the vast array of research by ARGOH and SOLGA scholars, but to its first decade of scholarship on berdache. The group's very different public profiling by the work of Gilbert Herdt—which, however, never eclipsed the publicity of berdache—is examined by Deborah Elliston in "Erotic Anthropology."

2. See, for example, Bayer, *Homosexuality and American Psychiatry.*

3. Taylor, "Homosexuality."

4. Taylor, "Background Information," 3–4.

5. Amory, "The History of SOLGA." See also Banner, *Intertwined Lives.*

6. Taylor, "Background Information."

7. Anthropological Research Group on Homosexuality, "A.R.G.O.H. Charter," 3.

8. Carrier, "Toward an A.A.A. Symposium on Homosexuality in 1980"; Williams, "Sessions on Homosexuality," 2.

9. Gross, "Messages from Our New Co-Presidents," 3; Carrier, "Notes on AAA Business Meeting of ARGOH," 2.

10. Kutsche, "A.R.G.O.H. in 1987," 2. The Political Action Committee is introduced in *ARGOH Newsletter* 4 (1982): 1–2. Kutsche's first campaign is announced in *ARGOH Newsletter* 4 (1983): 4. A history of antidiscrimination language in the AAA appears in *ARGOH Newsletter* 5 (1984): 1–2. An immediate response to the Committee on Ethics's negative response appears in *ARGOH Newsletter* 5 (1984): 3. Kutsche presents a final announcement of the positive results in *ARGOH Newsletter* 9 (1987): 1.

11. In 1986, the ARGOH Award was described as recognizing a "distinguished scholarly contribution with a cross-cultural perspective (including work on American culture) on the subject of lesbianism and/or male homosexuality." The first award announcement rephrased this as "Distinguished Scholarship on a Lesbian or Gay Topic." See Newton, "A.R.G.O.H. Annual Award," 4; Blackwood, "Winner of the 1986 A.R.G.O.H. Award," 8.

12. See, for example, Herdt, ed., *Ritualized Homosexuality in Melanesia.*

13. Anthropological Research Group on Homosexuality, "A.R.G.O.H. Charter," 3.

14. Mead, *Male and Female*, 142; Benedict, *Patterns of Culture*, 294.

15. Mead, *Sex and Temperament*, 294; Benedict, *Patterns of Culture*, 262, 264. See also Mead, *Coming of Age in Samoa.*

16. Ford and Beach, *Patterns of Sexual Behavior*, 130.

17. See Angelino and Shedd, "A Note on Berdache"; Jacobs, "Berdache"; Kroeber, "Psychosis or Social Sanction"; Sonenschein, "Homosexuality as a Subject of Anthropological Inquiry"; Stewart, "Homosexuality among American Indians and Other Native Peoples."

18. Callender and Kochems, "The North American Berdache," 443; Callender and Kochems, "Men and Not-Men," 168.

19. Whitehead, "The Bow and the Burden Strap," 108–9.

20. Raymond, *The Transsexual Empire.*

21. Blackwood, "Breaking the Mirror," 2.

22. Blackwood, ed., *The Many Faces of Homosexuality;* Blackwood, "Breaking the Mirror," 2.

23. Blackwood, "Sexuality and Gender in Certain Native American Tribes."

24. Williams, *The Spirit and the Flesh,* 207.

25. Blackwood, "Winner of the 1986 A.R.G.O.H. Award," 8.

26. Blackwood, "Report on the ARGOH Business Meeting," 3–4.

27. Mass, "On the Future of Lesbian and Gay Studies," 242. See also Roscoe, "Making History." Roscoe submitted records of his publications to the SOLGA newsletter and at least one research report: Roscoe, "History Comes Home."

28. Dickemann, "SOLGA Member Wins 1991 Margaret Mead Award."

29. Roscoe, "Comments on Receiving the Margaret Mead Award."

30. This quotation is not cited in SOLGA's reprinting of Roscoe's text.

31. Blackwood, "Review: The Zuni Man-Woman," 58.

32. On the history of *RFD* and back-to-the-land projects, see Herring, "Out of the Closets, into the Woods."

33. Treelove, "Spring, Spirit, and Faggotry," 44.

34. Issues 1–6 (fall 1974–winter 1975) were published from Iowa City. Issues 7–16 (spring 1976–summer 1978) were published from Wolf Creek, Oregon. Beginning with issue 17 (fall 1978), publication moved to Efland, North Carolina, after which sites continued to shift. Some issues were "farmed out": while RFD was published in North Carolina, New Orleans residents produced issues 18 and 22, and New England residents issue 21.

35. RFD Collective, "Collective Statement," 4.

36. Jerry, "RFD Reader Survey," 39.

37. Bob, Steve, and Allen, "Recipe for a Small Cabin"; John, "Gardening with the Fairies"; RFD Collective, "Uncle Ned Says, 'Let's Eat!'"

38. RFD Collective, "Collective Statement," 4.

39. Larry and Steven, "Our Theme . . . ," 8; Hermsen, "When the Sun Stands Still"; Steczynski, "Wholeness: Masculine & Feminine."

40. Phillips, "Electric Consciousness," 24.

41. Joyous, "We Circle Around," 13, 14.

42. Castaneda, *The Teachings of Don Juan.*

43. Caradoc, "Sharing the Mysteries," 25, 27.

44. RFD Collective, "Spiritual Soapbox," 30.

45. Lindner, "Letter," 3.

46. Holloway, "Letter," 2.

47. Manes, "Letter," 2.

48. Cornbelt, "Letter," 5.

49. Smoothstone, "Response to 'Arnold J. Cornbelt,'" 5.

50. Evans, "Things That Go Bump in the Night," 17.

51. Evans, *Witchcraft and the Gay Counterculture*, 111.

52. Carl, "Loving Circle," 31–32.

53. Phillips, "Electric Consciousness," 24.

54. Hay, "A Call to Gay Brothers." See also Clark, "The Native American Berdache."

55. Roscoe, *The Zuni Man-Woman*, vii; Williams, *The Spirit and the Flesh*.

56. Mass, "On the Future of Lesbian and Gay Studies," 244–45; Roscoe, *The Zuni Man-Woman*, vii.

57. Roscoe, "Dreaming the Myth," 116, 120, 123; emphasis in the original.

58. Mass, "On the Future of Lesbian and Gay Studies," 243–44.

59. On harassment faced by early organizers, see Medicine, "Changing Native American Roles in an Urban Context," 154.

60. See, for example, Anguksuar, "Angukcuaq Lafortune"; Burns, "American Indians Neglected"; Gays and Lesbians of the First Nations in Toronto, "The Greater Vancouver Native Cultural Society."

61. Burns, "Preface"; Pahe, "Speaking Up," 111.

62. Burns, "Preface," 5.

63. Gay American Indians, "Publication Proposal."

64. Kenney, "Tinselled Bucks"; Midnight Sun, "Sex/Gender Systems in Native North America."

65. Kenney, "Tinselled Bucks," 31.

66. Burns, "Preface," 4–5.

67. Hall, "Children of Grandmother Moon," 104.

68. Burns, "Preface," 2–3.

69. Burns describes the GAI History Project as having "compiled an extensive bibliography of sources on berdache" and "coordinated the development of this anthology." *Living the Spirit* is published with the designation "Compiled by Gay American Indians" while also indicating "Will Roscoe, Coordinating Editor." Some references to *Living the Spirit* omit Gay American Indians as an editing body and cite Roscoe as sole editor. The bibliography compiled by the History Project is printed in *Living the Spirit* without indication of authorship. Roscoe published an article separately that expanded upon this data. See Burns, "Preface," 4; Roscoe, "Bibliography of Berdache and Alternative Gender Roles among Native North American Indians," 81–171.

70. Pahe, "Speaking Up," 110.

71. Thomas and Jacobs, "'. . . And We Are Still Here,'" 92.

72. Anguksuar, "A Postcolonial Colonial Perspective," 221; Thomas and Jacobs, "'. . . And We Are Still Here,'" 92.

73. Little Thunder, "I Am a Lakota Womyn," 203.

74. Red Earth, "Traditional Influences on a Contemporary Gay-Identified Sisseton Dakota"; Wilson, "How We Find Ourselves."

75. Thomas, "Navajo Cultural Constructions of Gender and Sexuality"; Thomas and Jacobs, "'. . . And We Are Still Here,'" 92.

76. WeWah and BarCheeAmpe, "New Movement for Two Spirits."

77. Jacobs, Thomas, and Lang, "Introduction," 8.

78. Thomas and Jacobs, "'. . . And We Are Still Here,'" 91.

79. Jacobs, "Is the 'North American Berdache' Merely a Phantom in the Imagination of Western Social Scientists?" 21.

80. Jacobs, Thomas, and Lang, "Introduction," 8.

81. Jacobs, "Letter: 'Revisiting the "North American Berdache," Empirically and Theoretically,'" 3.

82. Tafoya, "M. Dragonfly," 195.

83. Little Thunder, "I Am a Lakota Womyn," 208.

84. Anguksuar, "A Postcolonial Colonial Perspective," 219.

85. Tafoya, "M. Dragonfly," 194. See also Patton, *Inventing AIDS*, 148.

86. Blackwood, "Native American Genders and Sexualities," 288–89.

87. Two-Spirit activism accomplished this by a critique of anthropology resonant with Johannes Fabian's *Time and the Other.*

88. See the different arguments in the *GLQ* issue on the topic "Sexuality, Nationality, Indigeneity": Driskill, "Doubleweaving Two-Spirit Critiques"; Justice, "Notes toward a Theory of Anomaly"; Stevens, "Poetry and Sexuality."

3. Authentic Culture and Sexual Rights

1. On the white-supremacist and settler colonial management and erasure of Native peoples, see Bruyneel, *The Third Space of Sovereignty;* Lawrence, *"Real" Indians and Others;* Turner, *This Is Not a Peace Pipe.*

2. Scholarship on queer citizenship that helps inspire this analysis includes Brandzel, "Queering Citizenship?"; Luibhéid, "Introduction"; Reddy, "Asian Diasporas, Neoliberalism, and Family."

3. Epstein, "Gay Politics, Ethnic Identity"; Halley, "'Like Race' Arguments"; Joseph, *Against the Romance of Community.*

4. Brown, *States of Injury.*

5. Povinelli, *The Cunning of Recognition.*

6. See Gordon and Newfield, eds., *Mapping Multiculturalism;* Jacobson, *Roots Too;* Lipsitz, *The Possessive Investment in Whiteness;* Takagi, *The Retreat from Race.*

7. Katz, *Gay American History,* 3.

8. Legg, "The Berdache and Theories of Sexual Inversion"; Stewart, "Homosexuality among American Indians and Other Native Peoples."

9. Katz, *Gay American History,* 329.

10. Devereux, "Institutionalized Homosexuality of the Mohave Indians."

11. Katz, *Gay American History*, 332–34.

12. See, for example, Murphy, Ruiz, and Serlin, eds., *Queer Futures*.

13. Marmor, "Homosexuality and Cultural Value-Systems." This and subsequent documentation of the early NGTF appear in the NGLTF Collected Papers, Human Sexuality Collection, Cornell University Library.

14. Blackswan, "It's a Shame We Don't Have More People of Color Participating," 27.

15. Hull, "The Posters Transformed the Landscape I Live In," 29.

16. White and Hull, "The Women Left Angry and Most Likely Disgusted with Us."

17. White and Hull, "As a Member of the Gay Community, I Am Affected by Racism Everyday."

18. Joseph, *Against the Romance of Community*.

19. See, for example, Anzaldúa, "Bridge, Drawbridge, Sandbar, Island"; Hemphill, ed., *Brother to Brother*; Ordoña, "The Challenges Facing Asian and Pacific Island Lesbians in the U.S."; Trujillo, ed., *Chicana Lesbians*; Trujillo, ed., *Living Chicana Theory*.

20. Diversity Center, *Annual Report* (2000): 1.

21. On historically concurrent political struggles see Irvine, "A Place in the Rainbow."

22. See diversitycenter.org, accessed September 30, 2010.

23. See Cantú, *The Sexuality of Migration*.

24. Personal communications from Randy Burns, Sharon Day, and Clyde M. Hall.

25. Lebsock, "North East Two-Spirit Society."

26. WeWah and BarCheeAmpe, "We Wah & Bar Chee Ampe."

27. WeWah and BarCheeAmpe, "We'wah and Bar Chee Ampe: Gay and Lesbian Indigenous People, New York City," 2.

28. Ibid. See also Roscoe, *The Zuni Man-Woman*.

29. Lebsock, "North East Two-Spirit Society," 14.

30. Cairos Collective, "Founding Matrons & Patrons."

31. WeWah and BarCheeAmpe, "What Are Two Spirits?" 4.

32. WeWah and BarCheeAmpe, "500 Years of Survival and Resistance," 16–17.

33. Romo-Carmona, Jackson, and Harris, "Activists Respond to the Quincentennial."

34. I discuss this latter implication by examining Romo-Carmona's contribution to the collective in chapter 5.

4. Ancient Roots through Settled Land

1. See Hennen, *Faeries, Bears, and Leathermen*; Povinelli, *The Empire of Love*; Stover, "When Pan Met Wendy."

2. Hay, "A Call to Gay Brothers"; Thompson, "This Gay Tribe."

3. Hennessy, "Fey Enough?"; Stover, "When Pan Met Wendy."

4. Radical Faerie demography defies quantitative accounting: no central database records historical demographics, and while the Holy Faerie Database recorded West Coast gatherers, no list collected racial or national identity. In chapter 5 I

explain my argument that Radical Faeries fully intersect the urban queer communities that historically formed and sustained them.

5. Povinelli, *The Empire of Love*, 4.

6. See Kasee, "Identity, Recovery, and Religious Imperialism."

7. These two key historical sites of Radical Faerie culture in the United States support its two oldest continuous networks. Each has a residential community; during my research, Wolf Creek housed up to six persons, while long-term visitors and residents at Short Mountain numbered ten to twenty. Major gatherings at Short Mountain occurred in May and October near neo-pagan festivals, while in 1995 an annual midsummer "spiritual gathering of Radical Faeries" was renewed at Wolf Creek.

8. Abelove, "New York City Gay Liberation and the Queer Commuters"; D'Emilio, "Foreword."

9. Milo Pyne, interview; Sears, *Rebels, Rubyfruits, and Rhinestones*.

10. Herring, *Queering the Underworld*; Valentine, "Making Space."

11. RFD Collective, "Faggots & Class Struggle."

12. Conner, *Blossom of Bone*; Hay, "Toward the New Frontiers of Fairy Vision"; Roscoe, "Dreaming the Myth"; Rose, *A Radical Fairy's Seedbed*; Thompson, "This Gay Tribe."

13. See Anderson, "On the Dangers of Faerie Anti-Intellectualism"; Royale, "As a Matter of Fact"; Weinstein, "Romancing the Stone Age." Faeries of All Colors Together, a first affinity group to support gay men of color and address racism among Radical Faeries, formed in 2000 at Short Mountain. Weinstein's critique of cultural appropriation is the only such text in the *RFD* special issue "Faerie Primitives."

14. Hay, *Radically Gay*, 254.

15. See Thompson, "This Gay Tribe."

16. Engstrom, "The Queer God Ritual."

17. Hay, "Toward the New Frontiers of Fairy Vision"; Circle of Loving Companions, "The Gays."

18. Brickman, *Aboriginal Populations in the Mind*.

19. Deloria, *Playing Indian*.

20. Clifford, *Routes*.

21. Kayal, *Bearing Witness*; Levine, Nardi, and Gagnon, eds., *In Changing Times*; Stoller, *Lessons from the Damned*.

22. Cohen, *The Boundaries of Blackness*; Rodriguez, *Queer Latinidad*; Vernon, *Killing Us Quietly*.

23. Blackswan, "It's a Shame We Don't Have More People of Color Participating," 27.

24. Royale, "As a Matter of Fact."

25. Muñoz, *Disidentifications*.

26. Braziel, "Dréd's Drag Kinging"; Baur, *Venus Boyz*.

27. Holmes, "Into the Woods."

28. Blackberri, "Searching for My Gay Spiritual Roots."

29. Blackswan, "It's a Shame We Don't Have More People of Color Participating," 28.

30. See, for example, Tiya Miles and Sharon Patricia Holland, eds., *Crossing Waters, Crossing Worlds.*

31. Hall, personal communication. See also Hall's biographical profile (http://www.ncpc.info/clyde_hall.html) and his "Children of Grandmother Moon."

32. Hall, personal communication. On the history of the northern Shoshone and Naraya, see Hultkrantz, *Belief and Worship in Native North America;* Liljeblad, *The Idaho Indians in Transition.*

33. Randy Burns affirms Hall's efforts in leading the Naraya as a form of Two-Spirit spiritual leadership, with Shoshone and other Native dance leaders, some of whom are also Two-Spirited. In 1991, on hearing of the first Naraya dance to admit non-Natives held in New York City in 1991, Curtis Harris and Kent Lebsock, writing for WeWah and BarCheeAmpe, wrote a strong critique of Hall in *Buffalo Hide* (Burns, personal communication; Harris and Lebsock, "Things Sacred"). Hall directs the nonprofit Naraya Cultural Preservation Council (NCPC), which describes the Naraya on its Web site as "A Dance for All Peoples." The dance is performed at a small set of sites across the continent in Native communities—including the Shoshone-Bannock reservation—and for non-Native or mixed non-Native/Native networks. Fees are not charged, and participants may contribute to "projects" initiated by the NCPC in Great Basin Native communities, which include oral history projects, the recording of traditional songs, and land preservation projects. See www.ncpc.info, accessed September 30, 2010.

34. Thompson, "Clyde Hall," 121, 122.

5. Global Desires and Transnational Solidarity

1. Altman, *Global Sex;* Boellstorff, *The Gay Archipelago;* Massad, *Desiring Arabs;* Rofel, *Desiring China.*

2. Alexander, *Pedagogies of Crossing;* Grewal, *Transnational America;* Manalansan, *Global Divas;* Rodriguez, *Queer Latinidad.*

3. Puar, *Terrorist Assemblages;* Alexander, *Pedagogies of Crossing;* King, "'There Are No Lesbians Here.'"

4. Sandoval, *Methodology of the Oppressed,* 27.

5. Deloria, *Playing Indian.*

6. By 2000, regional networks managed rural lands in Oregon, Minnesota, and Vermont, while residential collectives kept lands for gatherings in Tennessee, New Mexico, and New York. Toronto Radical Faeries managed rural land in Ontario, and in Australia a group of Radical Faeries also managed sanctuary land.

7. This is true even after Radical Faerie culture attracted international visitors and spread to Canada, Europe, Australia, or Asia, in that all its manifestations inherit a relationship to U.S. settler colonialism that must be explained.

8. Kreuter, *Drama in the Desert;* Starhawk, *Truth or Dare.*

9. Vale and Juno, *Modern Primitives.*

10. Hennessy, "Homohex," 14.

11. Vale and Juno, *Modern Primitives,* 34. See also Sprinkle, *Annie Sprinkle.*

12. Rosenblatt, "The Antisocial Skin," 299.

13. Portillo, "I Get Real"; Musafar, "Gryphon Blackswan Androgyne," 14; Mains, *Urban Aboriginals,* 179..

14. Mains, *Urban Aboriginals,* 179.

15. www.saratogasprings.com; accessed August 15, 2011.

16. Bean, "Magical Masochist."

17. See Vale and Juno, *Modern Primitives,* and Bean, "Magical Masochist."

18. Puar, *Terrorist Assemblages.*

19. Cruz-Malavé and Manalansan, eds., *Queer Globalizations.*

20. Manalansan, *Global Divas,* 123–24.

21. See also Saranillio, "Colonial Amnesia."

22. Rodriguez, *Queer Latinidad,* 74, 76.

23. Moraga, *The Last Generation,* 147.

24. Anzaldúa, *Borderlands/La Frontera;* Perez, *The Decolonial Imaginary.* See also Arrizón, *Queering Mestizaje.*

25. Contreras, *Bloodlines,* 131, 113.

26. Ibid., 130.

27. Saldaña-Portillo, *The Revolutionary Imagination in Latin America and the Age of Development,* 282.

28. Alarcón, "The Theoretical Subject(s) of *This Bridge Called My Back* and Anglo-American Feminism."

29. Mohanty, "Cartographies of Struggle," 7.

30. Anzaldúa, "Foreword," vii.

31. Anzaldúa and Keating, *Interviews/Entrevistas,* 132.

32. Saldaña-Portillo, *The Revolutionary Imagination in Latin America and the Age of Development,* 280.

33. Romo-Carmona, Jackson, and Harris, "Activists Respond to the Quincentennial," 11.

34. Saldaña-Portillo, *The Revolutionary Imagination in Latin America and the Age of Development,* 286.

35. Ashcroft, Griffiths, and Tiffin, eds., *The Empire Writes Back.*

36. Brooks, *The Common Pot;* Bruyneel, *The Third Space of Sovereignty.*

37. Alfred, *Wasa'se;* Smith, *Native Americans and the Christian Right.*

38. Anaya, *Indigenous Peoples in International Law;* de Costa, *A Higher Authority;* Niezen, *The Origins of Indigenism.*

39. For Indigenous feminist critiques of the nation-state form in work for decolonization, see Smith, *Native Americans and the Christian Right;* Smith and Kauanui, "Native Feminisms Engage American Studies."

40. See Rowell, "Developing AIDS Services for Native Americans."

Notes to Chapter 6   249

6. "Together We Are Stronger"

1. See, for example, Carson et al., eds., *Social Determinants of Indigenous Health;* Nebelkopf and Phillips, eds., *Healing and Mental Health for Native Americans.*

2. Bruyneel, *The Third Space of Sovereignty;* Allen, *Blood Narrative.*

3. Alfred, "Sovereignty."

4. Smith, *Native Americans and the Christian Right.*

5. Vernon, *Killing Us Quietly,* 1, 2.

6. National Alliance of State and Territorial AIDS Directors, "Native Americans and HIV/AIDS," 4.

7. U.S. Commission on Civil Rights, "A Quiet Crisis"; Vernon, *Killing Us Quietly,* 2, 8.

8. Walters and Simoni, "Reconceptualizing Native Women's Health"; Duran and Duran, *Native American Postcolonial Psychology.*

9. Duran and Walters, "HIV/AIDS Prevention in 'Indian Country,'" 194.

10. National Native American AIDS Prevention Center and the Rural Center for AIDS/STD Prevention, "HIV/STD Prevention Guidelines for Native American Communities," 15. The first quotation also quotes Walters and Simoni, "Reconceptualizing Native Women's Health," 522.

11. This history is discussed at length in Vernon, *Killing Us Quietly,* especially chapters 1 and 4. See also chapter 3 in Gilley, *Becoming Two-Spirit.*

12. Bouey and Duran, "The *Ahalaya* Case-Management Program," 38.

13. National Native American AIDS Prevention Center, "Gathering Our Wisdom II," 13, 15.

14. Minnesota American Indian AIDS Task Force, "The Ogitchidag Gikinooamaagad Players"; Rush, "Models of Prevention."

15. Human Health Organization, "*We Owe It to Ourselves and to Our Children,*" 4.

16. Smith, "*Her Giveaway.*"

17. Rush, "Her Giveaway," 4–5.

18. National Native American AIDS Prevention Center, "Creating a Vision for Living with HIV in the Circle of Life: Self-Care Manual for Native People Living with HIV/AIDS."

19. See Gilley, *Becoming Two-Spirit.*

20. WeWah and BarCheeAmpe, "Strength of Our Cultures," 2.

21. Albert, "Welcoming Remarks," 3.

22. Deschamps, "We Are Part of a Tradition."

23. WeWah and BarCheeAmpe, "Solidarity Statement—Two Spirits and HIV."

24. See Gilley, *Becoming Two-Spirit;* Medicine, "Changing Native American Roles in an Urban Context."

25. National Native American AIDS Prevention Center, "Leadership Development for Native American Gay/Bisexual/Two-Spirit Native American Men," 1; Rowell, "HIV Prevention for Gay/Bisexual/Two-Spirit Native American Men," 4, 5.

26. Rowell, "HIV Prevention for Gay/Bisexual/Two-Spirit Native American Men," 4–5.

27. Ibid., 37 (first quotation); National Native American AIDS Prevention Center, "Leadership Development for Native American Gay/Bisexual/Two-Spirit Native American Men," 2 (second quotation).

28. Pathmakers, "Pathmakers Organizational Meeting," 2.

29. Kairaiuak, *Addressing Two-Spirits*.

30. National Native American AIDS Prevention Center, "Together We Are Stronger" (designed by China Ching).

31. Tengan, "Ke Kulana He Mahu"; Xian and Anbe, *Ke Kulana He Mahu (the Rank of the Transgender)*.

32. Aspin, "Exploring Takatapui Identity within the Maori Community."

33. Patton, *Globalizing AIDS*.

34. Cameron, "Frybread in Berlin."

35. Junga-Williams, "Rodney's Journey."

36. Keck and Sikkink, *Activists beyond Borders*.

37. Grewal, *Transnational America*. See also: INCITE! Women of Color Against Violence, ed., *The Revolution Will Not Be Funded*.

38. Warrior, *The People and the Word*, 51, 53.

39. National Native American AIDS Prevention Center, "Landmark Charter Calls for Full Participation of Indigenous Peoples in HIV Programs."

40. Patton, *Globalizing AIDS* and *Inventing AIDS*.

41. Patton, *Globalizing AIDS*, 50.

42. Alfred, *Peace, Power, Righteousness*; Coulthard, "Subjects of Empire."

43. Barker, "Recognition."

44. See, for example, Epstein, *Impure Science*; Padilla, *Caribbean Pleasure Industry*; Treichler, *How to Have Theory in an Epidemic*.

45. Gilley, *Becoming Two-Spirit* and "'Snag Bags.'"

46. For a critique of culturally appropriate Native health care, see Smith, *Decolonizing Methodologies*.

47. Kairaiuak, *Addressing Two-Spirits*; Vernon, *Killing Us Quietly*.

Epilogue

1. Razack, *Casting Out*.

2. Denetdale, "Securing Navajo National Boundaries."

3. Butler, *Precarious Life*; Olwan, "Between Settlement and Indigeneity." A recent case was the roundtable "Turtle Island and Palestine: Forging Alliances against Settler Colonialism" at the Critical Ethnic Studies and the Future of Genocide conference, UC Riverside, March 2011.

4. Certain implications of this analysis are examined in Hochberg, ed., *Queer Politics and the Question of Palestine/Israel*.

5. Here I take particular inspiration from Alexander, *Pedagogies of Crossing,* and Tinsley, "Black Atlantic, Queer Atlantic."

6. Brooks, "Afterword"; Harjo, "Perhaps the World Ends Here."

7. Pulitano, *Toward a Native American Critical Theory.* See also Weaver, "Splitting the Earth"; Womack, "The Integrity of American Indian Claims."

8. Brooks, "Afterword," 237.

Bibliography

Archival Collections

Canadian Lesbian and Gay Archives, Toronto, Ontario
GLBT Historical Society, San Francisco, California
Human Sexuality Collection, Cornell University Library, Ithaca, New York
Jean-Nickolaus Tretter Collection in GLBT Studies, University of Minnesota Library,
Minneapolis, Minnesota

Abelove, Henry. "New York City Gay Liberation and the Queer Commuters." In *Deep Gossip*, 70–88. Minneapolis: University of Minnesota Press, 2003.

Adam, Barry. *The Rise of a Gay and Lesbian Movement*. New York: Twayne Publishers, 1995.

Agamben, Giorgio. *Homo Sacer: Sovereign Power and Bare Life*. Stanford, Calif.: Stanford University Press, 1998.

———. *State of Exception*. Chicago: University of Chicago Press, 2005.

Alarcón, Norma. "The Theoretical Subject(s) of *This Bridge Called My Back* and Anglo-American Feminism." In *Making Face, Making Soul Haciendo Caras: Creative and Critical Perspectives by Feminists of Color*, ed. Gloria Anzaldúa, 356–69. San Francisco: Aunt Lute, 1990.

Albert, Darcy. "Welcoming Remarks: Third Canadian Conference on HIV/AIDS and Related Issues in Aboriginal Communities" (1994). Canadian Lesbian and Gay Archives.

Alexander, M. Jacqui. *Pedagogies of Crossing: Meditations on Feminism, Sexual Politics, Memory, and the Sacred*. Durham, N.C.: Duke University Press, 2005.

Alexander, M. Jacqui, and Chandra T. Mohanty. "Introduction: Genealogies, Legacies, Movements." In *Feminist Genealogies, Colonial Legacies, Democratic Futures*, ed. M. J. Alexander and C. T. Mohanty, xii–xlii. New York: Routledge, 1997.

Alfred, Taiaiake. *Peace, Power, Righteousness: An Indigenous Manifesto*. New York: Oxford University Press, 1999.

———. "Sovereignty." In *Sovereignty Matters: Locations of Contestation and Possibility in Indigenous Struggles for Self-Determination,* ed. Joanne Barker, 33–50. Lincoln: University of Nebraska Press, 2005.

———. *Wasa'se: Indigenous Pathways of Action and Freedom.* Toronto: University of Toronto Press, 2005.

Allen, Chadwick. *Blood Narrative: Indigenous Identity in American Indian and Maori Literary and Activist Texts.* Durham, N.C.: Duke University Press, 2002.

Allen, Paula Gunn. *The Sacred Hoop: Recovering the Feminine in American Indian Traditions.* Boston: Beacon Press, 1986.

———. "Some Like Indians Endure." In *Living the Spirit: A Gay American Indian Anthology,* ed. Gay American Indians and Will Roscoe, 9–13. New York: St. Martin's Press, 1988.

Altman, Dennis. *Global Sex.* Chicago: University of Chicago Press, 2001.

Amadahy, Zainab, and Bonita Lawrence. "Indigenous Peoples and Black People in Canada: Settlers or Allies?" In *Breaching the Colonial Contract: Anti-Colonialism in the US and Canada,* ed. Arlo Kempf, 105–36. New York: Springer Publishing, 2009.

Amory, Deb. "The History of SOLGA." http://www.queeranthro.org/business; accessed May 29, 2011.

Anaya, S. James. *Indigenous Peoples in International Law.* New York: Oxford University Press, 2004.

Anderson, David. "On the Dangers of Faerie Anti-Intellectualism." *FDR: Faerie Dish Rag,* February 1996, 1, 6–7.

Anderson, Kim. *A Recognition of Being: Reconstructing Native Womanhood.* Toronto: Second Story Press, 2000.

Angelino, Henry, and Charles L. Shedd. "A Note on Berdache." *American Anthropologist* 57 (1955): 121–26.

Anguksuar Richard LaFortune. "Angukcuaq Lafortune." *Outweek,* July 3, 1991, 65.

———. "A Postcolonial Colonial Perspective on Western (Mis)Conceptions of the Cosmos and the Restoration of Indigenous Taxonomies." In *Two-Spirit People: Native American Gender Identity, Sexuality, and Spirituality,* ed. Sue-Ellen Jacobs, Wesley Thomas, and Sabine Lang, 217–22. Urbana: University of Illinois Press, 1997.

Anthropological Research Group on Homosexuality. "A.R.G.O.H. Charter." *ARGOH Newsletter* 2, no. 1 (1980): 3–4.

Anzaldúa, Gloria. *Borderlands/La Frontera: The New Mestiza.* San Francisco: Aunt Lute Books, 1987.

———. "Bridge, Drawbridge, Sandbar, Island: Lesbians of Color Hacienda Alianzas." In *Bridges of Power: Women's Multicultural Alliances,* ed. Lisa Albrecht and Rose M. Brewer, 216–31. Philadelphia: New Society, 1990.

———. "Foreword." In *Cassell's Encyclopedia of Queer Myth, Symbol, and Ritual: Gay, Lesbian, Bisexual, and Transgender Lore,* ed. Randy Conner, David Hatfield Sparks, and Mariya Sparks, vii–viii. London: Cassell, 1997.

Anzaldúa, Gloria, and AnaLouise Keating. *Interviews/Entrevistas*. New York: Routledge, 2000.

Arrizón, Alicia. *Queering Mestizaje: Transculturation and Performance*. Ann Arbor: University of Michigan Press, 2006.

Ashcroft, Bill, Gareth Griffiths, and Helen Tiffin, eds. *The Empire Writes Back: Theory and Practice in Post-Colonial Literatures*. New York: Routledge, 1989.

Aspin, Clive. "Exploring Takatapui Identity within the Maori Community: Implications for Health and Well-Being." In *Queer Indigenous Studies: Critical Interventions in Theory, Politics, and Literature*, ed. Qwo-Li Driskill, Chris Finley, Brian Joseph Gilley, and Scott Lauria Morgensen, 113–22. Tucson: University of Arizona Press, 2011.

Banner, Lois. *Intertwined Lives: Margaret Mead, Ruth Benedict, and Their Circle*. New York: Alfred A. Knopf, 2003.

Barker, Joanne. "Recognition." *American Studies* 46, no. 3/4 (2005): 117–45.

Barney, David, Betty Duran, and Caitlin Rosenthal. "HIV/AIDS Care Programs for American Indians and Alaska Natives." In *Healing and Mental Health for Native Americans*, ed. Ethan Nebelkopf and Mary Phillips, 149–58. Walnut Creek, Calif.: Altamira Press, 2004.

Battle, Juan, Cathy J. Cohen, Dorian Warren, Gerard Fergerson, and Suzette Audam. *Say It Loud, I'm Black and Proud: Black Pride Survey 2000*. New York: Policy Institute of the National Gay and Lesbian Task Force, 2002.

Baur, Gabriel. *Venus Boyz*. 104 min. United States: Icarus Films, 2001.

Bayer, Ronald. *Homosexuality and American Psychiatry: The Politics of Diagnosis*. Princeton, N.J.: Princeton University Press, 1987.

Bean, Joseph W. "Magical Masochist: A Conversation with Fakir Musafar." In *Leatherfolk: Radical Sex, People, Politics, and Practice*, ed. Mark Thompson, 303–19. Boston: Alyson Publications, 1991.

Bederman, Gail. *Manliness and Civilization: A Cultural History of Gender and Race in the United States, 1880–1917*. Chicago: University of Chicago Press, 1994.

Behrend-Martinez, Edward. "Manhood and the Neutered Body in Early Modern Spain." *Journal of Social History* 38, no. 4 (2005): 1073–93.

Benedict, Ruth. *Patterns of Culture*. Boston: Houghton Mifflin Company, 1934.

Bergland, Renée L. *The National Uncanny: Indian Ghosts and American Subjects*. Hanover, N.H.: University Press of New England, 2000.

Bérubé, Allan. "How Gay Stays White and What Kind of White It Stays." In *The Making and Unmaking of Whiteness*, ed. Birgit Brander Rasmussen, Irene J. Nexica, Eric Klinenberg, and Matt Wray, 234–65. Durham, N.C.: Duke University Press, 2001.

Blackberri. "Searching for My Gay Spiritual Roots." *BLK*, June 1990, 11.

Blackswan, Gryphon. "It's a Shame We Don't Have More People of Color Participating." *Lavender Reader* 7, no. 1 (1992): 26–28.

Blackwood, Evelyn. "Breaking the Mirror: The Construction of Lesbianism and the

Anthropological Discourse of Homosexuality." *Journal of Homosexuality* 11, no. 3/4 (1985): 1–17.

———. "Messages from Our Co-Presidents." *ARGOH Newsletter* 3, no. 4 (1982): 4.

———. "Native American Genders and Sexualities: Beyond Anthropological Models and Misrepresentations." In *Two-Spirit People: Native American Gender Identity, Sexuality, and Spirituality,* ed. Sue-Ellen Jacobs, Wesley Thomas, and Sabine Lang, 284–96. Urbana: University of Illinois Press, 1997.

———. "Report on the ARGOH Business Meeting." *ARGOH Newsletter* 9, no. 1 (1986): 3–4.

———. "Review: *The Zuni Man-Woman*." Will Roscoe. Albuquerque: University of New Mexico Press, 1991." *ARGOH Newsletter* 13, no. 3 (1991): 56–59.

———. "Sexuality and Gender in Certain Native American Tribes: The Case of Cross-Gender Females." *Signs* 10, no. 1 (1984): 27–42.

———. "Winner of the 1986 A.R.G.O.H. Award." *ARGOH Newsletter* 9, no. 1 (1987): 8.

———, ed. *The Many Faces of Homosexuality: Anthropological Approaches to Homosexual Behavior.* New York: Harrington Park Press, 1986.

Bob, Steve, and Allen. "Recipe for a Small Cabin." *RFD,* no. 7 (1976): 30–37.

Boellstorff, Tom. *The Gay Archipelago: Sexuality and Nation in Indonesia.* Princeton, N.J.: Princeton University Press, 2005.

Bouey, Paul, and Betty Duran. "The *Ahalaya* Case-Management Program for HIV-Infected American Indians, Alaska Natives, and Native Hawaiians: Quantitative and Qualitative Evaluation of Impacts." *American Indian and Alaska Native Mental Health Research* 9, no. 2 (2000): 36–52.

Boughter, Judith. *Betraying the Omaha Nation, 1790–1916.* Norman: University of Oklahoma Press, 1998.

Boyd, Nan Alamilla. *Wide-Open Town: A History of Queer San Francisco to 1965.* Berkeley: University of California Press, 2003.

Brandzel, Amy. "Queering Citizenship? Same-Sex Marriage and the State." *GLQ* 11, no. 2 (2005): 171–204.

Brant, Beth, ed. *A Gathering of Spirit: Writing and Art by North American Indian Women.* Rockland, Maine: Sinister Wisdom Books, 1984.

Braziel, Jana Evans. "Dréd's Drag Kinging of Race, Sex, and the Queering of the American Racial *Machine-Désirante*." *Women and Performance: A Journal of Feminist Theory* 15, no. 2 (2005): 162–87.

Brickman, Celia. *Aboriginal Populations in the Mind: Race and Primitivity in Psychoanalysis.* New York: Columbia University Press, 2003.

Brooks, Lisa. "Afterword." In *American Indian Literary Nationalism,* ed. Jace Weaver, Craig Womack, and Robert Allen Warrior, 225–52. Lincoln: University of Nebraska Press, 2006.

———. *The Common Pot: The Recovery of Native Space in the Northeast.* Minneapolis: University of Minnesota Press, 2008.

Brown, Wendy. *States of Injury: Power and Freedom in Late Modernity.* Princeton, N.J.: Princeton University Press, 1995.

Bruyneel, Kevin. *The Third Space of Sovereignty: The Postcolonial Politics of U.S.–Indigenous Relations.* Minneapolis: University of Minnesota Press, 2007.

Burns, Randy. "American Indians Neglected." *Bay Area Reporter,* March 31, 1988, 6.

———. "Gay Native Americans Find a Safe Harbor." Originally appears in *San Francisco Examiner,* Pride 2000 edition. Jean-Nickolaus Tretter Collection in GLBT Studies, Elmer L. Andersen Library, University of Minnesota.

———. "Preface." In *Living the Spirit: A Gay American Indian Anthology,* ed. Will Roscoe, 1–5. New York: St. Martin's Press, 1988.

Butler, Judith. *Precarious Life: The Powers of Mourning and Violence.* New York: Verso, 2006.

———. "The Question of Social Transformation." In *Undoing Gender,* 204–31. New York: Routledge, 2004.

Cairos Collective. "Founding Matrons & Patrons." *COLORLife!,* June 28, 1992, 32.

Callender, Charles, and Lee Kochems. "Men and Not-Men: Male Gender Mixing and Homosexuality." *Journal of Homosexuality* 11, no. 3/4 (1985): 165–76.

———. "The North American Berdache." *Current Anthropology* 24, no. 4 (1983): 443–70.

Cameron, Barbara. "Frybread in Berlin." *In The Wind: American Indian Alaska Native Community AIDS Network Newsletter* 4, no. 4 (1993): 1, 5.

Canadian Aboriginal AIDS Network. *An Aboriginal Strategy on HIV/AIDS in Canada: Summary of the Nine Key Strategic Areas Identified by ASHAC.* Ottawa: Canadian Aboriginal AIDS Network, n.d.

———. "Strengthening Ties—Strengthening Communities: An Aboriginal Strategy on HIV/AIDS in Canada for First Nations, Inuit, and Métis People." Ottawa: Canadian Aboriginal AIDS Network, 2003.

Cantú, Lionel, Jr. *The Sexuality of Migration: Border Crossings and Mexican Immigrant Men.* Ed. Nancy A. Naples and Salvador Vidal-Ortiz. New York: New York University Press, 2009.

Caradoc. "Sharing the Mysteries." *RFD,* no. 12 (1977): 25–27.

Carl. "Loving Circle." *RFD,* no. 4 (1975): 31–34.

Carpenter, Edward. *The Intermediate Sex.* London: George Allen and Unwin, 1908.

———. *Intermediate Types among Primitive Folks: A Study in Social Evolution.* New York: Mitchell Kennerley, 1914.

———. "Selected Insights." In *Gay Spirit: Myth and Meaning,* ed. Mark Thompson, 152–64. New York: St. Martin's Press, 1987.

Carrier, Joseph. "Notes on AAA Business Meeting of ARGOH." *ARGOH Newsletter* 3, no. 4 (1982): 1–2.

———. "Toward an A.A.A. Symposium on Homosexuality in 1980." *ARGOH Newsletter* 1, no. 2 (1980): 1.

Carson, Bronwyn, Terry Dunbar, Richard D. Chenhall, and Ross Bailie, eds. *Social Determinants of Indigenous Health*. Crows Nest, New South Wales: Allen and Unwin, 2007.

Carter, Julian. *The Heart of Whiteness: Normal Sexuality and Race in America, 1880–1940*. Durham, N.C.: Duke University Press, 2007.

Castaneda, Carlos. *The Teachings of Don Juan: A Yaqui Way of Knowledge*. Berkeley: University of California Press, 1968.

Child, Brenda. *Boarding School Seasons: American Indian Families, 1900–1940*. Lincoln: University of Nebraska Press, 1998.

Chrystos. *Dream On*. Seattle: Press Gang, 1991.

———. "Today Was a Bad Day like TB." In *Living the Spirit: A Gay American Indian Anthology*, ed. Gay American Indians and Will Roscoe, 180. New York: St. Martin's Press, 1988.

Circle of Loving Companions. "The Gays—Who Are We? Where Do We Come From? What Are We For?" *RFD*, no. 5 (1975): 38–39.

Clark, J. Michael. "The Native American Berdache: A Resource for Gay Spirituality." *RFD*, no. 40 (1984): 22–30.

Clifford, James. *Routes: Travel and Translation in the Late Twentieth Century*. Cambridge: Harvard University Press, 1997.

Cohen, Cathy. *The Boundaries of Blackness: AIDS and the Breakdown of Black Politics*. Chicago: University of Chicago Press, 1999.

Conner, Randy. *Blossom of Bone: Reclaiming the Connections between Homoeroticism and the Sacred*. San Francisco: HarperSanFrancisco, 1993.

Conner, Randy, David Hatfield Sparks, and Mariya Sparks, eds. *Cassell's Encyclopedia of Queer Myth, Symbol, and Spirit: Gay, Lesbian, Bisexual, and Transgender Lore*. London: Cassell, 1997.

Contreras, Sheila Marie. *Bloodlines: Myth, Indigenism, and Chicana/o Literature*. Austin: University of Texas Press, 2008.

Cornbelt, Arnold J. "Letter." *RFD*, no. 15 (1978): 5.

Coulthard, Glen. "Subject of Empire: Indigenous Peoples and the 'Politics of Recognition' in Canada." *Contemporary Political Theory* 6 (2007): 437–60.

Cox, James H. *Muting White Noise: Native American and European American Novel Traditions*. Norman: University of Oklahoma Press, 2006.

Cromwell, Jason. *Transmen and FTM's: Identities, Bodies, Genders, and Sexualities*. Urbana: University of Illinois Press, 1999.

Cruz-Malavé, Arnaldo, and Martin F. Manalansan IV, eds. *Queer Globalizations: Citizenship and the Afterlife of Colonialism*. New York: New York University Press, 2002.

D'Emilio, John. "Foreword." In *Out of the Closets: Voices of Gay Liberation*, ed. Karla Jay and Allen Young, xi–xxx. New York: New York University Press, 1992.

———. *Sexual Politics, Sexual Communities: The Making of a Homosexual Minority in the United States, 1940–1970*. 2d ed. Chicago: University of Chicago, 1998.

de Costa, Ravi. *A Higher Authority: Indigenous Transnationalism and Australia.* Sydney: University of New South Wales Press, 2006.

Deloria, Philip J. *Indians in Unexpected Places.* Lawrence: University Press of Kansas, 2006.

———. *Playing Indian.* New Haven: Yale University Press, 1998.

den Ouden, Amy. *Beyond Conquest: Native Peoples and the Struggle for History in New England.* Lincoln: University of Nebraska Press, 2005.

Denetdale, Jennifer. *Reclaiming Navajo History: The Legacies of Navajo Chief Manuelito and Juanita.* Tempe: University of Arizona Press, 2008.

———. "Securing Navajo National Boundaries: War, Patriotism, Tradition, and the Diné Marriage Act of 2005." *Wicazo Sa Review* 24, no. 2 (2009): 131–48.

Desai, Jigna, Danielle Bouchard, and Diane Detournay. "Disavowed Legacies and Honorable Thievery: The Work of the 'Transnational' in Feminist and LGBTQ Studies." In *Critical Transnational Feminist Praxis,* ed. Amanda Lock Swarr and Richa Nagar. Albany: State University of New York Press, 2010.

Deschamps, Gilbert. *We Are Part of a Tradition: A Guide on Two-Spirited People for First Nations Communities.* Toronto: 2-Spirited People of the 1st Nations, 1998.

Devereux, George. "Institutionalized Homosexuality of the Mohave Indians." *Human Biology* 9 (1937): 498–527.

Diaz, Rafael, and George Ayala. "Social Discrimination and Health: The Case of Latino Gay Men and HIV Risk." Washington, D.C.: Policy Institute of the National Gay and Lesbian Task Force, 2001.

Dickemann, Mildred. "SOLGA Member Wins 1991 Margaret Mead Award." *ARGOH Newsletter* 14, no. 1 (1992): 11.

Diversity Center. *Annual Report.* 2000.

Driskill, Qwo-Li. "Doubleweaving Two-Spirit Critiques: Building Alliances between Native and Queer Studies." *GLQ: A Journal of Lesbian and Gay Studies* 16, nos. 1–2 (2010): 69–92.

———. "Shaking Our Shells: Cherokee Two-Spirits Rebalancing the World." In *Beyond Masculinity: Essays by Queer Men on Gender and Politics,* ed. Trevor Hoppe, 2008. http://www.beyondmasculinity.com.

———. "Stolen from Our Bodies: First Nations Two-Spirits/Queers and the Journey to a Sovereign Erotic." *Studies in American Indian Literatures* 16, no. 2 (2004): 50–64.

———. *Walking with Ghosts: Poems.* Cambridge: Salt Publishers, 2005.

Driskill, Qwo-Li, Chris Finley, Brian Joseph Gilley, and Scott Lauria Morgensen. "Introduction." In *Queer Indigenous Studies: Critical Interventions in Theory, Politics, and Literature,* ed. Qwo-Li Driskill, Chris Finley, Brian Joseph Gilley, and Scott Lauria Morgensen, 1–28. Tucson: University of Arizona Press, 2011.

———. "The Revolution Is for Everyone: Imagining an Emancipatory Future through Queer Indigenous Critical Theories." In *Queer Indigenous Studies: Critical Interventions in Theory, Politics, and Literature,* ed. Qwo-Li Driskill, Chris Finley, Brian

Joseph Gilley, and Scott Lauria Morgensen, 211–22. Tucson: University of Arizona Press, 2011.

———, eds. *Queer Indigenous Studies: Critical Interventions in Theory, Politics, and Literature.* Tucson: University of Arizona Press, 2011.

Duggan, Lisa. *The Twilight of Equality: Neoliberalism, Cultural Politics, and the Attack on Democracy.* Boston: Beacon Press, 2003.

Duran, Bonnie, and Eduardo Duran. *Native American Postcolonial Psychology.* Albany: State University of New York Press, 1995.

Duran, Bonnie, and Karina Walters. "HIV/AIDS Prevention in 'Indian Country': Current Practice, Indigenist Etiology Models, and Postcolonial Approaches to Change." *AIDS Education and Prevention* 16, no. 3 (2004): 187–201.

Ellis, Havelock. *Studies in the Psychology of Sex,* vol. 2: *Sexual Inversion.* Philadelphia: F. A. Davis, 1915 (1897).

Elliston, Deborah. "Erotic Anthropology: 'Ritualized Homosexuality' in Melanesia and Beyond." *American Ethnologist* 22, no. 4 (1995): 848–67.

Eng, David. *Racial Castration: Managing Masculinity in Asian America.* Durham, N.C.: Duke University Press, 2001.

Engstrom, Donald L. "The Queer God Ritual: An Introduction to the Queer One." *Changing Men,* no. 23 (1991): 26–28.

Epstein, Stephen. "Gay Politics, Ethnic Identity: The Limits of Social Constructionism." *Socialist Review,* no. 17 (1987): 3–4.

———. *Impure Science: AIDS, Activism, and the Politics of Knowledge.* Berkeley: University of California Press, 1996.

Erai, Michelle. "A Queer Caste: Mixing Race and Sexuality in Colonial New Zealand." In *Queer Indigenous Studies: Critical Interventions in Theory, Politics, and Literature,* ed. Qwo-Li Driskill, Chris Finley, Brian Joseph Gilley, and Scott L. Morgensen, 66–80. Tucson: University of Arizona Press, 2011.

Evans, Arthur. "Things That Go Bump in the Night." *RFD,* no. 3 (1975): 16–17.

———. *Witchcraft and the Gay Counterculture.* Boston: Fag Rag Books, 1978.

Fabian, Johannes. *Time and the Other: How Anthropology Makes Its Object.* New York: Columbia University Press, 1983.

Fajardo, Kale. "Transportation: Translating Filipino and Filipino American Tomboy Masculinities through Global Migration and Seafaring." *GLQ* 14, nos. 2–3 (2008): 403–24.

Feinberg, Leslie. *Transgender Warriors.* Boston: Beacon Press, 1996.

Ferguson, Roderick. *Aberrations in Black: Towards a Queer of Color Critique.* Minneapolis: University of Minnesota Press, 2004.

———. "Of Our Normative Strivings: African American Studies and the History of Sexuality." *Social Text* 23, no. 3/4 (2005): 1–17.

Finley, Chris. "Decolonizing the Queer Native Body (and Recovering the Native Bull-Dyke): Bringing 'Sexy Back' and out of Native Studies." In *Queer Indigenous Studies: Critical Interventions in Theory, Politics, and Literature,* ed. Qwo-Li Driskill,

Chris Finley, Brian Joseph Gilley, and Scott Lauria Morgensen, 29–42. Tucson: University of Arizona Press, 2011.

Ford, Clellan S., and Frank A. Beach. *Patterns of Sexual Behavior.* New York: Harper, 1951.

Foucault, Michel. *The Birth of Biopolitics: Lectures at the Collège de France, 1978–1979.* Trans. Graham Burchell. New York: Picador, 2010.

———. *Discipline and Punish: The Birth of the Prison.* Trans. Alan Sheridan. New York: Vintage, 1977.

———. *The History of Sexuality: Volume 1: An Introduction.* Trans. Robert Hurley. New York: Vintage, 1978 (1976).

Foucault, Michel, Michel Senellart, and François Ewald. *Security, Territory, Population: Lectures at the Collège de France 1977–1978.* New York: Picador, 2009.

Frankenberg, Ruth. *White Women, Race Matters: The Social Construction of Whiteness.* Minneapolis: University of Minnesota Press, 1993.

Fujikane, Candace, and Jonathan Y. Okamura, eds. *Asian Settler Colonialism: From Local Governance to the Habits of Everyday Life in Hawai'i.* Honolulu: University Hawaii Press, 2008.

Gay American Indians. "Publication Proposal: Living the Spirit: A Gay American Indian Anthology." *ARGOH Newsletter* 9, no. 2 (1987): 19–20.

Gay American Indians and Will Roscoe. *Living the Spirit: A Gay American Indian Anthology.* New York: St. Martin's Press, 1988.

Gays and Lesbians of the First Nations in Toronto. "The Greater Vancouver Native Cultural Society." *The Sacred Fire,* August 1990, 2.

Gengle, Dean. "Reclaiming the Old New World: Gay Was Good with Native Americans." *Advocate,* 1976, 40–41.

Gilley, Brian Joseph. *Becoming Two-Spirit: Gay Identity and Social Acceptance in Indian Country.* Lincoln: University of Nebraska Press, 2006.

———. "'Snag Bags': Adapting Condoms to Community Values in American Indian Communities." *Culture, Health, and Sexuality* 8, no. 6 (2006): 1–12.

Gluck, Sherna Berger, with Maylei Blackwell, Sharon Cotrell, and Karen S. Harper. "Whose Feminism, Whose History? Reflections on Excavating the History of (the) US Women's Movement(s)." In *Community Activism and Feminist Politics: Organizing across Race, Class, and Gender,* ed. Nancy Naples. New York: Routledge, 1997.

Goeman, Mishuana, and Jennifer Nez Denetdale, eds. "Native Feminisms: Legacies, Interventions, and Sovereignties." *Wicazo Sa Review* 24, no. 2 (2009): 9–187.

Goldberg, Jonathan. "Sodomy in the New World: Anthropologies Old and New." In *Fear of a Queer Planet: Queer Politics and Social Theory,* ed. Michael Warner, 3–18. Minneapolis: University of Minnesota Press, 1993.

Gordon, Avery F., and Christopher Newfield, eds. *Mapping Multiculturalism.* Minneapolis: University of Minnesota Press, 1996.

Grahn, Judy. *Another Mother Tongue: Gay Words, Gay Worlds.* Boston: Beacon Press, 1984.

Green, Joyce, ed. *Making Space for Indigenous Feminism*. Halifax: Fernwood Publishers, 2007.

Grewal, Inderpal. *Transnational America: Feminisms, Diasporas, Neoliberalisms*. Durham, N.C.: Duke University Press, 2005.

Gross, Larry. "Messages from Our New Co-Presidents." *ARGOH Newsletter* 3, no. 4 (1982): 2–4.

Gustav-Wrathall, and John Donald. *Take the Young Stranger by the Hand: Same-Sex Relations and the YMCA*. Chicago: University of Chicago Press, 1998.

Hall, Clyde (M. Owlfeather). "Children of Grandmother Moon." In *Living the Spirit: A Gay American Indian Anthology*, ed. Gay American Indians and Will Roscoe, 97–105. New York: St. Martin's Press, 1988.

———. "Great Spirit." In *Gay Soul: Finding the Heart of Gay Spirit and Nature*, ed. Mark Thompson, 117–32. San Francisco: HarperSanFrancisco, 1994.

Halley, Janet. "'Like Race' Arguments." In *What's Left of Theory: New Work on the Politics of Literary Theory*, ed. Judith Butler, John Guillory, and Kendall Thomas, 40–74. New York: Routledge, 2000.

Hardt, Michael, and Antonio Negri. *Empire*. Cambridge: Harvard University Press, 2000.

Harjo, Joy. "Perhaps the World Ends Here." In *How We Became Human: New and Selected Poems*, 123–24. New York: W. W. Norton, 1994.

Harris, Curtis, and Kent Lebsock. "Things Sacred." *Buffalo Hide* 2, no. 4 (1993): 2–4.

Hartman, Saidiya V. *Scenes of Subjection: Terror, Slavery, and Self-Making in Nineteenth-Century America*. New York: Oxford University Press, 1997.

Hay, Harry. "A Call to Gay Brothers." *RFD* (summer 1979): 1.

———. "Prologue: How Did He Know?" In *Radically Gay: Gay Liberation in the Words of Its Founder*, ed. Will Roscoe, 17–58. Boston: Beacon Press, 1996.

———. "A Separate People Whose Time Has Come." In *Gay Spirit: Myth and Meaning*, ed. Mark Thompson, 279–91. New York: St. Martin's Press, 1987.

———. *Radically Gay: Gay Liberation in the Words of Its Founder*. Ed. Will Roscoe. Boston: Beacon Press, 1996.

———. "Toward the New Frontiers of Fairy Vision . . . Subject-Subject Consciousness." *RFD*, no. 24 (1980): 29–34.

Hemphill, Essex, ed. *Brother to Brother: New Writings by Black Gay Men*. Boston: Alyson Publications, 1991.

Hennen, Peter. *Faeries, Bears, and Leathermen: Men in Community Queering the Masculine*. Chicago: University of Chicago Press, 2008.

Hennessy, Keith. "Fey Enough?" *Anything That Moves*, no. 16 (1998): 21.

———. "HomoHex: A Public Queer Sex Ritual." *RFD*, no. 82 (1995): 14–15.

Herdt, Gilbert, ed. *Ritualized Homosexuality in Melanesia*. Berkeley: University of California Press, 1984.

Hermsen, Larry. "When the Sun Stands Still." *RFD*, no. 12 (1977): 9.

Herring, Scott. "Out of the Closets, into the Woods: *RFD, Country Women,* and the Post-Stonewall Emergence of Queer Anti-Urbanism." *American Quarterly* 59, no. 2 (2007): 341–72.

———. *Queering the Underworld: Slumming, Literature, and the Undoing of Lesbian and Gay History.* Chicago: University of Chicago Press, 2007.

Hobsbawm, Eric, and Terence Ranger, eds. *The Invention of Tradition.* Oxford: Cambridge University Press, 1983.

Hochberg, Gil Z., ed. *Queer Politics and the Question of Palestine/Israel. GLQ* 16 (2010).

Holloway, Bill. "Letter." *RFD,* no. 15 (1978): 2.

Holmes, Henry. "Into the Woods: Radical Faërie Movement Combines Earthy Spirituality with Insurgent Politics." *BLK,* June 1990, 7–8, 10, 12–13.

Horsman, Reginald. *Race and Manifest Destiny: The Origins of American Racial Anglo-Saxonism.* Cambridge: Harvard University Press, 1981.

Hull, Bryan. "The Posters Transformed the Landscape I Live In." *Lavender Reader* 7, no. 1 (1992): 24, 29.

Hultkrantz, Åke. *Belief and Worship in Native North America.* Ed. Christopher Vecsey. Syracuse, N.Y.: Syracuse University Press, 1981.

Human Health Organization. *We Owe It to Ourselves and to Our Children.* Berkeley: Human Health Organization, 1988.

INCITE! Women of Color Against Violence, ed. *The Revolution Will Not Be Funded: Beyond the Non-Profit Industrial Complex.* Boston: South End Press, 2007.

International Indigenous People's Satellite. *The Toronto Charter: Indigenous People's Action Plan on HIV/AIDS 2006.* Toronto: International Indigenous People's Satellite, 2006.

Intertribal Friendship House. *Urban Voices: The Bay Area American Indian Community.* Tucson: University of Arizona Press, 2002.

Irvine, Janice. "A Place in the Rainbow: Theorizing Lesbian and Gay Culture." *Sociological Theory* 12, no. 2 (1994): 232–48.

Isaac, Allan Punzalan. *American Tropics: Articulating Filipino America.* Minneapolis: University of Minnesota Press, 2006.

Jacobs, Sue-Ellen. "Berdache: A Brief Review of the Literature." *Colorado Anthropologist* 1, no. 2 (1968): 25–40.

———. "Is the 'North American Berdache' Merely a Phantom in the Imagination of Western Social Scientists?" In *Two-Spirit People: Native American Gender Identity, Sexuality, and Spirituality,* ed. Sue-Ellen Jacobs, Wesley Thomas, and Sabine Lang, 21–44. Urbana: University of Illinois Press, 1997.

———. "Letter: 'Revisiting the "North American Berdache," Empirically and Theoretically.'" 1993. Will Roscoe and Gay American Indians Papers (#1987–04), GLBT Historical Society.

Jacobs, Sue-Ellen, Wesley Thomas, and Sabine Lang. "Introduction." In *Two-Spirit People: Native American Gender Identity, Sexuality, and Spirituality,* ed. Sue-Ellen Jacobs, Wesley Thomas, and Sabine Lang, 1–20. Urbana: University of Illinois Press, 1997.

———, eds. *Two-Spirit People: Native American Gender Identity, Sexuality, and Spirituality.* Urbana: University of Illinois Press, 1997.

Jacobson, Matthew Frye. *Roots Too: White Ethnic Revival in Post-Civil Rights America.* Cambridge: Harvard University Press, 2006.

Jerry. "RFD Reader Survey." *RFD*, no. 8 (1976): 39.

John. "Gardening with the Fairies." *RFD*, no. 7 (1976): 4–6.

Johnson, E. Patrick, and Mae G. Henderson. *Black Queer Studies: A Critical Anthology.* Durham, N.C.: Duke University Press, 2005.

Joseph, Miranda. *Against the Romance of Community.* Minneapolis: University of Minnesota Press, 2002.

Joyous, Jada. "We Circle around (We Circle around the Boundaries of the Earth, Wearing Our Long-Winged Feathers as We Fly)." *RFD*, no. 12 (1977): 13–14.

Junga-Williams, Rodney. "Rodney's Journey." *Aboriginal and Islander Health Worker Journal* 30, no. sample (2006): 1–2.

Justice, Daniel Heath. "Notes toward a Theory of Anomaly." *GLQ: A Journal of Lesbian and Gay Studies* 16, nos. 1–2 (2010): 207–42.

Justice, Daniel Heath, and James H. Cox, eds. *Queering Native Literature, Indigenizing Queer Theory.* Vol. 20, *Studies in American Indian Literature*, 2008.

Justice, Daniel Heath, Mark Rifkin, and Bethany Schneider, eds. *Sexuality, Nationality, Indigeneity: Rethinking the State at the Intersection of Native American and Queer Studies.* Vol. 16, *GLQ: A Journal of Lesbian and Gay Studies*, 2010.

Kairaiuak, Larry. *Addressing Two-Spirits in the American Indian, Alaskan Native and Native Hawaiian Communities.* Oakland, Calif.: NNAAPC, 2002.

Karsch-Haack, Ferdinand. "Uranismus oder Päderastie und Tribadie bei een Naturvölkern." In *Jahrbuch für Sexuelle Zwischenstufen. Auswahl aus den Jahrgängen 1899–1923*, ed. Wolfgang Johann Schmidt, 229–96. Frankfurt and Paris: Qumran, 1983.

Kasee, Cynthia R. "Identity, Recovery, and Religious Imperialism: Native American Women and the New Age." *Journal of Homosexuality* 16, no. 2/3 (1995): 83–93.

Katz, Jonathan. *Gay American History: Lesbians and Gay Men in the U.S.A.* New York: Thomas Crowell, 1976.

Kauanui, J. Kehaulani. *Hawaiian Blood: Colonialism and the Politics of Sovereignty and Indigeneity.* Durham, N.C.: Duke University Press, 2008.

Kayal, Philip. *Bearing Witness: Gay Men's Health Crisis and the Politics of AIDS.* Boulder. Colo.: Westview Press, 1993.

Keck, Margaret E., and Kathryn Sikkink. *Activists beyond Borders: Advocacy Networks in International Politics.* Ithaca, N.Y.: Cornell University Press, 1998.

Kennedy, Hubert. *Ulrichs: The Life and Works of Karl Heinrich Ulrichs, Pioneer of the Modern Gay Movement.* Boston: Alyson Publications, 1988.

Kenney, Maurice. "Tinselled Bucks: A Historical Study in Indian Homosexuality." In *Living the Spirit: A Gay American Indian Anthology*, ed. Gay American Indians and Will Roscoe, 15–31. New York: St. Martin's Press, 1988.

King, Katie. *Theory in Its Feminist Travels: Conversations in U.S. Women's Movements.* Bloomington: Indiana University Press, 1994.

———. "'There Are No Lesbians Here': Lesbianisms, Feminisms, and Global Gay Formations." In *Queer Globalizations: Citizenship and the Afterlife of Colonialism,* ed. Arnaldo Cruz-Malavé and Martin F. Manalansan IV, 33–47. New York: New York University Press, 2002.

Krafft-Ebing, Richard von. *Psychopathia Sexualis.* 12th ed. Philadelphia: F. A. Davis, 1903.

Kreuter, Holly. *Drama in the Desert: The Sights and Sounds of Burning Man.* Berkeley: Raised Barn Press, 2002.

Kroeber, Alfred. "Psychosis or Social Sanction." *Character and Personality* 8 (1940): 204–15.

Kutsche, Paul. "A.R.G.O.H. in 1987: Report of the Co-Chair, Paul Kutsche." *ARGOH Newsletter* 9, no. 1 (1987): 2–3.

LaFortune, Richard. "A Cultural Marker." *Washington Blade,* March 21, 1997, 29.

Lapsley, Hilary. *Margaret Mead and Ruth Benedict: The Kinship of Women.* Amherst: University of Massachusetts Press, 1999.

Laqueur, Thomas. *Making Sex: Body and Gender from the Greeks to Freud.* Cambridge: Harvard University Press, 1990.

Larry and Steven. "Our Theme . . ." *RFD,* no. 12 (1977): 8.

Lawrence, Bonita. *"Real" Indians and Others: Mixed-Blood Urban Native People and Indigenous Nationhood.* Lincoln: University of Nebraska Press, 2004.

Lawrence, Bonita, and Enakshi Dua. "Decolonizing Antiracism." *Social Justice* 32, no. 4 (2005): 120–43.

Lawrence, Bonita, and Kim Anderson, eds. *Strong Women Stories: Native Vision and Community Survival.* Toronto: Sumach Press, 2002.

Lebsock, Kent. "North East Two-Spirit Society." *American Indian Community House Bulletin,* 2007.

Legg, Dorr. "The Berdache and Theories of Sexual Inversion." *One Institute Quarterly* 2, no. 2 (1959): 59–60, 63.

Levine, Martin, Peter Nardi, and John Gagnon, eds. *In Changing Times: Gay Men and Lesbians Encounter HIV/AIDS.* Chicago: University of Chicago Press, 1997.

Liljeblad, Sven. *The Idaho Indians in Transition, 1805–1960.* Pocatello: Idaho State University Press, 1972.

Lindner, Kelly. "Letter." *RFD,* no. 13 (1977): 3.

Lipsitz, George. *The Possessive Investment in Whiteness: How White People Profit from Identity Politics.* Philadelphia: Temple University Press, 2006.

Little, Ann. *Abraham in Arms: War and Gender in Colonial New England.* Philadelphia: University of Pennsylvania Press, 2007.

Little Thunder, Beverly. "I Am a Lakota Womyn." In *Two-Spirit People: Native American Gender Identity, Sexuality, and Spirituality,* ed. Sue-Ellen Jacobs, Wesley Thomas, and Sabine Lang, 203–9. Urbana: University of Illinois Press, 1997.

Lowery, Malinda Maynor. *Lumbee Indians in the Jim Crow South: Race, Identity, and the Making of a Nation.* Chapel Hill: University of North Carolina Press, 2010.

Luibhéid, Eithne. *Entry Denied: Controlling Sexuality at the Border.* Minneapolis: University of Minnesota Press, 2001.

———. "Introduction: Queering Migration and Citizenship." In *Queer Migrations: Sexuality, U.S. Citizenship, and Border Crossings,* ed. Eithne Luibhéid, ix–xlvi. Minneapolis: University of Minneapolis Press, 2005.

———. "Queer/Migration: An Unruly Body of Scholarship." *GLQ: A Journal of Lesbian and Gay Studies* 14, nos. 2–3 (2008): 169–90.

Mackenzie, Kent. *The Exiles.* United States: Milestone Films, 1961.

Mains, Geoff. *Urban Aboriginals: A Celebration of Leathersexuality.* San Francisco: Gay Sunshine Press, 1984.

Manalansan, Martin. *Global Divas: Filipino Gay Men in the Diaspora.* Durham, N.C.: Duke University Press, 2003.

Manes, Tom. "Letter." *RFD,* no. 14 (1977): 2.

Marmor, Judd. "Homosexuality and Cultural Value-Systems: Should Homosexuality Be Classified as a Mental Illness?" In *American Psychiatric Association Annual Meeting.* Honolulu, Hawaii, 1973.

Martin, Biddy, and Chandra Mohanty. "Feminist Politics: What's Home Got to Do with It?" In *Feminist Studies, Critical Studies,* ed. Teresa de Lauretis, 191–212. Urbana: University of Illinois Press, 1986.

Mass, Lawrence. "On the Future of Lesbian and Gay Studies: A Dialogue with Will Roscoe." In *Homosexuality as Behavior and Identity: Dialogues of the Sexual Revolution,* vol. 2, 234–52. New York: Harrington Park Press, 1990.

Massad, Joseph. *Desiring Arabs.* Chicago: University of Chicago Press, 2007.

Mbembe, Achille. "Necropolitics." *Public Culture* 15, no. 1 (2003): 11–40.

Mead, Margaret. *Coming of Age in Samoa: A Psychological Study of Primitive Youth for Western Civilisation.* New York: William Morrow and Company, 1928.

———. *Male and Female: A Study of the Sexes in a Changing World.* New York: Dell, 1949.

———. *Sex and Temperament in Three Primitive Societies.* New York: William Morrow and Company, 1935.

Medicine, Beatrice. "Changing Native American Roles in an Urban Context *and* Changing Native American Sex Roles in an Urban Context." In *Two-Spirit People: Native American Gender Identity, Sexuality, and Spirituality,* ed. Sue-Ellen Jacobs, Wesley Thomas, and Sabine Lang, 145–55. Urbana: University of Illinois Press, 1997.

Midnight Sun. "Sex/Gender Systems in Native North America." In *Living the Spirit: A Gay American Indian Anthology,* ed. Gay American Indians and Will Roscoe, 32–47. New York: St. Martin's Press, 1988.

Miles, Tiya, and Sharon Holland, eds. *Crossing Waters, Crossing Worlds: The African Diaspora in Indian Country.* Durham, N.C.: Duke University Press, 2006.

Minnesota American Indian AIDS Task Force. "The Ogitchidag Gikinooamaagad Players: Youth Peer Education 'Warrior Teachers.'" Minneapolis: Minnesota American Indian AIDS Task Force, n.d. Jean-Nickolaus Tretter Collection in GLBT Studies, Elmer L. Andersen Library, University of Minnesota.

Miranda, Deborah A. "Extermination of the *Joyas:* Gendercide in Spanish California." *GLQ: A Journal of Lesbian and Gay Studies* 16, nos. 1–2 (2010): 253–84.

Mohanty, Chandra Talpade. "Cartographies of Struggle: Third World Women and the Politics of Feminism." In *Third World Women and the Politics of Feminism,* ed. Chandra Talpade Mohanty, Ann Russo, and Lourdes Torres, 1–52. Bloomington: Indiana University Press, 1991.

———. "Under Western Eyes: Feminist Scholarship and Colonial Discourses." In *Third World Women and the Politics of Feminism,* ed. Chandra Talpade Mohanty, Ann Russo, and Lourdes Torres, 51–80. Bloomington: Indiana University Press, 1991.

Moraga, Cherríe. *The Last Generation: Prose and Poetry.* Boston: South End Press, 1993.

Morgensen, Scott Lauria. "The Biopolitics of Settler Colonialism: Right Here, Right Now." *Settler Colonial Studies* 1, no. 1 (2011): 52–76.

———. "Settler Homonationalism: Theorizing Settler Colonialism within Queer Modernities." *GLQ: A Journal of Lesbian and Gay Studies* 16, nos. 1–2 (2010): 105–31.

Mumford, Kevin. *Interzones: Black/White Sex Districts in Chicago and New York in the Early Twentieth Century.* New York: Columbia University Press, 1997.

Muñoz, José Esteban. *Disidentifications: Queers of Color and the Performance of Politics.* Minneapolis: University of Minnesota Press, 1999.

Murphy, Kevin, Jason Ruiz, and David Serlin, eds. *Queer Futures.* Vol. 100, *Radical History Review* (2008).

Musafar, Fakir. "Gryphon Blackswan Androgyne." *Body Play and Modern Primitives Quarterly* 1, no. 3 (1992).

National Alliance of State and Territorial AIDS Directors (NASTAD). "Native Americans and HIV/AIDS." Washington, D.C.: NASTAD, 2004.

National Native American AIDS Prevention Center (NNAAPC). "Creating a Vision for Living with HIV in the Circle of Life." Oakland, Calif.: NNAAPC, 2003.

———. "Creating a Vision for Living with HIV in the Circle of Life: Self-Care Manual for Native People Living with HIV/AIDS." *Seasons* (fall 2003): 6.

———. "Gathering Our Wisdom II: Proceedings and Recommendations." Oakland, Calif.: NNAAPC, 2003.

———. "Landmark Charter Calls for Full Participation of Indigenous Peoples in HIV Programs." *Seasons* (summer 2006): 6.

———. "Leadership Development for Native American Gay/Bisexual/Two-Spirit Native American Men." *In the Wind,* July/August 1995, 1–2.

———. "Together We Are Stronger." Poster Campaign. Oakland, Calif.: NNAAPC, 2006.

National Native American AIDS Prevention Center and the Rural Center for AIDS/ STD Prevention. "HIV/STD Prevention Guidelines for Native American Communities." Oakland, Calif.: NNAAPC, 2004.

Naylor, Celia. *African Cherokees in Indian Territory: From Chattel to Citizens.* Chapel Hill: University of North Carolina Press, 2008.

Nebelkopf, Ethan, and Mary Phillips, eds. *Healing and Mental Health for Native Americans: Speaking in Red.* Walnut Creek, Calif.: Altamira Press, 2004.

Newton, Esther. "A.R.G.O.H. Annual Award." *ARGOH Newsletter* 8, no. 1 (1986): 4.

Niezen, Ronald. *The Origins of Indigenism: Human Rights and the Politics of Identity.* Berkeley: University of California Press, 2003.

O'Brien, Jean M. *Firsting and Lasting: Writing Indians out of Existence.* Minneapolis: University of Minnesota Press, 2010.

Olwan, Dana. "Between Settlement and Indigeneity: Connecting Solidarity Struggles from Turtle Island to Palestine." *Settler Colonial Studies* 2, no. 1 (forthcoming 2012).

Oosterhuis, Harry. *Stepchildren of Nature: Krafft-Ebing, Psychiatry, and the Making of Sexual Identity.* Chicago: University of Chicago Press, 2000.

Ordoña, Trinity. "The Challenges Facing Asian and Pacific Island Lesbians in the U.S." In *The Very Inside: Asian and Pacific Islander Lesbians and Bisexual Women's Anthology,* ed. Sharon Lim Hing, 384–90. Toronto: Sister Vision Press, 1994.

Padilla, Mark. *Caribbean Pleasure Industry: Tourism, Sexuality, and AIDS in the Dominican Republic.* Chicago: University of Chicago Press, 2007.

Pahe, Erna. "Speaking Up." In *Living the Spirit: A Gay American Indian Anthology,* ed. Gay American Indians and Will Roscoe, 106–14. New York: St. Martin's Press, 1988.

Pathmakers. "Pathmakers Organizational Meeting: Meeting Minutes, March 28, 1998." Two-Spirit Collection, Jean-Nickolaus Tretter Collection in GLBT Studies, University of Minnesota Library.

Patton, Cindy. *Globalizing AIDS.* Minneapolis: University of Minnesota Press, 2002.

———. *Inventing AIDS.* New York: Routledge, 1990.

Perez, Emma. *The Decolonial Imaginary: Writing Chicanas into History.* Bloomington: Indiana University Press, 1999.

Phillips, Gary Lee. "Electric Consciousness." *RFD,* no. 12 (1977): 24.

Plane, Ann Marie. *Colonial Intimacies: Indian Marriage in Early New England.* Ithaca, N.Y.: Cornell University Press, 2002.

Portillo, Tina. "I Get Real: Celebrating My Sadomasochistic Soul." In *Leatherfolk: Radical Sex, People, Politics, and Practice,* ed. Mark Thompson, 49–55. Boston: Alyson Books, 1991.

Povinelli, Elizabeth. *The Cunning of Recognition: Indigenous Alterities and the Making of Australian Multiculturalism.* Durham, N.C.: Duke University Press, 2002.

———. *The Empire of Love: Toward a Theory of Intimacy, Genealogy, and Carnality.* Durham, N.C.: Duke University Press, 2006.

Pratt, Mary Louise. *Imperial Eyes: Travel Writing and Transculturation.* New York: Routledge, 1992.

Pratt, Minnie Bruce. "Identity: Skin Blood Heart." In *Yours in Struggle: Three Feminist Perspectives on Racism and Anti-Semitism,* ed. Elly Bulkin, Minnie Bruce Pratt, and Barbara Smith, 27–82. Ithaca, N.Y.: Firebrand Books, 1981.

Puar, Jasbir. *Terrorist Assemblages: Homonationalism in Queer Times.* Durham, N.C.: Duke University Press, 2007.

Pulitano, Elvira. *Toward a Native American Critical Theory.* Lincoln: University of Nebraska Press, 2003.

Ramirez, Renya. *Native Hubs: Culture, Community, and Belonging in Silicon Valley and Beyond.* Durham, N.C.: Duke University Press, 2007.

Raymond, Janice. *The Transsexual Empire: The Making of the She-Male.* Boston: Beacon Press, 1979.

Razack, Sherene. *Casting Out: The Eviction of Muslims from Western Law and Politics.* Toronto: University of Toronto Press, 2007.

———. "Introduction: When Place Becomes Race." In *Race, Space, and the Law: Unmapping a White Settler Society,* ed. Sherene Razack, 1–20. Toronto: University of Toronto Press, 2002.

Red Earth, Michael. "Traditional Influences on a Contemporary Gay-Identified Sisseton Dakota." In *Two-Spirit People: Native American Gender Identity, Sexuality, and Spirituality,* ed. Sue-Ellen Jacobs, Wesley Thomas, and Sabine Lang, 210–6. Urbana: University of Illinois Press, 1997.

Reddy, Chandan. "Asian Diasporas, Neoliberalism, and Family: Reviewing the Case for Homosexual Asylum in the Context of Family Rights." *Social Text* 84–85 (2005): 101–19.

Redwing, Jamal. "Untitled." *RFD,* no. 12 (1977): 18.

———. "Faggot Shaman Poet Butterfly Dancer." *RFD,* no. 12 (1977): 23.

RFD Collective. "Collective Statement." *RFD,* no. 10 (1976): 4.

———. "Faggots & Class Struggle." *RFD,* no. 10 (1976): 14.

———. "Spiritual Soapbox." *RFD,* no. 12 (1977): 30–33.

———. "Uncle Ned Says, 'Let's Eat!'" *RFD,* no. 3 (1975): 34.

Rifkin, Mark. "Indigenizing Agamben: Rethinking Sovereignty in Light of the 'Peculiar' Status of Native Peoples." *Cultural Critique* 73 (2009): 88–124.

———. *When Did Indians Become Straight? Kinship, the History of Sexuality, and Native Sovereignty.* Oxford: Oxford University Press, 2011.

Rodriguez, Juana Maria. *Queer Latinidad: Identity Practices, Discursive Spaces.* New York: New York University Press, 2003.

Rofel, Lisa. *Desiring China: Experiments in Neoliberalism, Sexuality, and Public Culture.* Durham, N.C.: Duke University Press, 2007.

———. "Qualities of Desire: Imagining Gay Identities in China." *GLQ: A Journal of Lesbian and Gay Studies* 5, no. 4 (1999): 451–74.

Romo-Carmona, Mariana, Lidell Jackson, and Curtis Harris. "Activists Respond to the Quincentennial: Lesbian/Gay/Bisexual/Two-Spirit in 1992." *COLORLife!*, June 28, 1992, 11–12.

Roscoe, Will. "Bibliography of Berdache and Alternative Gender Roles among Native North American Indians." *Journal of Homosexuality* 14, no. 3/4 (1987): 81–171.

———. *Changing Ones: Third and Fourth Genders in Native North America*. New York: St. Martin's Press, 1998.

———. "Comments on Receiving the Margaret Mead Award." *ARGOH Newsletter* 14, no. 1 (1991): 11–12.

———. "Dreaming the Myth: An Introduction to Mythology for Gay Men." In *Same-Sex Love and the Path to Wholeness*, ed. Robert Hopcke, Karen Lofthus Carrington, and Scott Wirth, 110–24. Boston: Shambhala Books, 1993.

———. "The Geography of Gender." In *Gay Soul: Finding the Heart of Gay Spirit and Nature*, ed. Mark Thompson, 99–116. San Francisco: HarperCollins, 1994.

———. "History Comes Home: Gay Studies on the Rez." *ARGOH Newsletter* 10, no. 1 (1988): 16–18.

———. "Making History: The Challenge of Gay and Lesbian Studies." *Journal of Homosexuality* 15, no. 3/4 (1988): 1–40.

———. *Queer Spirits: A Gay Men's Myth Book*. Boston: Beacon Press, 1995.

———. *The Zuni Man-Woman*. Albuquerque: University of New Mexico Press, 1991.

Rose, Bradley. *A Radical Fairy's Seedbed: The Collected Series*. San Francisco: Nomenus, 1997.

Rosenblatt, David. "The Antisocial Skin: Structure, Resistance, and 'Modern Primitive' Adornment in the United States." *Cultural Anthropology* 12, no. 3 (1997): 287–334.

Rowell, Ron. "Developing AIDS Services for Native Americans: Rural and Urban Contrasts." In *Two-Spirit People: American Indian Lesbian Women and Gay Men*, ed. Lester Brown, 85–96. New York: Harrington Park Press, 1997.

———. *HIV Prevention for Gay/Bisexual/Two-Spirit Native American Men: A Report of the National Leadership Development Workgroup for Gay/Bisexual/Two-Spirit Native American Men*. Oakland, Calif.: NNAAPC, 1996.

Royale, Rosette. "As a Matter of Fact . . . Musings on the First 'Fairies of All Colors Together' Gathering." *RFD* 28, no. 2 (2001): 29, 47.

Rush, Andrea Green. "Her Giveaway: A Spiritual Journey with AIDS." *Seasons* (1989): 5.

———. "Models of Prevention: Minnesota American Indian AIDS Task Force." *Seasons* (1989): 4–5.

Saldaña-Portillo, Maria Josefina. *The Revolutionary Imagination in Latin America and the Age of Development*. Durham, N.C.: Duke University Press, 2003.

Sandoval, Chela. *Methodology of the Oppressed*. Minneapolis: University of Minnesota Press, 2000.

Saranillio, Dean Itsuji. "Colonial Amnesia: Rethinking Filipino 'American' Settler

Empowerment in the U.S. Colony of Hawai'i." In *Asian Settler Colonialism: From Local Governance to the Habits of Everyday Life in Hawai'i*, ed. Candace Fujikane and Jonathan Y. Okamura, 256–78. Honolulu: University of Hawaii Press, 2008.

Sears, James. *Rebels, Rubyfruits, and Rhinestones: Queering Space in the Stonewall South*. New Brunswick, N.J.: Rutgers University Press, 2001.

Seligmann, C. G. "Sexual Inversion among Primitive Races." *Alienist and Neurologist* 23 (1902): 11–13.

Shah, Nayan. "Between 'Oriental Depravity' and 'Natural Degenerates': Spatial Borderlands and the Making of Ordinary Americans." *American Quarterly* 57, no. 3 (2005): 703–25.

Sharma, Nandita, and Cynthia Wright. "Decolonizing Resistance, Challenging Colonial States." *Social Justice* 35, no. 3 (2008): 93–111.

Shepard, Alexandra. *Meanings of Manhood in Early Modern England*. Oxford: Oxford University Press, 2003.

Simpson, Audra. "On Ethnographic Refusal: Indigeneity, 'Voice,' and Colonial Citizenship." *Junctures* 9 (2007): 69.

Smith, Andrea. *Conquest: Sexual Violence and American Indian Genocide*. Cambridge: South End Press, 2005.

———. *Native Americans and the Christian Right: The Politics of Unlikely Alliances*. Durham, N.C.: Duke University Press, 2007.

———. "Queer Theory and Native Studies: The Heteronormativity of Settler Colonialism." *GLQ* 16, nos. 1–2 (2010): 41–68.

Smith, Andrea, and J. Kehaulani Kauanui. "Native Feminisms Engage American Studies." *American Quarterly* 60, no. 2 (2008): 241–50.

Smith, Linda Tuhiwai. *Decolonizing Methodologies: Research and Indigenous Peoples*. New York: Zed Books, 1999.

Smith, Mona. *Her Giveaway: A Spiritual Journey with AIDS*. 21 min. United States: Women Make Movies, 1988.

———. *Honored by the Moon*. 15 min. United States: Women Make Movies, 1990.

Smoothstone, Candor. "Response to 'Arnold J. Cornbelt.'" *RFD*, no. 15 (1978): 5.

Somerville, Siobhan. *Queering the Color Line: Race and the Invention of Homosexuality in American Culture*. Durham, N.C.: Duke University Press, 2000.

Sonenschein, David. "Homosexuality as a Subject of Anthropological Inquiry." *Anthropological Quarterly* 39, no. 2 (1966): 73–82.

Sprinkle, Annie. *Annie Sprinkle: Post Porn Modernist: My 25 Years as a Multi-Media Whore*. San Francisco: Cleis Press, 1998.

Starhawk. *Truth or Dare: Encounters with Power, Authority, and Mystery*. San Francisco: Harper and Row, 1987.

Steakley, James. "Per Scientiam ad Justitiam: Magnus Hirschfeld and the Sexual Politics of Innate Homosexuality." In *Science and Homosexualities*, ed. Vernon Rosario. New York: Routledge, 1997.

Steczynski, John. "Wholeness: Masculine & Feminine." *RFD*, no. 12 (1977): 10–12.

Stevens, James Thomas. "Poetry and Sexuality: Running Twin Rails." *GLQ: A Journal of Lesbian and Gay Studies* 16, nos. 1–2 (2010): 191.

Stewart, Omer. "Homosexuality among American Indians and Other Native Peoples." *Mattachine Review* 6, nos. 1–2 (1960): 9–15.

Stoler, Ann Laura. *Carnal Knowledge and Imperial Power: Race and the Intimate in Colonial Rule.* Berkeley: University of California Press, 2002.

———. *Race and the Education of Desire: Foucault's History of Sexuality and the Colonial Order of Things.* Durham, N.C.: Duke University Press, 1995.

Stoller, Nancy. *Lessons from the Damned; Queers, Whores and Junkies Respond to AIDS.* New York: Routledge, 1997.

Stover, John Abraham. "When Pan Met Wendy: The Negotiation and Contention of Gendered Spiritualities in the Radical Faeries." Thesis, Loyola University Chicago, 2005.

Stryker, Susan, and Jim Van Buskirk, eds. *Gay by the Bay: A History of Queer Cultures in the San Francisco Bay Area.* San Francisco: Chronicle Books, 1996.

Suzack, Cheryl, Shari M. Huhndorf, Jeanne Perreault, and Jean Barman, eds. *Indigenous Women and Feminism: Politics, Activism, Culture.* Vancouver: University of British Columbia Press, 2010.

Tafoya, Terry. "M. Dragonfly: Two-Spirit and the Tafoya Principle of Uncertainty." In *Two-Spirit People: Native American Gender Identity, Sexuality, and Spirituality,* ed. Sue-Ellen Jacobs, Wesley Thomas, and Sabine Lang, 192–201. Urbana: University of Illinois Press, 1997.

Takagi, Dana. *The Retreat from Race: Asian-American Admissions and Racial Politics.* New Brunswick, N.J.: Rutgers University Press, 1992.

Tatonetti, Lisa. "The Emergence and Importance of Queer American Indian Literature; or, 'Help and Stories' in Thirty Years of Sail." *Studies in American Indian Literature* 19, no. 4 (2007): 143–70.

Taylor, Clark. "Background Information on the Organization of Gay Anthropologists and Researchers on Homosexuality." *ARGOH* 1, no. 1 (1979): 3–4.

———. "Homosexuality (A.A.A. Resolutions 11, 12, 13)." *ARGOH* 1, no. 1 (1979): 5.

Tengan, Ty P. Kawika. "Ke Kulana He Mahu: Remembering a Sense of Place (Review)." *Contemporary Pacific* 15, no. 1 (2003): 231–33.

Terry, Jennifer. *An American Obsession: Science, Medicine, and Homosexuality in Modern Society.* Chicago: University of Chicago Press, 1999.

Thobani, Sunera. *Exalted Subjects: Studies in the Making of Race and Nation in Canada.* Toronto: University of Toronto Press, 2007.

Thomas, Wesley. "Navajo Cultural Constructions of Gender and Sexuality." In *Two-Spirit People: Native American Gender Identity, Sexuality, and Spirituality,* ed. Sue-Ellen Jacobs, Wesley Thomas, and Sabine Lang, 156–73. Chicago: University of Illinois Press, 1997.

Thomas, Wesley, and Sue-Ellen Jacobs. "'. . . And We Are Still Here': From *Berdache* to Two-Spirit People." *American Indian Culture and Research Journal* 23, no. 2 (1999): 91–107.

Thompson, Mark. "Clyde Hall: Great Spirit." In *Gay Soul: Finding the Heart of Gay Spirit and Nature,* ed. Mark Thompson, 116—30. San Francisco: Harper-SanFrancisco, 1994.

———. "This Gay Tribe: A Brief History of Faeries." In *Gay Spirit: Myth and Meaning,* ed. Mark Thompson, 260–78. New York: St. Martin's Press, 1987.

———, ed. *Gay Soul: Finding the Heart of Gay Spirit and Nature.* San Francisco: HarperSanFrancisco, 1994.

———, ed. *Leatherfolk: Radical Sex, People, Politics, and Practice.* Boston: Alyson Publications, 1991.

Tinsley, Omise'eke Natasha. "Black Atlantic, Queer Atlantic: Queer Imaginings of the Middle Passage." *GLQ: A Journal of Lesbian and Gay Studies* 14, nos. 2–3 (2008): 191–215.

Torgovnick, Marianna. *Gone Primitive: Savage Intellects, Modern Lives.* Chicago: University of Chicago Press, 1990.

Tortorici, Zeb. "'Heran Todos Putos': Sodomitical Subcultures and Disordered Desire in Early Colonial Mexico." *Ethnohistory* 54, no. 1 (2007): 35–68.

Towle, Evan B., and Lynn M. Morgan. "Romancing the Transgender Native: Rethinking the Use of the 'Third Gender' Concept." *GLQ: A Journal of Lesbian and Gay Studies* 8, no. 4 (2002): 469–97.

Trask, Haunani-Kay. "Settlers of Color and 'Immigrant' Hegemony: 'Locals' in Hawai'i." *Amerasia Journal* 26, no. 2 (2000): 1–24.

Treelove, Don-Tevel. "Spring, Spirit, and Faggotry." *RFD,* no. 3 (1975): 42–44.

Treichler, Paula A. *How to Have Theory in an Epidemic: Cultural Chronicles of AIDS.* Durham, N.C.: Duke University Press, 1999.

Trinh T. Minh-ha. *Woman, Native, Other.* Bloomington: Indiana University Press, 1988.

Trujillo, Carla, ed. *Chicana Lesbians: The Girls Our Mothers Warned Us About.* Berkeley: Third Woman Press, 1991.

———, ed. *Living Chicana Theory.* Berkeley: Third Woman Press, 1997.

Tsing, Anna Lowenhaupt. *Friction: An Ethnography of Global Connection.* Princeton, N.J.: Princeton University Press, 2005.

Tsinhnahjinnie, Hulleah. "Hin-mut-toe-ta-li-ka-tsut (Thunder Clouds Going over Mountains)." In *Living the Spirit: A Gay American Indian Anthology,* ed. Gay American Indians and Will Roscoe, 135. New York: St. Martin's Press, 1988.

Turner, Dale. *This Is Not a Peace Pipe: Towards a Critical Indigenous Philosophy.* Toronto: University of Toronto Press, 2006.

U.S. Commission on Civil Rights. *A Quiet Crisis: Federal Funding and Unmet Needs in Indian Country.* Washington, D.C.: U.S. Commission on Civil Rights, 2003.

Vaid, Urvashi. *Virtual Equality: The Mainstreaming of Gay and Lesbian Liberation.* New York: Anchor, 1995.

Vale, V., and Andrea Juno. *Modern Primitives: An Investigation of Contemporary Adornment and Ritual.* San Francisco: RE/Search Publications, 1989.

Valentine, David. *Imagining Transgender: An Ethnography of a Category.* Durham, N.C.: Duke University Press, 2007.

Valentine, Gill. "Making Space: Lesbian Separatist Communities in the United States." In *Contested Countryside Cultures: Otherness, Marginalisation, and Rurality,* ed. Paul Cloke and Jo Little, 105–17. London: Routledge, 1997.

Vernon, Irene S. *Killing Us Quietly: Native Americans and HIV/AIDS.* Lincoln: University of Nebraska Press, 2001.

Visweswaran, Kamala. *Fictions of Feminist Ethnography.* Minneapolis: University of Minnesota Press, 1994.

Wallerstein, Immanuel. *World-Systems Analysis: An Introduction.* Durham, N.C.: Duke University Press, 2004.

Walters, Karina, and Jane Simoni. "Decolonizing Strategies for Mentoring American Indians and Alaska Natives in HIV and Mental Health Research." *American Journal of Public Health* 99, no. 1 (2009): 71–76.

———. "Reconceptualizing Native Women's Health: An Indigenist Stress-Coping Model." *American Journal of Public Health* 92, no. 4 (2002): 520–24.

Walters, Karina, Theresa Evans-Campbell, Jane Simoni, Theresa Ronquillo, and Rupaleem Bhuyan. "My Spirit in My Heart: Identity Experiences and Challenges among American Indian Two-Spirit Women." *Journal of Lesbian Studies* 10, nos. 1–2 (2006): 125–49.

Waltrip, Bob. "Elmer Gage: American Indian." *One: The Homosexual Viewpoint* 13, no. 3 (1965): 6–10.

Warrior, Robert Allen. *The People and the Word: Reading Native Nonfiction.* Minneapolis: University of Minnesota Press, 2005.

———. *Tribal Secrets: Recovering American Indian Intellectual Traditions.* Minneapolis: University of Minnesota Press, 1994.

Weaver, Jace. "Splitting the Earth: First Utterances and Pluralist Separatism." In *American Indian Literary Nationalism,* ed. Jace Weaver, Craig Womack, and Robert Allen Warrior, 1–90. Albuquerque: University of New Mexico Press, 2006.

———. *That the People Might Live: Native American Literatures and Native American Community.* New York: Oxford University Press, 1997.

Weinstein, MaxZine. "Romancing the Stone Age." *RFD,* no. 82 (1995): 32–33.

WeWah and BarCheeAmpe. "500 Years of Survival and Resistance." *Buffalo Hide* 2, no. 1 (1992): 16–17.

———. "New Movement for Two Spirits." *Buffalo Hide* (early spring 1991): 5.

———. "Solidarity Statement—Two Spirits and HIV: A Conference for Health of Gay and Lesbian Native Americans" (1991). Human Sexuality Collection, Cornell University Library.

———. "Strength of Our Cultures: Wewah & Barcheeampe Supports the A.I.C.H. HIV/AIDS Project of the American Indian Community House of New York City." *Buffalo Hide* (spring 1992): 2.

———. "We Wah & Bar Chee Ampe" (1990). Human Sexuality Collection, Cornell University Library.

———. "We'wah and Bar Chee Ampe: Gay and Lesbian Indigenous People, New York City" (1990). Human Sexuality Collection, Cornell University Library.

———. "What Are Two Spirits?" *COLORLife!* 1, no. 1 (1992): 4.

White, Robin, and Bryan Hull. "As a Member of the Gay Community, I Am Affected by Racism Everyday." *Lavender Reader* 7, no. 1 (1992): 25.

———. "The Women Left Angry and Most Likely Disgusted with Us." *Lavender Reader* 7, no. 1 (1992): 25.

Whitehead, Harriet. "The Bow and the Burden Strap: A New Look at Institutionalized Homosexuality in Native North America." In *Sexual Meanings: The Cultural Construction of Gender and Sexuality*, ed. Sherry Ortner and Harriet Whitehead, 80–115. Cambridge: Cambridge University Press, 1981.

Williams, Walter. "Sessions on Homosexuality at the 1984 American Anthropological Association Annual Meetings." *ARGOH* 6, no. 1 (1985): 2–4.

———. *The Spirit and the Flesh: Sexual Diversity in American Indian Culture*. Boston: Beacon Press, 1986.

Wilson, Alex. "How We Find Ourselves: Identity Development and Two-Spirit People." *Harvard Educational Review* 66, no. 2 (1996): 303–17.

Wilson, Waziyatawin Angela. *Remember This! Dakota Decolonization and the Eli Taylor Narratives*. Lincoln: University of Nebraska Press, 2005.

Wolf, Eric. *Europe and the People without History*. Berkeley: University of California Press, 1982.

Wolfe, Patrick. *Settler Colonialism and the Transformation of Anthropology*. London: Continuum Publishing Group, 1999.

———. "Structure and Event: Settler Colonialism and the Question of Genocide." In *Empire, Colony, Genocide: Conquest, Occupation, and Subaltern Resistance in World History*, ed. A. Dirk Moses, 102–32. Oxford: Berghahn Books, 2008.

Womack, Craig. "The Integrity of American Indian Claims (or, How I Learned to Stop Worrying and Love My Hybridity)." In *American Indian Literary Nationalism*, ed. Jace Weaver, Craig Womack, and Robert Allen Warrior, 91–178. Lincoln: University of Nebraska Press, 2006.

Wynter, Sylvia. *We Must Learn to Sit Down Together and Talk about a Little Culture: Anti-Colonial Essays, 1967–1981*. Leeds: Peepal Tree Press, 2011.

Xian, Kathryn, Brent Anbe. *Ke Kulana He Mahu (the Rank of the Transgender): Remembering a Sense of Place*. United States: Zang Pictures, 2001.

Young, Robert J. C. *Colonial Desire: Hybridity in Theory, Culture and Race*. New York: Routledge, 1994.

Zavella, Patricia. "Feminist Insider Dilemmas: Constructing Ethnic Identity with Chicana Informants." In *Feminist Dilemmas in Fieldwork*, ed. Diane Wolf, 138–59. Boulder, Colo.: Westview Press, 1996.

Index

Scott Lauria Morgensen is assistant professor of gender studies and cultural studies at Queen's University in Kingston, Ontario, Canada. He is coeditor of *Queer Indigenous Studies: Critical Interventions in Theory, Politics, and Literature.*